Aggression and Peacefulness in Humans
and Other Primates

AGGRESSION AND PEACEFULNESS IN HUMANS AND OTHER PRIMATES

Edited by

JAMES SILVERBERG and J. PATRICK GRAY

Department of Anthropology
University of Wisconsin—Milwaukee

New York   Oxford
OXFORD UNIVERSITY PRESS
1992

Oxford University Press

Oxford New York Toronto
Delhi Bombay Calcutta Madras Karachi
Petaling Jaya Singapore Hong Kong Tokyo
Nairobi Dar es Salaam Cape Town
Melbourne Auckland

and associated companies in
Berlin Ibadan

Library of Congress Cataloging-in-Publication Data
Aggression and peacefulness in humans and other primates
edited by James Silverberg and J. Patrick Gray.
p. cm. Includes bibliographical references and index.
ISBN 0-19-507119-0
1. Violence. 2. Aggressiveness (Psychology).
3. Primates—Behavior. 4. Human behavior.
I. Gray, J. Patrick. II. Title.
GN495.2.S55 1992 302.5'4—dc20
91-20318

9 8 7 6 5 4 3 2 1

Printed in the United States of America
on acid-free paper

Preface

The stimulus for this volume was a discussion about the Seville Statement on Violence (SSV, see Appendix) in a Business Meeting of the Anthropology Section of the American Association for the Advancement of Science. Responding to the discussion, Jim Silverberg agreed to organize a symposium to examine the present state of research on the phylogenetic and situational factors making for violence and nonviolence in primates. He and Pat Gray co-organized and co-chaired a session on 'The Ethology and Ethnography of Aggression and Nonaggression in Primates,' at the 1987 AAAS annual meeting. The research presented in the participants' papers illustrated some shortcomings of the SSV, while acknowledging its praiseworthy objectives by indicating ways to improve our understanding of the roles aggression and violence play in primate social life.

Panel members voted to publish the proceedings of the session and to invite a few additional papers. This volume, the product of that decision, illustrates important recent approaches to the issues of violence and nonviolence in primate species. Papers prepared for the session by panelists Baldwin, Dentan, Lauer, Pereira, Ross, Sade, Strayer, and de Waal, were revised in 1990, as were the invited papers by the Robarcheks and Strier.

The editors of the volume thank the contributors for their hard work, their willingness to consider the editors' suggestions, and their patience during the process of bringing the volume to press. We also express our gratitude to Joan Bossert, Bill Curtis, Kirk Jensen, and Donald Jackson of Oxford University Press for their aid and support. Silverberg is also indebted to formal and informal sessions with participants in the Commission on the Anthropological Study of Peace of the International Union of Anthropological and Ethnological Sciences, of which Commission he was a founding member.

James Silverberg
J. Patrick Gray

Contents

Contributors

John D. Baldwin
Department of Sociology, University of California, Santa Barbara, California

Robert Knox Dentan
Department of Anthropology, State University of New York, Buffalo, New York

J. Patrick Gray
Department of Anthropology, University of Wisconsin—Milwaukee, Milwaukee, Wisconsin

Carol Lauer
Department of Anthropology and Sociology, Rollins College, Winter Park, Florida

Michael E. Pereira
Duke University Primate Center, Duke University, Durham, North Carolina

Carole J. Robarchek
Department of Anthropology, Wichita State University, Wichita, Kansas

Clayton A. Robarchek
Department of Anthropology, Wichita State University, Wichita, Kansas

Marc Howard Ross
Department of Political Science, Bryn Mawr College, Bryn Mawr, Pennsylvania

Donald Stone Sade
Department of Anthropology, Northwestern University, Evanston, Illinois (and The North Country Institute for Natural Philosophy, Inc.)

James Silverberg
Department of Anthropology, University of Wisconsin—Milwaukee, Milwaukee, Wisconsin

F. F. Strayer
Laboratoire d'Ethologie Humaine, Département de Psychologie, Université du Québec à Montréal, Montréal, Québec

Karen B. Strier
Department of Anthropology, University of Wisconsin—Madison, Madison, Wisconsin

Frans B. M. de Waal
Wisconsin Regional Primate Research Center, University of Wisconsin—Madison, Madison, Wisconsin (and Yerkes Regional Primate Center, Emory University, Atlanta, Georgia)

Aggression and Peacefulness in Humans and Other Primates

Violence and Peacefulness as Behavioral Potentialities of Primates

JAMES SILVERBERG AND J. PATRICK GRAY

INTRODUCTION

The Seville Statement on Violence (SSV) was launched to counteract the aura of pessimism that its authors believe afflicts discussions on the possibility of eliminating or, at least, controlling war. The Statement (see Appendix, this volume) was to help that endeavor by refuting, as logically and scientifically invalid, the popular notion that we can blame war and violence on a genetically driven, precultural, human nature.

We have no quarrel with that point. We agree, however, with many commentators who feel that a narrow focus on what is scientifically incorrect formulates the issues incompletely and makes the SSV appear to be naive (see de Waal, Chapter 2, for a more complete examination of the SSV). Missing from the Statement is a sense of what science does know about aggression and violence in humans and other animals. Without this information we believe the SSV fails in its laudable purpose of alleviating pessimism about our ability to control violence. Simply to inform the public that "it's *not* biological"—that human nature or animal nature cannot be "blamed" for war and violence—provides no guidance on how to explain and thus possibly to control these phenomena. In other words, the SSV fails to provide grounds for the optimism that its signatories see as vital in efforts to promote peace.

If the SSV does generate an optimistic outlook on the possibility of controlling war and violence, we fear it will be an unreasoning and thus a vulnerable optimism. Our view derives from the fact that recent research on the multiplicity of biological, sociological and cultural factors relevant to violence among primates indicates that some level of violence, or the threat of violence, plays a vital role in the social life of some primate species. An important implication of this research is that, in commenting on the nature of violence, we must abandon the often unexamined equation of violence with social pathology. We must be willing to accept the possibility that in certain circumstances threatened and even actual violence might have pro-social outcomes (de Waal, Chapter 2, and Strayer, Chapter 7). An understanding of this dynamic is vital to the control of violence in human societies.

Of course, we must always confront, at the very least with skepticism, claims to be engaged in pro-social activity made by those who are using violence, as individuals or as representatives of social units. Analysis of the pro-social effects of violence does not commit us to the position that violence is inevitable, or to the position that people should not strive to change existing social situations where violence occurs. We hold that recognition of all the social effects of violence, pro-social as well as destructive, makes any social effort at change more effective.

Efforts to control violence will be more effective if we understand that primates use violence (often the mere threat of violence) as a tactic, one among many, in the pursuit of social goals. As social strategists, primates appear to evaluate the costs and benefits of different social behaviors in obtaining desired resources. Episodes of violence do not result from individuals "losing control," or from the "beast within" overwhelming the fragile control of sociability or civilization. Instead, violence is a tactic in social interaction, one that is used rarely because its potentially high costs can serve to make it less efficient than other tactics in most circumstances.

This view of primate social behavior gives us hope for the control of violence, for it suggests that changes in the distribution of social resources, manipulation of the costs and rewards of various social tactics, and socialization for peaceful interaction can serve to limit the situations in which violence occurs. The success of such strategies in human societies depends upon recognition that the capacity to use violence in social circumstances is part of the primate make-up.

The points reviewed are a basis for guarded optimism about our ability to limit violence in human societies. The recent volume edited by Groebel and Hinde (1989) marshals the evidence for the SSV's five propositions on what we should *not* say about violence. In this volume we move beyond the SSV to present research that illustrates what we can say about the role of violence in primate social life. Our hope is that an integrated view of violence—one that combines evolutionary considerations with ontogenetic, sociological and cultural perspectives as required— will provide some positive guidance in the effort to build a more peaceful world.

A major problem that confronts the task of creating an integrated view of violence's role in primate social life is that there is little agreement among the various research perspectives on how to define key terms such as aggression or violence. An integrated view requires the creation of interobserver reliability through shared definitions of key concepts, or at least a shared understanding of the issues raised by our use of such terms. We turn our attention to some of these terminological questions in the next section.

TERMINOLOGY

Aggression and Violence

The term *aggression* has proven remarkably difficult to define in a manner pleasing or useful to all disciplines. This difficulty stems in part from the heterogeneous collection of terms that bear a family resemblance to the concept (e.g., assertiveness, forcefulness, combativeness, ferocity, belligerence; and abuse, conflict, force, violence, war, etc.). Efforts to define aggression often attempt to handle, at least implicitly, several disparate concepts. That task, exacerbated by different disciplinary concerns, is probably impossible. Aggression is used in the behavioral domain as a synonym for an intense assault against some object(s) or some other being(s) (e.g., an act of violence); in the social domain, for the intersocietal situation that is characterized by such violence (e.g., war); in the communicative domain, for a suggestion or equivalent of violence (e.g., a threat or a verbal abuse); and in the psychic domain, for an emotional discharge (e.g., frustration-induced rage or hostility). Thus, it is used to characterize the acts of individuals and of social groups (from small to globe-spanning units). It is used for acts (threats, blows, etc.) and for a readiness to initiate an act (assertiveness, forcefulness, combativeness, belligerence).

The most cursory review of the social science and ethological literature reveals, then, that the definition of aggression is a muddle. The result has been an understandable tendency to accept the term as polythetic and to define it by adopting Justice Stewart's "I know it when I see it" stance on pornography. We do not presume to clear up the muddle here, but only comment on some issues raised by various definitions and to indicate where we stand on several points.

We begin by staking out our location in the muddle. We note first that the contributors to this volume do not share a single definition of aggression (or its derivatives, aggressive and aggressiveness). Yet they seem to have little trouble understanding one another when they use these terms. This is largely because most researchers see violent physical acts between individuals or groups as prototypes of the concept aggression. However, where internal consistency or interobserver reliability is lacking, to that extent it is difficult to mesh new research with earlier research and to build a common body of information. Thus, we believe that comparisons across species and across human societies will be rendered much easier if researchers separate the concept of violence from the concept of aggression.

Siann also distinguishes between *aggression*, which "involves the intention to hurt or emerge superior to others, [and] does not necessarily involve physical injury (violence). . . ." (1985:12), and *violence*, which "involves the use of great physical force or intensity and, while it is often impelled by aggressive motivation, may occasionally be used by individuals in a mutual interaction which is regarded by both parties as intrinsically rewarding" (1985:12).

Our quarrel with Siann's definition of violence is that it ignores an emerging and, as yet, inadequately specified *scale of behaviors ranging from violent to nonviolent (peaceful) and perhaps even on to anti-violent* (see Baldwin, Chapter 4, for efforts to scale specific acts, and de Waal, Chapter 2, on "affiliative acts," which might be seen as anti-violent). Siann's "intensity" may be more difficult to scale as a variable, but then "violence" needs much further effort in comparative research as well as in conceptualization. We also quarrel with defining aggression in terms of an actor's "intentions" (so elusive to observation, an issue we will discuss below). Aggression might be easier to observe if we define it as *the assertiveness (or forcefulness) indicated by one actor's initiating toward some other(s) of an act that is higher on the violence scale than the previous act in a given interaction sequence*, i.e., a readiness to initiate acts at higher levels of violence. A general characterization of particular actors as aggressive (combative, belligerent, etc.) would depend on their frequency of such assertiveness relative to other actors.

Discussion of three different views on aggression, currently prominent, will serve to highlight their implications for our decision to separate and then relate the concepts violence and aggression.

Genetic Fitness and Freedom

In his influential *Sociobiology: The New Synthesis*, E. O. Wilson defines aggression as "A physical act or threat of action by one individual that reduces the freedom or genetic fitness of another" (1975:577). If we substitute "violence" for "aggression"—meaning, thereby, an act high on our violence scale—this position is close to our own. Defining violence as the extent to which an act's recipient suffers a loss of freedom or genetic fitness would help resolve the difficulty we identified with Siann's definition of violence.

A related advantage of Wilson's definition is that it requires us to separate violent acts from what might be called aggressive "behavioral styles." The latter would be the equivalent of what we have referred to as assertiveness and would be observed as the frequency of escalating (or initiating higher) levels of violence. Among humans, for example, people in many of the societies profiled in Ashley Montagu's volume *Learning Non-aggression* (1978) appear to believe that a forceful demeanor is an undesirable trait that either signals a likelihood of acting violently or creates conditions in which violence will occur (see also Robarchek, Chapter 9, and Dentan, Chapter 10). On the other side of the coin, ethnographies of preindustrial societies, engaged in warfare around the time of their description, often depict the behavioral styles of males as "aggressive" or "commanding." The socialization material presented by Ross (Chapter 11) touches on the relationship between behavioral style and violence. Our violence scale, with aggression as an initiation marker, does much the same thing. The relationship between behavioral style (assertiveness, forcefulness, combativeness, belligerence) and violence as an act requires additional study.

At first glance a great advantage of Wilson's definition is that it permits us to judge behaviors as violent without having to concern ourselves with the intentions or motivations of the actors. This would be of great benefit in comparing violent behaviors across species and across human societies. Unfortunately, deeper reflection demonstrates that the definition does not avoid the issue of intention. Wilson's definition requires that we label as aggression only those violent acts that *succeed* in reducing the freedom or genetic fitness of another. But surely we would want to label as violent an attack by A to take a piece of food from B that *failed*. It makes little sense to judge B's successful defense of her food as violent or aggressive (since, at the very least, it reduced A's freedom to take food at will), but not so the attack that initiated B's violence. The ghost of intention materializes again, for we find that Wilson's definition unwittingly makes aggression a physical act or threat of action by one individual who *intends to reduce* the freedom or genetic fitness of another. However, the admission of intent into the definition leaves it vulnerable to traditional criticism that reading intent from behavior is a chancy procedure for both human and nonhuman animals. It also renders the comparison of aggression across species or across human societies more problematic.

Before we leave A's attack on B, we want to emphasize that, according to

Wilson's definition, B's successful defense of her food is an aggressive or violent act. We think it is worth remarking that this feature of Wilson's definition helps to control the tendency to judge acts as violent or not based on moral criteria. We assume that most people would agree that B was justified in defending herself against A, but we find this fact to be irrelevant to the decision to identify her behavior as violent. Most students of animal behavior adopt this position, speaking, for example, of a mother's violence against offspring during weaning. A common finding among nonhuman primates is that mothers often use mildly violent acts to control the behavior of their offspring. Such "discipline" is often seen as socializing the young into the social roles of the troop, trading mild violence by a close relative early in life against the possibility of more dangerous violence by nonrelatives later in life (see de Waal, Chapter 2). Thus, the mother's violence, while reducing the current freedom of her offspring, is ultimately in the genetic interest of her child. It is possible to argue that, since the mother's behavior is for the infant's "own good," her behavior should not be labelled as violent. Such a position requires that we know the costs and benefits of an act to all parties before we can label it as violent or not, a requirement that is frequently impossible to meet. We believe it more effective to note that the mother's acts appear to be similar to other behaviors we have no difficulty in labelling as violent (although probably they would be scored as mild violence).

Many cultural anthropologists hesitate to label as violent the acts of parents physically disciplining their children (we put to one side the problem of defining child abuse, although the difficulties with this concept also could illustrate our points). Yet they have no trouble making that judgement when the mothers and fathers are monkeys. And, even if they view such acts by human parents as (mild) violence, some might argue that there are human societies where the natives would not so judge them. The issue is this: is there a valid cross-cultural, "etic" definition of violence such that its use can command considerable interobserver reliability? We shall discuss the etic/emic problem in greater detail below. Here we cite Gerber at length on child-beating as an expression of the Samoan concept of "love":

> When I asked Samoan informants about the feeling of *alofa* "love" which exists between parents and children, I was surprised to learn that many of them believed a father's beating was an appropriate sign of his love. This was explained to me in the following way: fathers and children are closely identified, and the behavior of children reflects almost directly on the reputation of the parent. They are socially and legally responsible for any of their offsprings' wrongdoing, and are entitled to take credit for their achievements. Because of this close identification, fathers stand to be shamed if their children misbehave. They must therefore teach them right from wrong, but children, especially young children, learn only with the incentive of pain. Concerned fathers, who worry about their children's capacity to shame them and wish to make their children good people, therefore beat them. This logic is so compelling that several informants told me that if their fathers failed to beat them, they would be sad, since it would be a proof of paternal indifference (Gerber 1985:131).

In our view it makes sense to label a father beating his child as violent behavior, even though "Samoan culture" may classify the behavior as a manifestation of "paternal love," and some or even all individual informants agree. We are skeptical that beating recipients maintain this emic view during the actual act. We assume that the beating has the effect, at the very least, of limiting the child's freedom of action, thereby meeting Wilson's definition of an aggressive (violent) act. More important, the physical characteristics of the beating are similar to other behaviors that, we believe, both Samoans and outside observers would judge to be violent.

Agonistic and Affiliative Behavior

A focus that limits attention strictly to the most blatantly violent acts is too narrow to be useful in comparative research. Violent acts require interaction between at least two actors and are usually only a step in a complex social process. Two interrelated features of social interactions relevant to violent acts require us to widen our focus. First, animals frequently limit the freedom of other animals by performing acts that appear to communicate a likelihood that they will engage in violent behavior. Examples include the long noted, aggressive, canine-displaying "yawning threat" of baboons and other cercopiths (see Zuckerman 1932:249, 262, and the magnificent Plate XVIII facing page 244) and the erect penis display of *Saimiri* males, which, as Baldwin (Chapter 4) puts it, is "hard-wired" by evolution— it shows up in the newborn—but gets appropriately targeted through learning. To understand the role of violence in primate social life we must include acts that are lower on the violence scale (threat displays, mild chases, supplants, etc.) in our analysis.

The second feature that demands attention is that often only one actor engages in threat or violence; the other reacts with submission or even withdrawal, acts which could qualify as approaching a nonviolent sector of the violence scale.

These two features suggest the need to analyze the complex social dynamic that surrounds the potential occurrence of violence. Scott and Fredericson's (1951) term "agonistic" ("any activity related to fighting, whether aggression or concilia-tion and retreat" (Wilson 1975:578)), serves to capture this dynamic. The term is used widely in primatology and human ethology and we believe its wider use in social anthropology would serve to check the tendency to see each violent act as a momentary collapse of the social fabric due to individuals being overwhelmed by "the beast within." Interestingly, for all the concern with control of violence in human social life there are, outside of ethological studies of human children, very few detailed descriptions of agonistic patterns among humans. Robin Fox's (1989) analysis of the patterning of fights on Tory Island is an excellent example of the research required to understand some acts of violence. His article has the additional benefit of showing how the accounts of participants and bystanders may systematically distort both the degree and the pattern of violence that occurs.

In primatology and human ethology agonistic behaviors are usually contrasted with "affiliative" or "pro-social" behaviors (see Strayer, Chapter 7). The contrast between agonistic and affiliative behaviors raises the important conceptual and empirical problem of the relationship between aggression and nonaggression, or, in our terms, between violence and nonviolence, or (in the case of affiliative acts) anti-violence. Perhaps the path to a better definition of violence lies in identifying behaviors that are not solely at the upper extreme of the violence scale. To put the issue simply, what is the proper antonym for violence? One answer is obvious: in agonistic interactions the opposite of violent acts are the "loser's" nonviolent acts of submission or withdrawal that result in the "winner" ceasing to initiate violent acts. On the other hand, de Waal's work (Chapter 2) on reconciliation among primates suggests that behaviors opposed to violence are the anti-violent affiliative behaviors between former rivals after an agonistic episode ends.

Some researchers expect an inverse relationship between the incidence of violence and the incidence of affiliative behavior in primate groups, predicting that groups with high frequencies of violence will exhibit low frequencies of affiliative behavior, and vice versa. Other researchers do not predict an inherent inverse relationship between the two behavioral patterns, noting that groups with infrequent violence do not necessarily exhibit much affiliative behavior and that affiliative behavior frequently increases in the aftermath of violent episodes. This disagreement might be partially resolved by field research into inter- and intraspecific differences in the association between violence and affiliation.

There are difficult conceptual issues that require discussion. For example, some theorists emphasize that violence, or, for that matter, aggression (assertiveness) is a tactic animals use to resolve conflicts of interest (see Huntingford and Turner 1987). From this perspective, a fuller understanding of violence requires identifying behavioral tactics that resolve conflicts of interest but do not involve either the threat or use of violence. We doubt that all affiliative behaviors serve to settle conflicts of interest and therefore we do not expect the incidence of affiliative behavior in a group to be an accurate (inverse) gauge of the incidence of violent acts.

The antonym problem is especially troublesome for research on the control of human violence. If we commit ourselves to building societies with rare occurrences and/or low degrees of violence, what type of societies will result? If we confine ourselves to the most literal level, the required antonym for violence is either "nonviolence"—perhaps, "peace" if the term is defined simply as "lack of violence"—or it is "anti-violence" (e.g., affiliative behavior). This definition does not suggest how a society's frequency of violence relates to its frequency of cooperation or to its quality of life. Many people working toward a world with fewer violent acts might find this definition unsatisfactory, preferring to argue that the control of violence requires working to improve cooperation among potential opponents. Silverberg (1986:283), for example, makes the obvious point that cooperation to cope with commonly faced problems requires and generates inhibition of discord and conflict.

Much of the discussion of how best to socialize children into nonviolent behavior reflects a belief that teaching children how to behave effectively in pro-social ways reduces the probability they will resort to violence later in life. The ethnographic literature on so-called "nonviolent" peoples (Dentan, Chapter 10) suggests the need for a careful examination of this assumption. Many of these peoples appear to spend little time socializing for pro-social behaviors, but go to great lengths to prevent children from engaging in violence and ensuring that they are not positively reinforced when they do so.

Many ethnographies of "societies at peace" (see Howell and Willis 1989b) do not give the impression that conflicts of interest are so few as rarely to disrupt a Utopian state of happy cooperation. Instead, the striking image is one of people who so fear violence that they "walk on eggs" to prevent ruptures of relationships that might cause violence. This image could be an exaggeration created by the ethnographers' concentration on how such societies remain peaceful, but its presence poses an important challenge to attempts to create educational programs promoting peace.[1]

The concept of nonviolent peoples raises an issue touched on by Dentan (Chapter 10). A large domain of anthropology's own culture consists of typifications of other social realities to foreground specific theoretical problems. As Rosaldo puts it: ". . . go to India for hierarchy, New Guinea for pollution, Oceania for adoption, Africa for unilineal descent, and so on across the globe" (1988:79). The debate over the relative contribution of "nature" and "nurture" to patterns of human aggression and violence has frequently raged over a few ethnographic cases that have become the "type sites" for "peaceful" or "violent" peoples. The Semai, Eskimo, !Kung, Mbuti, and Hopi are models of nonviolence, while the Dani, Jivaro, Maring, Yanomamo, and Zulu serve as their violent counterparts. There is always a grain of ethnographic truth in such images although these groups have become types in part because their ethnographers focused research on the topics of peacefulness or violence.

We do not doubt the importance of these cases for the study of human aggression and violence, but we believe that to concentrate on them exclusively is to risk missing lessons about the control of violence in societies that fall more in the middle of the continuum anchored by the ideal poles of "peaceful" and "violent" peoples. A reading of the ethnographic literature suggests that both extremes are noteworthy for devoting a remarkable amount of social energy to controlling the inhibition or the expression of violence. As suggested above, this image of a high level of concern with preventing violence or promoting violence may result from ethnographic focus on these issues to the exclusion of other aspects of social behavior.

Further research will be needed to resolve this issue. Until the issue is decided, we suggest that it is important for theorists to identify what type of social reality they have in mind when they label societies as peaceful or violent. A distinction should be made between the extremes of the continuum and societies with more "relaxed" attitudes toward violence. This is as important when discussing violent societies as it is when the topic is peaceful societies. Many societies that have not engaged in warfare for long periods may be peaceful because they have few conflicts of interest with their neighbors, or because a colonial power used its superior force to prevent "illegitimate warfare," and not because their members are committed to nonviolence as a way of life in the manner of the Semai or the newly peaceful Waorani (Robarchek, Chapter 9, and Dentan, Chapter 10). On the other hand, not all groups with a reputation for violence engage in frequent warfare. With respect to this point, Ferguson makes an important distinction between war and "almost-war," which he defines as:

> a conflict between autonomous groups, characterized by those processes which precede actual wars—sharpening tensions and political polarization—but which does not culminate in lethal violence because of an ability to exit from the conflict situation and/or the expectable costs of launching an attack (Ferguson 1989:197).

We believe that it is worthwhile to ask if some societies with reputations for being "fierce" might not better exemplify conditions of almost-war than of frequent war.

Ferguson also questions the "unexamined premise that reported cases of war among nonstate or tribal peoples are self-generated phenomena" (1990:237). He traces the direct and indirect effects of European intrusion in Amazonia. European policies of expansion and resource extraction (including slaves) involved tribal groups in wars as mercenaries, allies, or subjects as well as victims. Such "warrification" (1990:239) and at other times pacification, a growing dependency on and fighting over European goods, and epidemics of newly introduced diseases, combined to destabilize severely the precontact population distributions—through loss, migration, displacement, and concentration—as well as social relations within and between tribal groups. Ferguson notes how such havoc frequently penetrated to groups well beyond the actual contact frontier and that the expansion of non-European states had similar consequences in other parts of the world. His work provides a check against the tendency to ignore historical circumstances and to label and count societies as "timelessly" warlike or peaceful in order to generate and "document" statements about "human violence" or "human peacefulness."

The Comparative Study of Violence

We believe that the study of violence among nonhuman animals can tell us something about the role of violence in human life, and vice versa. This is illustrated by the varied disciplinary affiliations of the contributors to this volume. By contrast, many of the cultural anthropologists who contributed to *Societies at Peace* (Howell and Willis 1989b), in struggling to define aggression, recommend positions that make the comparison of human behavior with that of nonhuman animals, and even comparisons among different human societies, more problematic than do the definitions we have examined previously. Their diverse critiques of the feasibility of universal definitions for aggression or violence invite students of animal behavior to reflect on their own efforts to conceptualize and explain agonistic behavior, especially with regard to three significant points. The first concerns the possibility of a universal definition of aggression. The second involves the problem of whether aggression (or violence) is an innate aspect of human nature. The final point focuses on the relationship between etics and emics in defining and explaining human violence.

As noted earlier, the possibility of finding a universal definition for aggression is stymied by the demand that any definition cope with a disparate collection of concepts. Howell and Willis note an important example of this problem:

> [There is] ... a common failure to clarify whether aggression is an experiential state or a way of behaving. The conflation of the two confuses the issue, and reinforces the tendency for the behaviour to be reduced to an inner state—and hence rendered less open to investigation (Howell and Willis 1989a:4).

As indicated earlier, we agree that conflation of inner states with overt behavior is to be avoided, and for that reason suggest that, for the comparative study of violence as a social tactic, guesses about the inner states of animals are best left aside.

Our tactic of studying violent acts rather than seeking to find a universal definition of aggression does not resolve the pseudo-question "Are humans innately violent (or aggressive)?" It is difficult to answer this question because it has many different meanings. Some are really asking "Are humans inevitably violent (and aggressive)," or, to put it more fully "Is it true that humans have a drive to engage in violence that must be expressed even in the face of extreme social pressures not to engage in violence?" The ethnographies in the Montagu (1978) and in the Howell and Willis (1989b) volumes, like the SSV, suggest that the answer to this inquiry is "no." However, if we widen the question to include the ill-assorted category of behaviors that have been at one time or another labelled as aggressive (including "verbal assaults," "re-directed" aggression against animals, and perhaps just general "bad vibes") the evidence in the ethnographies is not so definitively negative.

Others are asking "Is human nature fundamentally (or innately) endowed with a capacity for asserting violence, or, in other words, a capacity for aggression?" Howell and Willis (1989a:8) see that version of the question as taking for granted the capacity for violence, so that research is directed toward discovering how it is controlled. A society with little violence is assumed to be working constantly to prevent the outbreak of violence. The view that the whole of social life consists of constant vigilance against the outbreak of violence so obviously distorts social reality that we have no problem in asserting that violence is not fundamental to human nature in this way (or to the nature of any social animal).

Few researchers of nonhuman primate behavior would object to Howell and Willis's proposal to reconceptualize the place of violence, or aggression, in human nature; allowing for differences in cultural capacity, it applies equally well to most primate species:

> Human beings come pre-packaged with a set of potential capacities and constraints, but these in themselves are not fixed or determined. Rather, they are a set of directives for an imaginative negotiation which seek specific definition in the cultural setting. Among these may be listed the capacity for cooperative behaviour and the capacity for uncooperative competitive action (both conceptual and physical). The important point to stress is that humans appear to possess an innate capacity for finding common cause in a great number of cultural activities, a capacity Carrithers [1989] ... calls 'sociality'. Such a capacity would not explain the specific instances of human socio-cultural arrangements in their immense variety—that could only be done by reference to local histories, local circumstances, and local causes—but it could explain how such a range and history of variation was possible at all (Howell and Willis 1989a:19–20).

The concept of sociality leaves violence as an innate potential of human beings, just one among many of our social potentials (how could it be otherwise?) We believe the concept adds little to our scientific understanding of the role of violence in human life, but is advantageous in combating the political and moral connotations which unfortunately are associated with any statement that behavior "X" is part of "human nature," and, specifically the "violence is inevitable" pessimism that the SSV wishes to eradicate.

An "Emic" Alternative?

The last issue raised by the Howell and Willis volume concerns the role of "emic" (i.e., actor-conceptualized) and "etic" (i.e., observer-operationalized) strategies for identifying and explaining violence. Many papers in the volume illustrate the difficulty of finding a universal operational definition of aggression. Our suggestion that comparative research concern itself with violent acts and with the aggression (assertiveness, etc.) that characterizes their initiation, rather than trying to cope with all the behaviors that have been subsumed under the term aggression, stems in part from the difficulties discussed in these papers. However, for some scholars, finding a universal definition of violence is subject to the same pitfalls as is the search for a useful definition of aggression. We doubt that the following brief discussion will resolve this complex issue to everyone's satisfaction, but we hope it will help clarify some issues.

Paul Heelas's article "Identifying Peaceful Societies" is an excellent discussion of the etics and emics problem. He examines how various definitions of aggression apply to specific ethnographic cases and concludes:

> In short, that which only appears to be aggressive (or violent) in nature when divorced from full context cannot provide the basis for claiming that activities as a whole are aggressive. The 'etic' cannot override the 'emic'. Reliance on those core meanings which are meant to aid comparison only too readily result in impoverishment and distortion. Full justice must be done to participant understanding (Heelas 1989:236–237).

In contrast, we believe that etics must override emics if there is to be a productive comparative study of violence either across human societies or across species. Many examples used by Heelas do not, in our eyes, provide convincing reasons to reject the possibility of identifying violent behavior in different societies. Consider, for example, two definitions of aggression that he examines: (a) "... [behavior which] leads to another party's being hurt; this includes not only physical hurt (injury or destruction) but any kind of hurt including annoyance, taunts, or insults" (Eibl-Eibesfeldt 1979:29); and (b) "... any form of behavior directed toward the goal of harming or injuring another living being who is motivated to avoid such treatment" (Baron and Byrne 1977:405).

Heelas attempts to demonstrate the weaknesses of these definitions in two ethnographic cases: Yanomamo wife-beating and Samoan fathers beating their children. In the Yanomamo case he cites Chagnon on the reaction of women to violence against them:

> Women expect this kind of treatment. Those who are not too severely treated might even measure their husband's concern in terms of the frequency of minor beatings they sustain. I overheard two young women discussing each other's scalp scars. One of them commented that the other's husband must really care for her since he had beaten her on the head so frequently! (Chagnon 1983:113).

In this case, Heelas judges that Yanomamo husbands are aggressive under Eibl-Eibesfeldt's definition, but not under Baron and Byrne's definition since:

> That "women expect this kind of treatment" presumably diminishes or qualifies their "motivation to avoid" it, a consideration also supported by the suggestion that beatings can signify being "cared for" rather than (simply) being "harmed or injured" (Heelas 1989:228–229).

We do not find Heelas's analysis of this case to be persuasive. In the first place, we doubt that because women "expect" beatings their motivation to avoid being beaten is diminished. It is more likely that they have few alternative courses of action open to them. Chagnon's ethnography indicates that women reside in an environment of violence; it does not suggest that they do not try to avoid beatings and to minimize the frequency and degree of violence in those they cannot avoid.

Just because beatings may signify "caring" to some Yanomamo women (how many is unclear) does not negate the etic reality of the beatings as violent acts. If our goal is a complete understanding of the dynamics of violence in Yanomamo life, we must consider "participant understandings": i.e., how the emic interpretation of husbands beating wives structures violence. That approach would be especially relevant to a full explanation of any particular episode of violence. On the other hand, if our goal is to use evidence from the Yanomamo to arrive at a comparative understanding of the role of violence in primate sociality, we see little difficulty with abstracting the violent episodes of wife beatings out of their emic contexts and comparing them with episodes of wife beating in other human societies (with different emic interpretations). We are also willing to move to a higher level of abstraction by subsuming human "wife-beating" under a more general category, such as "male violence against females," and examining this category across primate species.

Similar considerations apply to the case of Samoan fathers beating their children. Heelas points out that Eibl-Eibesfeldt's definition of aggression leads to the paradoxical conclusion that violence may signify love.[2] Heelas argues that Baron and Byrne's definition of aggression does not apply here—that children have no apparent motivation to avoid beatings—an assertion we again find questionable.

Conclusions

We have highlighted some issues that arise from the different and overlapping definitions of aggression. We have indicated some preferences on our part. We have suggested scaling acts along a continuum of violence ranging from anti-violent, through nonviolent, to violent. We would then operationalize the concept of aggression and its many synonyms as the initiation or escalation of those acts that are classified more toward the violent end of the continuum. We hope this preliminary discussion will be followed by work that will enable all disciplines to agree on a definition of aggression.

However, our purpose was not to settle matters of definition, but to increase the utility of the research reported in this volume by alerting the reader to some problems that confront the scientific study of aggression and violence among primates. We hope that such alertness will be carried over into the political debate over the role of aggression and violence in human life.

Three Other Terminological Issues

Before leaving this section, three other matters of terminology must be mentioned. We asked the contributors to take each point into account in their chapters, and most have done so.[3] First, we believe it useful to distinguish carefully between the concepts of "status" and "rank." We hold that status is best used to identify different kinds of positions in a social structure, regardless of their relative locations within a hierarchy of rank. Thus "juvenile male," "female infant," "preschooler," are all statuses. We use rank to refer to the superordination (dominance) or subordination (submission) of one animal vis-à-vis another. When status is used inconsistently, both as a synonym for rank or prestige and as the label for types of social positions, ambiguity often results. Note, however, that once statuses are clearly identified as social units, it is valid to discuss if and how particular statuses are ranked or ordered in a hierarchy.

Second, we are wary of the common practice of identifying the behaviors observed in a single troop or colony as characteristics of an entire species. This practice is becoming less common as primatology becomes more aware of the need to study a species in many different ecological conditions. Given the comparative nature of most of the papers in this volume this has not been a major problem for our authors.

Finally, with many others (see e.g., Rowell 1988; Small 1990a), we believe care is needed in describing the mating systems of primates. For example, we question the use of the term "polygyny" to describe the situation where both males and females copulate with more than one individual of the opposite sex—all the more so when female choice determines copulatory partners as much as, if not more than, male choice. It is necessary to resist the common practice of labelling as "polygynous" any mating pattern where males have access to several females without examining the extent to which females have access to several males. In some cases "promiscuity" would be more appropriate (if the term were purged of the connotation that no selectivity is involved); in others, the old-fashioned "polygamy" might best be revived for obviously selective promiscuity. A word of caution, however. We are advocating the use of "polygamy" to enhance, not weaken, conceptual precision and descriptive reliability. The term has become virtually obsolete since a time, decades ago, when it referred to any non-monogamous mating (marriage, actually). It fell into disuse because cultural anthropologists now carefully distinguish between "polygyny" and "polyandry." We advocate the revival of "polygamy" with the same goal of precision; we do not wish to see it resuscitated as a residual term to justify carelessness or vagueness, nor to disguise indecision (for a more detailed review of efforts to define and explain primate mating systems, see also Gray 1985:65–75).

DOMINANCE RELATIONS AND AGONISTIC ACTIVITY

The ideas of dominance and aggression are linked intimately in the minds of most people. A popular misconception depicts agonistic behavior as the main pathway to position in a population's dominance hierarchy. (We shall use "dominance hierarchy" as a shorthand label for a concept that caution warns may be hypostatizing the ranking of individuals in terms of their tabulated dominance probabilities in a matrix of observed agonistic wins and losses.) Television nature shows rarely resist the temptation to illustrate dominance relations with visually exciting footage of threats, chases, attacks, and retreats. The intensive study of baboons and macaques, and the relative neglect of other primates, have also contributed to the idea that much primate social life involves violent fighting to establish and maintain dominance. Further, the tendency to study troops in open country, where animals can easily be monitored both by the primatologist and by one another, contributes to an exaggeration of the role dominance relationships play in primate social life (Rowell 1988).

The concepts of dominance and hierarchy have come to play an important role in the study of human violence. In part, this is because human ethologists find the dominance hierarchy an excellent focus for comparing human behavior, especially in children, to that of other primates. More significant, however, is the idea that hierarchy plays an important role in the political life of many human societies (see discussion in Masters 1989) which tempts some scientists from state societies to see the "seeds"—perhaps of class stratification, but certainly of economic, political, religious, health, educational, and military bureaucratic structure—in the dominance hierarchies of animals.

The 1980s witnessed debate among animal behaviorists, primatologists and human ethologists over the definition and utility of the concepts dominance and dominance hierarchy. Bernstein's 1981 target paper in *The Behavioral and Brain Sciences*, and the responses it generated, outlined the issues and provided glimpses of the directions research would take during the decade. As we enter a new decade it is clear that among primates the relationships between dominance, hierarchy, and agonistic behavior are not as simple as once thought.

Many chapters in this volume (2 through 8) illustrate different aspects of our evolving understanding of these relationships. We see six themes as especially significant in shaping current and future research on these issues:

1. The increasing availability of long-term data on dominance probability structures.
2. Improvements in the methodology of analyzing those structures.
3. Efforts to determine whether most primates, as social strategists, operate with a sophisticated awareness of their own specific dominance position and of the dominance hierarchy *per se*.
4. A shift away from analyzing dominance relationships as products solely of dyadic interactions and the development of ways to study polyadic interactions.
5. Analysis of how third party aggressive interference in the disputes between two individuals may be related to the maintenance of social order (the 'pro-social' function of aggression).
6. Exploration of how nonaggressive social tactics influence dominance relationships.

Use of Long-term Data

Sade (Chapter 3) illustrates the first three points. Although this paper is not a longitudinal analysis, his data are from one of several long-term projects that have tracked dominance relationships for an extended period. Sade et al.'s (1985) three volumes of demographic data from the Cayo Santiago rhesus colony is an important part of this literature. Pereira's study (Chapter 6) is part of a tradition of data collection on Amboseli yellow baboons that began in 1963 (Altmann et al. 1985; Samuels et al. 1987). Recently Mori et al. (1989) analyzed 29 years of data on female dominance relations in the Koshima troop of Japanese macaques. Data on the Arashiyama troop of Japanese macaques (with a daughter troop in Texas) started in 1954 (Koyama 1967, 1970; Fedigan et al. 1986).

Long-term data permit analysis of intergenerational change and stability in dominance relationships. We can begin to separate the individual characteristics (e.g., size, "personality") and social attributes (e.g., troop demography, lineage ranking, kin support) that decide an animal's dominance history. Further, multigenerational data permit us to correlate changes in dominance relationships with changes in environmental resources. The baboon population of Amboseli declined from 1963 to 1979 and stabilized in 1983. The Amboseli data thus permit study of how different demographic and resource regimes affected the relationship between agonistic behavior and dominance. Data from the Koshima troop show that dominance relationships were stable during a period of population growth, but major upheavals occurred during the population decline created by the restriction of artificial feeding. As most theories of dominance suggest that the amount of violence characteristic of a group is in some degree related to competition over scarce resources, the importance of these long-term studies is obvious.

Long-term studies of human dominance relationships are rare and confront several difficulties unique to our species. We need long-term studies in the type of societies traditionally studied by anthropologists. However, studies using a dominance matrix format are usually conducted in industrial societies which frequently lack the long-term stability of social relationships characteristic of many preindustrial societies. Strayer (Chapter 7) reports evidence of dominance as an important aspect of peer group relations from early childhood to adolescence. In most industrial societies the children from whom a child first learns about dominance are often not the peers he or she confronts two or three years later. This raises the interesting questions of what is learned in early dominance interactions and how it is transferred from one situation to another over a lifetime. Strayer's multiyear research in Montreal daycare centers is an excellent start toward answering such questions.

We need to examine the interrelationships between the dominance patterns of children and those of the more general society, especially how the latter influences the former. Lauer (Chapter 8) provides an example of how adults may affect the way children work out dominance relationships. She notes that the different idealizations of gender roles in American and Israeli societies, as transmitted through daycare teachers, influenced the dominance interactions between boys and girls in the groups she observed.

Improved Methodology

The development of new techniques for statistically analyzing dominance structures is a second recent advance illustrated in Sade's paper. Patterns of dominance are often difficult to describe statistically due to problems such as unobserved dyads, inconsistent outcomes for pairs of animals (sometimes A defeats B, other times the roles reverse), and lack of transitivity (as in the "cycles" where A defeats B, who defeats X, but X defeats A). Sade's procedure attempts to overcome some of these problems. More important, it allows the researcher to model different patterns of wins and losses predicted by competing theories of behavior and to test the observed pattern of interactions against these models. The technique thus offers a way of testing hypotheses about the behavioral processes underlying the agonistic patterns that we summarize as dominance hierarchies.

Sade's analysis permits him to reject the hypothesis that chance is responsible for the pattern of wins and losses in his rhesus data. It does not, however, allow him to reject the Equality (EQ) hypothesis stating that the pattern results from a situation where it is just as difficult for A to defeat X, who is far removed in the dominance hierarchy, as it is for A to defeat B, who is only one step below in the hierarchy. As Sade notes, this finding contradicts the common assumption that rank differences between animals correlate with differences in fighting ability, meaning that, at the very least, individuals in the lower portion of the hierarchy are significantly weaker or less capable in fighting, than those in the upper portion.

Inability to reject the EQ hypothesis has important implications for research on the processes responsible for creating and maintaining what are described as dominance hierarchies. As Sade notes:

> If EQ is in fact the usual condition then there must be social and psychological processes operating to ensure that the dominance order is not in continuous flux and upheaval, as should be the case under EQ alone (Sade, Chapter 3).

Much recent research on dominance among primates focuses on these social and psychological processes, including the strategic use of nonviolent as well as violent tactics. Since the late 1950s, we have had evidence that physical differences in size, strength, and fighting ability do not in all observed primate troops correlate highly with dominance ranking.

This should have come as no surprise. Over 50 years ago, a pioneer in "pecking order" research, warned against a simplistic assumption that dominance reflects a single factor:

> [V]ery often ... birds peck one another ... in a "triangle": a pecks b, b pecks c, and c again pecks a. ... [Perhaps] strength has given a despotism over b, courage has made b despot over c, and circumstances have caused c to become despot over a (Schjelderup-Ebbe 1935:952–953).

His admonitions about the single-determinant fallacy and the frequency of triangles (Sade's "cycles," Chapter 3) have often been ignored, as mass media popularizers and some scientific ethologists resonated back and forth to stereotype the dominance hierarchy as linear (transitive), rigid and based essentially on fighting ability.

The popular image still portrays a set of animals, born with different degrees of willingness and ability to fight, with the most "aggressive" individuals rising to highest rank. Francis (1988) used paradise fish to test the hypothesis that individual differences in "aggressive motivation" are responsible for the patterns of wins and losses in a dominance matrix. Noting that he had to measure their individual aggressiveness prior to their establishment of dominance relationships, he used a mirror display technique, measuring each fish's tendency to attack its own image or the image of another fish. Their differential aggressiveness did not correlate well with the dominance matrix that summarized their subsequent patterns of wins and losses in fighting. Francis invited scientists to consider the possibility that sometimes "aggressive motivation" (the ability and readiness to fight) plays only a small role in creating dominance orders. Studies in other fish populations find a positive correlation between aggressiveness and dominance, while still others find that such a correlation appears in some conditions, but not in others.

Such research seems to require going beyond the summary statistics of the dominance matrix to examine instead the historical processes responsible for the pattern of wins and losses observed by the researcher. For example, a history of frequent defeats in early life could create a mismatch between an animal's postulated level of "aggressive motivation," its size, and its dominance relationships. Jackson speculates on one way such mismatches can occur:

> If an individual is subjected to repeated defeat over a period of time it may learn that it is an individual with little dominance/fighting ability. ... If these defeats should happen early in life, that individual may refrain from challenging dominants later in life even though, for example, it may have grown larger than those potential opponents and therefore, if it challenged these smaller individuals, would be physically capable of defeating them (Jackson 1988:75).

The importance to any primate troop of the process modeled by Jackson depends upon a host of still not clearly understood factors. For example, the role dominance plays in the survival and reproductive success of individuals can affect what animals learn from early dominance interactions and the degree to which early experiences affect aggressiveness in later life.

We can no longer take each agonistic episode as an isolated event, but rather must view each act from the perspective of what de Waal (Chapter 2) labels the "relational approach." Adoption of the relational approach implies that for most primates it will be extremely difficult to use different levels of innate "aggressive motivation" in individuals as a simple explanation for the wins and losses in dyadic interactions that are summarized in a dominance matrix.

To analyze a specific agonistic episode between A and B in this perspective requires information on the interaction history of the two animals, their "motives" in the interaction (e.g., to gain a physical resource, to aid another animal, to punish for not sharing), and their current assets and options (e.g., their relative physical conditions, the location of potential allies, the possibility of sharing a disputed resource).

In many primates, for example, agonistic interactions between young animals rarely resemble Western one-on-one gunfights where the most skillful fighter (fastest, strongest, most motivated, etc.) wins. The more frequent situation is for close kin to become involved and for their relative dominance, rather than the relative strength of the initial combatants, to decide the issue.

The discovery by Japanese primatologists that matriline rank has a strong influence on the dominance position attained by female Japanese macaques was an important step in establishing the relevance of the relational perspective to studies of dominance among primates (Kawai 1958; Kawamura 1958). Kawamura's formulation of the principle of "youngest ascendancy" (i.e., while all daughters rank just below their mothers in the adult female order, younger sisters dominate older sisters), focused interest on the problem of how animals are socialized into dominance roles in ways that do not require constant agonistic episodes (Datta 1988).

Analyses of dominance relationships can no longer be mere summaries of assault records in the form of a dominance matrix, but must start to resemble continuing soap operas like the one described by Pereira (Chapter 6), starring the apparent social climber, "Sybil," or the one starring "D40," a female Barbary macaque, who used more pro-social tactics than "Sybil" (Small 1990b).

Some recent research in primate ethology resembles Francis's experiment with paradise fish that used a mirror stimulus in measuring aggressiveness. This research utilizes the "natural experiment" that occurs when individuals leave their natal troop and seek to join a new troop. We can observe how the learning experiences in their natal troop affect the "fighting ability" of individuals in their new troop (see Hamilton and Bulger 1990).

The American pattern of childhood, with its constantly changing cohorts in daycare centers and in schools, provides an excellent opportunity to investigate this dynamic in detail. It might be possible to obtain measurements of individual "aggressiveness" before combining children who are strangers to one another into a new class and then to match those measurements with achieved dominance in the new class.

Dominance Consciousness

A flowering of the relational perspective was a salubrious outcome of the ferment over sociobiology in the late 1970s. Researchers attempting to test theories of inclusive fitness and kin selection concentrated on the genetic relationships between the actors in agonistic episodes (early work reviewed in Gray 1985). Much of this research used the metaphor of animals as strategists who attack, defend, share resources, or withhold violence based on a calculus of genetic relatedness and reproductive potential. Applying this calculus in practice is difficult, but the attempt to do so stimulated innovative research. Strum and Latour summarize the effect of this focus on research among baboons:

> The trend has been in the direction of granting baboons more social skill and more social awareness than the sociobiological "smart biology" argument allowed. These skills involve negotiating, testing, assessing, and manipulating. A male baboon, motivated by his genes to maximize his reproductive success, cannot simply rely on his size, strength, or dominance rank to get him what he wants. Even if dominance was sufficient, we are still left with the question: how do baboons know who is dominant or not? Is dominance a fact or an artefact? If it is an artefact, whose artefact is it—is it the observer's, who is searching for a society into which he can put the baboons. ... Or is it a universal problem, one that both observer and baboon have to solve? (Strum and Latour 1987:788, references omitted).

Strum and Latour's mention of social awareness identifies our third theme: the role that dominance relationships play in the social awareness of primates. As

Bernstein (1981) and many others note, just because human observers can place animals in a dominance matrix does not mean that the idea of relative or absolute rank influences the behavior of individual animals. A consistent pattern of wins and losses, which an observer can summarize as a dominance hierarchy, can be obtained if animals operate without being aware of a hierarchy or being motivated to attain or maintain high rank. It can be obtained, for example, if animals act according to a simple rule of categorizing their troop mates into those who usually dominate them and those they usually dominate. It can even be obtained where the pattern of wins and losses is an observer's tabulation of what, in reality, are individual instances of fighting, each episode a time-bound conflict of interest.

Researchers have recently addressed the issue of primate awareness of social rank systematically (e.g., several papers in Byrne and Whiten 1988). Pereira's work (Chapter 6) on rank acquisition by juvenile baboons suggests that the animals he observed act as if they are aware of the relative ranking of others. Pereira suggests that when cercopithecine females intervene in fights between two other females they follow the behavioral algorithm "support the member of the higher ranking family." This algorithm requires us to postulate that a female, "contemplating" intervention in an agonistic episode, looks beyond such simple characteristics as the relative size and fighting ability of the combatants or their different degrees of relatedness to her, to evaluate the relative ranks of their families. This requires that a juvenile female associate each fighter with the proper adult female relatives and then evaluate the relative rankings of those adults.

Johnson's (1989) research on "food supplants" (expropriation of food sources) among juvenile olive baboons at Gilgil also suggests that juvenile baboons distinguish the relative ranks of other troop members. Although supplants usually do not involve physical force or threats, the dynamics Johnson postulates are the types of processes required to understand agonistic episodes. Johnson identifies two reasonable presuppositions: we expect animals to complete agonistically when the resource they desire is of great value to them or when the potential costs of fighting are low.[4] We have little trouble understanding why an animal in either of these circumstances might use violence in competing for a resource. We have more difficulty understanding an animal who competes violently when the resource in dispute is of little value and when the potential costs of violence are high.

Johnson compares supplants over corms, a highly valued and highly nutritious food source, with those over grasses, a less valued and less nutritious resource. As expected, given the relative resource value of the foods, most supplants involved corms. Supplants over grasses did occur, however, and were correlated with previously observed dominance relationships of juveniles. As grasses have low resource value we might expect animals to compete only when the potential costs were low. Johnson suggests that the potential costs of competition are lowest for a higher ranking animal when the gap between its rank and that of its competitor is widest (note that this interpretation requires rejecting the Equality hypothesis retained in Sade's research on Cayo Santiago rhesus, Chapter 3). Johnson tested the hypothesis that the probability that animal A will supplant animal B from grasses increases as the gap between their ranks increases. The reverse situation occurred, with animals close in rank supplanting over grasses more frequently than predicted.

Johnson argues that juvenile baboons use supplants over grasses to reinforce their positions in the dominance hierarchy. As the relationships between adjacent ranks are the most unstable, animals direct supplants toward those near them in rank. Johnson notes that supplants are low cost behaviors that rarely escalate into agonistic episodes, but observes that unprovoked attacks and agonistic displays observed in other populations might be explained by the same dynamics.

Polyadic Interactions

The question of whether awareness of a dominance hierarchy *per se* influences the behavior of individual primates is vital to the fourth theme shaping recent research on dominance: the emphasis on examining both agonistic interactions and achieved dominance as the result of polyadic, instead of solely dyadic, interactions. There are several reasons for the focus on polyadic interactions. As noted above, studies testing predictions from kin selection theories examined coalitions in primate troops. Reciprocal altruism theory, with its attention to cooperation among nonkin, also provided an impetus for the study of polyadic interactions (e.g., Packer 1977).

Research on the relationship between male dominance and mating success has been an important stimulus to our understanding of polyadic interactions. The view that dominance rankings are structures created by interactions between animals striving to obtain the resources (e.g., food, safety, matings) necessary for maximization of inclusive fitness, suggests a set of simple predictions that have stimulated much research in the last decade. For example, since males in many primate populations spend a good deal of time and energy in what appear to be efforts to acquire and defend rank, it can be argued that high rank must bring important benefits that translate into increased reproductive success or higher inclusive fitness. This leads to the prediction that in multimale troops dominance will correlate strongly with reproductive success (usually measured with the proxy variable, mating success).

Efforts to verify this prediction have met with mixed results (for reviews, see Fedigan 1983; Gray 1985; McMillian 1989) and have revealed complex social processes relating agonistic activity and dominance to male reproductive strategies. Smuts's (1985) work on the life trajectory of agonistic success and mating success in male baboons is an outstanding example of recent work (see also Noe and Sluijter 1990). She finds that males who have recently joined a troop establish their dominance rank through agonistic behavior, but that high rank is not strongly correlated with mating success. Males do not increase mating success directly through their dominance interactions with other males, but through their abilities to form nonagonistic relationships ("friendships") with females and their offspring (see also Strier, Chapter 5).

Smuts's research suggests that females may play an important role in shaping male dominance interactions, and that males may sometimes be important in female dominance relationships. The primatological literature contains many anecdotal accounts of how relationships with some member(s) of the opposite sex affected an animal's rise to, or maintenance of, its dominance rank. Systematic investigations of such processes have started only recently. For example, Raleigh and McGuire (1989) analyzed how adult females affected male dominance acquisition in captive vervets. In ten social groups the experimenters removed the alpha (most dominant) male and observed which of two subordinate males became the new alpha male. Surprisingly, neither the previous dominance relations between the two males, nor the previous interactions between the males and females predicted the male who became dominant. Instead, in the period before the new rank order stabilized, females engaged in more positive social interactions with the male who became dominant than with the one who remained subordinate. The study also found that the support of high ranking females carried more weight in the outcome than the support of lower ranking females.

This research must still confront important questions. What criteria did females use in deciding which male to support? To what extent did the housing system play a role in making female support effective? Where males can escape from interactions and perhaps engage in agonistic episodes away from females, female support may not be as influential in shaping male dominance relations. Raleigh and McGuire's work is an exciting development that requires extension both by applying the procedure to other populations and by studying the roles males play in female dominance interactions.

The study just reviewed demonstrates that adults of one sex can influence the rank of adults of the opposite sex. Pereira (Chapter 6) suggests that this dynamic varies across species and provides an interesting conjecture for such variation. Discussing how adult females manipulate juvenile male and female dominance interactions, he identifies species differences in the sexual dimorphism of body weight and in seasonality of breeding as features that might affect opposite sex interference. Baldwin's analysis of agonistic behavior in relatively nonviolent troops of *Saimiri* (Chapter 4) also contains several points relevant to these processes, as does Strier's discussion of the monomorphic woolly monkeys (*Muriqui*), also residing in troops where agonistic behavior is rare (Chapter 5).

Pro-social Aggression

Systematic studies of polyadic interactions in human dominance behavior are beginning to appear (see Strayer and Noel 1983). Many of them relate to our fifth theme: the study of the pro-social effects of aggression. As we discussed above, this concept is problematic. The least controversial use is to remind us that not all agonistic episodes threaten to destroy social life. The difficulty with this usage is that the term "pro-social" connotes something more than the point that violence may occur without totally destroying the flow of social behavior. Further, the distinction between an agonistic episode that is pro-social and one that is resolved quickly is difficult to operationalize. Strayer and Noel's discussion captures the positive connotation of the term and suggests some political implications of its use:

> Both the ultimate strength and the inevitable weakness of this [prosocial versus antisocial] distinction arise from its direct focus on the complex relationship between the individual and his social world. A special preoccupation with the individual in relation to society was evident in the earliest formulations of the emerging social sciences. However, the historical roots of the prosocial–antisocial distinction can be traced to earlier political and moral reflections on the nature of "good" and "evil." In

its simplest form, prosocial activity can be defined as that which is good or beneficial for the social group; by contrast, antisocial refers to that which is harmful to, or disruptive of social life (Strayer and Noel 1986:107, references omitted).

Notice that this definition does not require that the animal engaging in violence "intend" its behavior to benefit the social group. The intervention of high ranking adult yellow baboon females in the squabbles of juvenile females (Pereira, Chapter 6) provides an example: such acts need not be altruistic—in the sense that adults sacrifice their inclusive fitness to maintain a group peace that increases the inclusive fitness of other troop members—to be classified as pro-social. Pereira argues that the behavior of these females can be explained if we assume that the longer dominance relations among juveniles remain unsettled, the higher the probability that a high ranking family will lose its position. Thus the high ranking females are acting in ways that benefit themselves and their families.

If we eliminate the element of intention or motive in deciding whether a particular agonistic act is pro-social or antisocial we still require some way of distinguishing pro-social violence from quickly resolved agonistic episodes that do not disrupt social life greatly. One possibility is to identify as pro-social any act consistent with existing dominance relations (i.e., higher ranking animals attacking lower ranking ones, or higher ranking animals intervening on the side of the higher ranking of two animals involved in an agonistic episode) and to label all other agonistic acts as antisocial. This, however, too easily identifies the good of the troop with the continuation of existing dominance relations. There are many difficulties in taking such a position with regard to nonhuman primates, but they pale when considering the moral and political implications of applying it to human societies (see Trivers 1985:77–79).

The idea of pro-social violence will continue to be a controversial topic in the study of primate sociality. Several lines of research discussed in this volume capture the logic behind the concept. For example, de Waal (Chapter 2) suggests that "moralistic aggression" among chimpanzees serves to reinforce a system of social understandings or rules. De Waal's discussion of aggressive socialization among rhesus macaques illustrates how pro-social aggression may function in dyadic interactions. Among rhesus, as among Japanese macaques (Kurland 1977), high levels of both affiliative and agonistic behavior characterize the relations between close kin. De Waal's results suggest that older relatives use mild violence to teach their younger relatives "rules of conduct," rules of behavior that must be learned if the younger animals are to mature socially. This use of what de Waal labels "constructive aggression" may benefit the younger animal later in life by saving it from making social blunders in situations with potential for serious aggression.

Nonviolent Tactics

Moving from the pro-social effects of violence to our sixth topic, the analysis of how nonagonistic social tactics influence dominance relationships, we again find little research confronting major theoretical and methodological problems. The most significant methodological problem is that to identify nonagonistic tactics often requires us to notice that an animal does *not* do something. It is usually difficult to fathom the meaning of a behavior that does not occur. For example, if animal A sees animal B with a resource but does not attack, is it because animal A: (1) is not interested in the resource (e.g., perhaps he or she is sated); (2) is subordinate to animal B; (3) is dominant to animal B, but in the context does not wish to risk a confrontation (e.g., perhaps animal B is near relatives); (4) is attempting to gain animal B's favor (e.g., to establish a "friendship"); or (5) is attempting to gain the favor of animal C by not attacking animal B (e.g., a male gains the friendship of a female by not harassing her juvenile offspring)? Of course, even to ask these questions requires that observers view the animal as choosing between courses of action in the first place. An additional problem for unsystematic research, especially in terms of time-sampled observation, is a tendency not to notice or record the less dramatic, more humdrum activities that comprise the greatest part of social life.

Many field anecdotes describe circumstances in which it appeared that animals who could have used violence with little risk did not do so, but this topic has not been addressed systematically in any field study. An ingenious study by Hector et al. (1989) suggests the potential reward from such research. The experiment sought to discover: (1) if captive vervet adult males would adjust their behavior toward an infant as a function of the perceived presence of the infant's mother, and (2) if the mother's subsequent behavior toward males was affected by the way the males treated her infant. Such adjustments by males might be expected if females based mating choices on male behaviors communicating a readiness to provide paternal investment. The tests isolated adult male–infant dyads under three conditions. In one, the adult male could see the mother behind a Plexiglass partition from which she observed the dyad. In the second the mother was invisible to the adult male behind a one-way mirror, but she could see the dyad. In the final condition a metal partition prevented any visual contact between the mother and the dyad.

Both male rank and visibility of the mother affected male behavior toward the infants. All males (alphas, subordinates, and new members of the group) were less aggressive toward infants when the mothers were visible. Highly ranked males were friendly to infants even if the mothers were not in sight, especially if the infants were likely to be their own offspring. Subordinate males were less friendly when the mothers were not in sight. There was some evidence that a female's subsequent interaction with an adult male was influenced by his treatment of her infant. Females tended not to act affiliatively with subordinate males, but they were more violent towards those subordinates who behaved aggressively toward infants.

The image of primates as social strategists aware of complex histories of polyadic interaction will continue to inspire research on how nonagonistic behaviors function as tactics of resource acquisition in those populations where dominance relations play a major role in the structuring of social life. Such research will provide a more balanced picture of the role that agonistic behavior plays in the life of these populations. We need to remind ourselves frequently, however, that the importance of both dominance and violence varies widely both within and between primate troops, species and even higher taxonomic units.[5]

Baldwin (Chapter 4) and Strier (Chapter 5) provide excellent additions to the literature on populations in which violence seems somewhat rarer and dominance relations less important than among most baboons and macaques. Strier combines her new field data on the woolly spider monkey with an interesting discussion of the evolutionary socioecology involved with the selection of monomorphism and nonviolent reproductive strategies in this population. Baldwin, synthesizing his own field observations on squirrel monkeys with the work of many others, illustrates the advantages of combining socioecological, ontological and physiological approaches when explaining nonviolent and agonistic behavior. Both papers are far too rich to summarize, but their content is vital for comparative studies of dominance relations and agonistic behavior. For example, Baldwin suggests that pain thresholds play an important role in the ontogeny of violence and dominance. It might be noted that remembered experience with, and the potentiality of, pain is much more likely to be a matter of conscious awareness and cost/benefit calculation than are "positions" in a dominance structure. This should be considered by comparing the actual physical risks juveniles of different populations encounter as they achieve adulthood. The willingness of some animals to challenge others may be determined in part by their ability to tolerate pain. This factor must surely influence the aggression, violence, agonistic activity, or the general peacefulness and nonviolence, that may be characteristic of a population.

WAR AND PEACE

As dominance is the leitmotif of research on violence among nonhuman primates, so warfare plays the central role in the anthropological study of violence among humans. Robarchek (Chapter 9), Dentan (Chapter 10), and Ross (Chapter 11) move away from the microlevel of individual acts of violence and affiliation to macrolevel analysis of the peaceful or warlike posture of entire societies or subcultures. We shall not make detailed comments on these three ambitious papers, but focus on what each adds to the debate over how humans can construct more peaceful societies.

At the outset, however, questions arise: are studies of agonistic behavior among nonhuman primates relevant to the understanding of human violence and nonviolence and, if so, in what ways? Two interconnected points are paramount in attempting to answer them. The first is that there is no single pattern of agonistic and/or affiliative behavior among nonhuman primates. The importance of dominance, violence, reconciliation, and so on varies greatly among different species and among different populations of the same species. Further, longitudinal studies of single troops indicate that the relative importance of the various components of agonistic and affiliative behavior varies with changes in resource and demographic regimes.

The second vital point is that there is no single nonhuman primate species that can serve as a referential model for analyzing the role violence played in the social life of extinct hominids (Tooby and DeVore 1987; see also Silverberg 1980:59–60) or in the interactions of present-day humans. Studies of agonistic behavior among troops of living baboons, macaques, gorillas, chimpanzees, etc. tell us about the dynamics of violence in those populations and may inspire testable hypotheses about relationships between the "violence variable" and other variables that may be applicable across species. However, there is no reason to choose one species of nonhuman primate and argue that it is the best model for explaining the role of violence in human social life. An implication of these two points is that there is little hope of constructing a "precultural" ethogram of human agonistic behavior based on the study of a single nonhuman primate species.

Some scientists and some TV nature programs support a claimed biological basis for the violent side of human nature by advancing, as candidates to be our closest evolutionary behavioral models, the open ground-dwelling cercopithecine monkeys of Africa and Eurasia. They emphasize the analogies that they discern in open ground as opposed to forest adaptations. Thereby, however, at one stroke, they undermine their own biological determinism of human violence: they ignore (1) the overwhelming array of homologies that document our closest evolutionary kinship with the forest-dwelling African apes (bonobos, chimpanzees, lowland and mountain gorillas), (2) the extent to which the African apes are ground-dwellers, (3) the forest-dwelling adaptations of many food-collecting human bands, and (4) the tree-using abilities and practices of the open ground-dwelling monkeys.

We do not study the agonistic and affiliative behaviors of baboons and bonobos to discover if human nature is "really" a baboon or a bonobo nature molded to at least some extent by our capacity for culture. Instead, we use the results of studies of violence and nonviolence in primate species to construct and test *conceptual models*: "sets of concepts or variables that are defined, and whose interrelationships are analytically specified" (Tooby and DeVore 1987:183). Results of a study linking the variability of macaque dominance relationships with the distribution of resources might be applicable to the behavior of school children, not because the latter carry within them a "macaque psychology" or a "macaque ethogram" of dominance, but because there might be a more abstract relationship between the distribution of resources and the social tactics used to obtain them.

A conceptual model is useful in explaining the range of behavior exhibited by a particular species only when combined with much additional data concerning the species in question. In the case of humans, for example, any conceptual theory of violence and nonviolence must consider how the human capacity for culture shapes the operations of variables implicated in the theory.

Before we can use a conceptual theory for cross-species comparisons of behavioral patterns, we must be sure that we have identified the equivalent phenomena in each species. This requirement is especially important when we deal with such ill-defined concepts as aggression or peacefulness. In the context of the present discussion, we need to ask if the behaviors involved in descriptions of dominance and violence among nonhuman primates bear any but the most superficial resemblance to the phenomenon of human warfare. If we decide that they do, we still must identify which aspects of human warfare and "almost-war" can be illuminated by conceptual theories relevant to violence among nonhuman primates. Will insight be limited to the small scale, personalized "almost-war" of traditional hunting–gathering and horticultural societies or will we gain some significant understanding of the massive, frequently remote and impersonal, violence characteristics of warfare in industrialized societies?

In his 1990 Croonian lecture on "The Interdependence of the Behavioural

Sciences" Hinde raises the possibility that the portrayal of, say, "aggressive" baboons fighting one another might have little to tell us about human warfare because war is a social institution, a collection of prescribed roles:

> [I]t is the rights and duties attendant on their roles in the institution of war that constitute the primary motivating forces for individuals in wartime. Elementary aggressiveness plays little part in the actions of combatants: they are guided by obedience, a propensity to cooperate, above all by duty consequent upon the role that they occupy (Hinde 1990:225).

Hinde is not implying that the conceptual models developed from analyses of primate behavior are irrelevant to understanding human warfare: just that these models may explain only a portion of the societal phenomenon called war. And, as anthropologists and sociologists have long noted—especially in the tradition of "social facts to explain social facts" (Durkheim 1938) or "culturological vs. psychological" explanations (White 1949)—social processes generate dynamics that are not predictable from the summation of the motivations or emotional states of the individuals involved in them. Wars do not occur because a critical mass of people on either side reaches a "boiling point," resulting in an attack on a different social unit. The reverse is usually true, with war creating the requirement that the military and other political bureaucracies bring numbers of people to their "boiling points." However, this is as true for the smaller scale wars and "almost-wars" of preindustrial societies as it is for the wars of industrialized states.

Most researchers agree that conceptual models of violence and nonviolence among nonhuman primates will be useful in explaining patterns of human violence only when the complications created by the human capacity for culture are integrated with the models. There is great debate over how such an integration is to be achieved.

One of the many possible positions in the debate is illustrated by Robarchek's comparison of the "peaceful" Semai and the "warlike" Waorani (Chapter 9). He uses ethnographic data on both societies to critique psychobiological, socio-biological and ecological explanations of preindustrial violence and warfare. He argues that such explanations are simplistic: they neglect the role human consciousness plays when actors interpret social events as situations where violence is an acceptable, or even the only possible, response. Robarchek (1989) labels these approaches as "deterministic" and argues that they manifest a "ratomorphic" (Koestler 1967) image of humans that sees human behavior as ("basically," "ultimately," "most importantly," etc.) determined by forces that individuals cannot control. Robarchek seeks to replace this image of humans as reactive entities and to explain violence and war as resulting from the behavior of humans who are:

> active decision makers picking their ways through fields of options and constraints in pursuit of individually and culturally defined goals in a culturally constituted reality which they themselves are actively constructing (Robarchek 1989:904; for a similar perspective on the role of human cognition in explaining preindustrial warfare, see Vayda (1989)).

Robarchek suggests (1989:904) that the problem with psychobiological, sociobiological or ecological explanations of warfare is not that they are necessarily wrong (this must be determined on a case by case basis), but that they are necessarily incomplete. A complete explanation of an act of violence (or concilia- tion) or a pattern of war (or peace) requires information on the symbolic world and the motives of the participants.

The issue of what constitutes an adequate explanation of social action is, of course, a passionately debated topic in the social sciences. On one hand, many of the scientists whose orientations Robarchek disparages as ratomorphic argue that statistical regularities in human behavior can be explained adequately by consider- ing variables that are measurable without taking into account how people conceptualize them (e.g., resource depletion, mating patterns). This approach does not deny that human consciousness mediates the social impact of these variables. In fact, some theorists argue that the symbolic world is a straightforward reflection of the operation of these variables. The approach asks if consideration of human consciousness adds significantly to the power of our explanatory models. For example, we might ask whether the different understandings individuals or even whole societies hold—about human nature and the acceptability or inevitability of conflict, violence, or war—play a major explanatory role when we examine cross-cultural variations in terms of variables such as resource depletion. If such understandings do not, accurate conceptual models of war and peace may be constructed without referring to them.

Approaches that assign the major role in the explanation of war and violence to human consciousness often reject attempts to develop what are labelled as "deterministic" explanations of these phenomena. A frequent complaint is that such approaches find empirical support only by ignoring (or distorting) ethno- graphic particularities. Theorists seeking to explain patterns of violence and war without recourse to the analysis of the symbolic systems through which individuals construct their reality, often respond by noting that all conceptual models require abstraction and that any demand to incorporate the uniqueness of each ethno- graphic case destroys our ability to generalize about human behavior. The current debate over "anthropology as science" and "anthropology as interpretive en- deavor" is well documented; we shall not pursue it here. We do wish, however, to highlight an issue raised by the debate: the role of peace education in building more peaceful societies.

A major difference between many "deterministic" theories and most theories focusing on human consciousness is how the two approaches evaluate the likelihood of changing human behavioral patterns by changing human conscious- ness. Robarchek's paper is therefore particularly important for its argument that the major factor in the Waorani switch from a pattern of frequent feuds to one of no feuding was a change in consciousness rather than the political or economic changes the society has undergone. More important, his data suggest that the new Waorani attitudes effectively prevent the outbreak of feuding in conditions that would have resulted in violence in the recent past.

Approaches to human violence that emphasize the role of cognition often are seen as conducive to greater optimism about the possibility of reducing the frequency of violence than those theories that give less weight to human consciousness. Social scientists debating these issues usually realize that the argument is over assigning relative weights in explanatory models; few suggest we ignore completely the contributions of different factors. Once the debate reaches a public forum matters become much less ambiguous. The claims often become simplistic: deterministic theories are pessimistic confessions of our inability to change human behavior in the face of forces beyond our control; to the deterministic camp it is wishful thinking to suggest that changes in human consciousness alone can play an important role in changing the frequency of violence and war.

Both characterizations are gross distortions that make for exciting debates, but are irresponsible given the gravity of the problems under discussion. Most deterministic theories argue merely that programs to change human consciousness will be less effective in reducing violence within and between societies than will programs that address the economic, social or political factors that such theories identify as important in explaining violence and war.

A second, more controversial, suggestion arising from deterministic theories is that forces creating the conditions for peace (or war) will determine the state of affairs at a given time, regardless of changes in human cognition, which are assumed to catch up in due course. One deterministic view (e.g., Silverberg 1986) argues that (1) social integration occurs when shared adaptive problems are most critical; (2) the world-spanning impact of many adaptive stresses that today confront humanity in its entirety provides grounds for optimism about world peace through increased global integration; (3) there is abundant ethnographic evidence of social cooperation, despite claims advanced by some that individual interest maximization will always stymie collective action; and that (4) millions of years of band-level existence, on the one hand, and a few hundred years of inter- and supranational organization, on the other, may make five or six thousand years of city–state and even fewer of nation–state experience, a poor basis for insisting that nationalism will inevitably block global cooperation.

Even if we accept both controversial points, we need not conclude that education for peace—shaping the way people view themselves, their world, and the acceptability or inevitability of violence—is futile. Most theorists who emphasize the necessity of changing perceptions to build a more peaceful world also argue for the need to establish a more just distribution of resources and power to support the perceptions that will dispose people toward resolving conflicts of interest without violence.

Dentan's analysis of peaceful polities, including peaceable enclaves within modern nation-states (Chapter 10), is an exciting work that attempts to explain common characteristics of two types of peaceful societies: refugee societies and cenobite enclaves. The paper is valuable because it rescues the anthropology of peaceful societies from being perceived as restricted to a few, ahistorical, ethnographic curiosities and therefore as irrelevant to modern societies. Dentan challenges us to consider how lessons about violence and peacefulness learned from study of these two social types apply to the task of building peace in more open and pluralistic societies.

The ideologies of such groups seem to have little to offer more open societies. Dentan argues that the peaceable attitudes of refugee populations are based on fear of invaders who wield superior force. It is unlikely that industrial societies can build a stable peace based on a similar fear, although there is evidence that the fear of nuclear weapons may operate in a manner analogous to the Semai fear of invaders. The xenophobia Dentan identifies as the central dynamic of refugee groups will not serve for a world where increasingly all-threatening earth-spanning crises demand a global scale integration of all peoples (Silverberg 1986). Nor do the "we–they" attitudes of the cenobite enclaves in industrial societies offer more hope.

If the ideologies of the groups analyzed by Dentan offer little guidance, does their behavior provide help? Perhaps their child-rearing practices or rules of social interaction can be divorced from their ideologies and used as guides for socializing children and adults to be less violence-prone? Discussions about peace education in the United States often center on the issue of how the power differentials between adults and children and between males and females relate to the level of violence within and between societies. Are there ways of raising children that produce more peaceable adults? Are power differentials between male and female gender roles correlated with levels of violence?

Both Dentan and Ross (Chapter 11) touch on these issues. Dentan's description of the inculcation of fear in refugee populations suggests that children in such societies are seldom harshly punished. He notes, however, that many peaceable cenobite communities in Western societies discipline children harshly, which suggests that peaceable adults may result from very different child-rearing regimes.

Ross's holocultural study of factors correlated with levels of internal and external violence examines child training in a much wider range of societal types than those addressed by Dentan. We will not discuss Ross's important findings on the internal vs. external targeting of violence, but restrict our attention to his material on socialization. Ross finds that the level of social violence correlates inversely with the degree to which socialization is affectionate. He also finds that both harsh child rearing and gender identity conflict in males predict higher levels of violence (for a recent review of holocultural research on male gender identity, see Broude 1989). His results hold out the promise that careful attention to how we socialize children can affect their willingness to engage in violence both as children and as adults. Ross's socialization variables are necessarily defined at a rather abstract level ("harsh vs. affectionate") and may offer few specific suggestions for parents and educators desiring to shape the behavior of children. However, research programs such as Lauer's (Chapter 8) and Strayer's (Chapter 7) can provide a wealth of practical techniques.

Ross's work raises the important question of what factors are responsible for a society's pattern of child-rearing practices, a problem requiring much additional research. For example, of the socialization variables in Ross's study, only the role of the father during childhood has received a good deal of attention (West and Konner 1976; Mackey 1981, 1985; Draper and Harpending 1982; Hewlett 1988). Societies characterized by close contact between adult males and children generally exhibit low levels of warfare, but the social factors leading to close father–child relations have not been identified.

Both Dentran and Ross touch on the relationships between a society's gender prestige system and its socialization regime. Are different distributions of power among the sexes correlated with levels of violence within or between societies?

A review of the ethnographies of several societies at peace led Howell and Willis to identify a correlation between "'peacefulness' as a moral value and gender equality" (1989a:24). Is this correlation one that would hold in a larger sample of societies? We briefly examined this problem using Ross's methodology and conclude this section with our results.

Using a holocultural sample, Whyte (1978) demonstrated that female status (prestige) is not a unified trait, but is best measured on several subscales that vary independently within societies. Ideally, we would have correlated Ross's scores on socialization practices and on level of violence with Whyte's scores on various scales of female prestige. Unfortunately, Ross scored the even numbered societies of the Standard Cross-Cultural Sample (Murdock and White 1969) while Whyte coded female prestige for the odd numbered societies. We therefore correlated Sanday's (1981) "Female economic and political power or authority scale" with Ross's scores on several variables.

Surprisingly, we found no relationship between Sanday's scores on amount of female power and level of either internal or external violence. Further, female power did not correlate significantly with either affectionate or harsh socialization practices, nor with the degree of male gender identity conflict. Our failure to find significant correlations between these variables may be because Sanday's scale measures female power using both economic and political factors. Ross (1986) found significant relationships between his socialization scores and level of violence scores and two measures of female political power. One, a high score on a scale of "female political activity," was positively associated with both level of "internal conflict and violence" and "warm and affectionate socialization practices" and was negatively associated with level of "external conflict and warfare." The second, probability that a society exhibits "female controlled organizations and positions," was also negatively correlated with level of "external conflict and warfare."

These results should be replicated using Whyte's codes on female prestige, but they do suggest that the relationship between child-rearing practices, differential gender prestige and power, and levels of violence are complex. Research on the topic of female prestige and power requires close attention to the measures used in defining gender inequality. Careful work in this area is vital, for there are preliminary indications of important connections between child-rearing, gender prestige and power, and violence. For example, using Ross's scores for female political participation, Coltrane (1988) found that female political activity correlates positively with male involvement in child care, but increased male involvement in child rearing does not result in greater indulgence of children. His findings must be integrated with both our and Ross's results. At present the entire issue of how gender inequality relates to levels of violence is an important open question.

SUMMARY

Violent acts capture the attention of those who observe nonhuman primates both because they are bits of excitement in otherwise seemingly uneventful stretches of social life and because the control of violence is a major human concern. Thus there is a tendency to exaggerate the importance of violence in primate life and to stereotype animals as either "dominant aggressors" or "low ranking victims."

Newer views of primate life manifest a more subtle approach: the analysis of factors that determine the release and intensity of violence in specific social circumstances. The study of violent episodes requires information such as the value of resources to potential competitors, the options competitors have to obtain resources without violence, their sensitivity to pain, the learning history of the competitors, and the possible intervention of other animals. In short, we will understand how and why violent acts occur only when we understand how and why animals forego violence. Work along these lines will make discussion of how to limit violence in human life more realistic.

This volume reports recent research on violence and nonviolence in humans and other primates. We have noted how the scientific study of violence and peacefulness—as also the political debate over their role in human life—is bedeviled by the different and overlapping definitions of principal concepts. We have tried to clarify the terminology by distinguishing *behavioral acts* from *behavioral styles* and specifying a relationship between the two. Thus, many terms help to identify different acts as score points along a *violence scale*. This scale ranges in its *peaceful* sector from *anti-violent behavior*, notably *affiliative* acts and perhaps *conciliatory* acts, through *nonviolent behavior* such as *withdrawal, retreat, deference, submission, displacement, supplant*, and on toward the *violent behavior* sector of the scale with acts such as *threat displays, lunges, chases*, and outright *violence*. We have identified terms that bespeak of a behavioral style, which in general is measured as the frequency with which any actor is the *initiator* of agonistic activity. That is what we call *aggression* or *aggressiveness* or *assertiveness* and a host of terms which simultaneously reflect such *assertiveness* and some point along the violence scale where the initiation occurs: *competitiveness, intensity, forcefulness, hostility, combativeness*, etc. Much remains to be done to refine, operationalize, and utilize these concepts, but we believe this helps to clarify the relation between aggression and violence.

In complex animals, all behaviors reflect an interaction between evolved physiological and behavioral adaptations and developmental events (e.g., learning, environmental circumstances). Social animals are strategists whose behaviors closely track environmental change. Knowledge of how behaviors have evolved is one basis for manipulating the environment to regulate behavior (e.g., to inhibit violence).

Emphasis on an evolved "predisposition" for violence in certain social circumstances cannot overlook evolved attributes that serve to limit the expression of violence, such as sensitivity to pain or tactics to avoid other costs incurred by violence. Nor can it overlook data on peace-making.

Recent studies on dominance relationships profit from the increasing availability of long-term observations of some primate populations and improvements in methods of analyzing dominance structures. Clearly dominance structures can no longer be studied as mere summaries of dyadic assault records. Primate groups are structured by more then dyadic agonistic bouts. A need to cope with polyadic interactions is recognized—a relational approach—including study of interventions by third parties in the conflicts of other individuals, apparent cross-sex "friendships" and female or male mate choices. Future research on dominance must explore two questions in more detail: (1) whether the acquisition and maintenance of high rank is itself an incentive for aggression, and (2) whether high rank correlates with genotypic or phenotypic superiority and/or reproductive success.

Affiliative acts (including peace-making) seem important in structuring primate groups. However, the level of affiliative behavior does not seem to be inversely correlated with the level of agonistic behavior, perhaps because some affiliative behavior is rewarding in ways other than in the service of conflict resolution. On the other hand, violence can have "pro-social" (group structure-preserving) consequences, but always with some costs to "losers." Operationalizing "pro-social" is, of course, highly controversial, and vulnerable to ideological bias.

In human groups of small children, violence is a major force structuring relationships early in life, but very quickly, and increasingly as children get older, affiliative acts play a more important role in group dynamics. In such groups, external factors—e.g., group constancy and cultural values transmitted through the interventions of adults—strongly affect group structure.

With a more complete understanding of the roles of violence and peacefulness derived from recent research on nonhuman primate populations and on small groups of human children, we can, with some trepidation, approach the complex question of violence within and between human societies.

Papers in this volume suggest several interesting correlations that touch upon the possibility of peace education and lowering the potential for violence between human populations:

1. Nonviolent children with nonviolent adults, indeed, nonviolent societies with affectionate socialization.
2. Successful peace education with minimal age hierarchy.
3. Extent of nonviolence with degree to which social integration is promoted by coping successfully with adaptive problems.
4. Extreme gender inequality with harsh socialization and with an orientation toward violence.
5. Female prestige with affectionate socialization and nonviolent intersocietal relations.

We believe the message of these correlations is that socialization for nonviolence is possible, although not easily, not simply, and not isolated from other behavioral domains. In this connection we have suggested that, notwithstanding the raging philosophical debates—"anthropocentrism" vs. "ratomorphism," emics vs. etics, consciousness vs. determinism, idealism vs. materialism—most theories that emphasize the importance of changing perceptions to build a more peaceful world, also recognize the need for a more universally satisfying distribution of resources and power to support the perceptions that incline people towards nonviolence.

NOTES

1. We are not casting doubt on the accuracy of the ethnographic work in these societies. The problem is one that haunts all ethnographic descriptions focused on a specific topic.

The place of that topic in the total social life of the society is bound to be distorted to some extent.

2. This seems to be reversed in Heelas's text (1989:229), which reads: "'love' is seen as signifying aggression."

3. Although we did discuss terminological issues with contributors they were not obliged to accept any of the recommendations we discuss in this chapter.

4. There is, of course, a prior presupposition: nonhuman primates will not prefer "junk food."

5. For example, partly at an infra-order level, as long ago as 1942, in his popular *Man's Poor Relations*, Hooten characterized "totalitarian" Old World Cercopithecoids as "vicious, cruel, domineering, hypersexual, and given to tyrannical social groupings," contrasting them with the New World "democratic" anthropoids, who "show a diminution in degree of such behavior which may amount to a difference in kind" (1942:326–327). He added: "If you have any fascist leanings you will prefer macaques and baboons to howlers and spider monkeys, but if you are democratic or communistic you will share my partiality for American monkey institutions" (Hooten 1942:234).

REFERENCES

Altmann, J., G. Hausfater, and S. Altmann. 1985. Demography of Amboseli baboons, 1963–1983. *American Journal of Primatology* 8:113–125.

Baron, R. and D. Byrne. 1977. *Social Psychology*. London: Allyn and Bacon.

Bernstein, I. 1981. Dominance: The baby and the bathwater. *The Behavioral and Brain Sciences* 23:146–181.

Broude, G. 1989. Revisiting status-envy: Does the theory hold up? *Behavioral Science Research* 23:146–181.

Byrne, R. and A. Whiten. 1988. *Machiavellian Intelligence: Social Expertise and the Evolution of Intellect in Monkeys, Apes, and Humans*. Oxford: Clarendon Press.

Carrithers, M. 1989. Sociality, not aggression, is the key human trait, pp. 187–209. In *Societies at Peace: Anthropological Perspectives*, S. Howell and R. Willis, eds. London: Routledge.

Chagnon, N. 1983. *Yanomamo: The Fierce People*. New York: Holt, Rinehart and Winston.

Coltrane, S. 1988. Father–child relationships and the status of women: A cross-cultural study. *American Journal of Sociology* 93:1060–1095.

Datta, S. 1988. The acquisition of dominance among free-ranging rhesus monkey siblings. *Animal Behaviour* 36:754–772.

Draper, P. and H. Harpending. 1982. Father absence and reproductive strategy: An evolutionary perspective. *Journal of Anthropological Research* 38:255–273.

Durkheim, E. 1938. *The Rules of the Sociological Method*, S. Solovay and J. Mueller, trans. New York: Free Press (originally 1895).

Eibl-Eibesfeldt, I. 1979. *The Biology of Peace and War*. London: Thames and Hudson.

Fedigan, L. M. 1983. Dominance and reproductive success in primates. *Yearbook of Physical Anthropology* 26:91–129.

Fedigan, L. M., L. Fedigan, S. Gouzoules, H. Gouzoules, and N. Koyama. 1986. Lifetime reproductive success in female Japanese macaques. *Folia Primatologica* 47:143–157.

Ferguson, R. 1989. Game wars? Ecology and conflict in Amazonia. *Journal of Anthropological Research* 45:179–206.

———. 1990. Blood of the Leviathan: Western contact and warfare in Amazonia. *American Ethnologist* 17(2):237–257.

Fox, R. 1989. The inherent rules of violence, pp. 150–170. In *The Search for Society: Quest for a Biosocial Science and Morality*, R. Fox, ed. New Brunswick, NJ: Rutgers University Press (originally 1975).

Francis, R. 1988. On the relationship between aggression and social dominance. *Ethology* 78:223–237.

Gerber, E. 1985. Rage and obligation. Samoan emotion in conflict, pp. 121–167. In *Person, Self, and Experience: Exploring Pacific Ethnopsychologies*, G. White and J. Kirkpatrick, eds. Berkeley: University of California Press.

Gray, J. P. 1985. *Primate Sociobiology*. New Haven: Human Relations Area Files Press.

Groebel, J. and R. Hinde, eds. 1989. *Aggression and War: Their Biological and Social Bases*. Cambridge: Cambridge University Press.

Hamilton, W. and J. Bulger. 1990. Natal male baboon rank rises and successful challenges to resident alpha males. *Behavioral Ecology and Sociobiology* 26:357–362.

Hector, A., R. Seyfarth, and M. Raleigh. 1989. Male parental care, female choice and the effect of an audience in vervet monkeys. *Animal Behaviour* 38:262–271.

Heelas, P. 1989. Identifying peaceful societies, pp. 225–243. In *Societies at Peace: Anthropological Perspectives*, S. Howell and R. Willis, eds. London: Routledge.

Hewlett, B. 1988. Sexual selection and parental investment among Aka Pygmies, pp. 263–276. In *Human Reproductive Behaviour: A Darwinian Perspective*, L. Betzig, M. Borgerhoff Mulder, and P. Turke, eds. Cambridge: Cambridge University Press.

Hinde, R. A. 1990. The interdependence of the behavioural sciences. *Philosophical Transactions of the Royal Society of London*, B 329:217–227.

Hooten, E. A. 1942. *Man's Poor Relations*. Garden City, NY: Doubleday Doran and Company.

Howell, S. and R. Willis. 1989a. Introduction, pp. 1–28. In *Societies at Peace: Anthropological Perspectives*, S. Howell and R. Willis, eds. London: Routledge.

Howell, S. and R. Willis, eds. 1989b. *Societies at Peace: Anthropological Perspectives*. London: Routledge.

Huntingford, F. and A. Turner. 1987. *Animal Conflict*. London: Chapman and Hall.

Jackson, W. 1988. Can individual differences in history of dominance explain the development of linear dominance hierarchies? *Ethology* 79:71–77.

Johnson, J. 1989. Supplanting by olive baboons: Dominance rank difference and resource value. *Behavioral Ecology and Sociobiology* 24:277–283.

Kawai, M. 1958. On the system of social ranks in a natural group of Japanese monkeys. *Primates* 1:111–148 (in Japanese, with English summary).

Kawamura, S. 1958. Matriarchal social order in the Minoo-B group: A study on the rank system of Japanese macaques. *Primates* 1:149–156 (in Japanese, with English summary).

Koestler, A. 1967. *The Ghost in the Machine*. Chicago: Henry Regnery.

Koyama, N. 1967. On dominance rank and kinship of a wild Japanese monkey troop in Arashiyama. *Primates* 8:189–216.

———. 1970. Changes in dominance rank and division of a wild Japanese monkey troop in Arashiyama. *Primates* 11:335–390.

Kurland, J. 1977. *Kin Selection in the Japanese Monkey. Contributions to Primatology 12*. Basel: Karger.

Mackey, W. 1981. A cross-cultural analysis of adult–child proxemics in relation to the Plowman-protector complex: A preliminary study. *Behavior Science Research* 16:187–223.

———. 1985. *Fathering Behaviors: The Dynamics of the Man–Child Bond*. New York: Plenum.

McMillian, C. 1989. Male age, dominance, and mating success among rhesus macaques. *American Journal of Physical Anthropology* 80:83–89.

Masters, R. D. 1989. *The Nature of Politics*. New Haven: Yale University Press.

Montagu, A., ed. 1978. *Learning Non-aggression: The Experience of Non-literate Societies*. Oxford: Oxford University Press.

Mori, A., K. Watanabe, and N. Yamaguchi. 1989. Longitudinal changes of dominance rank among the females of the Koshima group of Japanese macaques. *Primates* 30: 147–173.

Murdock, G. and D. White. 1969. Standard cross-cultural sample. *Ethnology* 8:329–369.

Noe, R. and A. A. Sluijter. 1990. Reproductive tactics of male savanna baboons. *Behaviour* 113:117–170.

Packer, C. 1977. Reciprocal altruism in *Papio anubis*. *Nature* 265:441–443.

Raleigh, M. and M. McGuire. 1989. Female influences on male dominance acquisition in captive vervet monkeys, *Cercopithecus aethiops sabaeus*. *Animal Behaviour* 38:59–67.

Robarchek, C. 1989. Primitive warfare and the ratomorphic image of mankind. *American Anthropologist* 91:903–920.

Rosaldo, R. 1988. Ideology, place, and people without culture. *Cultural Anthropology* 3:77–87.

Ross, M. H. 1986. Female political participation: A cross-cultural explanation. *American Anthropologist* 88:843–858.

Rowell, T. 1988. Beyond the one-male group. *Behaviour* 104:189–201.

Sade, D., B. Chepko-Sade, J. Schneider, S. Roberts, and J. Richtsmeir. 1985. *Basic Demographic Observations on Free-ranging Rhesus Monkeys*. New Haven: Human Relations Area Files Press.

Samuels, A., J. Silk, and J. Altmann. 1987. Continuity and change in dominance relations among female baboons. *Animal Behaviour* 35:785–793.

Sanday, P. 1981. *Female Power and Male Dominance: On the Origins of Sexual Inequality*. Cambridge: Cambridge University Press.

Schjelderup-Ebbe, T. 1935. Social behavior of birds, pp. 947–972. In *A Handbook of Social Psychology*, C. Murchison, ed. Worchester, MA: Clark University Press.

Scott, J. and E. Fredericson. 1951. The causes of fighting in mice and rats. *Physiological Zoology* 24:273–309.

Siann, G. 1985. *Accounting for Aggression: Perspectives on Aggression and Violence*. Boston: Allen and Unwin.

Silverberg, J. 1980. Sociobiology, the new synthesis? An anthropologist's perspective, pp. 25–74. In *Sociobiology: Beyond Nature/Nurture?* G. Barlow and J. Silverberg, eds. Boulder, CO: Westview Press.

———. 1986. The anthropology of global integration: Some grounds for optimism about world peace, pp. 281–291. In *Peace and War: Cross-cultural Perspectives*, M. Foster and R. Rubinstein, eds. New Brunswick, NJ: Transaction Books.

Small, M. F. 1990a. Consortships and conceptions in captive rhesus macaques (*Macaca mulatta*). *Primates* 31:339–350.

———. 1990b. Social climber: independent rise in rank by a female Barbary macaque (*Macaca sylvanus*). *Folia Primatologica* 55:85–91.

Smuts, B. 1985. *Sex and Friendship in Baboons*. New York: Aldine.

Strayer, F. F. and J. Noel. 1986. The prosocial and antisocial functions of preschool aggression: An ethological study of triadic conflict among young children, pp. 107–131. In *Altruism and Aggression: Biological and Social Origins*, C. Zahn-Waxler, E. Cummings, and R. Iannotti, eds. Cambridge: Cambridge University Press.

Strum, S. and B. Latour. 1987. Redefining the social link: From baboons to humans. *Social Science Information* 26:783–802.

Tooby, J. and I. DeVore. 1987. The reconstruction of hominid behavioral evolution through strategic modeling, pp. 183–237. In *The Evolution of Human Behavior*, W. Kinzey, ed. Albany, NY: State University of New York Press.

Trivers, R. 1985. *Social Evolution.* Menlo Park, CA: Benjamin Cummings.

Vadya, A. 1989. Explaining why Marings fought. *Journal of Anthropological Research* 45:159–175.

West, M. and M. Konner. 1976. The role of the father: An anthropological perspective, pp. 185–217. In *The Role of the Father in Child Development*, M. Lamb, ed. New York: John Wiley and Sons.

White, L. A. 1949. *The Science of Culture.* New York: Grove Press.

Whyte, M. 1978. *The Status of Women in Preindustrial Societies.* Princeton: Princeton University Press.

Wilson, E. O. 1975. *Sociobiology: The New Synthesis.* Cambridge, MA: Harvard University Press.

Zuckerman, S. 1932. *The Social Life of Monkeys and Apes.* New York: Harcourt, Brace and Company.

2

Aggression as a Well-integrated Part of Primate Social Relationships: A Critique of the Seville Statement on Violence

FRANS B. M. DE WAAL

INTRODUCTION

> Why should our nastiness be the baggage of an apish past and our kindness uniquely human? Why should we not seek continuity with other animals for our "noble" traits as well? (Gould 1980:261).

The message of the Seville Statement on Violence (see Appendix, this volume) is summed up in one of its closing lines: "The same species who invented war is capable of inventing peace." The emphasis is on the verb, *to invent*.

While welcoming the spirit of the Statement (SSV), I shall use this space to question the wisdom of its signatories in downplaying the importance of biology (read: genetics) relative to other influences on human behavior. Admittedly, biologists have promoted a rather narrow view of human and animal nature, with great emphasis on competition. Their world is filled with winners and losers. The risks and costs associated with overtly aggressive competition are often ignored, and it is only recently that principles of peaceful coexistence are beginning to be studied. Partly as a result of this one-sidedness in biology, the self-image of our species is often quite cynical. A more balanced and moderate view can be achieved, however, without abandoning previous valuable insights.

It must be obvious that war and violence are not human inventions in the same sense as are, say, the wheel and parliamentary government. Aggressive patterns are too transcultural and too similar to patterns observed throughout the animal kingdom. Neither can peacemaking be regarded as a uniquely human capacity. Over the past decade, my research team and several other primatologists have documented powerful behavioral mechanisms of social repair after aggressive disturbance among monkeys and apes. These mechanisms allow aggressive behavior to become a well-integrated part of relationships, so much so that it is fruitless to discuss this behavior outside the relational context. We need to think of aggression as one way in which conflicts of interest are expressed and resolved, and be open to the possibility that its impact on future relationships ranges all the way from harmful to beneficial.

TRADITIONAL EMPHASIS IN BIOLOGY

> Be warned that if you wish, as I do, to build a society in which individuals cooperate
> generously and unselfishly towards a common good, you can expect little help from
> biological nature (Dawkins 1976:3).

Biology adopted a competitive world view with the idea of a "struggle for
existence" among animals. This phrase caught on as no other, even though Charles
Darwin and most of his followers must have realized that it was not to be taken
literally. Malnutrition and disease cause more animal deaths than fighting, hence
natural selection chiefly operates through *indirect* competition. The champions of
the game are those individuals who are most successful in obtaining food, resisting
disease, attracting members of the opposite sex, and raising offspring. Although
doing so undoubtedly requires some aggressiveness, the bloody gladiators' show
described by Huxley (1888) was an exaggeration. Kropotkin, the most influential
opponent of these views, observed that some naturalists see pure harmony among
animals, whereas others see nothing but a field of slaughter. "Rousseau had
committed the error of excluding the beak-and-claw fight from his thoughts;
Huxley committed the opposite error" (Kropotkin 1972 [1902]:30).

If we look at biology today, it is evident which side has prevailed. The metaphor
of ruthless competition among animals is so well accepted that one is not surprised
to hear Wall Street being described as a "Darwinian jungle." Many remarkable
instances of cooperation and support among animals are known to science, yet
even these instances are commonly explained from the perspective of competitive
relations. Thus, an influential book on the evolution of "altruism" is paradoxically
entitled *The Selfish Gene* (Dawkins 1976). Note how emotions are projected onto
entities that obviously lack them (i.e., genes do not have a "self" that can make
them "selfish"). The terminology refers to a passive process of natural selection
that favors genetic traits which promote the procreation of their carrier and its
relatives. To call this selfishness is yet another intriguing metaphor, but one that
carries great danger. The danger is that the nonexistent emotions of genes are
mistaken for those of their animal and human carriers, the only entities that do
possess an emotional life (Midgley 1979). The height of confusion is reached when
Badcock (1986) attaches greater value to the motives projected onto genes than
to introspectively perceived motives. Discrepancies between the two are reconciled
by the argument that human consciousness must be based as much on self-
deception as on self-awareness.

A bird alarming another of a nearby predator may be perfectly unselfish in
the psychological sense, that is, the safety of the other may be all it has in mind.
Whether animals communicate intentionally or not is a matter of debate, but it
is evident that this is the *only* level at which cognitive/emotional terminology can
be appropriately applied. The picture emerging from ethological research on
animal behavior is not one of continuous strife and cut-throat competition. Social
species live congenially most of the time; they would obviously not be seeking the
company of others if cooperation were not at least as important as competition.

If a connecting line—albeit not a straight one—can be drawn from Hobbes
(1950 [1651]) and Huxley (1888) to contemporary biologists who regard society
as an abstraction and individual reproductive interests as the only reality, a second

line can perhaps be drawn from Kropotkin (1902) to modern primatology, which increasingly regards individuals as embedded in a network of social relationships. Not the anonymous relationships of many invertebrates, but the partner-specific relationships of animals capable of individual recognition and of evaluating entire histories of positive and negative interaction (Hinde and Stevenson-Hinde 1976). At some point these two lines join, because social relationships and individual interests need to be in harmony (i.e., relationships serve the parties involved rather than the reverse). For the sake of argument, however, it is good to stress the second line's distinctiveness and importance. We may call it the *relational*, as opposed to individualistic, approach to social behavior.

Because relationships among primates are advantageous and may last a lifetime, they have been compared to long-term investments (Kummer 1979). Primates spend hours grooming their friends and kin, and fend off others who wish to develop bonds with the same partners. Yet, the greatest threat to their social investments does not come from the outside, but from the inside, through conflict and competition. There is a limit to the amount of aggression a cooperative relationship can endure. For this reason, a primate will generally not initiate an aggressive incident for trivial reasons, even if victory is guaranteed. In other words, competition is constrained by the value of the competitor as a partner and ally in other contexts.

The relational approach is gaining ground in studies of animal behavior, as is evidenced by attempts to improve upon traditional cost/benefit analyses of competition, which paid exclusive attention to the physical risks of fighting (e.g., Maynard Smith and Price 1973; Popp and DeVore 1979). Recent analyses have begun to consider the *social* costs of competition as well (Vehrencamp 1983; Hand 1986; de Waal 1989a). These new developments within biology can resolve some of the problems that the SSV tries to resolve by getting *around* biology.

THE STATEMENT'S IDEOLOGICAL NATURE

> Only by redefining the words "innateness" and "aggression" to the point of uselessness might we correctly say that human aggression is not innate (Wilson 1978:99).

The SSV voices important and legitimate concerns about the common misconception that genes require people to act one way or another (SSV: "While genes are co-involved in establishing our behavioral capacities, they do not by themselves specify the outcome"). That behavior is determined by a complex interplay of genetic and environmental influences, rather than by either influence alone, is of course known to every biologist. Yet, it cannot be denied that some biologists have been less than even-handed in discussing the origins of human behavior. A correction of their writings is perhaps timely. In providing this correction, however, the SSV makes essentially the same mistake: it emphasizes one influence at the expense of the other.

Not satisfied with the full recognition of environmental factors, the SSV tends to dismiss human nature altogether: "Violence is neither in our evolutionary legacy nor in our genes." Curiously, this reckless statement immediately follows a rather thoughtful paragraph discussing both the cohesive function of social dominance and the dramatic results of experimental selection for aggressive behavior. The fact that artificial selection can rapidly produce hyper-aggressive animals indicates, according to the SSV, that aggression is not maximally selected under natural conditions. This is true and important, but how can a demonstration of genetic selection for high aggressivity ever be taken to mean that violence is not in our genes?

This is quite a statement considering *Homo sapiens*'s amply documented proclivity to maim, torture, and eliminate conspecifics. If this were primarily a cultural phenomenon, as the SSV wants us to believe, the question arises as to how it could have originated independently in such a large majority of cultures. Culture and language do provide powerful explanations of variation in human behavior, but are of considerably less help in dealing with behavior that is virtually universal. The SSV ignores the widespread occurrence of war by stressing two arguments that rather miss the point: that cultures are not in a continual state of war, and that a number of cultures have not waged war for centuries.

The document also attaches special importance to tools designed to be weapons, thus laying the groundwork for the SSV claim that "warfare is apeculiarly human phenomenon and does not occur in other animals." But is technology the *essence* of warfare? Are not the *means* by which people kill one another secondary to the *fact* that they do so, and the *reasons* for it? We would not think of reserving the word "eating" for the act of transporting nutrients to the mouth by means of tools, which definition would make eating a cultural expression, absent in animals and human infants. Instead, we recognize that a cat lapping up her milk is doing basically the same as Mrs. X sipping from a glass of Beaujolais.

The essence of warfare is, in my opinion, that members of one community organize themselves to fight those of another community over a piece of land and associated resources. This is not only a widespread human pattern, but similar behavior has been observed in another primate, which—and this can hardly be coincidental—is our closest relative. No one reading Goodall's (1986) dramatic chapter on the territoriality of the chimpanzees in Gombe National Park, along with evidence from the other long-term field study of wild chimpanzees by Nishida et al. (1985), can escape the impression that chimpanzees stand at the threshold of planned, organized intercommunity conflict. Adult males silently stalk males of neighbouring communities, attack and exterminate them as a team, and eventually take over their territory. Goodall (1986:531) regards the patrolling of borders, close cooperation, and extreme brutality as preadaptations for warfare.

It has been argued that this behavior may be an artefact of human food provisioning (e.g., Power 1986). Even if true, this by no means diminishes the importance of the observations. There is no reason why we should limit our enquiries to "naturally living species" (SSV) given that, as stated so emphatically in the SSV, behavioral *potentials* are what genes are all about. There evidently are circumstances under which male chimpanzees exhibit the potential to carry out violent raids to expand their territory and gain access to females. In their critique of the SSV, Manson and Wrangham (1987) propose that the phenomenon of intergroup aggression across territorial boundaries has adaptive significance, i.e., that human and chimpanzee males can increase their reproductive success by engaging in raids and wars. In response, one signatory of the SSV has clarified that biological considerations are, in his opinion, not irrelevant to understanding the dynamics of warfare, and that biologists have a great deal to say about the bases of human violence (Hinde 1987). This standpoint, however, does not come through loud and clear in the SSV. It would have interfered with the document's stated purpose, which is to cure humanity of "biological pessimism."

Questionnaires apparently show that people who believe that war is intrinsic to human nature are more likely to believe that there is nothing they can do about it (Adams and Bosch 1987). The SSV is intended to change these defeatist views in order to encourage action for world peace. This is an ideological objective, not a scientific one. Perhaps the SSV does not aspire to provide a balanced survey of factors underlying human aggression and violence, and can therefore be excused for underrepresenting biological factors. Yet, the person claiming to have conceived the need for a Statement on Violence, describes the SSV in a letter to the UNESCO as "clarifying what science knows about violence" (Genoves 1988).

By presenting the majority view *outside biology* as the academic consensus, the SSV is driving a wedge between ethology and the other behavioral sciences. This is an unfortunate development that needs to be countered both by pointing out the weaknesses and internal contradictions of the document itself, and by a search for common ground. Biologists obviously know that the learning component of behavior is highly developed not only in humans but in many animals as well; that attitudes toward war and peace can be molded through education and culture; that genes create potentials, not inevitabilities; and that aggressive behavior is not the only behavior selected for in our evolutionary history.

If these trite insights have not reached the general public and scientists in other disciplines—and they evidently have not—this may be because biologists have not been careful enough in their explanations. Alternatively, and this seems the real problem, biologists who have tried to present all sides to the issue have not reached as wide an audience as their more provocative colleagues. The SSV reads like a belated response to the "instinctivism" of authors such as Ardrey (1966), Lorenz (1967), and Morris (1967). Recent theories of the evolution of animal social behavior, which theories are highly relevant to the problem of human aggression, are not at all incompatible with a belief in cultural flexibility.

One aspect of the SSV that is particularly disturbing is its intolerant language. The document opens each of its statements with the capitalized dictum: "IT IS SCIENTIFICALLY INCORRECT to say . . . " In view of the elusive character of scientific truth, this language is basically unscientific. Lack of appreciation of the scientific endeavor is further indicated by attempts to obtain endorsement of the document by majority votes from professional organizations. Not surprisingly, some commentators have seen hints in the whole affair of the darkest periods in the history of science (Fox 1988; Zenner 1988; Somit 1990).

No one would even think of writing a manifesto similar to the SSV with the purpose of questioning a genetic substrate for patterns of attachment, sex, language, or cooperation. Most people readily accept these behavioral universals as core elements of human nature without in any way implying that this makes them immune to cultural modification. What is special about aggression is that it is the one behavioral universal that the human species does not like to see when it looks in the mirror. This is based on the unexamined assumption that aggression is an exclusively harmful trait, one that we could easily do without. I shall argue instead that elimination of aggression is not only an unrealistic goal, it is a misguided one. A friction-free social system has yet to be found, and the ones that come closest lack the structural complexity and individual differentiation that we value so much in human society.

THE PARADOX OF CONSTRUCTIVE AGGRESSION

> American social science has traditionally been somewhat remiss in examining social conflict and social violence because of its excessive commitment to models of social harmony; this has resulted in a tame view of social structures (Coser 1966:8).

Human aggressive behavior runs the entire spectrum from the little family quarrels, with which we are comfortable most of the time, to socially detrimental forms, such as child abuse, rape, and murder. When the focus is on the most extreme expressions, there is a risk of generalizing our concern and condemnation to all forms of aggression. The result is a totally unworkable mix of value judgements, policy suggestions, and scientific insights. Thus, one of the main difficulties of research in this area has been our inability to shake loose from centuries of religious attitudes and moral philosophy (Bohannan 1983). Similar problems in the field of sex research have led Money (1988:5) to complain that "what is actually applied ideology gets by, with its basic ideology unquestioned, as if it were scientific." At the risk of being accused of "justifying" aggression and violence (*vide* the SSV), my purpose here is to question the tenet that aggressive behavior is by its very nature antisocial.

Hinde (1970) reviewed reasons why aggression cannot be regarded as beneficial to society, going so far as to compare individual acts of aggression to the threat of the hydrogen bomb in terms of their cumulative effect on human unhappiness. Yet, conflict is often a well-integrated component of cooperative relationships, so that a dichotomy between aggressive and socially positive behavior has limited value. Both aspects of social life interact in a dynamic equilibrium, each aspect, as it were, feeding on the other. This insight can be found throughout the ethological literature, from Lorenz's (1967) studies of pair-bonding in geese, and his contention that "there is no love without aggression" (p. 186), to Crook's (1970) speculation that higher-order cooperation evolved in the context of competitive relationships, and that "men, like monkeys, appear to cooperate best when at their most competitive" (p. 176).

Similarly, aggression among preschool children may serve "pro-social" functions through its structuring effect on the peer group (Strayer and Noel 1986, and Strayer, Chapter 7). On a larger scale, many of humanity's most cherished social institutions are firmly rooted in and upheld by aggressive behavior. Our systems of justice, for example, can be regarded as the successful transformation of a deep-seated urge for revenge—euphemized as retribution—which transformation keeps this urge within acceptable boundaries (Jacoby 1983). There also exist abundant historic examples of violence as a means of effectuating much-needed societal change, the threat of which makes elites realize that they can can ignore the plight of the poor and disadvantaged only at their own peril (Coser 1966). The opposite is law enforcement, which is little else than governmental violence— euphemized as force—often, but by no means always, sanctioned by the majority of the population.

Hinde (1970) has addressed the idea that enforcement of the social hierarchy serves to maintain order. This may appear a constructive use of aggression, he argued, but an imposed order "may conceal untold tensions," and there would be no need for this if a potential for aggressive disturbance did not exist in the first place. In other words, the use of aggresson to minimize aggression is, on logical grounds, rejected as a genuine function. This logic, however, fails to recognize conflict as a fact of life. When demand exceeds supply—a common condition in nature as well as human society—conflict, in one form or another, is simply inevitable. Given this inevitability, aggressive behavior is not by definition antisocial or maladaptive. It depends on how and when it is used, and what effect it has on the survival chances of both aggressors and recipients. The adaptiveness of observed aggression is more realistically estimated by measuring its con- sequences against the hypothetical impact of unrestrained competition than against the utopia of absolute peace.

At the same time that aggressive behavior poses a serious problem to group life, it has become part of the solution. Certain types of aggressive interaction modify the expression of other types, including the "raw" hostilities springing from unevenly distributed resources. Some aggressive acts serve as statements of individual frustration or interest in resources, other acts back up or stake out priority rights which in the long run help to reduce conflict, and again other aggressive acts prevent physical harm to the young and weak through protective interference in fights. For example, Hall (1964) and Bernstein and Gordon (1974) emphasize the role aggression plays in enforcing the social codes in monkey groups. It is through these regulatory functions that an order is created which in complexity far exceeds that of animals, such as herds of bovids, characterized by low levels of competition due to evenly distributed resources.

Ultimately, the social processes creating order at the group level are the combined efforts of all individuals to achieve predictability in their social relationships, and to protect relatives and other valuable partners. The way aggressive behavior structures relationships will be illustrated below with the examples of food sharing among chimpanzees, and socialization of young rhesus monkeys.

Moralistic Aggression in Chimpanzees

Originally, noncompetitive mechanisms of food distribution were thought to be uniquely human, closely linked to the emergence of cooperative hunting (Washburn and Lancaster 1968; Tiger and Fox 1971). Since humans exchange goods and services on the basis of mutual obligations (e.g., Sahlins 1965; Mauss 1970 [1925]), the human capacity to exchange goods and services was considered a departure from the ape mode of life. In the words of Tiger and Fox (1971:148): "Of all the social bonds that exist, those between debtor and creditor are the most characteristically human, and depart furthest from the basic biogrammar of primate bonding." When field studies produced the first evidence of predation, cannibalism, and meat sharing in chimpanzees (Goodall 1963; Suzuki 1971; Teleki 1973), the sharing was dismissed as "tolerated scrounging" since human systems of reciprocity needed emphasis as a major evolutionary advance (Isaac 1978).

Already half a century ago Yerkes and Yerkes (1935:1024) considered it a "securely established fact that the chimpanzee is not necessarily utterly selfish." Aside from an early study by Nissen and Crawford (1936), the possibility that our closest relative exhibits reciprocal food sharing has only recently been the subject of systematic investigation. Because it is virtually impossible in the natural habitat to collect the large amount of data necessary for such an analysis, a captive study was conducted at the Field Station of the Yerkes Regional Primate Research Center (de Waal 1989b). Provisioning of branches and leaves to 19 chimpanzees (*Pan troglodytes*) in an outdoor corral resulted in 4,653 interactions over food, half of which involved a transfer of food from one chimpanzee to another (Figure 2-1). The food trials were characterized by increased levels of both aggressive and appeasement behavior, i.e., a remarkable, more than one hundredfold increase in the rate of calming body contact (e.g., kissing, touching, embracing), and only a ninefold increase in aggressive encounters.

Food exchanges among the adult members of the group (one male, eight females) were remarkably balanced within each dyadic combination, and the frequency of sharing by individual A with B correlated positively with sharing of

Figure 2-1 A cluster of peacefully co-feeding chimpanzees at the Field Station of the Yerkes Regional Primate Research Center. The cluster consists of one adult male (upper left), three adult females, and one infant hidden under the foliage. (Photograph by de Waal.)

B with A (Pearson $r = 0.552$, $p = 0.001$). This result corroborates other behavioral studies of captive chimpanzees that indicate their great potential to establish mutually supportive relationships (de Waal 1982; de Waal and Luttrell 1988). Here, we are particularly interested in the possible maintenance and shaping of these relationships through what has been termed "moralistic aggression," i.e., aggressive responses to perceived injustice, unfairness, and lack of reciprocity (Trivers 1971).

Wrangham (1975) expressed disagreement with earlier descriptions of meat consumption among the wild chimpanzees of Gombe as a leisurely activity. He observed frequent aggression during meat eating. Curiously, this behavior rarely seemed to increase the aggressor's chances of obtaining a share. Wrangham reasoned that the effect may be more indirect. Since aggressive behavior could disturb or harm food possessors, possessors learn to use part of the meat to "pay" others to leave them alone. Distribution of the meat reduces the number of frustrated individuals, hence the general level of aggression. Sharing is thus seen as the least costly consequence of the competitive behavior of others. This sharing-under-pressure hypothesis was tested on data obtained in the captive group.

The rate of food distribution of each adult chimpanzee was defined as the number of food transfers to other adults divided by the possession time of a shareable quantity of food. This measure was then compared with the number of aggressive acts received from other adults during food trials. As predicted by Wrangham (1975), a negative correlation was found. Yet, when we looked further into this relation it became evident that the bulk of the aggression was received, not by individuals in the possession of food, but by those requesting food from others (i.e., 2.5% of the interactions among adults involved aggression against food requesters, compared to 0.6% against food possessors). Figure 2-2 illustrates the negative correlation between an individual's rate of food distribution and the probability of an aggressive response when this individual approached a food possessor. This result means that individuals who were least "generous" as food possessors were most likely to meet resistance on occasions when they had no food and tried to obtain a share from others. By definition, the two compared behaviors were separated in time, indicating a mediating role of memory in producing this effect.

Conceivably, then, the reciprocity in food sharing demonstrated for this group of chimpanzees depended at least partly on aggressive sanctions against individuals who were reluctant to share. Note that, if aggressive behavior indeed served this function, it did so in a rather unobtrusive manner, involving a very small proportion of interactions. Moreover, food-related aggression rarely escalated to violence.

Aggressive Socialization in Rhesus Monkeys

The matrilineal hierarchy of cercopithecine monkeys is no doubt one of the most intensely studied social systems in the animal kingdom. Its basic features are:

1. Female offspring develop lifelong bonds with their mothers and other female relatives.

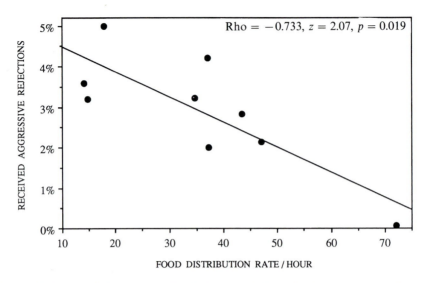

Figure 2-2 Relation between an individual's rate of food distribution (i.e., number of food transfers to others per hour of food possession), and the probability that others aggressively reject food requests by this individual when he or she has no food (expressed as a percentage of approaches to food possessors). Each dot represents one of nine captive adult chimpanzees studied by de Waal (1989b).

2. Male offspring develop somewhat looser bonds with their matriline, and tend to leave the group during puberty.
3. Matrilines act both as cohesive units, in terms of grooming and other affiliative contact, and as large coalitions during intragroup conflict.
4. Daughters reach positions closely below their mothers in the adult dominance hierarchy (see reviews by Gouzoules and Gouzoules 1987, and Pereira, Chapter 6).

In addition to intimate and supportive relationships, disproportionally high levels of aggression among kin have been reported in one field study and one captive study (Kurland 1977; Bernstein and Ehardt 1986). Bernstein and Ehardt (1986) explain the frequent aggression against relatives as part of socialization processes. Older relatives (e.g., mothers) use aggressive behavior to punish and inhibit "unacceptable" behavior patterns in young monkeys. They tend to use threats for this purpose, but can do so only after threats have become effective through previous association with physical punishment. Thus, in the rhesus monkey, it is not unusual to see a female bite her own offspring (Figure 2-3).

Since Bernstein and Ehardt's (1986) analysis pools the data for an entire monkey group (which precludes an adequate statistical evaluation of the results), we decided to replicate it on a captive rhesus group (*Macaca mulatta*) while taking care to measure individual variation (de Waal and Luttrell 1989). Figure 2-4 shows the mean rate of aggressive acts of any intensity per adult rhesus monkey (20 females, four males) against four victim categories: adult kin and nonkin, and juvenile kin and nonkin (kinship refers to matrilineal relations regardless of genetic

Figure 2-3 A rhesus monkey bites her own infant, which responds with a scream and a submissive facial expression. The mother did so after unsuccessful nonaggressive attempts to loosen the infant from her ventrum. (Photograph from de Waal (1989c).)

distance and paternity). The data have been corrected for the number of potential partners per category.

It is evident from Figure 2-4 that a disproportionate amount of aggression is aimed at kin, particularly immature kin. Using Wilcoxon tests to compare the rate of aggression by each adult against the various victim categories, the kin-bias toward juveniles was found to be significant ($z = 2.58$, $p = 0.01$), but not the bias

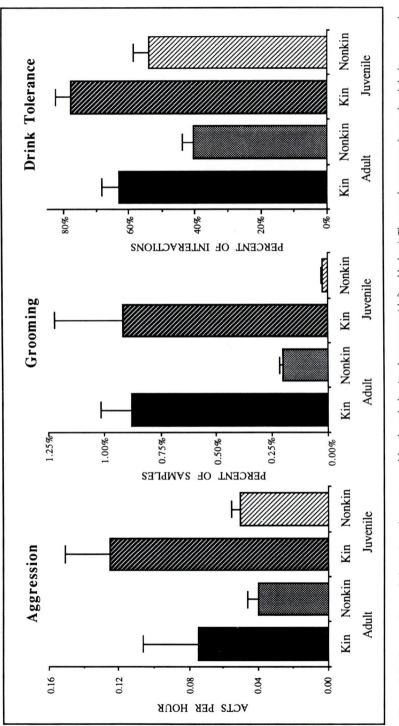

Figure 2-4 Four partner–victim categories are scored for three behavioral measures (defined below). The graph presents for each adult rhesus monkey, per partner in each category, the mean and standard error for each measure. Aggression is measured as the number of acts (of any intensity) initiated per hour; grooming is expressed as the percentage of 10-minute point samples during which it was observed, and drink tolerance as the percentage of interactions around a water basin resulting in co-drinking or co-occupation by two individuals (the remaining proportion represents intolerant interactions, such as withdrawal and aggressive exclusion). (Data from de Waal and Luttrell (1989).)

toward adults ($z = 1.46$). No kin-bias in the intensity of aggression could be demonstrated. To illustrate the pro-social aspects of kinship relations among rhesus monkeys, Figure 2-4 also provides the grooming data for adults. Social grooming, the most common affiliative activity of this species, is heavily kin-biased ($z = 4.07$ towards juveniles; $z = 3.91$ toward adults; both $p < 0.001$).

The high aggression rate against the very partners who are favored with most affectionate behavior might be explained as a product of proximity. That is, if aggression were indiscriminately directed against individuals that happen to be in the vicinity, relatives would automatically receive a relatively large share. We found, however, selective tolerance toward relatives. When brought in close proximity in a competitive situation, competitive tendencies were more pronounced against nonkin than against kin. The test paradigm consisted of a sharable basin filled with water made available after three hours of water deprivation. The monkeys could either drink together or exclude one another. Tolerance was defined as co-drinking and co-occupying as a proportion of all encounters around the basin (cf. de Waal 1986). As shown in Figure 2-4, drink tolerance was higher among kin than nonkin ($z = 3.25$ toward juveniles; $z = 2.61$ toward adults; both $p < 0.01$). Because this measure weighs tolerant against intolerant encounters, the result means that, at least in this situation, the proximity of kin provokes fewer aggressive and withdrawal responses than the proximity of nonkin.

In summary, the special kinship relationships of rhesus monkeys are reflected in close association, frequent grooming, and greater social tolerance. Yet, at the same time, these monkeys attack their relatives more, especially the younger ones. Rather than a mere result of proximity, this aggression probably reflects active socialization. Older relatives teach youngsters "rules of conduct," a process culminating in but not ending with weaning. As observed by Bernstein and Ehardt (1986:746): "When aggression is no more severe than necessary to modify unacceptable behavior, and when unacceptable behavior may provoke more serious aggression from nonkin, then aggressive socialization of immatures by their older relatives may improve the inclusive fitness of the relatives."

HOW RELATIONSHIPS ARE MAINTAINED

Surely, no matter how complexly social their lives become, individuals continue to have divergent needs. But these diverging needs result in their competing with each other *in addition* to cooperating, not instead of cooperating (Smith 1986:74).

When speaking of so-called constructive aggression we have to keep several distinctions in mind. First of all, a behavior that is "adaptive" in the eyes of a biologist is not necessarily "good" in the eyes of a particular human culture. The concept of biological adaptivity refers to a behavior's impact on the survival and reproduction of the performer and its relatives, which is not always the criterion underlying our moral standards, although the two are probably not independent (Alexander 1987).

Second, just as a plant is condemned as a weed if found in the wrong place, aggression can occur with the wrong intensity in the wrong context. So, even if a certain form of aggression is considered adaptive, this cannot be generalized to the same form under different circumstances, and even less to different forms. This would be the opposite error of those who define all aggressive behavior as antisocial. The distinctions are far from clear-cut, however: adaptive and maladaptive aggression often form a continuum. A mother threatening or physically disciplining her child for his own benefit, a mother beating her child harder than necessary for an offense, and a mother seriously abusing her child engage in similar behavior with different intensities. Both the crucial distinctions with respect to intention, context, and consequences, and the common thread deserve recognition.

Third, judging a particular aggressive act to be adaptive does not mean that it carries benefits only. The so-called "moralistic aggression" discussed above, for example, may promote rather egalitarian give-and-take relationships among chimpanzees, something we value highly in some societies. Yet, the same aggressive behavior also disturbs relationships. Positive functions have to be weighed against possible physical and social damage. The difference between a socially acceptable and unacceptable dose of aggression depends on this balance as well as on the coping capacity of the relationship, i.e., the capacity to continue the beneficial side of a relationship despite occasional conflict. The most basic manifestation of this coping capacity is the restoration of physical closeness following aggression (de Waal 1989c).

Traditionally, aggressive behavior has been viewed as a dispersive behavior, that is, a behavior of which the predominant effect is spacing among animals (e.g., Hediger 1941; Scott 1958; Marler 1976). Yet, the opposite may be observed in primates: aggression may actually lead to *decreased* interindividual distances within a group. Continuous video recording of the large chimpanzee colony at Arnhem Zoo (Netherlands) revealed that, after a fight had occurred, the contenders were within 2 meters of one another more often than before the fight. Obviously, aggressors were avoided during the incident itself, but rapprochement often began as soon as the hostilities had ceased. This was not due to lack of space as the Arnhem colony lives on an island of nearly 1 hectare with plenty of room for adversaries to stay out of each others' way (de Waal and van Roosmalen 1979). If this result contradicts the view of aggression as a dispersive behavior, we have to keep in mind that the early ethologists who developed this idea focused on territorial species. Aggressive confrontation between territory owners differs from intragroup conflict in that an increase in distance is not merely an effect but the *goal* of such behavior (i.e., the behavior is regulated by its effect on interindividual distance).

Another method of study in Arnhem was to record the behavior of a chimpanzee for 45 minutes after he or she had been in conflict with another. We found that opponents seek contact relatively shortly after the conflict, and that these reunions involve special behavior patterns. Typically, contact between former combatants is preceded by an invitational hand gesture, with outstretched arm and open hand. If the other accepts the invitation, the two embrace and kiss in chimpanzee fashion, with an open mouth pressed on the partner's open mouth (de Waal and van Roosmalen 1979).

These observations led us to formulate a *reconciliation* hypothesis, according to which primates try to "undo" the damage that their relationships incur from aggression. The only cognitive capacities strictly required for this process are individual recognition and a good memory (i.e., the animals need to remember with whom they fought). Both capacities are present in a wide range of species, from elephants to zebras, and from dolphins to hyenas. There is no *a priori* reason, therefore, to assume that reconciliation behavior is limited to the primate order. Yet, it is only in this order that reconciliation has thus far been demonstrated, using the following three criteria:

1. *Contact increase.* Following aggression, the probability of contact between two individuals is higher than usual.
2. *Partner specificity.* The increase in contact specifically concerns the former adversaries.
3. *Behavioral distinctness.* Reunions between former opponents involve special reassurance behavior rarely observed in other contexts.

Several systematic studies have tested these requirements following the paradigm of the first controlled investigation into these issues by de Waal and Yoshihara (1983). This study concerned the rhesus monkey, an interesting species because of its reputation as one of the most aggressive primates, both in captivity and in the wild. We assumed that if reconciliation behavior can be demonstrated in this belligerent species, it must be a widespread phenomenon indeed.

Data collection concerned spontaneous aggressive incidents in a captive group. Let us say that a female named Ommie chases another female, named Beatle, at 1415 h today. We activate a stopwatch as soon as the conflict is over, and observe one of the two contestants, say Ommie, for 10 minutes, recording all her interactions with other monkeys. This is called the post-conflict observation. Tomorrow, again at 1415 h, we will follow Ommie again, collecting the same data, but this time without any preceding aggression. This is called the matched-control observation. As a result of this procedure, the control observations have the same distribution over the individuals in the group, the time of day, and the seasons of the year as the post-conflict observations. This means that differences between the two types of observation are probably caused by the factor in which we are interested, that is, the previous occurrence of aggression. This procedure was followed for 350 aggressive incidents.

The data confirmed that rhesus monkeys meet the criteria for reconciliation. They more often initiate friendly contact following aggression than during control periods, and show a preference for contact with the former opponent. Reassurance behavior, such as lipsmacking and embracing, occurs more often during these reunions than during normal contacts. We also found that reconciliation was most predictable between individuals with close social bonds. For example, if a mother punished her adult daughter in a fight the two females would almost certainly come together afterwards. If the same female attacked another female with which she had no special relationship she might subsequently ignore her. The correlation with bond strength supports the idea that post-conflict contact serves to repair a relationship; the most valuable relationships are the most in need of repair.

Recently, this work has been replicated on a variety of other primates by de

Waal (1987), de Waal and Ren (1988), York and Rowell (1988), and Aureli et al. (1989). The main difference between these studies and the one above is an improvement in control procedures. For example, de Waal (1987) compared the post-conflict behavior of bonobos, or pygmy chimpanzees, with both their baseline activity and behavior immediately preceding the aggressive incident. In another approach, de Waal (1984) and Cords (1988) experimentally induced aggression with attractive foods. All studies report an increase in friendly contact following aggression among primates. The reconciliation hypothesis is strongly supported, therefore. The next step will be to determine the conditions under which primates seek reunion with opponents, and the consequences of this behavior for long-term relationships (de Waal, n.d.).

The discovery of reconciliation behavior opens a new perspective on the role of aggression in conflict resolution; it can help us understand the compatibility of high aggression levels and social bonding, as demonstrated in the previous section for kinship relations among rhesus monkeys. In this light it is hardly surprising to hear a prominent human family being described as engaging in "a lot of good healthy fights that brought us all closer" (Neil Bush in *The New York Times*, 15 January 1989). The existence of mechanisms of social repair means that confrontation should not be viewed as a barrier to sociality but rather as an unavoidable element upon which relationships can be built and strengthened.

CONCLUSION

Aggression can be both adaptive and maladaptive, just as it can be both an integrated part of relationships and thoroughly disturb them. These fundamental distinctions are largely ignored by ideological approaches to "the problem" of aggression as these approaches tend to focus on extreme forms, and to isolate the phenomenon of aggression from the social context. Because in this frame of thinking scientific explanation amounts to moral justification, the development of explanatory models, particularly functional ones, is seriously discouraged.

Recent work on conflict resolution in primates suggests a more profitable approach. Instead of treating peacemaking as a victory of reason over instinct, or as a human invention, there is now a possibility to seek continuity with other animals in this area. The key element is to move from an individualistic perspective on behavior to a relational perspective, including attention to mechanisms that cancel some of the harmful consequences of aggression. That aggressive behavior evolved in tandem with the means to control it was, of course, already Lorenz's (1967) message, but this point has been largely forgotten as critics focused their attention on his drive concept.

Refutations of so-called biological determinism, however well-intentioned, create a serious dilemma because, as Manning (1989, p. 56) warned, "... by their apparent denial of genetically based biasses [they] seem to imply that, if such biasses were found, they would seal our fate." A quarter-century after Lorenz's book, we understand enough of both aggression and its controlling mechanisms to solve this dilemma through a research program that pays equal attention to genetic and environmental factors without in any way giving in to the "biological pessimism" that worries the authors of the Seville Statement.

SUMMARY

The Seville Statement on Violence, which attacks the belief that human nature stands in the way of world peace, is criticized for its ideological nature. The Statement is shown to caricature the biological approach to aggressive behavior by suggesting that this approach excludes environmental and cultural influences. Also criticized, however, is the one-sided attention by some evolutionary biologists to competition, and their terminological confusion between reproductive success in relation to natural selection and selfishness at the psychological level. It is argued that, instead of investigating social behavior entirely from the individual perspective, more attention should be paid to long-term social relationships, and to the structuring role of aggressive behavior. Primates possess powerful mechanisms of reassurance and reconciliation that allow them to cope with most of the socially negative effects of intragroup aggression. As a result, aggression can be a well-integrated part of and can contribute constructively to social relationships. Two examples are discussed, i.e., the use of "moralistic aggression" among chimpanzees to promote egalitarian food sharing relationships, and the role of threats and punishment in the socialization of young rhesus monkeys by older relatives.

ACKNOWLEDGMENTS

The macaque studies reported in this paper were supported by the National Science Foundation (BNS-8311595 and BNS-8616853) and by grant RR-00167 from the National Institutes of Health to the Wisconsin Regional Primate Research Center. The food sharing study on chimpanzees was supported by the H. F. Guggenheim Foundation and by NIH grant RR-00165 to the Yerkes Regional Primate Research Center. I thank Mary Schatz and Jackie Kinney for typing of the manuscript, and the book editors for detailed comments. This is publication No. 28-025 of the WRPRC.

REFERENCES

Adams, D. and S. Bosch. 1987. The myth that war is intrinsic to human nature discourages action for peace by young people, pp. 121–137. In *Essays on Violence*, J. Ramirez, R. Hinde, and J. Groebel, eds. Publicaciones de la Universidad de Sevilla.

Alexander, R. D. 1987. *The Biology of Moral Systems*. New York: Aldine.

Ardrey, R. 1966. *The Territorial Imperative*. New York: Atheneum.

Aureli, P., C. van Schaik, and J. A. R. A. M. van Hooff. 1989. Functional aspects of reconciliation among captive long-tailed macaques (*Macaca fascicularis*). *American Journal of Primatology* 19:39–52.

Badcock, C. R. 1986. *The Problem of Altruism: Freudian–Darwinian Solutions*. Oxford: Blackwell.

Bernstein, I. S. and C. Ehardt. 1986. The influence of kinship and socialization on aggressive behaviour in rhesus monkeys (*Macaca mulatta*). *Animal Behaviour* 34:739–747.

Bernstein, I. S. and T. P. Gordon. 1974. The function of aggression in primate societies. *American Scientist* 62:304–311.

Bohannan, P. 1983. Some bases of aggression and their relationship to law, pp. 147–158. In *Law, Biology and Culture*, M. Gruter and P. Bohannan, eds. Santa Barbara, CA: Ross-Erikson.

Cords, M. 1988. Resolution of aggressive conflicts by immature long-tailed macaques (*Macaca fascicularis*). *Animal Behavior* 36:1124–1135.

Coser, L. A. 1966. Some social functions of violence. *The Annals of the American Academy of Political and Social Science* 364:8–18.

Crook, J. H. 1970. Sources of cooperation in animals and man, pp. 160–178. In *Aggression and Evolution*, C. Otten, ed. Xerox College Lexington, MA: Xerox College Publishers.

Dawkins, R. 1976. *The Selfish Gene.* Oxford: Oxford University Press.

Fox, R. 1988. The Seville Declaration: Anthropology's auto-da-fé. *Academic Questions* 1:35–47.

Genoves, S. 1988. Correspondence with UNESCO. *The Seville Statement on Violence Newsletter* 3 (1).

Goodall, J. 1963. My life among wild chimpanzees. *National Geographic* 124:272–308.

———. 1986. *The Chimpanzees of Gombe: Patterns of Behavior.* Cambridge, MA: Belknap.

Gould, S. J. 1980. *Ever since Darwin.* Harmondsworth, UK: Penguin.

Gouzoules, S. and H. Gouzoules. 1987. Kinship, pp. 299–305. In *Primate Societies*, B. B. Smuts, D. L. Cheney, R. M. Seyfarth, R. W. Wrangham, and T. T. Struhsaker, eds. Chicago: University of Chicago Press.

Hall, K. R. L. 1964. Aggression in monkey and ape societies, pp. 51–64. In *The Natural History of Aggression*, J. Carthy and F. Ebling, eds. New York: Academic Press.

Hand, J. 1986. Resolution of social conflicts: Dominance, egalitarianism, spheres of dominance, and game theory. *Quarterly Review of Biology* 61:201–220.

Hediger, H. 1941. Biologische gesetzmässigkeiten im verhalten von wirbeltieren, pp. 37–55. *Mitteilungen Naturforschungs Gesellschaft Bern.*

Hinde, R. A. 1970. Aggression, pp. 1–23. In *Biology and the Human Sciences*, J. Pringle, ed. Oxford: Clarendon Press.

———. 1987. Reply to Manson and Wrangham. *Human Ethology Newsletter* 5:4–5.

Hinde, R. A. and J. Stevenson-Hinde. 1976. Towards understanding relationships: Dynamic stability, pp. 451–479. In *Growing Points in Ethology*, P. Bateson and R. Hinde, eds. New York: Cambridge University Press.

Hobbes, T. 1950 [1651]. *Leviathan.* New York: Dutton.

Huxley, T. H. 1888. The struggle for existence: A programme. *Nineteenth Century*, February, quoted in Kropotkin (1902).

Isaac, G. 1978. The food-sharing behavior of protohuman hominids. *Scientific American* 238:90–108.

Jacoby, S. 1983. *Wild Justice: The Evolution of Revenge.* New York: Harper and Row.

Kropotkin, P. 1972 [1902]. *Mutual Aid: A Factor of Evolution.* New York: New York University Press.

Kummer, H. 1979. On the value of social relationships to nonhuman primates: A heuristic scheme. *Social Science Information* 17:687–705.

Kurland, J. 1977. *Kin Selection in the Japanese Monkey. Contributions to Primatology 12.* Basel: Karger.

Lorenz, K. 1967. *On Aggression.* London: Methuen.

Manning, A. 1989. The genetic bases of aggression, pp. 48–57. In *Aggression and War*, J. Groebel and R. Hinde, eds. Cambridge: Cambridge University Press.

Manson, J. H. and R. W. Wrangham. 1987. Is human aggression nonbiological? Problems with the Statement on Violence. *Human Ethology Newsletter* 5:3–4.

Marler, P. 1976. On animal aggression. *American Psychologist* 31:239–246.

Mauss, M. 1970 [1925]. *The Gift*. London: Routledge & Kegan Paul.

Maynard Smith, J. and G. Price. 1973. The logic of animal conflict. *Nature* 246:15–18.

Midgley, M. 1979. Gene-juggling. *Philosophy* 54:439–458.

Money, J. 1988. Current status of sex research. *Journal of Psychology and Human Sexuality* 1:5–16.

Morris, D. 1967. *The Naked Ape*. London: Jonathan Cape.

Nishida, T., M. Hiraiwa-Hasegawa, T. Hasegawa, and Y. Takahata. 1985. Group extinction and female transfer in wild chimpanzees in the Mahale National Park, Tanzania. *Zeitschrift für Tierpsychologie* 67:284–301.

Nissen, H. and M. Crawford. 1936. A preliminary study of food-sharing behavior in young chimpanzees. *Journal of Comparative Psychology* 22:383–419.

Popp, J. L. and I. DeVore. 1979. Aggressive competition and social dominance theory: Synopsis, pp. 317–338. In *The Great Apes*, D. Hamburg and E. McCown, eds. Menlo Park, CA: Benjamin Cummings.

Power, M. 1986. The foraging adaptation of chimpanzees, and the recent behaviors of the provisioned apes in Gombe and Mahale National Parks, Tanzania. *Human Evolution* 1:251–266.

Sahlins, M. 1965. On the sociology of primitive exchange. pp. 139–236. In *The Relevance of Models for Social Anthropology*, M. Banton, ed. London: Tavistock.

Scott, J. P. 1958. *Animal Behavior*. Chicago: University of Chicago Press.

Smith, W. J. 1986. An "informational" perspective on manipulation. pp. 71–86. In *Deception: Perspectives on Human and Nonhuman Deceit*, R. Mitchell and N. Thompson, eds. Albany, New York: SUNY Press.

Somit, A. 1990. Humans, chimps, and bonobos: The biological bases of aggression, war, and peacemaking. *Journal of Conflict Resolution* 34:553–582.

Strayer, F. F. and J. M. Noel. 1986. The prosocial and antisocial functions of preschool aggression: An ethological study of triadic conflict among young children, pp. 107–131. In *Altruism and Aggression: Biological and Social Origins*, C. Zahn-Waxler, E. M. Cummings and R. Iannotti, eds. Cambridge: Cambridge University Press.

Suzuki, A. 1971. Carnivority and cannibalism among forest-living chimpanzees. *Journal of the Anthropological Society of Nippon* 79:30–48.

Teleki, G. 1973. *The Predatory Behavior of Wild Chimpanzees*. Lewisburg: Bucknell University Press.

Tiger, L. and R. Fox. 1971. *The Imperial Animal*. New York: Dell.

Trivers, R. L. 1971. The evolution of reciprocal altruism. *Quarterly Review of Biology* 46:35–57.

Vehrencamp, S. 1983. A model for the evolution of despotic versus egalitarian societies. *Animal Behaviour* 31:667–682.

de Waal, F. B. M. 1982. *Chimpanzee Politics*. London: Jonathan Cape.

———. 1984. Coping with social tension: Sex differences in the effect of food provisioning to small rhesus monkey groups. *Animal Behaviour* 32:765–773.

———. 1986. Class structure in a rhesus monkey group: The interplay between dominance and tolerance. *Animal Behaviour* 34:1033–1040.

———. 1987. Tension regulation and nonreproductive functions of sex among captive bonobos. *National Geographic Research* 3:318–335.

———. 1989a. Dominance "style" and primate social organization. pp. 243–263. In *Comparative Socioecology: The Behavioural Ecology of Humans and Other Mammals*, V. Standen and R. Foley, eds. London: Blackwells.

de Waal, F. B. M. 1989b. Food sharing and reciprocal obligations among chimpanzees. *Journal of Human Evolution* 18:433–459.

———. 1989c. *Peacemaking Among Primates.* Cambridge, MA: Harvard University Press.

———. n.d. The biological basis of peaceful co-existence: A review of reconciliation research on monkeys and apes. In *What we Know about Peace.* T. Gregor, ed.

de Waal, F. B. M. and L. M. Luttrell. 1988. Mechanisms of social reciprocity in three primate species: Symmetrical relationship characteristics or cognition? *Ethology and Sociobiology* 9:101–118.

———. 1989. Toward a comparative socioecology of the genus *Macaca*: Intergroup comparisons of rhesus and stumptail monkeys. *American Journal of Primatology* 10:83–109.

de Waal, F. B. M. and R. Ren. 1988. Comparison of the reconciliation behavior of stumptail and rhesus macaques. *Ethology* 78:129–142.

de Waal, F. B. M. and A. van Roosmalen. 1979. Reconciliation and consolation among chimpanzees. *Behavioral Ecology and Sociobiology* 5:55–66.

de Waal, F. B. M. and D. Yoshihara. 1983. Reconciliation and re-directed affection in rhesus monkeys. *Behaviour* 85:224–241.

Washburn, S. and J. Lancaster. 1968. The evolution of hunting, pp. 293–303. In *Man the Hunter*, R. Lee and I. DeVore, eds. Chicago: Aldine.

Wilson, E. O. 1978. *On Human Nature.* Cambridge, MA: Harvard University Press.

Wrangham, R. 1975. The behavioral ecology of chimpanzees in Gombe National Park, Tanzania. Unpublished Ph.D. dissertation, Cambridge University.

Yerkes, R. and A. Yerkes. 1935. Social behavior in infrahuman primates, pp. 973–1033. In *A Handbook of Social Psychology*, C. Murchinson, ed. Worcester: Clark University Press.

York, A. and T. Rowell. 1988. Reconciliation following aggression in patas monkeys, *Erythrocebus patas. Animal Behaviour* 36:502–509.

Zenner, W. P. 1988. Making scholarly decisions. *Anthropology Newsletter*, February: 2.

3

Dominance Hierarchies as Partial Orders.
A New Look at Old Ideas

DONALD STONE SADE

When agonism is observed among individual monkeys living in social groups, the observer can rank any two monkeys by the frequency of wins over losses in their fights, the most frequent winner being termed dominant. An overall pattern of interaction often becomes apparent in which all animals come to be ranked in order of such wins and losses of fights. The monkey who usually beats each other monkey is called the alpha (or dominant) animal. The monkey who usually loses to each other monkey is the omega (or most subordinate) animal. The order itself, the agonistic network, is often called a dominance hierarchy.

It is often assumed that animals fight over scarce resources, such as food or mates, and that fighting is therefore an aspect of inter-individual competition. The winners of fights are assumed to be superior to the losers in some way, such as in size, strength, ability, vigor. If competitive superiority is assumed to be due to genetic superiority then fights, or dominance interactions, mediate genetic competition.

Now, although these statements are deliberately something of a caricature of what is actually in the literature, ignoring as they do all the qualifications and complexities that in fact are widely recognized, the following is still a fair summary of current thinking: The higher ranking animals are better in some way than the lower ranking ones, and therefore it should be easier for a monkey to beat another that is much lower in rank than one who is of nearly the same rank. If this were found to be not the case, it would be necessary to re-evaluate the assumption that rank in a hierarchy reflects individual ability, and therefore also the assumption that dominance interactions mediate genetic competition.

These issues can be modeled with mathematical structures and the assumptions tested statistically. The assumption that the further removed in rank that an individual is from a dominant monkey the easier it is for the dominant to beat him is an assumption of "Strong Stochastic Transitivity" (SST). This is expressed as follows: Let p_{ij} be the probability that the ith monkey will beat the jth monkey in a fight and let p_{jk} be the probability that the jth monkey will beat the kth monkey in a fight. If p_{ij} and p_{jk} are both greater than 0.5 (that is, the dominant member of the dyad has a better than random probability of winning the fight), then SST implies that $p_{ik} \geq \max\{p_{ij}, p_{jk}\}$ for all ijk.

In contrast to SST, suppose that the ease with which a monkey wins a fight is independent of the distance between the ranks of the dominant and subordinate members of the pair. This implies that $p_{ij} = p_{jk} = p_{ik} =$ a constant. This latter condition is called Equality (EQ).

Methods have been developed to distinguish SST and EQ in dominance orders (Iverson and Sade 1990). They are applied in the present paper to the analysis of the agonistic network among male rhesus monkeys. To anticipate, EQ fits the data as well as or better than does SST. This has been found in red deer, baboons, and rhesus monkeys (Iverson and Sade 1990) and in emperor tamarins (Knox 1989; Knox and Sade 1991). The usual assumptions about dominance hierarchies should be re-examined.

REVIEW

The mathematical structure usually used to model animal dominance hierarchies is a completely connected, transitive directed graph (digraph) (Harary et al. 1965). Each node of the digraph represents an individual animal. The arrows (edges) connecting the nodes show which pairs of individuals (dyads) have established dominance relations, and the direction of dominance within each such dyad. Generally the edges are not valued, that is the frequency with which individuals interact is not shown. The matrix representation of this model $M = \{m_{ij}; i, j \leq k\}$ is a binary matrix with ones in every cell above the main diagonal and zeros in every cell below it, the main diagonal itself being undefined (or by convention $m_{ij} = 0$ for all $i = j$). Matrices recording actual dominance relations have generally been evaluated (if at all) by the degree to which they depart from transitivity due to the presence of *cycles* (*i* beats *j* beats *k* beats *i*). Still the best known of such methods is the familiar Landau Index of Hierarchy, H (Landau 1951), which, varying between zero and one, characterizes with a single number the degree to which the observed ranking approaches perfect transitivity. Landau's Index is purely descriptive and does not indicate the likelihood that any particular value could have been obtained by a chance ordering of the individuals in the hierarchy.

Appleby (1983) applied statistical procedures developed by Kendall to an adaptation of Landau's Index. Appleby concluded that, although high values of Landau's Index H are usually reported in the literature, chance alone could account for an unacceptably large proportion of the reported linear or nearly linear hierarchies, especially when k, the number of individuals, is small.

Two aspects of empirical dominance records are not well modeled by Landau's (1951) method or its statistical extension by Appleby (1983). The first aspect is that, especially in field observations, interactions are lacking for some dyads. This means that the graphs representing the dominance relations are at best *partial* rather than complete orders (Harary et al. 1965:265–267), leaving aside the question of whether the graph contains cycles. For some *ij* dyads both the cells m_{ij} and m_{ji} will equal zero in the matrix representation of the graph. Landau's method requires all dyads to have been observed. Appleby arbitrarily assigns one-half to each cell of an unobserved dyad.

The second aspect is that, especially in naturalistic studies, in which encounters between individuals are observed as they happen rather than being prearranged by an experimenter, the number of interactions varies from dyad to dyad. Usually it is thought desirable to observe as many interactions as possible within each dyad in order to strengthen the investigator's confidence in the usual direction of dominance within the relation. However, both Landau's method and Appleby's statistical extension of it censor the observations so that the cells of the dominance matrix contain only ones or zeros. Any information contained in multiple observations is thus discarded.

Therefore there is a need for methods for the analysis of partial orders and digraphs with valued edges as more realistic models of dominance relations. Several approaches toward this goal have appeared.

Boyd and Silk (1983) developed a model that assigned cardinal ranks to individuals using the Bradley–Terry–Luce model from the literature on paired comparisons. Use of this model assumes a strictly decreasing interval scale at least. Boyd and Silk (1983) assume that a stochastically transitive hierarchy exists in the dominance data and then fit the data to the model. The assumptions are not directly tested in their approach. However, their method makes use of all the information available in the raw dominance matrix, in contrast to the approaches mentioned earlier.

McMahan and Morris (1984) used a maximum likelihood procedure to discover the best ranking of a group of individuals, assuming weak stochastic transitivity as the model of dominance relations. Their procedure makes use of all the information in the dominance matrix and does not require that interactions within all dyads be observed. Whether weak stochastic transitivity is the best model was not tested in their paper.

Iverson and Falmagne (1985) and Iverson and Harp (1987) explore statistical methods for assessing how closely empirical observations (measurements) approach underlying conditions of various theoretical order restrictions, such as the forms of stochastic transitivity assumed by Boyd and Silk (1983) and by McMahan and Morris (1984) as underlying properties of the dominance hierarchy.

These methods were adapted by Iverson and Sade (1990) to re-evaluate the dominance data presented by Appleby (1983) and by McMahan and Morris (1984) against the null hypotheses of Chance as well as against the strong models of hierarchy, Strong Stochastic Transitivity (SST) and Equality (EQ). The findings of Iverson and Sade (1990) were that in all sets of data examined, including those of Appleby, Chance was easily rejected. EQ, curiously, was not rejected as a valid underlying structure for any of the three sets of data, and EQ provided at least as adequate a model for the three hierarchies as did SST. Therefore the present paper will focus on EQ as the characteristic of interest underlying the dominance hierarchy.

EQUALITY

Equality (EQ) is a model of stochastic transitivity. If p_{ij} is the probability that the ith individual dominates the jth individual, then $p_{ij} + p_{ji} = 1$. EQ implies that there is a rank ordering of individuals for which p_{ij} equals a constant, θ, for all

$i < j \le k$, where k is the number of individuals considered. This implies that it is no easier for the dominant monkey to beat the lowest ranking monkey than it is for the dominant to beat the one next lower ranking than himself. Conversely, a low ranking monkey should be able to rise in rank over the dominant one as easily as over the one just above him in the hierarchy. θ is estimated from the ratio of wins to total encounters within each dyad. If n_{ij} is the total number of encounters between the ith and jth individual and r_{ij} is the number won by i, $i < j$, then $\theta = r_{ij}/n_{ij}$ summed over all $(k * (k - 1))/2$ dyads in the group. Computationally this is equivalent to summing the above diagonal cells of the dominance matrix and dividing by the sum for the entire matrix, after the rows and columns of the matrix have been arranged to represent the proposed ordering of individuals in the dominance hierarchy.

OUTLINE OF THE PROCEDURE

The present paper applies the approach of Iverson and Sade (1990) to the male dominance hierarchy in a large group of rhesus monkeys living on Cayo Santiago, Puerto Rico. The conditions of the monkey colony and the detailed demographic history of the population is given in Sade et al. (1985). *A priori* knowledge suggests that this group of animals, as well as being larger than the groups considered in previous papers, is composed of several subgroups and therefore may not form a single well-ordered set of dyads. The full matrix is given in the Appendix to this chapter. The matrix records the number and direction of all the agonistic interactions observed among these animals during the mating season of 1974. Row labels indicate the winner, or dominant individual, for each dyad. Column labels indicate the loser, or subordinate individual, for each dyad. The criteria for determining the dominant and subordinate individuals in an interaction are given in earlier papers (Sade 1967, 1972, 1973).

The matrix was arranged by ordering the rows and columns so as to reduce the number of values below the main diagonal. In the present case this was done by inspection. This is the proposed hierarchy evaluated in the sections that follow. If it were thought worth the computational effort, the best possible ordering (or the set of best orderings if there were no unique best hierarchy) might be found by applying the maximum likelihood algorithm used by McMahan and Morris (1984). However, this was not done in the present case.

Chance was then tested against EQ for the ordering of Table 3-1. The computational formula

$$p \ge k! \binom{N}{r*}\left(\frac{1}{2}\right)^N \left(\frac{r*/2}{r* - N/2}\right), \tag{3-1}$$

where $r* = \sum_{i<j} r_{ij}$, gives the probability that the observed ordering could have arisen by chance, in which case there would be no evidence for a hierarchy, here one characterized by EQ.

To account for the unobserved dyads $k!$ should be replaced by a smaller number, the count of acyclical graphs possible among the total number of possible graphs that could be constructed given the number of observed dyads. In the present case this means finding the number of acyclical graphs among the 288! that could be constructed, a formidable, if not impossible task. However, as Iverson and Sade (1990) show by example, the p values for actual data are so small that even enormous increases in p still result in rejection of Chance as a reasonable hypothesis.

Having shown that Chance is unlikely as an explanation for the observed ordering of individuals in the dominance hierarchy, it is still necessary to enquire whether EQ is an adequate characterization of the model by applying a goodness of fit test. Iverson and Sade (1990) develop a likelihood ratio statistic and a Pearson chi-square statistic, both of which should approximate the chi-square distribution. In fact the asymptotic behaviors of these two tests are not known in the present application. The computational formula for the likelihood ratio stochastic, lambda, used in the present paper is

$$\text{Lambda} = 2 \sum_{i<j}^{k} \sum_{j>i}^{k} m_{ij} * \ln((m_{ij}/(m_{ij} + m_{ji}))/\theta)$$

$$+ 2 \sum_{i>j}^{k} \sum_{j<i}^{k} m_{ij} * \ln((m_{ij}/(m_{ij} + m_{ji}))/(1 - \theta)) \qquad (3\text{-}2)$$

for all $(m_{ij} + m_{ji}) > 0$.

The computational formula for the corresponding Pearson chi-square statistic is

$$\text{Pearson} = \sum_{i<j}^{k} \sum_{j>i}^{k} (m_{ij} - (\theta(m_{ij} + m_{ji})))^2/((m_{ij} + m_{ji})\theta(1 - \theta)) \qquad (3\text{-}3)$$

for all $(m_{ij} + m_{ji}) > 0$.

The degrees of freedom of each of these statistics are simply one less than the number of observed dyads. Thus the degrees of freedom are reduced by the number of dyads for which no data are available.

THE FULL MATRIX

Applying these formulae to the dominance matrix (listed in the Appendix to this chapter) for the rhesus monkey males yields the results given in Table 3-1.

The extremely low value of p makes it unlikely that Chance would be a reasonable hypothesis even if the unobserved dyads were taken into account. However, whether EQ should also be rejected is unclear. The likelihood statistic Lambda does not exceed the estimated critical value of chi-square for the 0.05 level of rejection, but the Pearson statistic greatly exceeds it. Iverson and Sade (1990) discovered that the Pearson statistic was more sensitive to cycles in the data than was the likelihood ratio statistic and thus might be the preferable test. Faced with this contradiction between the two tests, one has several choices, given the fact that some sort of underlying structure is indicated by the very strong rejection of Chance as an explanation of the ordering. One might test whether Strong Stochastic Transitivity fits the observations better than does EQ. However,

Table 3-1 Analysis of the Dominance Matrix for Cayo Santiago Group F Adult and Adolescent Males for the Mating Season of 1974. Observations were made by Douglas Rhodes.

$$k = 35$$
$$N = 857$$
$$\text{Estimate of } R = 825$$
$$\theta = 0.96$$
$$\text{No. observed dyads} = 288$$
$$\text{No. unobserved dyads} = 307$$
$$p \geq 1.7e - 160$$
$$\text{Lambda} = 231.65$$
$$\text{Pearson} = 660.41$$
$$\text{DF} = 287$$
$$\text{Approximate critical value} = 335.34, \alpha = 0.05$$

prior knowledge of the composition of the group of monkeys suggests that the dominance matrix as given actually contains several hierarchies that are inappropriately combined.

It would be possible to decompose the partial order represented by the entire matrix into its several complete orders and examine each for biological correlates of interest. Such a procedure would be using the complete order as a grouping criterion. Although this would be of interest an alternative procedure is followed here. Here subgroups of individuals are identified on demographic and biological grounds and the dominance order within each subgroup evaluated using the methods illustrated above.

Three subgroups are examined. The first consists of the adult males who had been members of the group for at least one year (an arbitrary period) prior to the study. The second subgroup consists of the adult males who were recent immigrants and who therefore might be expected to have not yet established social relations, including agonistic ones, with the central portion of the group. These might loosely be called "peripheral males." The third subgroup consists of the group's adolescent natal males. Their subsequent history suggests that they formed a relatively cohesive unit within the group, but at the time of the observations reported on here had not yet become integrated into the dominance hierarchy of the adults.

THE OLD MALES

The dominance matrix for the adult males who had been members of the group for at least one year is given in the Appendix to this chapter. The statistics evaluating this matrix are given in Table 3-2.

Here again we see the discrepancy between the likelihood ratio statistic and Pearson's chi-square. In this matrix the effect is due largely to the presence of a single male R009 whose relations account for all the cycles in the hierarchy. Without him it is possible to find a rank order containing no cycles. There is some biological justification for not including R009 in the same category as the other

Table 3-2 Analysis of the Dominance Matrix for Cayo Santiago Group F Adult Males who had been Members for a Year or More Prior to the Mating Season of 1974 (Appendix to this chapter). Observations were made by Douglas Rhodes.

$$k = 13$$
$$N = 309$$
Estimate of $R = 303$
$$\theta = 0.98$$
No. observed dyads $= 60$
No. unobserved dyads $= 18$
$$p \geq 7.0e - 77$$
Lambda $= 48.86$
Pearson $= 226.72$
$$DF = 59$$
Approximate critical value $= 81.62$, $\alpha = 0.05$

Table 3-3 Analysis of the Dominance Hierarchy Among the Old Male Members of Group F after Removing the Castrate R009 from the Matrix (Appendix to this chapter).

$$k = 12$$
$$N = 280$$
Estimate of $R = 279$
$$\theta = 1.00$$
No. observed dyads $= 51$
No. unobserved dyads $= 15$
$$p \geq 6.9e - 74$$
Lambda $= 6.76$
Pearson $= 27.10$
$$DF = 50$$
Approximate critical value $= 70.92$, $\alpha = 0.05$

old members. Castrated as a subadult, R009's position in the group in some respects more resembled that of a female or subadult male rather than a full adult male. This was shown in an earlier analysis of the grooming network (Sade 1972). The consequence of removing R009 from the hierarchy is shown in Table 3-3.

This analysis shows both the likelihood ratio statistic and the Pearson statistic well below the critical value. Removing R009 from the matrix of all males, however, did not alter the statistics (not shown) to any appreciable degree.

THE NEW OR "PERIPHERAL" MALES

The dominance relations among the new immigrants to Group F are shown in the Appendix to this chapter. The statistical analysis of this matrix is summarized in Table 3-4.

As is to be expected for males peripheral to the main social group and who do not necessarily form a cohesive unit, the number of interactions, N, is rather

Table 3-4 Analysis of Dominance Relations among the New Male Immigrants of Group F. One male, B4, was in the group for only a short time, did not interact with the other new males, and is excluded from the matrix.

$$k = 8$$
$$N = 34$$
Estimate of $R = 34$
$$\theta = 1.00$$
No. observed dyads $= 18$
No. unobserved dyads $= 10$
$$p \geq 2.3e-6$$
Lambda $= 0.00$
Pearson $= 0.00$
DF $= 17$
Approximate critical value $= 29.68$, $\alpha = 0.05$

low and the unobserved dyads amount to a relatively large proportion of the total. Although the uncorrected p value is still small one might begin to wonder to what degree correcting for the number of unobserved dyads would move p toward the chosen alpha. On the other hand, there are no cycles in this hierarchy and no reversals within dyads. Is this due to the small number of observations? In any case $\theta = 1$ and there is no variation on which to base a statistical evaluation of the hypothesis EQ. Both the likelihood ratio statistic and the Pearson statistic are undefined. At least there is no basis for rejecting EQ as a characteristic of this hierarchy.

THE YOUNG NATAL MALES

The final subgroup to consider is composed of the young natal males. Two of these, 407 and 457, left the group during the mating season and were not observed interacting with the others. Therefore they are omitted from the analysis. Table 3-5

Table 3-5 Analysis of Dominance Relations among the Young Natal Males of Group F, Omitting 407 and 457, who Emigrated during the Mating Season and did not Interact with the Others.

$$k = 11$$
$$N = 106$$
Estimate of $R = 102$
$$\theta = 0.96$$
No. observed dyads $= 34$
No. unobserved dyads $= 21$
$$p \geq 2.5e-18$$
Lambda $= 20.88$
Pearson $= 41.74$
DF $= 33$
Approximate critical value $= 50.22$, $\alpha = 0.05$

gives the statistical evaluation of the hierarchy. The matrix for these males is given in the Appendix to this chapter.

In this case the statistics show in a straightforward manner that while Chance is firmly rejected there is no evidence that EQ is not an adequate model with which to characterize the hierarchy.

MATRIX PERMUTATION PROCEDURES FOR EVALUATING EQ AND SST

Matrix permutation procedures have been applied recently to a variety of problems in the social and biological sciences (Dow 1985; Dow and Cheverud 1985; Hubert 1987). These procedures offer nonparametric tests of the similarity of structure between two conforming matrices. Both matrices may contain data, or one may contain data and the other a set of theoretical expectations based upon a particular hypothesis. The similarity of structure between the two matrices is expressed in a score, which must be devised in such a way as to reflect the hypothesis under consideration. In general, the theoretical probability distribution of the score will be unknown. However, the observed score can be compared to the distribution of a sample of scores drawn at random from the theoretical distribution. This is accomplished by repeatedly permuting the matrix subscripts at random. Each permutation results in a new matrix with the original rows and columns in the order of the randomized subscripts. The score is calculated for each randomized matrix. The proportion of scores that exceed the observed score can be used to compute the likelihood of the observed structure in the data.

These procedures were applied to the dominance matrices of the present paper to answer the following question: Given an ordering of animals into a linear or near-linear dominance hierarchy and an order restriction hypothesis, such as Equality (EQ) or Strong Stochastic Transitivity (SST), are there other orderings that conform closer to the proposed hypothesis than does the observed order? The randomization procedure samples, from the unknown theoretical distribution of all possible orderings and scores, each randomized matrix for its agreement with the hypothesis under consideration. In the present application it was not necessary to construct a matrix representing the theoretical structure of the data under the proposed null hypotheses. Rather the scores were calculated directly from the randomized matrices themselves.

EQ was tested by computing the Pearson and likelihood ratio statistics discussed earlier for each randomized matrix and counting the number of matrices whose scores exceeded the magnitude of the observed statistic and therefore were further from EQ than the observed dominance matrix. The score used to test SST was the count of dyads that conformed to SST. This score was computed as follows. The probability p_{ij} that the ith monkey dominates the jth monkey was calculated as described earlier for all m_{ij}, $i < j$. Each p_{il}, $l = ((i + 2)\cdots k)$ was compared to the maximum p_{iq}, $q = ((i + 1)\cdots(l - 1))$ and the matrix score was incremented by one for each $p_{il} > p_{iq}$. The number of matrices that scored higher than the observed matrix is the probability that reordering the original dominance matrix would result in a condition closer to SST. The results are given in Table 3-6.

Table 3-6 Evaluation of EQ and SST by the Matrix Permutation Procedure. Each value is the percentage of the distribution of randomized scores that exceeded the observed score after 1,000 trials. For Pearson and likelihood the values indicate the percentage of the randomized matrices that were further from EQ than the observed dominance matrix. For SST the values indicate the percentage of the randomized matrices that were closer to SST than the observed dominance matrix.

	Percentage of sample greater than observed score		
Dominance matrix	Pearson	Likelihood	SST
Group F 1974 males	100.000	100.000	99.401
Old males	100.000	100.000	23.801
Old males omitting castrated R009	100.000	100.000	21.301
New males	99.901	99.901	11.901
Young natal males	100.000	100.000	49.201

The results of the matrix permutation procedure show that if the rows and columns of the dominance matrices are ordered so as to approximate a linear dominance hierarchy as closely as possible, the matrix will also be as close to EQ as possible. The ordering of the observed dominance matrices does not place them particularly close to SST. Even in the worst case among this set of examples (New Males) there is a greater than 1 in 10 chance that a random reordering would produce a matrix closer to SST than the observed dominance matrix. These results confirm the conclusions reached earlier.

CONCLUSION AND PROSPECTUS

This analysis of the dominance relations among the adolescent and adult male members of a social group of rhesus monkeys shows that, when the group is partitioned according to reasonable demographic and biological criteria, the dominance hierarchies within each subgroup are characterized by the condition EQ. Although statistical questions still remain, due to uncertainty about the asymptotic behavior of the likelihood and Pearson statistics, and the uncertain behavior of the Pearson statistic when θ is near unity, the results of these tests seem to be confirmed through nonparametric, matrix permutation procedures. In particular, the matrix permutation procedure gives completely consistent results when both the Pearson statistic and the likelihood ratio statistic are used to score the observed and randomized matrices, and the results firmly support EQ as the order restriction hypothesis that best characterizes the linear dominance hierarchy.

The approach illustrated in this paper has the potential of contributing to a new understanding of dominance relations. If EQ were to be shown generally to describe the structure of dominance relations as well as or better than alternative models it would be a finding as counter-intuitive as Landau's earlier finding that differences in individual characteristics were insufficient in general to account for the observed linearity (H) of hierarchies. As with Landau's finding, it would further weaken the argument that animals who are somehow phenotypically or genetically superior occupy the higher ranks. If the latter notion were true then the data should show much higher probabilities for winning encounters with lower ranking animals than with those closer in rank (SST), although such a finding would not be sufficient to demonstrate phenotypic or genetic superiority of the dominant individuals.

It is difficult to reconcile the finding of EQ with both the assumption that straightforward competition for rank and its presumed advantages underlie the observed ordering of dominance relations and also with the usual observation that changes in dominance rank generally occur between individuals close together in the hierarchy. If EQ is in fact the usual condition then there must be social and psychological processes operating to ensure that the dominance order is not in continuous flux and upheaval, as should be the case under EQ alone.

Future research should focus on these issues.

SUMMARY

The usually implicitly assumed mathematical structure underlying discussions of animal dominance hierarchies is a completely connected, transitive digraph. However, field observations seldom provide the completed matrices of un-ambiguous agonistic relations necessary to satisfy the very stringent requirements of the assumed underlying structure. A statistical procedure that takes into account the number and direction of agonistic encounters within each dyad and the number of dyads for which the number of interactions $n_{ij} = 0$, was developed to test the model EQ (equality). EQ states that it is possible to find a rank order such that with respect to that rank order the probability p_{ij} that the ith animal dominates the jth animal in any encounter equals a constant θ for all $i < j$ and $1 - \theta$ for all $i > j$. This means that the structure represented in the actual data in any dominance matrix can be represented by a single number more appropriate than Landau's H. In the present paper this procedure is used to evaluate the dominance structure of males in a large group of monkeys, in which a partial ordering of animals, but not a single linear hierarchy, is the most appropriate model. The dominance hierarchies of several natural partitions of the male membership by age and migration history conformed closely to EQ. EQ implies that individuals at any distance in the hierarchy should be able to exchange rank with equal ease, in apparent contradiction to the actually observed stability and predictability of the dominance order. This implies that as yet undiscovered social or psychological processes, rather than resource competition alone, maintain the dominance hierarchy.

ACKNOWLEDGMENTS

The author thanks Geoffrey J. Iverson for his collaboration in developing the original method and Malcolm Dow for helpful advice and discussions. Any errors are solely the author's. Preparation of this paper was aided in part by a grant to The North Country Institute for Natural Philosophy, Inc. from the H. F. Guggenheim Foundation. The original data were collected under a grant from the NSF to Northwestern University. The Cayo Santiago colony was supported by a contract from the DRR, NIH to the University of Puerto Rico.

REFERENCES

Appleby, M. C. 1983. The probability of linearity in hierarchies. *Animal Behaviour* 31:600–608.

Boyd, R. and J. B. Silk. 1983. A method for assigning cardinal dominance ranks. *Animal Behaviour* 31:45–58.

Dow, M. M. 1985. Nonparametric inference procedures for multistate life table analysis. *Journal of Mathematical Sociology* 11:245–263.

Dow, M. M. and J. M. Cheverud. 1985. Comparison of distance matrices in studies of population structure and genetic microdifferentiation: Quadratic assignment. *American Journal of Physical Anthropology* 68:367–373.

Harary, F., R. Z. Norman, and D. Cartwright. 1965. *Structural Models: An Introduction to the Theory of Directed Graphs*. New York: John Wiley and Sons.

Hubert, L. 1987. *Assignment Methods in Combinatorial Data Analysis*. New York: Dekker Press.

Iverson, G. J. and J.-C. Falmagne. 1985. Statistical issues in measurement. *Mathematical Social Sciences* 10:131–153.

Iverson, G. J. and S. A. Harp. 1987. A conditional likelihood ratio test for order restrictions in exponential families. *Mathematical Social Sciences* 14:141–159.

Iverson, G. J. and D. S. Sade. 1990. Statistical issues in the analysis of dominance hierarchies in animal societies. *Journal of Quantitative Anthropology* 2:61–83.

Knox, K. L. 1989. Observations on dominance relations among *Saguinus imperator*, the emperor tamarin (family: Callitrichidae). Doctoral dissertation, Department of Anthropology, Northwestern University, Evanston, Illinois.

Knox, K. L. and D. S. Sade. 1991. Social behavior of the emperor tamarin in captivity. Components of agonistic display and the agonistic network. *International Journal of Primatology* 12:439–480.

Landau, H. G. 1951. On dominance relations and the structure of animal societies. I: Effect of inherent characteristics. *Bulletin of Mathematical Biophysics* 13:1–19.

McMahan, C. A. and M. D. Morris. 1984. Application of maximum likelihood paired comparison ranking to estimation of a linear dominance hierarchy in animal societies. *Animal Behaviour* 32:374–378.

Sade, D. S. 1967. Determinants of dominance in a group of free-ranging rhesus monkeys, pp. 91–114. In *Social Communication Among Primates*, S. A. Altmann, ed. Chicago: University of Chicago Press.

———. 1972. Sociometrics of *Macaca mulatta*. I. Linkages and cliques in grooming matrices. *Folia Primatologica* 18:196–223.

———. 1973. An ethogram for rhesus monkeys. I. Antithetical contrasts in postures and movement. *American Journal of Physical Anthropology* 38:537–542.

Sade, D. S., B. D. Chepko-Sade, J. M. Schneider, S. S. Roberts, and J. T. Richtsmeir. 1985. *Basic Demographic Observations on Free-ranging Rhesus Monkeys*. New Haven: Human Relations Area Files.

APPENDIX: DOMINANCE MATRICES

Group F males mating season 1974 complete matrix

	EE	L7	UB	298	TJ	309	415	056	AL	ZW	R009	DW	JX	K8	2C	292	5D	K7	2E	349	UD	ZH	D2	257	282	254	B4	436	407	409	410	412	414	439	457
EE	0	0	0	0	0	0	0	0	0	0	0	0	0	0	0	0	0	0	0	0	0	0	0	0	0	0	0	10	1	5	6	6	1	0	0
L7	0	0	0	0	0	0	0	0	0	0	0	0	0	0	0	0	0	0	1	0	1	0	0	1	1	1	0	0	0	0	0	0	1	0	0
UB	0	0	0	5	8	1	0	0	0	0	0	0	0	0	0	3	8	2	3	1	0	4	0	3	1	0	0	4	0	6	2	3	0	0	0
298	0	0	0	0	2	5	7	8	9	3	1	0	6	8	0	2	3	0	0	5	1	0	0	3	0	0	0	6	0	1	2	3	1	0	0
TJ	0	0	5	0	0	0	4	1	14	6	5	1	3	1	0	4	3	0	0	5	0	5	1	4	0	2	0	5	0	2	5	0	0	1	1
309	0	0	1	0	0	0	0	0	14	6	5	3	1	6	0	4	3	0	0	0	0	0	0	0	0	0	0	5	0	1	1	0	0	0	0
415	0	0	0	0	0	0	0	1	4	0	5	3	3	6	0	0	7	1	2	1	0	4	1	6	4	0	0	2	0	7	12	4	1	2	0
056	0	0	0	0	0	0	0	0	9	1	0	0	1	0	0	3	3	1	2	1	0	1	0	12	1	2	0	6	0	1	4	1	1	4	0
AL	0	0	0	0	0	0	0	0	0	1	8	0	6	5	0	0	7	2	2	1	1	0	0	4	0	0	0	1	0	3	1	1	1	1	0
ZW	0	0	0	0	0	0	0	0	0	0	3	2	2	6	0	2	10	2	3	0	4	0	0	5	1	2	0	1	0	1	3	1	0	4	0
R009	0	0	0	0	0	0	0	0	0	0	0	0	2	1	1	0	4	3	3	0	1	1	0	4	0	1	0	0	0	0	0	1	0	0	0
DW	0	0	0	0	0	0	0	0	0	0	0	0	3	2	0	2	2	1	1	0	2	3	4	7	4	1	0	2	0	0	0	1	0	0	0
JX	0	0	0	0	0	0	0	0	0	0	0	0	0	2	1	0	4	2	1	0	0	0	0	4	1	1	0	2	0	1	4	0	2	0	0
K8	0	0	0	0	0	0	0	0	0	0	0	0	0	0	0	1	11	6	2	4	4	3	0	4	3	1	0	2	0	4	1	2	2	0	0
2C	0	0	0	0	0	0	0	0	0	0	0	0	0	0	0	2	0	0	0	0	0	0	0	0	1	0	0	0	0	1	0	1	0	0	0
292	0	0	0	0	0	0	0	0	0	0	0	0	0	0	0	0	1	1	3	1	0	1	0	4	3	3	0	2	0	2	2	1	0	0	0
5D	0	0	0	0	0	0	0	0	0	0	0	0	0	0	0	0	0	1	3	0	2	2	2	9	0	1	0	0	0	1	1	1	0	0	0
K7	0	0	0	0	0	0	0	0	0	0	0	0	0	0	0	0	0	0	3	0	3	0	0	4	0	3	0	1	0	1	3	1	0	0	0
2E	0	0	0	0	0	0	0	0	0	0	0	0	0	0	0	0	0	0	0	1	5	5	2	3	1	3	0	1	0	3	1	0	0	0	0
349	0	0	0	0	0	0	0	0	0	0	0	0	0	0	0	0	0	0	0	0	1	0	0	1	0	0	0	0	0	0	0	0	0	0	0
UD	0	0	0	0	0	0	0	0	0	0	0	0	0	0	0	0	0	0	0	0	0	1	0	0	1	1	0	1	0	0	0	1	0	0	0
ZH	0	0	0	0	0	0	0	0	0	0	0	0	0	0	0	0	0	0	0	0	0	0	0	0	1	0	0	2	0	0	0	0	0	0	0
D2	0	0	0	0	0	0	0	0	0	0	0	0	0	0	0	0	0	0	0	0	0	0	0	0	0	0	0	0	0	0	0	0	0	0	0
257	0	1	0	0	0	0	0	0	0	0	0	0	0	0	0	0	0	0	0	0	0	0	0	0	1	0	0	0	0	0	0	0	0	0	0
282	0	0	0	0	0	0	0	0	0	0	0	0	0	0	0	0	0	0	0	0	0	0	0	20	0	0	0	0	0	0	0	0	0	0	0
254	0	0	0	0	0	0	0	0	0	0	0	0	0	0	0	0	0	0	0	0	0	0	0	0	10	0	0	0	0	0	0	0	0	0	0
B4	0	0	0	0	0	0	0	0	0	0	0	0	0	0	0	0	0	0	0	0	0	0	0	0	0	4	0	0	0	0	0	0	0	0	0
436	0	0	0	0	0	0	0	0	0	0	0	0	0	0	0	0	0	0	0	0	0	0	0	0	0	0	0	0	0	4	2	3	1	2	0
407	0	0	0	0	0	0	0	0	0	0	0	0	0	0	0	0	0	0	0	0	1	0	0	0	0	0	0	2	0	0	0	1	0	0	0
409	0	0	0	0	0	0	0	0	0	0	0	0	0	0	0	0	0	0	0	0	0	0	0	0	0	0	0	0	0	0	7	4	0	0	0
410	0	0	0	0	0	0	0	0	0	0	0	0	0	0	0	2	0	0	0	0	0	0	0	0	0	0	0	2	0	0	0	6	1	0	0
412	0	0	0	0	0	0	0	0	0	0	0	0	0	0	0	0	0	0	0	0	0	0	0	0	0	0	0	0	0	0	0	0	0	0	0
414	0	0	0	0	0	0	0	0	0	0	0	0	0	0	0	0	0	0	0	0	0	0	0	0	0	0	0	1	0	0	1	0	0	0	0
439	0	0	0	0	0	0	0	0	0	0	0	0	0	0	0	0	0	0	0	0	0	0	0	0	0	0	0	0	0	0	0	0	0	0	0
457	0	0	0	0	0	0	0	0	0	0	0	0	0	0	0	0	0	0	0	0	0	0	0	0	0	0	0	0	0	0	0	0	0	0	0

Group F old males 1974

	EE	UB	TJ	056	AL	DW	R009	ZW	JX	K8	2C	5D	257
EE	0	0	6	2	9	3	0	3	0	5	0	5	0
UB	0	0	8	8	9	1	0	3	6	8	0	8	3
TJ	0	0	0	10	14	3	5	6	3	6	0	6	4
056	0	0	0	0	9	0	1	1	0	5	0	7	6
AL	0	0	0	1	0	3	8	1	6	7	0	10	12
DW	0	0	0	0	0	0	0	1	3	2	1	4	4
R009	0	0	0	0	0	2	0	0	2	1	0	2	5
ZW	0	0	0	0	0	0	2	0	0	6	0	4	4
JX	0	0	0	0	0	0	0	0	0	2	0	7	7
K8	0	0	0	0	0	0	0	0	0	0	0	11	4
2C	0	0	0	0	0	0	0	0	0	0	0	0	4
5D	0	0	0	0	0	0	1	0	0	0	0	0	9
257	0	0	0	0	0	0	0	0	0	0	0	0	0

Group F old males 1974 omitting castrated R009

	EE	UB	TJ	056	AL	DW	ZW	JX	K8	2C	5D	257
EE	0	0	6	2	9	3	3	0	5	0	5	0
UB	0	0	8	8	9	1	3	6	8	0	8	3
TJ	0	0	0	10	14	3	6	3	6	0	6	4
056	0	0	0	0	9	0	1	0	5	0	7	6
AL	0	0	0	1	0	3	1	6	7	0	10	12
DW	0	0	0	0	0	0	1	3	2	1	4	4
ZW	0	0	0	0	0	0	0	0	6	0	4	4
JX	0	0	0	0	0	0	0	0	2	0	7	7
K8	0	0	0	0	0	0	0	0	0	0	11	4
2C	0	0	0	0	0	0	0	0	0	0	0	4
5D	0	0	0	0	0	0	0	0	0	0	0	9
257	0	0	0	0	0	0	0	0	0	0	0	0

Group F new males 1974

	L7	K7	2E	UD	ZH	D2	282	254
L7	0	0	1	1	0	0	1	1
K7	0	0	3	5	2	0	3	3
2E	0	0	0	0	1	1	0	1
UD	0	0	0	0	1	0	2	2
ZH	0	0	0	0	0	0	1	1
D2	0	0	0	0	0	0	0	0
282	0	0	0	0	0	0	0	4
254	0	0	0	0	0	0	0	0

Group F young natal males 1974

	298	415	436	409	309	410	292	439	412	349	414
298	0	4	6	1	5	5	2	0	0	5	1
415	0	0	2	7	0	12	3	1	4	0	0
436	0	0	0	4	0	2	1	2	3	1	1
409	0	0	2	0	1	7	1	0	4	0	0
309	0	0	0	0	0	0	0	2	2	1	0
410	0	0	0	0	0	0	2	1	6	0	1
292	0	0	0	0	0	2	0	0	0	0	0
439	0	0	0	0	0	0	0	0	1	0	0
412	0	0	0	0	0	0	0	0	0	0	0
349	0	0	0	0	0	0	0	0	0	0	1
414	0	0	0	0	0	0	0	0	0	0	0

4

Determinants of Aggression in Squirrel Monkeys (*Saimiri*)

JOHN D. BALDWIN

INTRODUCTION

A broad-based biosocial theory of aggression would integrate evolutionary, physiological, and environmental–developmental determinants of behavior: Evolutionary processes select various physiological mechanisms that influence and are influenced by behavior during the developmental processes in each individual's unique environmental setting. To date, there has been considerable research on and theory proposed for the physiological and environmental–developmental determinants of aggression in *Saimiri*, but no integration of the evolutionary perspective relevant to this behavior. Coe and Levine (1983), Coe et al. (1985), and others present good analyses of the role of hormones in *Saimiri* aggression; and the social and environmental determinants of the development of aggressive behavior have been described by Ploog et al. (1967), Baldwin (1969), Rosenblum (1974), Hopf et al. (1985), and others.

The present paper draws upon the literature on *Saimiri* ecology and behavior to develop a series of 14 mostly descriptive hypotheses about the major patterns of aggression typically seen in the species. The present analysis of *Saimiri* should facilitate further research on evolutionary, physiological and environmental–developmental determinants of aggression in *Saimiri* and other species by clarifying certain relationships between aggressive behavior and evolutionary adaptations. It also demonstrates that evolutionary variables can be interwoven with physiological and environmental–developmental factors to construct more comprehensive theories of aggression. The paper begins with descriptive data on *Saimiri* ecology, behavior, and aggression to provide the background for an analysis of *Saimiri* evolutionary adaptations and later discussions of more comprehensive theories.

SAIMIRI: GENERAL ADAPTATIONS

Saimiri are small, agile, arboreal omnivores that are indigenous to many parts of the Amazon basin, the Guianas, and parts of Panama and Costa Rica (Thorington

1985). Adult females typically reach 500 to 750 g, while adult males attain weights of 700 to 1,170 g (Long and Cooper 1968; Cooper 1968; Middleton and Rosal 1972; Mendoza et al. 1978a, b). During mating season the males may gain up to 30% in body weight, developing a "fatted" appearance (DuMond 1968).

Saimiri eat various ripe fruits and spend many hours each day searching the foliage for insects and other small prey (Terborgh 1983). They supplement their standard diet of fruits and insects with a variety of other foods, including nuts, flowers, buds, seeds, leaves, gum, snails, crabs, and some small vertebrates, such as frogs, bird eggs, and bats (Sanderson 1957; Izawa 1975; Moynihan 1976; Boinski and Timm 1985). They are light enough to be able to utilize the tips of branches and vines as leaf gleaners.

Saimiri tend to travel in medium to large multi-male troops—typically of 20 to 50 or more individuals—and are neither territorial nor monogamous. Each day troops move long distances, finding insects whenever they can and feasting when they discover a source of ripe fruit (Terborgh 1983). The patchy distribution of prized foods leads the animals to have large home ranges—which can exceed 250 ha—that overlap extensively with those of other troops. When neighboring troops intermingle in fruiting trees or while foraging for insects, they typically show little or no aggressiveness or territorial defensiveness.

Saimiri troops are loosely structured around one or more cohesive groups of adult females, accompanied by their offspring, while a small group of adult males ("insider males") is attached to the troop closely before and during mating season and loosely outside of mating season. Separate all-male satellite groups and occasional solitary males are sometimes attracted to the female-centered troops, especially before and during mating season. These out-group males appear to have little or no opportunity to mate with the adult females of the troop, because the insider males chase them away when they approach the troop. Although there are no observations of females selecting to mate with out-group males, the possibility of this happening cannot be ruled out.

Aggression

The gradually accumulating data from field studies reveal that *Saimiri* in natural environments spend very little time in social interaction; and aggressive behaviors are usually minimal, except before and during mating season, when males engage in dominance displays, chases, and fights. The levels of aggression seen in different studies are variable, and apparently depend on ecology, troop size, age–sex composition, social stability, possibly genetic differences between species, and other factors. Although no dominance rank order has been seen in some troops, males in other troops have linear or near linear dominance hierarchies based on fights and reasserted through stereotyped genital displays, in which one male exhibits an erect penis toward one or more others (Ploog 1967). Genital displays are given at various intensities from the relatively "half hearted" ones given to individuals who pose little threat to the very intense ones before challenges to insider-group positions (Baldwin 1968). In contrast, adult females and young are usually less aggressive than males, though female rank orders have been reported in some circumstances.

There appear to be four different subspecies of *Saimiri sciureus* in South America and only a small enclave of *S. oerstedii* in Central America (Thorington 1985).[1] Various behavioral and social differences have been reported among a few of the subspecies (MacLean 1964; Winter 1969; Hopf et al. 1974; Mendoza et al. 1978b); but some of the differences in the field observations (reported below) may result from differences in troop composition and ecology, rather than species or subspecies genetic differences. Given the tentative nature of our present knowledge about *Saimiri* ecology, the behavioral data are presented in two general clusters, to contrast the studies of *Saimiri sciureus* in Colombia and Peru with those of *S. oerstedii* in Central America. Laboratory research suggests that future field studies may well reveal other patterns besides the two general patterns presented here (Mendoza et al. 1978b).

Saimiri sciureus *in South America*

Thorington's (1967, 1968) study on the llanos of Colombia provided some of the first systematic data on *Saimiri* social ecology. The main study troop lived in a 14.7 ha forest and consisted of 22 *S. sciureus*—three adult males, five adult females, and 14 immature animals. Except for a 1–2 hour rest period in the heat of the day, the animals seemed to be "incessantly active" (Thorington 1968:76), foraging and moving between foraging areas within their forest. When hunting for insects, *Saimiri* are leaf gleaners, hunting quickly and cursorily through the understory, grabbing mostly cryptic and immobile prey—such as caterpillars—from the leaves. There was little food stealing or other forms of aggression. Genital displays were observed only six times in the 10-week study. Thorington (1968:82) noted that "[t]he foraging behavior of squirrel monkeys seems to be a significant determinant of their social behavior and of their troop structure. While foraging, the animals are more isolated from one another visually, and agonistic behavior is correspondingly restricted."

Terborgh (1983, 1985) conducted a lengthy study on the ecology and behavior of five species of New World primates at Cocha Cashu, Peru. The *Saimiri* traveled in noisy troops of 30–40 individuals, using large home ranges which may have exceeded 250 ha. There was extensive overlap of home ranges and the monkeys showed no signs of territoriality. Different troops often joined or traveled in parallel while foraging for insects or converging on the same fruit tree. No aggression was observed when troops met or traveled together.

At all seasons of the year, the monkeys' daily patterns were "remarkably constant" (Terborgh 1983:56). The *Saimiri* spent about 50% of their waking hours foraging for arthropods and other small prey, 11% foraging for fruit, another 11% resting, and 27% traveling between foraging areas. Troops often moved at a steady pace for long periods, each individual picking its own separate pathway through the trees, cursorily searching for food. No single animal appeared to serve as troop leader. Every monkey fended for itself.

The monkeys' feeding activities affected much of their social life. They ate a variety of ripe fruits, but showed a strong preference for figs. Because fig trees were widely scattered and fruited at irregular times, the monkeys had large home ranges that overlapped with those of other troops, and they criss-crossed their ranges frequently in search of fruit. The fig trees often produced large quantities of fruit, and the monkeys were tolerant of other troops and individuals while foraging in them. Although *Saimiri* feasted on figs when possible, they foraged for insects for at least half of each day. When fruit was scarce for long periods (during May and July), the *Saimiri* worked especially hard, doing little else but foraging for insects most of the day. "*Saimiri* hunts by dogged persistence" (Terborgh 1983:100), rather than by craft, cunning, or strength.

Saimiri were the least social of the five species studied at Cocha Cashu: Only 2% of their day involved directed social interactions. Apparently, the monkeys were too busy searching for food to have much time for social activity. The data on social behavior are sketchy: Huddling together and roughhouse social play were the most commonly observed social activities. Grooming was rare. During the brief mating season, the adult males curtailed their foraging activities and "engaged each other in incessant dominance interactions and mutual sexual displays" (Terborgh 1983:51).

Saimiri sciureus often forage in mixed troops with *Cebus appella* or *C. albifrons*.[2] Although the *Cebus* control the direction of the troop travel, the *Saimiri* travel ahead of the *Cebus*, snatching the more visible and easily obtained insect prey. *Saimiri* benefit from traveling with *Cebus* (primarily by responding to *Cebus* alarm calls when there is danger); and "the *Cebus* either gain little or lose slightly" (Terborgh 1983:166). *Cebus* sometimes displace or show anger toward *Saimiri*; but the two species usually travel together peacefully. *Cebus* appear to have an atttitude of "passive resignation to the presence of *Saimiri*" (Terborgh 1983:186).

In sum, the *Saimiri* at Cocha Cashu are hard-working omnivores that spend approximately 90% of each day busily traveling and foraging. For *Saimiri*, foraging is a "tireless hunt" that leaves little time for resting or socializing (Terborgh 1983:124). Since they are usually busy foraging, *Saimiri* benefit from safety in numbers, hence from traveling in large troops and being with the more vigilant *Cebus*. Scattered resources favor nomadic travel, opportunistic foraging, and tolerance of other troops (Terborgh 1983:213–214).

Mitchell's (personal communication) more recent study on behavior and social organization at Cocha Cashu revealed larger troop sizes—50 animals or more— with the study troops averaging in the 70s. There was little food stealing and responses to it varied: from tolerance, to avoidance, to threats or fights. When two troops traveled next to each other, the adult males of each troop tended to avoid each other, though some males made noisy displays, such as branch shaking.

One well-studied troop had three insider adult males; and another varied from seven to 10. Fights were common among insider males before and during mating season, and a relatively linear dominance hierarchy was established. The largest male was the most dominant: Large size appeared to be an advantage in the numerous dominance displays, wrestling matches, and fights. Most male aggression was among the insider adult males. Some was directed toward outsider males, who were attracted to the troop before and during mating season, apparently to repel these out-group males, especially before mating season. All 15 insider and out-group males in the principal study troop were wounded, some wounds being so serious that the male could not engage in mating activities. Adult females could be ranked into three general dominance levels (high, medium, and low), as revealed mainly by grabbing. Females "harassed" males and appeared to have considerable power, since males cowered, displayed fear grimaces, and moved away from the adult females when harassed. The receptive females only allowed themselves to be courted by the most dominant male; and this largest male accounted for almost all recorded successful copulations. A successful male tended to remain with the troop during the following year; but unsuccessful males often changed troops after mating season. A male who had success in one mating season was unlikely to have success the next year.

Saimiri oerstedii *in Central America*

Baldwin and Baldwin (1972, 1973) observed two troops of *Saimiri oerstedii* in a narrow coastal forest of 400+ ha in southwestern Panama. The two troops had home ranges of 17.5 and 24+ ha. In the main study troop of 23 animals, there were two adult males; and a peripheral young adult male accompanied the troop, though he avoided the troop's two insider adult males. The two adult males traveled together in a coordinated manner with a minimum of overt interactions; but they did chase and get chased by other troop members, especially the adult females. Not a single fight was observed during the 10-week study. The monkeys spent almost all of their 14-hour waking days foraging and moving between foraging areas. The adult females and young were very tolerant of physical contact with others—except for adult males—when foraging. When concentrated around a fruiting plant, the animals sometimes walked over each others' limbs; but they seldom interacted. Attempts to steal food occurred about 0.5 times per hour; and half were successful. Food stealing was never observed to evoke threats or aggression. When one animal grabbed a piece of food that another was holding or eating, the two monkeys might tug once or twice at the food; but the monkey which held onto the food for one or two tugs usually became the owner, and the other monkey showed no further attention.

Aggressive chases and displays were observed about 40 to 45 times per day. Chases occurred 1 to 20 times per hour. Most chases occurred after one or both of the troop's males rushed up to an adult female for investigation of her odors and were chased away either before or after they made contact. Olfactory investigation helps males assess which phase of a female's estrous cycle she is in (Hennessy et al. 1978). Usually, a lone female would tolerate a male's approach; but several females, when near to one another, would not. The higher the ratio of females to males in the area near the male–female interaction, the more likely the male approach was terminated before contact was made, as several females and young chased the male(s) away. Though noisy, these chases between adult males and females never led to fights. The second and less common type of chasing involved one or both of the adult males chasing the peripheral young adult male when he approached the troop. The two troop males never chased each other, and only two genital displays were observed between them.

Boinski (1987a) reported very low levels of aggression in troops of *Saimiri oerstedii* in the Parque Nacional Corcovado, in Costa Rica. The troop varied in size between 38 and 45 individuals, containing four fully adult males and a young adult male. This younger adult male remained separate from the other adult males, had a "ragged" appearance, and disappeared before the end of mating season. The four adult insider males were never observed to engage in aggressive behavior.

Due to the infrequency of displays, avoidance, and food competition, no domin-ance hierarchy was identifiable among the males. Boinski points out that a male dominance hierarchy could have gone unnoticed because (1) dominance inter-actions were too subtle or infrequent, and/or (2) dominance relations were established during play interactions before adulthood. The troop's subadult and young adult males engaged in roughhouse play, but not fighting. There was almost no competition over food. Even mild forms of aggression—such as "a full adult male lightly batting away a too-inquisitive juvenile male"—were infrequent (Boinski 1987a:14).

The *Saimiri* foraged 64% of the time in the worst food season; and 43–47% in other seasons (Boinski 1987c). Individuals avoided each other while foraging, which appeared to increase their foraging efficiency. Adult males engaged in "high levels of vigilance and direct interventions in situations of possible threat to neonates and other troop members" (Boinski 1987a:19). Since males did not switch troops, they probably had sufficient reproductive investment in the troop's young to explain their levels of vigilance. Mothers increased the time they spent in vigilance during the period in which their infants were small and most vulnerable to predation and they were observed to mob predators at this phase of the year (Boinski 1987b).

The most common forms of aggression were seen when adult males cooperated with each other in mobbing females in order to evaluate the females' estrous condition by olfactory cues, especially before and during breeding season (Boinski 1987a). The males would leave females who were not in estrus, but they showed prolonged interest in receptive females. Females resisted male approaches when they were not in estrus; but they actively solicited sexual contact when they were in estrus. "No successful forced copulation was ever observed; the full cooperation of the female was almost certainly required" (Boinski 1987a:16). Boinski's observations indicate that mating is based on female choice. The younger adult females were less selective than the more experienced females who showed a strong preference for mating with the largest male. Large size could indicate to a female that the male is likely to stay in the troop and to provide vigilance and protection for her infants throughout the year.

If female choice is based on body size, it could help explain why *Saimiri* males are 35–45% (50%?) larger than females and/or become "fatted" in mating season. The other naturalistic studies do not provide enough information to determine whether the largest male was most likely to reproduce successfully, or if other traits—including behavioral traits—could be crucial determinants of female choice.

Saimiri sciureus *in Seminatural Environments*

There have been several studies in a 1.5 ha seminatural environment established by Frank DuMond in 1960 in southern Florida. DuMond (1968) and Baldwin (1968) observed the troop in 1966 and 1967, when it contained 110 monkeys, and grew to 136 in the 1967 birth season. During most of the study, there were 34 fully adult females and four fully adult insider males in the troop. There was also a small group of subadult and young adult males that traveled separately from the main troop. Before and during mating season, some of these out-group males attempted to join the insider-male group; but they were chased away by the insider adult males, and none was observed to gain entry to the insider group. When not in mating season, the four insider adult males traveled together, loosely attached to the rest of the troop. Before the onset of mating season, they began approaching the troop's adult females for olfactory investigation; and as mating season approached, the males became increasingly active, excitable, and aggressive. When spermatogenesis began, before mating season, they gained approximately 30% extra weight, taking on a "fatted" appearance (DuMond 1968). At this time, a highly contested dominance hierarchy could be inferred from fights and genital displays. When the less dominant member of a genital display dyad did not remain submissive, firm grasping or fights sometimes occurred. Fights between the lower members of the hierarchy were generally less intense than fights between higher ranking members—in part because the presence of high ranking individuals tended to suppress fights between the lower ranking individuals. Three extremely violent fights were observed when there were successful challenges for the highest rank position in the hierarchy, and these led to very serious wounds. The loser usually withdrew from the troop for several days to recuperate and was too weakened to take any position other than the lowest rank.

High rank in the dominance hierarchy appeared to confer no special advantages for reproductive success nor for gaining access to food or other resources. The two most excitable, active, and aggressive males—Scar Eye and Pink— occupied the top position in the troop's dominance hierarchy; but neither of these males was ever observed to copulate to ejaculation. In interactions with the adult females, it was the less excitable, less active, and less aggressive males that had the greater success in approaching adult females and carrying out the lengthy chain of behaviors needed to succeed in copulating to ejaculation: namely, following the female, waiting until the troop had moved away from her, approaching and synchronizing with the female, then mounting. It appeared that the females were disturbed and angered by the most aggressive males and preferred interacting with—and mating with—the less aggressive ones. This observation is partly compatible with Boinski's theory of female choice, except that in this case the females' choice appeared to be based on the males' behavior, not body size (Baldwin 1968). Although none of the records from this study indicate any noticeable difference in the body sizes of the four males, it is possible that the less dominant insider males were the largest.

Scollay and Judge (1981) reported that the troop in DuMond's seminatural forest had increased to about 200 animals then leveled off to a constant size. At the beginning of their study in 1975, there were three large troops containing both males and females, and they were organized around three separate female cores. In addition, there were several smaller groups of juvenile, subadult and adult males along with two solitary males that did not associate with the larger mixed-sex troops. The three large troops mingled and fed together peacefully, but usually foraged in different areas. At the onset of 1977, several changes in the forest led to a shift in social organization, bringing about a fusion of the three large troops into one extra large troop. However, six months later, this troop divided into three separate smaller troops; and these three troops rarely intermingled, even though there was a complete overlap of home ranges among them. Each of these three troops had almost the same female composition as it had one year before. Scollay and Judge attributed the stability of the three troops to the lasting social bonds among the females. The males switched from one troop to another as the female-centered troops joined and split over the year's time.

THEORETICAL INTEGRATION

Observations on *Saimiri* ecology and behavior in natural environments—in conjunction with laboratory research on *Saimiri* and comparative data on other primates—allow the development of several descriptive hypotheses relevant to the evolutionary adaptiveness of aggression in *Saimiri*. Although *Saimiri* have been studied in considerable detail in laboratories, there have only been a small number of field studies on the species, and much remains unknown about the natural variation in *Saimiri* ecology and behavior. Thus, at present, it is appropriate that a theory of the evolutionary adaptations of *Saimiri* aggression be presented tentatively, as a series of empirically based hypotheses that are open to much further research, evaluation, and modification. The available laboratory and field studies reveal enough on general patterns in *Saimiri* aggression to warrant a preliminary attempt at theoretical integration. If this theory can serve as a tentative first outline of a more comprehensive theory, it may stimulate further study and facilitate the development of more sophisticated theories. There is no doubt that evolutionary theories of this type can be greatly expanded and refined.

Evolutionary theories of behavior can be quite speculative and difficult to evaluate (Welker 1971; Rowell 1972, 1979; Lewontin 1979). The present theory of *Saimiri* adaptations is admittedly speculative, but each descriptive hypothesis presented below can be tested and either rejected or refined using comparative methods—comparing *Saimiri* in different environments and comparing *Saimiri* with other species. Given the limited number of field studies on *Saimiri* in natural environments to date, unexpected new findings could easily emerge in the coming years that would falsify any of the hypotheses presented here. Thus, all the descriptive hypotheses can be viewed as predictions about *Saimiri* behavior that can be tested and either modified or rejected by future research. Hopefully by focusing attention on some key variables that appear to relate aggression to ecology, these hypotheses will help advance future studies on aggression in *Saimiri*—and perhaps in other species.

Since there is only limited information about *Saimiri* responses to various predators, it is difficult to evaluate the forms or frequencies of aggression against predators. Thus, the following discussion is limited to a discussion of aggression among conspecifics, beginning with the selective pressures for nonaggressive behavior, then considering those favoring aggression.

General Adaptations for Nonaggressive Living

Saimiri typically live in multi-male troops of 20 to 50 or more individuals. Large troop size appears to be an adaptation that reduces predation (Alexander 1974; van Schaik 1983; Terborgh 1986; de Ruiter 1986). As small primates *Saimiri* are "vulnerable to predators and give alarm calls to large carnivores, boas, and almost any large flying bird" (Robinson and Janson 1986:69). When traveling with conspecifics or with *Cebus*, *Saimiri* benefit from safety in numbers and from hearing the alarm calls of other individuals. Such benefits can lead to the evolution of psychological mechanisms that facilitate living in large troops. There appears to be only one major cost: Animals in large troops have to travel further and work harder to satisfy the hunger of all members. However, when resources permit, large troops are possible. *Saimiri* troops are not territorial, and neighboring troops can travel peacefully together when they find a large fruiting tree or are foraging for insects near each other. These considerations lead to the first descriptive hypothesis: 1 Saimiri *have evolved to be relatively nonaggressive and tolerant of conspecifics—especially when they are somewhat familiar with them—allowing them to form large troops (when forest structure and food distribution permit).* Although subsequent hypotheses will amend this first general hypothesis, all the existing studies in natural environments report low levels of fighting for most of the year, even when neighboring troops travel together. In addition, the adult females and young—who form the main body of *Saimiri* troops—usually interact with a minimum of aggression.

Terborgh's (1986) theory indicates that as a species evolves to live in large troops, it is likely to live in multi-male troops. Although monogamous and one-male groups are found in species with small basic social units, the difficulties of excluding large numbers of adult males from large troops reduces the chances that large stable troops will contain only one adult male. The next step of Terborgh's (1986) logic suggests that as *Saimiri* evolved to live in large multi-male troops, other variables—type of mating season, body size, diet, mode of sexual selection, and so forth—contributed to molding other details of their social system.

Ridley (1986) presents data showing that the length of the breeding season is associated with harem versus multi-male social organization. In species with long breeding seasons, it is typical for one male to control a harem of females; whereas species with short breeding seasons typically have multi-male troops. In *Saimiri*'s case, the evolution of large multi-male troops would favor the emergence of brief mating seasons—which in fact rarely exceed two months in length. Other factors can favor brief mating seasons, since highly synchronized births allow each mother to benefit from giving birth when other mothers have babies and are most vigilant for predators (Boinski 1987b). This leads to a second hypothesis: 2 *A short breeding season tends to limit the number of weeks per year in which sex-related aggression—both competition between males and chases between males and females—is most likely to occur.* It is important to note that in nature *Saimiri* show very little aggression other than these two forms seen just before and during mating season. Having short mating seasons restricts aggression temporally to a small fraction of the year.

Saimiri body size is an important determinant of their dietary specializations for eating both fruit and insects, use of the forest, risk of predation, and so forth (Fleagle et al. 1981).[3] *Saimiri* fruit sources usually provide abundant crops that neither necessitate competition nor facilitate monopolization by aggressive individuals. Field observations indicate that competition over fruits is usually rare. Also, there are no observations of individuals using aggression to exclude others from fruiting plants (Baldwin and Baldwin 1972:175). *Saimiri* insect foods are scattered throughout the forest; and typically individuals hunt alone, though maintaining proximity to the troop. Even in the laboratory, *Saimiri* appear to be relatively asocial feeders (Fragaszy and Mason 1983). Working alone with minimal competition or fighting over insect sources appears to work quite well for *Saimiri*, allowing them to capture about one prey per minute, which is a relatively high rate—e.g., twice as high as that of *Cebus*.[4] Hypothesis 3: *The abundance of fruits and patchy distribution of insects create little selection pressure for aggressiveness while feeding or traveling between foraging areas (about 45 to 90% of each day).* In both the laboratory and the field, food stealing tends not to evoke much aggression, even when preferred foods are taken. Spending many hours of each day in noncompetitive foraging creates a busy but relatively nonaggressive behavioral routine.

Boinski's (1987a) observations indicate that *Saimiri* reproduction is based on female choice. Females either seek out certain males or only allow certain males to court them. Data from other natural and captive environments are compatible with this conclusion (Baldwin 1968; Mendoza et al. 1978a; Mitchell, personal communication). It is not known if these patterns obtain in the large troops seen in South America. Theoretically, a female would be expected to choose to mate with a male who will maximize her reproductive success by protecting her and her infants against predators and other dangers (Boinski 1987a). Trivers (1972), Symons (1978), and others argue that selection favors females who mate with males displaying signs of fitness. Thus, a large, strong, active, vigilant, protective male with a well-established position in the troop would be expected to be attractive to adult females. In addition, females would be expected to prefer mating with a male who cooperated with, or at least controlled his aggressiveness with females. The admittedly limited data lead to the tentative presentation of hypothesis 4: *When female choice obtains, females prefer males who are vigilant, protective, and cooperative—rather than aggressive—with females, which would favor the evolution of behavioral mechanisms that limit male aggressiveness in the presence of females.* Although males sometimes make excited approaches to adult females for olfactory investigation before and during mating season—which females appear to dislike—this is the most adversive experience that males impose on females.

Since *Saimiri* males cannot know which or how many infants in a troop are their offspring, there would be few selection pressures for adult males to give the kind of direct paternal care that monogamous *Callicebus* males give to the infants that they father (Mason 1968). However, there may still be selective pressures to show some care for the young. Especially in stable troops with only a small number of adult males—some of which may not mate—any male that did mate might be the father of some of the infants. This suggests hypothesis 5: *Especially in stable troops with a small number of adult males, there may be a tendency for any male that does mate (1) to help to protect not only the females with whom he has mated but also their offspring, or (2) at least to inhibit aggression around those females and their offspring.* *Saimiri* males have been observed to provide some protection for their troop by being vigilant for predators and intervening to protect various troop mates (Boinski 1987a), and by investigating causes of alarm during certain kinds of danger (Baldwin 1968; DuMond 1968). Adult males also show minimal aggression to adult females and infants—even when adult females threaten and chase them or when infants direct genital displays to those males. Although limited aggression with females could be predicted from hypotheses 4 and 5, limited aggression with infants is evidence to support hypothesis 5. In places where males transfer between troops (as at Cocha Cashu, Peru), the males would not be highly related to other troop members. In such cases, the males would be expected to invest less in troop vigilance and spend more time competing with other males for reproductive success.

Adult Male Aggression

Although there appear to be selection pressures for males to be nonaggressive with females and perhaps with their infants, other facets of male reproductive life create selection pressures that favor male aggressiveness toward unfamiliar and/or assertive adult males. Observations in nature and in a seminatural environment in Florida indicate that males may need to compete aggressively with other males to gain and retain a position in a troop's insider-male subgroup *before* they even have a chance to mate.

From the existing data in the seminatural environment, it appears that subadult or young adult males may be forced to leave their natal troops by the insider males. Once excluded from their troop, these young males usually travel with other out-group males in satellite groups, though a few may travel alone. Before and during mating season, some of the mature males from these outside groups approach large troops containing females, even though they are usually threatened and chased by the stronger and more aggressive insider males who can successfully fend off competitors. An out-group male's chances for reproductive success appear to depend on his being able to (1) fight and win a place in a troop's insider-male subgroup, which mates with the troop's adult females, and then (2) ward off challenges from other males seeking to displace him from the insider-male group. (Although young adult males might be able to join a troop that had no insider males, field observations suggest that few troops exist very long with no insider males.) Hypothesis 6: *Selection pressures on males favor the aggressiveness needed in order to join and stay in an insider-male group, especially before and during mating season, since such behavior appears to be essential for reproductive success.*

Male aggression toward strange and assertive males is most common just before and during mating season, when males show the greatest attraction to adult females and membership in a troop's insider-male subgroup is most vigorously contested. At the end of mating season, out-group males cease approaching troops closely and all forms of male aggression decline in frequency. It is as if a "truce" were called after mating season.

Although the entry of a new male or males into a troop's insider-male group apparently depends on aggressive behavior, especially in mating season, low levels of aggression among insider males have been reported in *S. oerstedii*, even in mating season. This may be due to genetic differences, smaller troop size (which allows insider-male relations to stabilize more easily), or other environmental causes. Hypothesis 7: *Once a male has joined an insider-male group, there are benefits for the males' developing tolerance and cooperation if the instigations to or benefits of aggression are not too great.* However, for large troops this hypothesis does not appear to apply. In the large troops of *S. sciureus* at Cocha Cashu, with up to seven or 10 insider males, the males may not attain stable, cooperative, nonaggressive relations (Mitchell, personal communication).

There may be many factors that influence the costs and benefits of aggression and tolerance in insider-male groups. The following are some of the more obvious possibilities. The costs to a given male for fighting to expel or kill other insider males from a large troop may be greater than the benefits of monopolizing the females—since those costs include loss of membership in the insider-male group, a high risk of injury, or loss of life. Mechanisms that limit aggression can promote individual fitness, since an overly pugnacious individual increases its risk of injury or death (Maynard Smith and Price 1973; Maynard Smith 1974; Fry 1980). In addition, each insider male benefits if he cooperates to form a united coalition. First, a coalition of insider males can mob groups of adult females for olfactory investigation more easily than can a single male. Second, there is less fighting and risk of injury for a male who belongs to a coalition—compared with a single male—in excluding strange out-group males who try to force their way into a troop. Other costs and benefits may contribute to male tolerance of familiar male group-mates. Their relative importance is unknown at present. More field observations and comparative data are needed to refine this hypothesis.

When males fight, they learn their relative strengths and propensities to fight, which, if consistent, suggest a rank order based on dominance and submission. The information on strength and inclination to fight that males communicate, especially through the genital display, allows dominance to be asserted without physical fighting. Thus, it provides a behavioral mechanism that can limit aggression.

Hypothesis 8: *An adult male dominance hierarchy, along with ritualized genital displays, helps limit aggression among adult males.* When genital displays do not succeed in cuing a subordinate individual to act in a submissive manner, stronger forms of threat—grabbing, and firm holding—may be used before actual fights break out. In insider-male groups where all the males accept their status, they gradually devote less time to threats or fights, and eventually even genital displays become less intense and less frequent. In highly stable groups with low levels of aggression, where the males have become familiar and increasingly cooperate with each other, the male rank order may be rarely or subtly expressed, in the sense that the males are aware of each other's fighting powers and less dominant individuals avoid provoking fights.

Subadult and Young Adult Male Aggression

Although females typically become reproductively mature at 2.5 years, males pass through a 2 year or longer subadult phase before becoming fully mature (Hopf 1979). There is no sharp boundary demarcating the end of the subadult phase; and a given male's age of transition to full adulthood may depend on a number of factors, such as his health, "personality," motivation to join a male-insider group, his aggressiveness and that of the subadult and adult males with whom he interacts. Hypothesis 9: *The postponement of full male maturity for young males lengthens the period for attaining the strength and skill needed to compete successfully for a place in an insider-male group.* As a side-effect of postponed male maturation, each troop has fewer fully adult males fighting to enter or stay in the insider-male group—thus, less aggression—than would be expected if males became fully mature and began competing for a position in the insider-male group at 2.5 years of age.

In their early subadult phase, males may stay in their natal troop, traveling and foraging with the troop. Subadult males learn many skills needed for successful adult competitive and reproductive behavior through both playful interactions and nonplayful experiences. Most *Saimiri* males make a gradual shift from playful learning with juveniles and subadults to more serious, nonplayful learning experiences with adults. Subadult males have been reported to engage in play fights and sexual play (Latta et al. 1967; Baldwin 1969). Although it is difficult to demonstrate functional benefits of play (Martin and Caro 1985), and mammals appear to be able to develop normal adult behavior in the absence of play (Baldwin and Baldwin 1973, 1974; Berger 1979, 1980), play can develop some skills (Biben 1986). For example, play fights may help males develop physical strength, agility, balance, strategy, and other skills needed for fighting (Symons 1978). Sexual play with juvenile females may help subadult males learn how to approach, mount, gently hold, and thrust with juvenile females in ways that minimize being rejected later on by adult females (Baldwin 1969:66). Between the early and late subadult phase, "[i]t seems likely that the subadult males [learn] to be gentle with their play partners in order not to disturb the juveniles and hence to prolong the interaction" (Baldwin 1969:66). If adult females choose males in part for their cooperative and nonaggressive behavior, a subadult's learning experiences during sexual play may enhance his chances in later years of being chosen by receptive females for sexual interaction. Sexual play also acquaints males with the positive reinforcers of sexual interaction, which may enhance their motivation to enter insider-male groups at a later time.

However, social play may not be essential. Male social skills can apparently be learned through nonplayful experiences with adults (Baldwin and Baldwin 1973). During mating season, subadult males mob adult females to investigate their odors (Boinski 1987a); and this learning experience may enhance reproductive motivation or skills (Baldwin 1969). Since female odors appear to function as positive reinforcers, smelling them may help subadult males acquire positive associations with adult females and thus increase their motivation to approach females once they reach adulthood; and this motivation may be important for a male's gaining entry into an insider-male group. In addition, even in mobbing females some subadults may learn the skills for approaching females for copulation without disturbing them.

The growing success of subadult males in interacting with adult females in an adult-like manner may be among the stimuli that lead adult males to direct increasing threats, chases, or more serious forms of aggression toward these younger males. Also, the subadult males' increasing size, strength, assertive behavior—and perhaps the development of the "fatted" condition prior to mating season—make them more conspicuous to the adult males. To the degree that the subadult males direct aggressive responses to adult males, there are additional stimuli that could trigger the adult males' aggression toward them. Once adult males begin threatening, chasing, sparring, and fighting with the subadult males, the subadults are forced to learn how to deal with adult male aggression—by avoiding confrontations and/or acquiring increased skills for aggressive interactions.

At some phase of the subadult or young adult period, it appears that all or almost all subadult males leave their natal troop. Most observations suggest that the insider males drive the younger males out, but the young males might leave of their own accord outside the mating season if they were attracted to neighbor troops, all-male satellite groups, or other stimuli outside their natal troop. Much is still unknown about the male transition to out-group status.

After leaving their natal troop, some subadult and young adult males travel alone, but most appear to join all-male satellite groups. These groups are most likely to be seen near large multi-male troops just before and during mating season. Observations from the seminatural environment suggest descriptive hypothesis 10: *There is relatively little aggression among the young adult males within all-male satellite groups, and these males show little resistance to the entry of new males.* There may be a deference hierarchy based on individuals' avoiding adversive contacts with males perceived as stronger or more belligerent (Baldwin 1969:65), but there appears to be little or no serious fighting in satellite groups. This hypothesis complements hypothesis 6: Males are not likely to show aggressive responses to other males except when competing for proximity to adult females before and during mating season.

Observations in natural and seminatural environments suggest that during their transition from juvenile to fully adult status, young males have a higher than average chance of becoming injured, disappearing, or dying (DuMond 1968; Baldwin 1968, 1969; Boinski 1987a). Active and sometimes playful young adult males traveling in small groups may be more exposed to predation than are males in large troops. In addition, when young adult males have violent encounters with fully adult males, who are stronger and more skillful fighters, they risk being injured or killed. Heightened mortality during the subadult and young adult years would have the side-effect of decreasing the number of adult males in *Saimiri* populations, hence decreasing adult male competition and aggression. Clearly, future research on males' transition to adult status can help clarify much about aggression, the interactions between satellite groups and insider-male groups, male mortality, and much more.

Adult Females and Young

Descriptive hypotheses 1 and 3—which are relevant to all *Saimiri*, not just to males—suggest that *Saimiri* benefit from low levels of aggressiveness; and there appear to be few selection pressures on the females or the young to cause them to deviate from this pattern. Hypothesis 11: *Young* Saimiri *engage in little serious aggression, although they use mild threats in daily social adjustments and mock aggression in play fights.* During weaning, infants exchange threats with their mothers. During daily troop activities, the young may use threats to negotiate social spacing and ward off unwanted interactions. During play, threats and mock fighting are common. But, consistent with hypotheses 1 and 3, none of these forms of aggression appears to result in serious fighting.

In their natural habitats, female aggression is minimal. Females appear to form stable clusters based largely on personal friendships though rank orders based on mild or moderate aggression exist in some troops (Baldwin 1971; Scolly and Judge 1981; Mitchell, personal communication). Hypothesis 12: *Aggression in females is limited to a few situations that are of special significance to their own welfare and reproductive success.*

First, the most intense, active and vocal forms of female aggression are directed to males before and during mating season. After nonreceptive adult females have been mobbed by excited males for olfactory investigation, they are likely to chase the males to a more peripheral part of the troop. These chases involve vocalizations, lunges, and other threats, but not actual fighting; and usually it takes two or more females to successfully chase one highly motivated male. Receptive females tend not to respond aggressively to male approaches, and they may actively seek sexual interactions with some males (Boinski 1987a). Since mobbing by excited adult males interferes with normal adult female traveling and foraging activities, there may be selective pressures for adult females, except when sexually receptive, to terminate these disruptive male–female interactions.

Second, mothers of small infants are sometimes approached by juveniles and adult females who visually inspect, touch, smell, or otherwise attempt to interact with the infant (Baldwin 1969). In these cases, mothers sometimes leave or threaten the approaching individuals, which at least temporarily curtails their involvement with the infant. Since relatively simple threats are effective in deterring individuals who might cause an infant to fall or become injured, the benefits of protective maternal behavior far outweigh the costs. (Boinski (1987b:398) reported that adult females also show increased vigilance when their infants are small and they mob predators at this time.)

Third, when weaning their infants, mothers use mild aggression, such as vocal threats, placing a hand on the infant's head or shoulders, or grabbing it somewhat vigorously. By the time of weaning, the infants are relatively independent and becoming increasingly burdensome to their mothers, suggesting that the costs of continued support exceed the benefits to the mother (Wilson 1975). However, mothers show only limited aggression to their offspring—as would be expected, since a mother would reduce her own inclusive fitness if she seriously injured her infant (Fry 1980).

Fourth, when other individuals come too close to or interfere with a given adult female, she may use vocalizations, holding, grabbing, and other forms of limited aggression to warn the approacher and increase the social spacing. Similar self-protective responses are seen in individuals of all age–sex classes, and they probably reflect the benefits of reducing interference from others. Apparently such self-protective behavior rarely escalates to serious fighting—as expected from *Saimiri* adaptations for generally peaceful and tolerant social relations (hypotheses 1 and 3).

Consistent patterns of holding and grabbing have been observed among adult female *Saimiri* in some laboratory studies, making it possible to identify linear rank orders based on mild aggression (Castell and Heinrich 1971; Talmage-Riggs and Anschel 1973; Mendoza et al. 1978a). To date, field studies have not reported conspicuous rank orders among females, though subtle ones may exist. Naturally, it is possible that a more visible and influential female rank order might emerge in nature in hard times *if* the females were forced to compete for very scarce and highly clustered resources. In some other species, where females compete for food or other resources, female hierarchies are apparent (Hrdy 1986). In the seminatural environment, some identifiable females grabbed, held, threatened or displaced other females more than was done to them; and Mitchell (personal communication) reports a ranking of females in three general levels of assertiveness. Although it may be possible to rank order females in other natural settings based on measures of grabbing and holding, a female rank order based on mild threats is considerably different from the type of rank order seen in males, which can involve serious fighting; but the presence of subtle rank orderings should not obscure the fact that female social relations are based more on positive social bonds than on aggression. At present, the data suggest hypothesis 13: *If female rank orders exist in* Saimiri *in nature, they are based on mild aggression and play a relatively small role in organizing adult female social relations.*

The final topic of concern is the relative power of females and males in *Saimiri* troops, especially as seen in (1) the chases between females and males and (2) the contrast between the females' central position in the troops and the males' peripheral position. After adult males approach adult females for olfactory investigation, adult females sometimes chase them to a more peripheral position in the troop. In addition, males spend much of their time at the periphery, especially outside of mating season. Although adult males typically are stronger and more aggressive than adult females,[5] females have a numerical superiority that might give them greater social power. Such considerations led Leger et al. (1981) to ask if the relatively peripheral position of males in *Saimiri* troops is due to "female power" or "male choice." Do females force males out of the troop's core, or do males seek a peripheral position by choice?

The currently available data suggest hypothesis 14: *Male choice is more important than female power in* Saimiri *spatial organization.* Leger et al. (1981) conclude that the balance of power "depends very much on [a male's] motivational state" (p. 178). When males are highly motivated, they can approach females and travel wherever they choose in the troop, and adult females show little resistance; however, "if males do not show signs of being highly motivated ... females readily display threats or other behaviors that seem to deter males" (Leger et al. 1981:178). The most obvious motivation that males have for approaching females is sexual attraction (Strayer and Harris 1979), though a fruiting tree can simultaneously attract males and females into the same area. Outside of mating season, males show little attraction to adult females; but before and during mating season, males frequently approach adult females for olfactory investigation and sexual interaction. Females only attempt to drive males out to a peripheral position when the females are nonreceptive and the males show no strong motivation to stay; and these chases do not involve serious aggression. In addition, both laboratory and field data indicate that males have several attractions to the periphery of the troop (Perloe 1983): chasing out-group males away from the troop, curiosity, possibly troop defense, and perhaps decreased foraging competition. However, given the paucity of data from natural environments, much remains to be clarified about the relative strength of the various motivations that attract males to the female core and to the troop's periphery.

Evolutionary Selection and the Costs/Benefits of Aggression

The above data-based descriptive hypotheses lead to the following general picture of *Saimiri* aggression. In nature, *Saimiri* are basically nonaggressive and mutually tolerant animals that work long hours each day to obtain their food. These patterns result, in part, from their living in large troops—an adaptation that provides the benefits of increased protection against predators at the cost of increased time needed for foraging (van Schaik 1983; Terborgh 1986). The typical daily patterns of prolonged foraging and low aggression are seldom broken except in the several weeks before and during mating season, at which time some adult males engage in serious fights to enter or remain in the insider-male group that travels in proximity to the troop's adult females. Also, males mob females for olfactory investigation, after which nonreceptive females may chase the males toward the troop's periphery; but these cases of mobbing and chasing do not involve serious aggression. Males do not fight over females; mating is apparently determined by female choice; and female choice does not favor the males who direct the most aggression toward females. Naturally, the form and frequency of aggression within any given troop depends a great deal on local variations in troop composition, the composition of all-male satellite groups, the strength and assertiveness of males competing to gain proximity to the adult females, and other factors.

In the laboratory, a high ratio of males to females, the introduction of strange males, unstable social organization, crowding, lack of visual cover, and so forth provide situations that can trigger aggression or make it difficult to limit. However, stable laboratory groups can have low levels of aggression.

The descriptive hypotheses about aggression in *Saimiri* have relied solely on explanations in terms of individual selection and inclusive fitness, without reference to group selection. *Saimiri* provide several examples of social situations that support Fry's (1980) hypothesis that even the more altruistic facets of aggression—the self-restraint shown in limiting aggression against a conspecific—actually increase the individual's own fitness.

The data on which hypotheses 1 through 5 are based reveal selective pressures on individuals that could lead to low levels of aggression without postulating group selection, even though the whole group may benefit by the lower levels of turmoil and injury which result from limited aggression. All during the year, infants and juveniles engage in only low levels of aggression. The limited nature of a mother's aggression when weaning her infants appears to be explained adequately in terms of inclusive fitness (Wilson 1975): the mother's inclusive fitness would be reduced if her weaning activities injured her infant. The only other common display of female aggression is toward males who approach in an excited manner; and each female benefits from chasing males, by reducing the disruption of her daily foraging activities.

Adult males fight to enter or remain in the insider-male group that travels in proximity to adult females, since this provides the males with a chance to mate.

However, there are costs of hyperaggressive behavior and benefits for exercising restraint. The inclusive fitness of hyperaggressive males is reduced by the tendency of females to reject them as mates. Besides, a male who limits his aggressiveness reduces his risk of serious injury, since being overly pugnacious can stimulate others to fight back in desperation rather than acquiescing to limited aggression in a submissive manner (Fry 1980:73). In addition, once in the insider-male group, *Saimiri* males who cease fighting with each other can gain the benefits of forming coalitions with other males for mobbing females and repelling out-group males.

In insider-male groups with stable composition, genital displays and subtler forms of communication benefit *both* sender and receiver of the information because they communicate each male's relative aggressiveness and help males avoid serious fights and possible injury. Apparently, subtler communication— vocalizations, body postures, speed and noisiness of movement, and so forth—is so effective that genital displays are rarely needed in some troops (Baldwin and Baldwin 1972; Boinski 1987a). No hypothesis of group selection is needed. Nor is group selection needed to explain why genital displays and dominance rank orders sometimes fail to constrain male aggression, when a lower rank male challenges a higher rank male.

There are at least two mechanisms that reduce the frequency of serious aggression in *Saimiri* troops by reducing the number of potentially competing adult males per troop. First, because males pass through a 2 year or longer subadult period before reaching full adult status, there are fewer fully adult males per troop than if all males became adult at 2.5 years of age, as females do. However, group selection is not needed as an explanation: Each individual male benefits from the extended subadult year(s) as a time in which to mature and gain skills before having to compete with a troop's strongest adult males for insider-male status. Second, the elevated mortality of subadult and young adult males during the period when they have been forced out of their natal troops reduces the number of adult males available to compete and fight for insider positions in a troop; and again, group selection is not needed as an explanation. It is not altruistic for males to die while going through the subadult and young adult periods: The benefits of a successful attempt to gain insider-male status offset the risks of injury or death while fighting to gain that status, since *not* attempting to do so virtually assures that a male would have no access to adult females and no opportunity to reproduce.

The male aggression that forces some males to join all-male satellite groups and others to travel alone, segregates the males into spatially separate groups, which may reduce the number of times that unfriendly males come close enough to fight. Perhaps the out-group males have less motivation to fight than if they were closer to the females. Since such spatial segregation also decreases the number of insider males who are near the females, it may make it easier for insider males to develop stable relations, familiarize, learn their relative levels of aggressiveness, and avoid unnecessary fights. By excluding out-group males and keeping the insider group small, each insider male has an increased chance of reproducing; thus, there is no need to postulate group selection to explain why insider males act in ways that create all-male satellite groups and solitary males.

TOWARD A COMPREHENSIVE THEORY

This paper's extensive focus on *Saimiri* evolutionary adaptations is not intended to suggest that this alone can explain everything of importance about *Saimiri* aggression. A comprehensive theory of aggression needs to interweave evolutionary, physiological, and environmental–developmental determinants of behavior.

Exemplifying the Theory

Although there is too little space here to outline such a comprehensive theory, it is possible to provide several brief examples that show how evolutionary, physiological, and environmental–developmental data can be integrated. Several mechanisms that influence *Saimiri* aggressiveness reveal the interplay of all three factors. Evolutionary processes shape and adjust the design of the physiological mechanisms which in turn influence and are influenced by environmental factors during the developmental process.

Learning to Use the Ritualized Genital Display

First, the developmental data on genital displays demonstrate the interaction of evolutionary, physiological, and environmental influences. The ritualized genital display in adult males communicates an individual's readiness to fight. Since he may be able to avoid real fights by using and responding appropriately to genital displays, one can explain the evolution of such displays by their ability to enhance individual fitness. Furthermore, since genital displays appear in infancy (Ploog 1967), it is reasonable to assume that the neural mechanisms for producing the displays are well-programmed by selective processes and are "hard wired" to be operational at birth. However, young infants perform genital displays in various inappropriate situations, for example, displaying to fully adult males who could easily injure them. Apparently, the infant's response can be triggered by a variety of different stimuli; and it may take years before an individual develops or learns the discriminations needed to use the display appropriately.

Differential reinforcement provides a possible means by which an individual could acquire the relevant discriminations needed to use the genital display appropriately. Although infants who are traveling with their mothers perform genital displays to adult males and others with impunity, juveniles and especially subadult males who display in inappropriate circumstances may be punished by threats, chases, or attacks from larger and stronger individuals. As a result of such social punishment, maturing individuals would learn to behave submissively in the presence of stronger, more aggressive individuals, while continuing to display toward less aggressive individuals. The fact that some recipients of displays become less assertive provides negative reinforcement for displayers to direct genital displays to them. Such differential reinforcement would lead to the emergence of controlled aggression as individuals learned to use an "innate" display correctly. Differential reinforcement also helps explain how individuals learn to display with different frequency and intensity toward specific partners in the troop and how the use of genital displays with any given partner changes over time, if that individual's patterns of aggression change.[6]

Testosterone Levels and Aggression

Second, selective processes shape and adjust hormonal mechanisms, which in turn influence and are influenced by behavior during the developmental process. In their review of the literature, Coe and Levine (1983) present data indicating that in many primate species (including *Homo sapiens*), testosterone has little *direct* influence on aggression. In *Saimiri*, high testosterone levels do not cause males to be aggressive nor do low testosterone levels cause nonaggressiveness (Coe et al. 1985). However, winning a fight leads to increased testosterone production, and losing has the opposite effect. The two best documented effects of testosterone on aggressive behavior are *indirect* effects:

1. Prenatal exposure to testosterone appears to organize the central nervous system of infant males differently from that of females, causing young males to seek more active and stimulating play—such as rough and tumble wrestling.
2. The rise in testosterone levels at puberty increases general arousal and behavioral activity in pubertal males.

In a study of *Saimiri* mothers and infants living in relatively complex laboratory environments, Rosenblum (1974) found that "male infants show a greater readiness to move toward moderately novel, complex, or arousing stimuli than do females" (p. 139). Rosenblum suggested that males may prefer a higher level of external sensory stimulation than do females. Apparently, males need higher levels of sensory inputs than do females for sensory stimulation to function as a positive reinforcer; and this may be one way that prenatal testosterone produces sex differences in behavior—by biasing the neural mechanisms that mediate sensory stimulation reinforcement. Sensory stimulation appears to be the main unconditioned reinforcer for exploration and play, and various evolutionary explanations for this have been presented in the literature (Baldwin and Baldwin 1981). Such reinforcement mechanisms help explain why infant and juvenile *Saimiri* males prefer higher levels of play activity than do females, seeking out more rowdy play, engaging in more play fights, hence learning more play-fight skills than do females (Ploog et al. 1967; Baldwin 1969; Biben 1986). Thus, the natural selection of hormonal and neural mechanisms that create sex differences in sensory stimulation reinforcement helps explain biological variables that affect the differences in male and female socialization. Such a model clearly links evolutionary, physiological, and environmental–developmental factors—including learning— into an integrated theoretical system.

At puberty, the rising titers of testosterone tend to increase the arousal and activity levels of males, leading them to engage in more vigorous play fights. The young adults' heightened activity and larger body size also make them increasingly salient to the adult males, which may increase the probability of aggressive responses from the adult males; and the adults' aggressive threats, chases, and fights force the subadult males to learn to deal with more serious forms of aggression than they face in play or real fights with peers. Naturally, the hormonal effects interact with individual differences in aggressiveness and inhibition. At puberty, an inhibited male might respond to adult males with increasing avoidance, flight, and perhaps early withdrawal to all-male satellite groups; whereas a male with more fighting skills and fewer inhibitions might remain in the troop and interact with the adult males, thereby learning increasing fighting skills, until he gained a place in the insider-male group or was forced out of the troop.

The Social Environment and Individual Learning of Aggressive Behavior

Third, aggression is influenced by reinforcers and punishers other than sensory stimulation. Various reinforcers—such as food, female odors, and sexual interaction—can provide incentives to fight by rewarding aggressive behavior; while the punishments of painful fights can inhibit aggressive behavior, especially in those who lose more fights than they win. Sensitivity to all the unconditioned reinforcers and punishers is influenced by selective processes, thus the proximal rewards and costs of aggression can be adjusted by selective processes (Baldwin and Baldwin 1981). Each individual's genetic inheritance sets its base level of responsiveness to all the unconditioned reinforcers and punishers; then that individual's aggressive behavior is molded by the social models it sees and the patterns of reinforcement and punishment it experiences during the developmental process.

Reinforcers. Although sensory stimulation reinforces early play wrestling and fighting, other reinforcers motivate and reward the more serious aggression seen in mature individuals. Food, of course, can motivate and reinforce food stealing, which in turn can lead to aggression, though this is uncommon in *Saimiri*.

Before and during mating season, female odors appear to function as strong positive reinforcers for *Saimiri* males: Even immature males repeatedly approach adult females for olfactory investigation (Boinski 1987a). This suggests that the neural mechanisms that make female odors an unconditioned reinforcer for males have been established by selective processes and are operational before adulthood. Such a reinforcement mechanism would be adaptive for adult males, since preadult rewards for approaching females establish a motivation to approach adult females—when they have the opportunity to mate—even when faced with aggressive responses from other males. When immature males engage in sexual play, they learn how to copulate and gain experience in synchronizing with females for the positive reinforcers of sexual interaction. In adulthood, the positive reinforcers of female odors and copulation motivate approach to and interactions with adult females.

Punishers. Although the reinforcers of female odors and sexual interaction attract males to the female core, the need to fight other males to gain insider status introduces punishers that inhibit some males' approaches. A species level of sensitivity to pain affects the degree to which males will fight to attain reinforcers. Sensitivity to pain is, no doubt, adjusted through the selective processes. Selection for brain mechanisms that reduce sensitivity to pain would decrease the degree to which an individual would be punished by painful stimuli during serious fights. Hence, an individual with little sensitivity to pain would be less inhibited about engaging in aggression. In contrast, the selection of brain structures that heighten a species' sensitivity to pain would increase the chances that individuals would learn to avoid excessive aggressiveness during play fights early in life and during real fights at any age.[7]

Theories of reinforcement and punishment help clarify how even small variations in social environments contribute to the emergence of individual differences in aggressiveness during the socialization process. In order to understand how an individual might learn to be more or less aggressive than troop mates, data would be needed on the individual's history of reinforcement and punishment for aggression, along with its observational learning from relevant social models. For example, if an infant had an unusually large number of adversive experiences during play fights, this punishment might cause it to avoid vigorous play fights more than its peers did. This avoidance would, in turn, lead it to have less learning experience in play fights than would peers who did not avoid such play; and limited experience in play fights would limit its chances to learn and practice the running, jumping, sparring, and other skills that are useful in real fights.

In contrast, an infant who had an assertive and protective mother might be sheltered from adversive contact while young, which would increase the chances that it would enter into early play in an uninhibited and bold manner. Its own mother and/or her close associates—if bold and assertive—would be social models further increasing its tendency to learn assertive skills and use them fearlessly and boldly. *Saimiri* are capable of learning by imitation (Huebner et al. 1979). The infant's assertive, unfearful behavior in play fights would increase its chances to experience sensory stimulation reinforcers of play without too much punishment from adversive experiences; thus it would show less tendency to avoid such mock aggression than would less bold and skillful peers. Naturally, large body size, strength, high activity level, and other variables would increase an individual's chances for success and reinforcement in play fights. Those individuals with the physical and learned advantages needed for success in play fights would be expected to gain increasing skill and boldness, facilitating the continued learning of aggressive skills, both during play and later in serious fights. Individual differences in physiology and learning could be critical determinants of a male's maturing skills for successfully challenging adult males for a place in an insider-male group. A male with extensive play-fight experience would be better prepared to deal with the adult males during the transition to adulthood and more likely to succeed in entering an insider-male group.

This type of approach to reinforcers and punishers clearly interweaves all three variables—evolutionary, physiological, and environmental–developmental. Presumably, selective processes adjust the neural mechanisms for sensitivity to various stimuli—such as odors, sexual contact, and pain—as unconditioned reinforcers and punishers, adjusting them toward levels that are suited to a species' typical social ecology. Then, depending on its unique life experiences with observational learning and differential reinforcement, each individual learns the form and frequency of aggression that are compatible with the type of reinforcement and punishment it experiences in its particular social setting. In addition, the relative power of stimuli to function as primary reinforcers or punishers can be modified by learning experiences in which those stimuli are paired with other reinforcers and punishers (Baldwin and Baldwin 1981).

Developing a Comprehensive Theory?

Purely evolutionary theories sometimes create the impression that a species' behavioral patterns are determined solely by evolutionary processes. Such a conclusion is completely unwarranted. Hopefully, these three examples are adequate to demonstrate the feasibility and value of interweaving evolutionary, physiological, and environmental–developmental factors in explaining certain aspects of *Saimiri* aggressiveness. Other behavioral mechanisms doubtlessly influence *Saimiri* aggression, helping to explain other features of aggression within the genus.

A comprehensive theory of aggression requires an integration of evolutionary, physiological, and environmental–developmental factors: There are quite a few species—including our own—for which adequate data are available to begin to develop comprehensive theories. Even in research on the less well-understood species, an awareness of the need to interweave all three types of data can help researchers, who are dealing with any specific topic, to conceptualize the overall design features of such a comprehensive theory and begin to structure their work in ways that will be compatible and easily integrated with work on other components of the larger theory. Researchers in each discipline can continue to study the issues best suited to their specialty; but a sensitivity to the demands of a larger, integrated theory can help guide their work and coordinate their contribution with those from other fields.

SUMMARY

1. A comprehensive theory of aggression interweaves data and theories on all three major determinants of behavior—evolutionary, physiological, and environmental–developmental. One of the main goals of this chapter is to advance the work on such comprehensive theories: first by developing a missing element of such a theory for *Saimiri*; and second, by demonstrating how data on evolutionary, physiological, and environmenal–developmental variables can be synthesized into one integrated theory.

2. At present there has already been a reasonably good start at developing the data and theories concerning the physiological and environmental–developmental determinants of aggression in *Saimiri* troops. However, there is no adequate analysis of the evolutionary adaptiveness of aggression in such troops.

3. A tentative evolutionary analysis of *Saimiri* aggression is developed from the existing literature on diverse troops. Fourteen empirically based descriptive hypotheses are presented, each of which is open to falsification or further refinement.

4. If these hypotheses are reasonably correct, they reveal that *Saimiri* are relatively nonaggressive, the only serious aggression being limited to competition among males for the chance to travel near the adult females during a relatively

brief mating season. In Central America, very little aggression has been reported in the insider-male group that travels closest to the adult females in mating season—though insider males do chase and fight out-group males and males from other troops. In South America, where troops are larger, considerable aggression has been reported among the insider adult males and between insider males and out-group males that follow near the troop in mating season. Overall, other troop members (and adult males out of mating season) seldom engage in aggressive behavior.

5. Even though there are several social mechanisms that can reduce aggression in *Saimiri* troops, the data presented here reveal that group selection is not needed to explain any of these.

6. The last section of the chapter demonstrates how evolutionary, physiological, and environmental–developmental determinants of behavior can be interwoven: Evolutionary processes select various physiological mechanisms that influence and are influenced by behavior during the developmental processes in each individual's unique environmental setting.

7. For example, *Saimiri*'s highly stereotyped genital display is doubtlessly a product of natural selection; and its early emergence in infancy suggests that it is based on "hard wired" physiological mechanisms. However, infants display in inappropriate social situations; and developmental processes such as differential reinforcement are needed for them to learn the appropriate use of this "innate" behavior.

8. The role of testosterone in promoting differences in male and female behavior also reveals how selective processes can shape physiological mechanisms that in turn lead males and females to have different learning experiences, which train males to develop more strength and aggressive skills.

9. A species' sensitivity to all the primary reinforcers and punishers is established by the natural selection of the brain mechanisms that mediate reinforcement and punishment; and these physiological mechanisms in turn influence the learning of aggressive behavior and are themselves modifiable by various learning experiences.

10. Comprehensive theories of aggression can be constructed by linking data and theories on the evolutionary, physiological, and environmental–developmental determinants of behavior in the manner demonstrated here.

ACKNOWLEDGMENTS

I thank Carol Mitchell, the editors of this book, and unknown reviewers for reading and commenting on this manuscript.

NOTES

1. The taxonomy of *Saimiri* has not been resolved, and other authorities subdivide the genus differently (Cabrera 1958; Hill 1960).

2. The combined troops are noisy, and birds probably capture many of the insects that are flushed by the advancing troop (Terborgh 1983); thus the *Cebus* lose access to the easily

obtained insects taken by the birds and *Saimiri*. *Saimiri* are "commensal or mildly parasitic" (Terborgh 1983:220): It is the *Saimiri* who join *Cebus* groups, not *Cebus* who join *Saimiri* troops. Mittermeier and van Roosmalen (1981) also concur that *Saimiri* gain the major advantage in mixed troops with *Cebus*; and *Cebus* puts up with *Saimiri*.

3. In comparing body size with diet, Fleagle (1985) found that very small primates typically eat insects; and as body size increases to 1 kg, primates increasingly supplement insect food with fruit. Insects provide an excellent source of protein and calories; however, as body size increases, few primates can catch enough insects per day to meet their daily energy requirements. Thus, primates of *Saimiri* size typically rely heavily on fruit to supplement their insect diet. *Saimiri* have specialized to take advantage of abundant sources of ripe fruit when possible and insects much of the rest of the time.

4. *Saimiri* weighing 800 g can catch twice as much insect prey per hour as *Cebus* weighing 3 kg (Terborgh 1985:301–302).

5. Mendoza et al. (1978b) report that males and females of the Guyanese subspecies of squirrel monkeys are more similar in size than are some of the other subspecies, but Guyanese males are still approximately 250 g heavier than females.

6. Experiments using intracranial reinforcement could evaluate the effect of differential reinforcement to change genital displays in various social situations.

7. This model can be investigated in the laboratory by comparing several species to determine if the less aggressive species are more sensitive to pain, at least when that variable is measured by the ability of adversive stimuli to serve as punishers that suppress aggressive behavior.

REFERENCES

Alexander, R. D. 1974. The evolution of social behavior. *Annual Review of Ecology and Systematics* 5:325–383.
Baldwin, J. D. 1968. The social behavior of adult male squirrel monkeys (*Saimiri sciureus*) in a seminatural environment. *Folia Primatologica* 9:281–314.
———. 1969. The ontogeny of social behavior of squirrel monkeys (*Saimiri sciureus*) in a seminatural environment. *Folia Primatologica* 11:35–79.
———. 1971. The social organization of a semifree-ranging troop of squirrel monkeys (*Saimiri sciureus*). *Folia Primatologica* 14:23–50.
Baldwin, J. D. and J. I. Baldwin. 1972. The ecology and behavior of squirrel monkeys (*Saimiri oerstedii*) in a natural forest in western Panama. *Folia Primatologica* 18:161–184.
———. 1973. The role of play in social organization: Comparative observations on squirrel monkeys (*Saimiri*). *Primates* 14:369–381.
———. 1974. Exploration and social play in squirrel monkeys. *American Zoologist* 14:303–315.
———. 1981. *Beyond Sociobiology*. Elsevier: New York.
Berger, J. 1979. Social ontogeny and behavioural diversity: Consequences for Bighorn Sheep *Ovis canadensis* inhabiting desert and mountain environments. *Journal of Zoology* 188:251–266.
———. 1980. The ecology, structure and functions of social play in Bighorn Sheep (*Ovis canadensis*). *Journal of Zoology* 192:531–542.
Biben, M. 1986. Individual- and sex-related strategies of wrestling play in captive squirrel monkeys. *Ethology* 71:229–241.
Boinski, S. 1987a. Mating patterns in squirrel monkeys (*Saimiri oerstedii*). *Behavioral Ecology and Sociobiology* 21:13–21.

Boinski, S. 1987b. Birth synchrony in squirrel monkeys (*Saimiri oerstedii*). *Behavioral Ecology and Sociobiology* 21:393–400.

———. 1987c. Habitat use by squirrel monkeys (*Saimiri oerstedii*) in Costa Rica. *Folia Primatologica* 49:151–167.

Boinski, S. and R. M. Timm. 1985. Predation by squirrel monkeys and double-toothed kites on tent-making bats. *American Journal of Primatology* 9:121–127.

Cabrera, A. 1958. Catálogo de los mamíferos de América del Sur. *Revista del Museo Argentino de Ciéncias Naturales "Bernardino Rivadavia" e Instituto Nacional de Investigación de las Ciéncias Naturales. Zoología* 4(i–iv):1–307.

Castell, R. and B. Heinrich. 1971. Rank order in a captive female squirrel monkey colony. *Folia Primatologica* 14:182–189.

Coe, C. and S. Levine. 1983. Biology of aggression. *Bulletin of the American Academy of Psychiatry and the Law* 11:131–148.

Coe, C. L., E. R. Smith, and S. Levine. 1985. The endocrine system of the squirrel monkey, pp. 191–218. In *Handbook of Squirrel Monkey Research*, L. A. Rosenblum and C. L. Coe, eds. New York: Plenum Press.

Cooper, R. W. 1968. Squirrel monkey taxonomy and supply, pp. 1–29. In *The Squirrel Monkey*, L. A. Rosenblum and R. W. Cooper, eds. New York: Academic Press.

DuMond, F. V. 1968. The squirrel monkey in a seminatural environment, pp. 87–145. In *The Squirrel Monkey*, L. A. Rosenblum and R. W. Cooper, eds. New York: Academic Press.

Fleagle, J. G. 1985. Size and adaptation in primates, pp. 1–19. In *Size and Scaling in Primate Biology*, W. L. Jungers, ed. New York: Plenum Press.

Fleagle, J. G., R. A. Mittermeier, and A. L. Skopec. 1981. Differential habitat use by *Cebus apella* and *Saimiri sciureus* in central Surinam. *Primates* 22:361–367.

Fagaszy, D. M. and W. A. Mason. 1983. Comparisons of feeding behavior in captive squirrel and titi monkeys (*Saimiri sciureus* and *Callicebus moloch*). *Journal of Comparative and Physiological Psychology* 97:310–326.

Fry, D. P. 1980. The evolution of aggression and the level of selection controversy. *Aggressive Behavior* 6:69–89.

Hennessy, M. B., C. L. Coe, S. P. Mendoza, E. L. Lowe, and S. Levine. 1978. Scent-marking and olfactory investigatory behavior in the squirrel monkey (*Saimiri sciureus*). *Behavioral Biology* 24:57–67.

Hill, W. C. O. 1960. *Primates, Comparative Anatomy and Taxonomy. IV. Cebidae. Part A.* New York: Interscience.

Hopf, S. 1979. Development of sexual behaviour in captive squirrel monkeys (*Saimiri*). *Biology of Behaviour* 4:373–382.

Hopf, S., E. Hartmann-Wiesner, B. Kuhlmorgen, and S. Mayer. 1974. The behavioral repertoire of the squirrel monkey (*Saimiri*). *Folia Primatologica* 21:225–249.

Hopf, S., M. Herzog, and D. Ploog. 1985. Development of attachment and exploratory behavior in infant squirrel monkeys under controlled rearing conditions. *International Journal of Behavioral Development* 8:55–74.

Hrdy, S. B. 1986. Sources of variance in the reproductive success of female primates. *Accademia Nazionale dei Lincei* 259:191–203.

Huebner, D. K., J. L. Lentz, M. J. Wooley, and J. E. King. 1979. Responses to snakes by surrogate- and mother-reared squirrel monkeys. *Bulletin of the Psychonomic Society* 14:33–36.

Izawa, K. 1975. Foods and feeding behavior of monkeys in the upper Amazon basin. *Primates* 16:295–316.

Latta, J., S. Hopf, and D. Ploog. 1967. Observation on mating behavior and sexual play in the squirrel monkey (*Saimiri sciureus*). *Primates* 8:229:246.

Leger, D. W., W. A. Mason, and D. M. Muckenbeck Fragaszy. 1981. Sexual segregation, cliques, and social power in squirrel monkey (*Saimiri*) groups. *Behaviour* 76:163–181.

Lewontin, R. 1979. Sociobiology as an adaptationist program. *Behavioral Science* 24:5–14.

Long, J. O. and R. W. Cooper. 1968. Physical growth and dental eruption in captive-bred squirrel monkeys, *Saimiri sciureus* (Leticia, Colombia), pp. 193–205. In *The Squirrel Monkey*, L. A. Rosenblum and R. W. Cooper, eds. New York: Academic Press.

MacLean, P. D. 1964. Mirror display in the squirrel monkey. *Science* 146:950–952.

Martin, P. and T. M. Caro. 1985. On the functions of play and its role in behavioral development. *Advances in the Study of Behavior* 15:59–103.

Mason, W. A. 1968. Use of space by *Callicebus* groups, pp. 200–216. In *Primates: Studies in Adaptation and Variability*, P. C. Jay, ed. New York: Holt, Rinehart and Winston.

Maynard Smith, J. 1974. The theory of games and the evolution of animal conflict. *Journal of Theoretical Biology* 47:209–221.

Maynard Smith, J. and G. R. Price. 1973. The logic of animal conflict. *Nature* 246:15–18.

Mendoza, S. P., E. L. Lowe, J. A. Resko, and S. Levine. 1978a. Seasonal variations in gonadal hormones and social behavior in squirrel monkeys. *Physiology & Behavior* 20:515–522.

Mendoza, S. P., E. L. Lowe, and S. Levine. 1978b. Social organization and social behavior in two subspecies of squirrel monkeys (*Saimiri sciureus*). *Folia Primatologica* 30:126–144.

Middleton, C. C. and J. Rosal. 1972. Weights and measurements of normal squirrel monkeys (*Saimiri sciureus*). *Laboratory Animal Science* 22:583–586.

Mittermeier, R. A. and G. M. van Roosmalen. 1981. Preliminary observations of habitat utilization and diet in eight Surinam monkeys. *Folia Primatologica* 36:1–39.

Moynihan, M. 1976. *The New World Primates*. Princeton, NJ: Princeton University Press.

Perloe, S. I. 1983. Affiliation within and between the sexes and the use of space in a captive group of squirrel monkeys (*Saimiri sciureus*). Presented at the American Society of Primatologists Meeting, East Lansing, Michigan.

Ploog, D. W. 1967. The behavior of squirrel monkeys (*Saimiri sciureus*) as revealed by sociometry, bioacoustics, and brain stimulation, pp. 149–184. In *Social Communication among Primates*, S. A. Altmann, ed. Chicago: University of Chicago Press.

Ploog, D. W., S. Hopf and P. Winter. 1967. Ontogenese des Verhaltens von Totenkopf-affen (*Saimiri sciureus*). *Psychologische Forschung* 31:1–41.

Ridley, M. 1986. The number of males in a primate troop. *Animal Behavior* 34:1848–1858.

Robinson, J. G. and C. H. Janson. 1986. Capuchins, squirrel monkeys, and atelines: Socioecological convergence with Old World primates, pp. 69–82. In *Primate Societies*, B. B. Smuts, D. L. Cheney, R. M. Seyfarth, R. W. Wrangham, and T. T. Struhsaker, eds. Chicago: University of Chicago Press.

Rosenblum, L. A. 1974. Sex differences in mother–infant attachment in monkeys, pp. 123–141. In *Sex Differences in Behavior*, R. C. Friedman, R. M. Richart and R. L. Vande Wiele, eds. New York: John Wiley & Sons.

Rowell, T. E. 1972. *The Social Behaviour of Monkeys*. Baltimore: Penguin.

———. 1979. How would we know if social organization were *not* adaptive? pp. 1–22. In *Primate Ecology and Human Origins: Ecological Influences on Social Organization*, I. S. Bernstein and E.O. Smith, eds. New York: Garland.

de Ruiter, J. R. 1986. The influence of group size on predator scanning and foraging behaviour of wedgecapped capuchin monkeys (*Cebus olivaceus*). *Behaviour* 98:240–258.

Sanderson, I. T. 1957. *The Monkey Kingdom*. Philadelphia: Chilton.

van Schaik, C. P. 1983. Why are diurnal primates living in groups? *Behaviour* 87:120–144.

Scollay, P. A. and P. Judge. 1981. The dynamics of social organization in a population of squirrel monkeys (*Saimiri sciureus*) in a seminatural environment. *Primates* 22:60–69.

Strayer, F. F. and P. J. Harris. 1979. Social cohesion among captive squirrel monkeys (*Saimiri sciureus*). *Behavioral Ecology and Sociobiology* 5:93–110.

Symons, D. 1978. *Play and Aggression: A Study of Rhesus Monkeys*. New York: Columbia University Press.

Talmage-Riggs, G. and S. Anschel. 1973. Homosexual behavior and dominance hierarchy in a group of captive female squirrel monkeys (*Saimiri sciureus*). *Folia Primatologica* 19:61–72.

Terborgh, J. 1983. *Five New World Primates*. Princeton, NJ: Princeton University Press.

———. 1985. The ecology of Amazonian primates, pp. 284–304. In *Key Environments: Amazonia*, G. T. Prance and T. E. Lovejoy, eds. New York: Pergamon Press.

———. 1986. The social systems of New World primates: An adaptionist view, pp. 199–211. In *Primate Ecology and Conservation*, J. G. Else and P. C. Lee, eds. New York: Cambridge University Press.

Thorington, R. W., Jr. 1967. Feeding and activity of *Cebus* and *Saimiri* in a Colombian forest, pp. 180–184. In *Progress in Primatology*, D. Stark, R. Schneider and H.-J. Kuhn, eds. Stuttgart: Gustav Fischer Verlag.

———. 1968. Observations of squirrel monkeys in a Colombian forest, pp. 69–85. In *The Squirrel Monkey*, L. A. Rosenblum and R. W. Cooper, eds. New York: Academic Press.

———. 1985. The taxonomy and distribution of squirrel monkeys (*Saimiri*), pp. 1–33. In *Handbook of Squirrel Monkey Research*, L. A. Rosenblum, and C. L. Coe, eds. New York: Plenum Press.

Trivers, R. L. 1972. Parental investment and sexual selection, pp. 136–171. In *Sexual Selection and the Descent of Man 1871–1971*, B. Campbell, ed. Chicago: Aldine-Atherton.

Welker, W. I. 1971. Ontogeny of play and exploratory behaviors: A definition of problems and a search for new conceptual solutions, pp. 171–228. In *The Ontogeny of Vertebrate Behavior*, H. Moltz, ed. New York: Academic Press.

Wilson, E. O. 1975. *Sociobiology: The New Synthesis*. Cambridge, MA: Harvard University Press.

Winter, P. 1969. Dialects in squirrel monkeys: Vocalization of the Roman arch type. *Folia Primatologica* 10:216–229.

5

Causes and Consequences of Nonaggression in the Woolly Spider Monkey, or Muriqui (*Brachyteles arachnoides*)

KAREN B. STRIER

INTRODUCTION

Aggression and overt competition are commonly observed in multi-male, multi-female primate societies. In general, females compete over access to preferred food resources while males compete for access to sexually receptive females (Wrangham 1979a). Intragroup feeding competition between females usually involves mild forms of agonistic behavior, such as displacements (Smuts 1987); in extreme cases, it may lead to the fission–fusion social systems characteristic of chimpanzees (Wrangham 1979b) and spider monkeys (McFarland 1986). In these species, females avoid high costs associated with intragroup feeding competition at small fruit patches by dispersing into small or independent foraging units. Agonistic interactions between females occur infrequently because females avoid each other.

Competition between males, by contrast to females, is more frequent and more likely to escalate into full-fledged fights because of the greater, more direct importance of females to male reproductive success (Smuts 1987). This is especially true among the well-studied Old World semiterrestrial monkeys where males are also unrelated to one another (Strier 1990, submitted). Rates of agonistic interactions in savanna baboons, for example, may be as high as 0.24/hour when sexually receptive females are present (Hausfater 1975).

Because male reproductive success is potentially more variable than that of females, sexual selection pressures are stronger on males than females. Sexual selection is believed to account both for the intense competition over access to mates and for the fact that males in polygynous species are typically larger than females in both body and canine size (Clutton-Brock and Harvey 1978). Males are better equipped for fighting, so agonistic interactions are more dangerous for males than for females. In addition, sexual dimorphism may explain why males in these species are individually dominant over females (Smuts 1987; Strier 1990).

Woolly spider monkeys, or muriquis (*Brachyteles arachnoides*) (Figure 5-1) are striking exceptions to this general pattern (Milton 1985a). Although they live in multi-male, multi-female groups (Milton 1985a; Strier 1986), the data published

Figure 5-1   An adult female muriqui (*Brachyteles arachnoides*) rests calmly after being sexually inspected. Her $2\frac{1}{2}$-year-old son, who is now fully weaned, forages nearby (left background). (Photograph by K. B. Strier.)

so far suggest that males and females appear to be monomorphic in body size (Milton 1985a; Rosenberger and Strier 1989). Moreover, they exhibit comparatively little (Kay et al. 1988) or no (Milton 1985a; Rosenberger and Strier 1989) dimorphism in canine size.

Fossil records of *Brachyteles* are nonexistent, but it has been hypothesized that this species diverged from a smaller, more sexually dimorphic atelin ancestor (Rosenberger and Strier 1989). It is difficult to evaluate the historical reasons for their morphological changes, and efforts to reconstruct scenarios of behavioral evolution must be considered tentative. Nonetheless, the low dimorphism found today in this monkey is likely to reflect constraints on the expression of sexual selection pressures that are associated with intrasexual competition. While these constraints may inhibit overt agonistic behavior between male muriquis, the exceptionally large size of muriqui testes suggests that selection pressures favoring more subtle forms of competition are operating (Milton 1985a, b; Strier 1986, 1987b).

Cross-species comparisons have found strong correlations between testis size and both sperm production and high levels of male competition for mates

(Harcourt et al. 1981). Selection for large testis size is more likely to occur in multi-male polygamous species where individual males are unable to monopolize receptive females and females mate with a number of males. Large testis size enables males to compete for fertilizations both through greater sperm production and higher sperm quality (Moller 1988). However, in most species with large testes, males also compete agonistically for access to females.

The unique combination of low sexual monomorphism and large testis size observed in muriquis appears to reflect an extreme condition in which sexual selection pressures favoring overt agonistic competition between males are fully replaced by more subtle, nonaggressive competitive strategies. What limits overt agonistic competition in muriquis, and therefore constrains sexual selection in males? How does muriqui behavior reflect these constraints on agonism? To address the first question, it is necessary to consider the costs of agonistic competition in this species. To address the second question, it is necessary to examine muriqui social behavior for evidence of nonaggression.

CONSTRAINTS ON AGGRESSION

Muriquis are the largest New World primates, with adults reported to weigh up to 15 kg (Aguirre 1971). As in other mammals, large size in muriquis is likely to be an adaptive response to the pronounced seasonality in their food resources (Lindstedt and Boyce 1985; Strier 1986; Rosenberger and Strier 1989). Indeed, their large body size (Gaulin 1979), together with their specialized cranio-dentition (Zingeser 1973) and digestive system (Hill 1962), enable muriquis to rely heavily on leaves when preferred fruit resources are scarce (Milton 1984; Strier 1986, 1991a).

Muriquis also share with their smaller atelin relatives a suspensory mode of locomotion. Suspensory locomotion has been attributed to selection favoring rapid travel between widely dispersed fruit sources in spider monkeys (Cant 1977); it is likely to be similarly involved in enabling muriquis to minimize travel time, and thus include a greater proportion of fruit in their diet than would be expected from body size energetics alone (Strier 1987c, 1991a).

The importance of rapid travel in an arboreal niche for both sexes may offset selection pressures for larger male than female body size. The other primate genera which routinely employ suspensory locomotion (*Ateles* and *Hylobates*) are also sexually monomorphic, or nearly so, in body size (Leighton 1987; Kay et al. 1988). Although sexual monomorphism in *Hylobates* has been associated with their monogamous social system, it is striking that spider monkeys and muriquis, which are both polygamous, also exhibit relatively low levels of dimorphism. Despite their quite different social systems, similar ecological constraints on increased male body size may counteract sexual selection pressures in these primates.

It is more difficult, however, to explain the low degree or near absence of muriqui canine dimorphism. Kay et al. (1988) have suggested that different selection factors control body size dimorphism and canine dimorphism. In a comparison among New World primates, they demonstrate that canine dimorphism is associated with the degree of mating competition between males. In their study, muriquis fell in the low range of dimorphism.

Milton (1984, 1985a) has proposed that energetic constraints imposed by a low quality, highly folivorous diet may have selected for large body size, and may leave muriquis little surplus energy for overt competition. If agonistic behavior is prohibitive, males may be forced to rely on more subtle reproductive strategies, such as sperm competition, rather than aggression. While energetic constraints are undoubtedly important, not all muriqui populations are as folivorous as the one Milton observed (e.g., Strier 1986, 1991a; Lemos de Sa 1988). Furthermore, in more folivorous primates such as howler monkeys, overt competition between males may be severe (Crockett and Eisenberg 1987).

Muriquis, however, are much larger than howler monkeys (Rosenberger and Strier 1989). It is possible that the physical risks involved in rapid movements onto untested branches during agonistic interactions are greater for muriquis than for smaller arboreal species. Muriquis move slowly and more cautiously when they are not following one another along familiar travel routes, and they rarely rely on a single branch to support their weight at these times (Strier 1986). While risks of falling are likely to be present for all arboreal primates, they may be even greater for large-bodied species such as muriquis. Such risks, combined with the opportunities in a three-dimensional niche to anticipate and avoid agonistic confrontations, may be important ecological correlates that clearly distinguish arboreal and semiterrestrial primates.

The benefits of agonistic competition between male muriquis may be reduced both by the costs of aggression and by the overriding effects of female choice (Strier 1990). Because male muriquis are not physically able to dominate females, female choice is likely to be enhanced. Female choice may have important consequences both for the relationships between males and females and competition between males. First, if males cannot dominate females, they also may be unable to monopolize females or coerce them into copulating. Second, if females avoid mating with aggressive males, female choice may override the benefits that males might otherwise derive through direct agonistic competition.

Both ecological constraints on aggression and the resulting strength of female choice may reduce the net benefits of male–male aggression, as depicted in Figure 5-2. Nonaggression, on the other hand, is simultaneously reinforced by the large testes of male muriquis, and should be reflected in muriqui social behavior.

In the following section I examine data on muriqui social behavior collected during a systematic study of one muriqui group consisting of 23–26 individuals at the time (Table 5-1). The study described here was conducted from June 1983 through July 1984 at Fazenda Montes Claros, in Minas Gerais, Brazil. A detailed description of the study site can be found elsewhere (Strier 1986). The research methodology is provided in the appendix to this chapter.

EVIDENCE OF NONAGGRESSION

Agonistic Behavior

Aggression in muriquis is exceptionally rare, and when it does occur, it is mild in form. During over 1,200 contact hours during this study period, only 31 agonistic

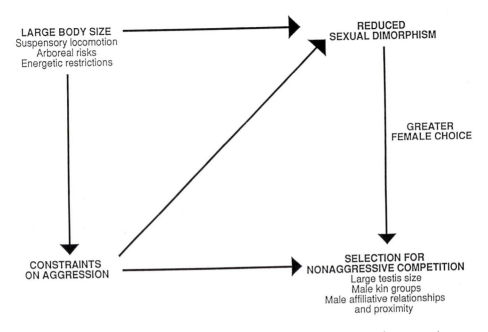

Figure 5-2   Schematic representation of some causes and consequences of nonagression.

interactions among group members were observed (Table 5-2). A total of five of the agonistic interactions involved adult females chasing or supplanting subadult females who ultimately succeeded in migrating into the group. Twenty-two interactions were displacements, in which one animal supplanted another from its position and activity; the remaining interactions were chases.

Agonistic interactions occurred too infrequently to determine dominance relationships based on consistent patterns between "winners" and "losers." For example, of the seven supplants between adult males, two involved MR and CL. Yet, each of these males supplanted the other once. Similarly, females displaced

Table 5-1   Composition of Study Group During Study Period—see Strier (1987a, 1991b) for details on age class categories

Age–sex class	July 1983	July 1984
Adult male	6	6
Adult female	8	8
Subadult male	2	2
Subadult female	0	2[a]
Juvenile-2	0	6
Juvenile-1	6	1
Infant	1	1
Total	23	26

[a] Both subadult females immigrated into group during 1983–1984.

Table 5-2 Interactions are listed separately for each combination of age–sex classes observed.

Age–sex class	Supplants	Chases	Total
Adult male	7	1	8
Adult male–adult female	2	0	2
Adult female–adult male	3	0	3
Adult female	3	4	7
Adult male–subadult male	1	0	1
Adult female–subadult male	1	0	1
Adult female–subadult female	3	2	5
Adult female–unknown immature	2	1	3
Adult male and female–adult male	0	1	1
Total	22	9	31

males in three of the five dyadic interactions that occurred between adult males and females, suggesting that males were not dominant over females.

None of the agonistic interactions occurred over access to obvious resources such as food or mates. Although four of the seven displacements between males occurred during sexual inspections of females (see following text), none of these inspections resulted in subsequent copulations.

Spatial Relations

The low frequency of agonistic behavior is particularly surprising because muriquis spend substantial proportions of their time in close proximity to one another. Data on muriqui spatial relationships, obtained from 4,334 scan samples involving a total of 16,587 individual observations, indicate that muriquis spent over 30% of their time less than 1 m, and over 50% of their time less than 5 m from at least one other individual (Strier 1990).

Muriqui spatial relationships also differ depending on whether they are resting or feeding, suggesting that they actively avoid agonistic contests over food by avoiding one another (Strier 1990). First, they tend to be in closer proximity to their nearest neighbors when they are resting than when they are feeding. Sixty-five per cent of all resting observations involved nearest neighbors less than 1 m apart, in contrast to only 44% of all feeding observations. Even more striking, there were clear differences in the identities of muriqui nearest neighbors depending on activity. In nearly every case, the most frequent nearest neighbor of each resting adult differed from the most frequent nearest neighbor of each adult when feeding (Table 5-3). Because muriquis spend an average of 49% of their daylight hours resting (Strier 1987d), it is likely that these spatial relationships occur between individuals with the strongest social bonds. Yet, the fact that muriquis do not feed in proximity to the individuals with whom they otherwise spend most of their time suggests that they avoid potential competition with their closest associates.

Muriquis' avoidance of feeding competition enables them to remain in cohesive

Table 5-3 Most Frequent Nearest Neighbors. Initials indicate individual muriquis. In the case of tied scores, all individuals are listed. Parentheses designate the second most frequent nearest neighbor when the difference between first and second is small. Female data are discussed elsewhere (Strier 1990).

	Rest	Feed
Males		
SC	CL	IV
CL	SC	IV
MR	CL	SC
IV	SC (CL)	SC(CY)
MK	SC (CL)	SC (IV)
PR	IV	MR
Females		
SY	BS	LS
NY	BS	IV
AR	LS	JU
BS	NY, SY	CH
RO	SC, IV	SC, NY, MO
DD	NY	MR
MO	NY	SC, BS, RO, LS
LS	AR, SY	SC

groups while feeding rather than fissioning into smaller feeding parties (Strier 1989). In other primates, group cohesion has been seen as associated with the benefits to individuals either because of improved predator detection (van Schaik and van Hooff 1983) or because of the competitive advantages groups have in intergroup resource defense (Wrangham 1980, 1982). However, as the size of the group expands, intragroup feeding competition is likely to increase. If intragroup feeding competition does increase, the frequency of agonistic interactions also increases, and may ultimately result in group fissioning.

The long-term data on muriquis at Fazenda Montes Claros may shed light on this process. In the eight years that these muriquis have been monitored, for example, the group has increased from 22 to 43 individuals, and the group has begun to show correspondingly greater tendencies toward fragmentation (Strier 1991b). During the first six years of the study, group members maintained vocal contact and coordinated their movements when they were too dispersed to see one another (Strier 1986, 1989). More recently, however, smaller parties have been separated by distances too great to permit communication and coordinated movements. The feeding requirements of the group may have begun to approach a critical limit that exceeds food patch size.

After six years of group cohesion, these muriquis appear to be adopting the more fluid patterns of association that characterize both their closest relative, *Ateles* (Klein and Klein 1977; McFarland 1986), and another population of muriquis studied elsewhere (Milton 1984). By fissioning into smaller subgroups, it appears that the muriquis can continue to avoid overt confrontations over access to food. Indeed, it is possible that constraints on aggression make group fissioning their only alternative in the absence of mechanisms to resolve conflicts (see de Waal 1986).

Avoiding feeding competition may reflect the high costs of aggressive confrontations. Yet, if preferred foods are sufficiently abundant (see following text), there may be little reason to compete for food resources. The absence of overt competition between males, in contrast, is more difficult to explain because the number of sexually receptive females in this group was undeniably limited.

Sexual Behavior

Muriqui reproduction was asynchronous during the 14-month study period described here. All of the eight adult females but one, who was nursing a new infant, became sexually receptive at different times (Strier 1987b, but see also Strier 1991b). Female muriquis do not exhibit any visual signs of sexual receptivity. Rather, information about their reproductive state appears to be transmitted through pheromonal cues (see Milton 1985c). Sexual inspections are an important context for this chemical communication.

Sexual inspections occurred when a male sniffed a female's genitals. Females have pendulous genitalia which males also sometimes pulled on. This elicited a liquid secretion which the male then smelled, and sometimes tasted, from his fingers.

A total of 117 sexual inspections were observed during the present study period. Females approached and presented their perinea to males in 46% of the 28 inspections in which the initiator was recorded. Males initiated inspections by approaching resting females from the rear or side.

Except in the four cases mentioned earlier, other group members did not interfere with sexual inspections. In three of the cases in which males were supplanted during inspections, the newly arrived male also inspected the female. Males would also inspect females whom they had watched being inspected by a different male without attempting to supplant the latter.

Forty-eight copulations were observed during this period (Strier 1987b). All copulations occurred in full view of other group members, and sometimes in the same tree where other males were resting. Copulations averaged 6.48 minutes (sd = 3.74, $N = 27$, median = 5), but lasted up to 18 minutes. Yet, except for the curiosity exhibited by the females' youngest offspring, copulations were never interrupted or disturbed by other group members.

Some males copulated more frequently than others. However, there was no significant relationship between how often a male inspected females and how often he copulated with them (Table 5-4; $r_s = 0.29$, $n = 7$, $p > 0.05$), nor between the number of different females a male inspected and the number he copulated with ($r_s = 0.39$, $n = 7$, $p > 0.05$).

Four of the seven receptive females conceived during the study period. For three of these females, at least two different males were possible fathers. The three males who copulated most frequently (IV, MR, and CL) were among the possible fathers although they were not the only possible fathers (Strier 1987b).

The long duration of copulations and their open occurrence in the presence

Table 5-4 Frequency of Sexual Inspections and Copulations by Different Males. Initials indicate individual adult males except as noted otherwise.

Male	Sexual inspection	Copulation
SC	29	3
IV	26	15
MR	13	7
CL	12	6
PR	12	3
MK	4	1
AM[a]	17	9
CY[b]	4	4
Total	117	48

[a] Includes adult males who could not be identified individually.
[b] Subadult male who began copulating toward end of study period.

of the other males indicate that muriquis do not attempt to conceal their reproductive activities for fear of inciting aggression. Indeed, muriquis not only tolerate one another in potentially competitive contexts, they also exhibit strongly affiliative relationships.

Affiliative Relationships

Spatial Associations

In their spatial relationships, adults and subadults preferred the company of members of their own sex (Strier, in press). Adult males spent 69% of their time in proximity to other adult males, whereas females divided their time between other females and their dependent young (Strier, submitted).

Individual nearest neighbors were neither randomly nor evenly distributed across group members (Figure 5-3). That is, all muriquis spent significant proportions of their time in proximity to only a few other individuals.

Nearest neighbors were often, although not always, reciprocal (see Appendix). The same individuals were often among one anothers' most frequent nearest neighbors. However, for most of these pairs, one individual was more responsible for maintaining the association than the other (Strier, submitted).

Male muriquis differed from one another in their degree of popularity, or the proportion of time spent in the proximity of others relative to the total number of minutes each male was observed during the focal samples (see Appendix; Strier, submitted). The two most popular males, MR and IV, were often among the most frequent nearest neighbors of other males (Figure 5-3). Yet their popularity appears to have been imposed upon them largely through approaches initiated by others (Strier, submitted).

Embraces

Unlike most other group living primates, muriquis do not groom one another. Their primary forms of physical contact occur during rest (see preceding text) and

Figure 5-3 Matrix of nearest neighbors.

	ADULT MALES							ADULT FEMALES									SUBADULT MALES			SUBADULT FEMALES			JUVS	PROXIMITY SCANS (N)
	SC	CL	MR	IV	MK	PR	AM	SY	NY	AR	BS	FD	DD	MO	LS	AF	SO	CY	SM	CH	BL	SF	JV	
SC		13	5	15	3	2	14	1	1		2			1	4	14	4	4	4				10	421
CL	28		10	14	6	3	8	1	2		1	2			3	2	6	8	2	2			3	209
MR	10	12		17	2	6	11	3	2	1	2	1	2	2	1	10	3	6	2	1	1		5	166
IV	21	10	17		4	7	7	1	1	1	2	4		1	3	11	2	6	3				5	281
MK	20	23	8	14			3	2			2				4	6	5	9					3	66
PR	10	7	11	23			14					1		1	5	10	5	10	1	1			1	84
AM	22	1	1	1		2		2		1	2		1		1	10	1	4	5				4	2337
SY	3	3	3	2	1		4		2	7	5		2	2	10	5	1	1		2			48	137
NY	1	2	2	14			3	14		5	12		6	8	5	8	1	1		2			42	213
AR	1		3	1			7	7	13		5			4	19	4		2		1			31	94
BS	4	2		3			4	4	16			1	2	2	2	9	2	2	2	2			37	162
FD	10		1	12			5	1	14	4	1			6	4	3				4			45	78
DD	2	1	3	1		1	1	1	7	1	2			9	7	8		1		2			44	86
MO	1	1	1	1			1	6	5	8	3	3	2		5	18		1		1			50	277
LS	6	3	1	4		2	9		5	8	3	1	2	6		25		3		1			13	221
AF	2		1	2			11	6	1		1	1	2	2	2				1	1			38	2255
SO	10	6	2	2		2	11		1		2	1	1	2	1	5		20		4			28	157
CY	8	7	4	3	2	3	39	1	1		2			1	2	3	13			1			12	253
SM	6	1	1	3			57				1					11		4					13	276
CH	2	2	3	2		2	3	5	5	2	3	7	2	2	2	13	15	5					22	60
BL			10										10	10									70	10
SF	8						23								54								15	13
JV	1	1	1	1			4	3	5	2	3	2	2	6	1	37	2	2	1	1			26	2195

Values are expressed as the proportion of all observations during scan samples in which proximity was less than 5 m. All initials refer to individuals except: AM, unidentified adult male; AF, unidentified adult female; SM, unidentified subadult male; SF, unidentified subadult female; and JV, includes all infants and juveniles.

during "embraces." Embraces occurred during or immediately following tense periods such as when they were startled by an observer or during intergroup encounters. Embraces, which appeared to serve a reassurance function, varied from one animal touching another with its hand or foot to full body contact, in which two or more individuals hang suspended by their tails and wrap their arms and legs around one another ventrally. Only full body embraces are discussed below.

Muriquis appear calm and relaxed after embracing. No tension is evident between embrace partners, although embrace huddles involving multiple males sometimes appear more agitated. At these times, the soft "chuckle" that routinely accompanies dyadic embraces becomes louder, and gradually becomes a more intense, throaty "warble" (Strier 1986).

A total of 122 embraces were observed in the scan samples, focal samples, and *ad libitum* monitoring combined (Figure 5-4). The majority (83.61%) was dyadic, and occurred when two animals moved toward one another simultaneously so that initiation was not scored. Males are more likely than females to participate in multiple-partner embraces. Of the 26 polyadic embraces observed, 61.5% involved at least two males.

Embraces, like spatial relationships, were not evenly distributed across all group members. A comparison of Figures 5-3 and 5-4 reveals that embrace partners were also likely to be most frequent nearest neighbors.

CONSEQUENCES OF NONAGGRESSION

Constraints on agonism appear to have profound consequences for the competitive strategies available to male muriquis. As noted above, their large testes strongly indicate selection for sperm competition. What is striking, however, is that males do not behave agonistically toward one another in either reproductive or nonreproductive contexts.

Male muriquis also do not direct aggression toward females. Rather, their relationships involve both avoidance at feeding sites and affiliative contact. Some females spent disproportionate amounts of their time in proximity to only one or two different males (Figure 5-3). These associations may reflect heterosexual "friendships" similar to those described by Smuts (1985) among baboons. In baboons, male efforts to establish and maintain special relationships with particular females have been attributed to strategies for subordinate males that increase their probabilities of mating. In chimpanzees (Tutin 1979) as well as baboons, females may be more likely to mate with males who are also their friends. Although some female muriquis copulated with close male associates, sample sizes are at present too small to permit a systematic analysis.

Muriquis, however, differ from both baboons and chimpanzees in their low sexual dimorphism and in the apparent codominance of males and females. Females were responsible for initiating nearly half of all sexual inspections, and when females terminated the inspections by moving away, they were not pursued or harassed by any males. This deferential behavior may reflect both constraints on agonism and the effects of female choice on male mating success, although it is still unclear what female muriquis are choosing in their mates.

Figure 5-4 Matrix of embrace partners. Values represent the frequency of each embrace dyad. The sum of all embrace dyads (n = 271) is greater than the total number of embraces observed because polyadic embraces are broken down into their dyadic components here. Initials are the same as in Figure 5-3.

	ADULT MALES							ADULT FEMALES									SUBADULT MALES			SUBADULT FEMALES			JUVS	EMBRACES (N)
	SC	CL	MR	IV	MK	PR	AM	SY	NY	AR	BS	FD	DD	MO	LS	AF	SD	CY	SM	CH	BL	SF	JV	
SC		4		2		2	3	7									2	2		1				19
CL	4		1	1	1	1	2		1						3	1	1	1						13
MR		1		3			3	1	1					1	1	1								8
IV	2	1	3		1	2	2				1			1	1	1		1	1					10
MK	1	2	1	1																				3
PR	2	1		2				1	1					2				1	1				1	8
AM	3	2	3	2			16	1	1					2	2	5	5	5	3		1	1		28
SY	7	1	1	1					1	1	1		1	1	1	2	2	1		1			2	5
NY	1	1	1				1	1		1	8			7	1	2				1			2	28
AR								1							2						1			3
BS	1	1	1					1	8			1	2	1	2	1	1		1				1	17
FD											1		1	2	1	1								6
DD	1										2	1		1		1		1						6
MO	1	2	1	1		2	2	1	7		1	2	1		3	2							2	24
LS	3	5	1	2				1	1	2	2	1		3		2								15
AF	1	1	1	1			5	2	2		1	1	1	2	1	10		1	2	1	1		3	35
SD	2	1																1		1			2	5
CY	2	1		1			5		1		1					1	1		1	1			1	6
SM			1	1		1	3									2								6
CH	1							1								1	1	1				3	2	7
BL																						3	1	3
SF																1	3	1	1	3	3			
JV						1		1	2		3	1	1	2		3	2	1	1	1	1		11	16

High costs of agonism and the overriding effects of female choice prevent males both from competing with one another directly and from monopolizing access to females. If males must share copulations, and thus the probability of paternity, higher inclusive fitness is achieved if they "share" with the close relatives.

During the eight years that the study group has been monitored systematically, no males have emigrated from the group. All four immature males present when the study began are now fully mature and reproductively active, and routinely associate without tension with the older adult males.

Although far from conclusive, these records suggest male muriquis remain in their natal groups and are thus related to one another. In most other primates in which male kin groups occur (see Pusey and Packer 1987), females have fluid and unpredictable patterns of association. Male kinship in these species has been attributed to selection for males to cooperate in patrols of the community's range. Male kin groups in muriquis may reflect a phylogenetic condition in which females disperse (Rosenberger and Strier 1989; Strier 1990), while males maximize their inclusive fitness by remaining in their natal group where conventional forms of competition are prohibitive.

Another corollary of nonaggression in muriquis may be the strong affiliative relationships between males. Indeed, male muriquis spend more time in close proximity to one another than has been reported in any other species. Males may even benefit by maintaining proximity because it permits them to monitor one another's activities. This surveillance may be particularly important if it enables males to monitor one another's sexual activities.

It is significant that MR and IV, the two most popular males, together accounted for 56% of the 39 copulations in which the identity of the male could be positively determined. One or both of these males were also among the most likely fathers of all four of the infants conceived during this study period. These males were important nearest neighbors to other males, yet they were not directly responsible for their popularity (see Strier, submitted).

While it is difficult to demonstrate the causal relationships between popularity and mating success, these males may have been more popular with other males *because* they were more adept at detecting female receptivity (see Milton 1985b). By contrast, the male who demonstrated the strongest tendencies for initiating and maintaining proximity with other males (SC) was involved in nearly twice as many embraces as any other male. Although he also inspected females more than any other male, he neither copulated often nor was he a probable father of any of the infants conceived during this time.

Affiliative interactions may help ensure that relationships between males remain nonaggressive. More importantly, they may enable younger males to monitor and learn from the activities of their more experienced adult male relatives (Strier, in press).

SUMMARY

Constraints on aggression moderate sexual selection by restricting sexual dimorphism and agonistic competition between male muriquis (Figure 5-2). Males are not dominant over females, and female choice may further reduce the net benefits of male intrasexual aggression. Within these constraints, males have few options other than to: (1) compete through testes size indication of sperm quantity and quality; (2) defer to females; (3) monitor one another's activities by maintaining close proximity and strong affiliative relationships; and (4) associate with their male kin.

While other primates may exhibit any subset of these characteristics, the complete combination has not been reported for groups of any other species. Muriquis, therefore, provide a unique opportunity to evaluate alternatives to agonism and the ways in which constraints on sexual selection may influence primate social behavior.

ACKNOWLEDGMENTS

I am grateful to the Brazilian government and CNPq for permission to work in Brazil, and to Professor Celio Valle for his encouragement. Generous financial support was provided by NSF grants BNS-8305322, BNS-8619442, and BNS-8959298, the Fulbright Foundation, the Joseph Henry Fund grant no. 213, the L. S. B. Leakey Foundation, the World Wildlife Fund, and the Department of Anthropology at Harvard University. E. Veado, F. Mendes, J. Rimoli, and A. O. Rimoli contributed to the long-term data collection. K. Bassler and L. Johnson helped prepare figures. I thank J. Silverberg and P. Gray for inviting me to contribute this paper to their volume and for their comments, as well as those of T. Boswell and F. de Waal, on an earlier draft.

REFERENCES

Aguirre, A. C. 1971. *O Mono* Brachyteles arachnoides (*E. Geoffroy*). Rio de Janeiro: Academia Brasileira de Ciencias.

Altmann, J. 1974. Observational study of behavior: Sampling methods. *Behaviour* 49:227–267.

Cant, J. G. H. 1977. Ecology, locomotion, and social organization of spider monkeys (*Ateles geoffroyi*). Ph.D. thesis, University of California, Davis.

Clutton-Brock, T. H. and P. H. Harvey. 1978. Mammals, resources, and reproductive strategies. *Nature* 273:191–195.

Crockett, C. M. and J. F. Eisenberg. 1987. Howlers: Variations in group size and demography, pp. 54–68. In *Primate Societies*, B. B. Smuts, D. L. Cheney, R. M. Seyfarth, R. W. Wrangham, and T. T. Struhsaker, eds. Chicago: University of Chicago Press.

Gaulin, S. J. C. 1979. A Jarman/Bell model of primate feeding niches. *Human Ecology* 7:1–20.

Harcourt, A. H., P. H. Harvey, S. G. P. Larson, and R. V. Short. 1981. Testis weight, body weight and breeding system in primates. *Nature* 293:55–57.

Hausfater, G. 1975. *Dominance and Reproduction in Baboons* (Papio cynocephalus). *Contributions to Primatology* 7. Basel: Karger.

Hill, W. C. O. 1962. *Primates: Comparative Anatomy and Taxonomy V: Cebidae Part B.* New York: Interscience.

Hinde, R. A. 1977. On assessing the basis of partner preferences. *Behaviour* 62:1–9.

Kay, R. F., J. M. Plavcan, K. E. Glander, and P. C. Wright. 1988. Sexual selection and canine dimorphism in New World monkeys. *American Journal of Physical Anthropology* 77:385–397.

Klein, L. L. and D. J. Klein. 1977. Feeding behavior of the Colombian spider monkey, pp. 153–181. In *Primate Ecology*, T. H. Clutton-Brock, ed. New York: Academic Press.

Leighton, D. R. 1987. Gibbons: Territoriality and monogamy, pp. 135–145. In *Primate Societies*, B. B. Smuts, D. L. Cheney, R. M. Seyfarth, R. W. Wrangham, and T. T. Struhsaker, eds. Chicago: University of Chicago Press.

Lemos de Sa, R. M. 1988. Situação de uma população de Mono-Carvoeiro, *Brachyteles arachnoides*, em fragmento de Mata Atlántica (M.G.), e implicaçoes para sua conservação. Master's thesis, Universidade de Brasília, Brasília.

Lindstedt, S. L. and M. S. Boyce. 1985. Seasonality, fasting endurance, and body size in mammals. *American Naturalist* 125:873–878.

McFarland, M. J. 1986. Ecological determinants of fission–fusion sociality in *Ateles* and *Pan*, pp. 181–190. In *Primate Ecology and Conservation*, J. G. Else and P. C. Lee, eds. Cambridge: Cambridge University Press.

Milton, K. 1984. Habitat, diet, and activity patterns of free-ranging woolly spider monkeys (*Brachyteles arachnoides* E. Geoffroy 1806). *International Journal of Primatology* 5:491–514.

———. 1985a. Multimale mating and absence of canine tooth dimorphism in woolly spider monkeys (*Brachyteles arachnoides*). *American Journal of Physical Anthropology* 68:519–523.

———. 1985b. Mating patterns of woolly spider monkeys, *Brachyteles arachnoides*: Implications for female choice. *Behavioral Ecology and Sociobiology* 17:53–59.

———. 1985c. Urine washing behavior in the woolly spider monkey (*Brachyteles arachnoides*). *Zeitschrift für Tierpsychologie* 67:154–160.

Moller, A. P. 1988. Ejaculate quality, testes size and sperm competition in primates. *Journal of Human Evolution* 17:479–488.

Pusey, A. E. and C. Packer. 1987. Dispersal and philopatry, pp. 250–266. In *Primate Societies*, B. B. Smuts, D. L. Cheney, R. M. Seyfarth, R. W. Wrangham, and T. T. Struhsaker, eds. Chicago: University of Chicago Press.

Rosenberger, A. and K. B. Strier. 1989. Adaptive radiation in the ateline primates. *Journal of Human Evolution* 18:717–750.

van Schaik, C. P. and J. A. R. A. M. van Hooff. 1983. On the ultimate causes of primate social systems. *Behaviour* 85:91–117.

Smuts, B. B. 1985. *Sex and Friendship in Baboons*. New York: Aldine.

———. 1987. Sex, aggression, and influence, pp. 400–412. In *Primate Societies*, B. B. Smuts, D. L. Cheney, R. M. Seyfarth, R. W. Wrangham, and T. T. Struhsaker, eds. Chicago: University of Chicago Press.

Strier, K. B. 1986. The behavior and ecology of the woolly spider monkey, or muriqui (*Brachyteles arachnoides* E. Geoffroy 1806). Ph.D. thesis, Harvard University, Cambridge.

———. 1987a. Demographic patterns of one group of free-ranging woolly spider monkeys. *Primate Conservation* 8:73–74.

———. 1987b. Reproducao de *Brachyteles arachnoides*, pp. 163–175. In *A Primatologia no Brasil–2*, M. T. de Mello, ed. Brasilia: Sociedade Brasileira de Primatologia.

———. 1987c. Ranging behavior of woolly spider monkeys. *International Journal of Primatology* 8:575–591.

———. 1987d. Activity budgets of woolly spider monkeys, or muriquis. *American Journal of Primatology* 13:385–395.

———. 1989. Effects of patch size on feeding associations in muriquis. *Folia Primatologica* 52:70–77.

Strier, K. B. 1990. New World primates, new frontiers: Insights from the woolly spider monkey, or muriqui (*Brachyteles arachnoides*). *International Journal of Primatology* 11:7–19.

———. 1991a. Diet in one group of woolly spider monkeys, or muriquis (*Brachyteles arachnoides*). *American Journal of Primatology* 23:113–126.

———. 1991b. Demography and conservation in an endangered primate, *Brachyteles arachnoides*. *Conservation Biology* 5:214–218.

———. In press. Development in a patrilocal monkey society: Sex differences in the behavior of immature muriquis (*Brachyteles arachnoides*). In *Juvenile Primates: Life History, Development, and Behavior*, M. E. Pereira and L. A. Fairbanks, eds. New York: Oxford University Press.

———. Submitted. Subtle cues of social relations in muriquis: Relevance for understanding social relationships in humans. *American Journal of Physical Anthropology*.

Tutin, C. E. G. 1979. Mating patterns and reproductive strategies in a community of wild chimpanzees (*Pan troglodytes schweinfurthii*). *Behavioral Ecology and Sociobiology* 6:29–38.

de Waal, F. B. M. 1986. The integration of dominance and social bonding in primates. *Quarterly Review of Biology* 61:459–479.

Wrangham, R. W. 1979a. On the evolution of ape social systems. *Social Science Information* 18:334–386.

———. 1979b. Sex differences in chimpanzee dispersion, pp. 481–499. In *The Great Apes*, D. A. Hamburg and E. R. McCown, eds. London: Benjamin/Cummings.

———. 1980. An ecological model of female-bonded primate groups. *Behaviour* 75:262–299.

———. 1982. Mutualism, kinship, and social evolution, pp. 269–290. In *Current Problems in Sociobiology*. King's College Sociobiology Group, eds. Cambridge: Cambridge University Press.

Zingeser, M. R. 1973. Dentition of *Brachyteles arachnoides* with reference to alouattine and ateline affinities. *Folia Primatologica* 20:351–390.

APPENDIX: RESEARCH METHODOLOGY

Systematic data on muriqui social behavior were obtained from scan samples and focal samples (Altmann 1974). The scan samples, which comprise the majority of the data, were conducted at 15-minute intervals throughout the study. During each sample, the identity, activity, and nearest neighbors were recorded for all individuals in view (see Strier 1987d for more details). Because muriquis have distinct natural markings, it was possible to identify them individually except when poor light or foliage interfered with visibility. Activities were described as resting, feeding, traveling, or socializing.

Nearest neighbors were distinguished by their proximity to the scanned individual within the following three categories: in contact; less than 1 m; and less than 5 m. Only nearest neighbors within the closest proximity category were recorded, so that if individuals A and B were in contact, and C was within 5 m of B, A and B would be scored as one another's nearest neighbors, while B would be scored as C's nearest neighbor. Unless otherwise noted in the analyses, nearest neighbors from different proximity categories are assigned equal value and are considered to be "in proximity" if they were within 5 m of one another.

Focal samples involving adult males were conducted on preselected days from

August 1983 through June 1984 (see Strier, submitted). Focal subjects were chosen in sequence from a predetermined list; however, if the individual slotted could not be located within 5 minutes, the next individual on the list was sought. At 1-min intervals, the activity of the focal subject, the distance between him and his nearest neighbors, and the identity of his nearest neighbors were recorded as described above. I also kept track of which individual in each dyad was responsible for approaching and avoiding proximity. These data were analyzed following Hinde (1977) to evaluate which individuals were responsible for maintaining spatial relationships (Strier, submitted). Focal samples were strongly biased against traveling individuals because poor visibility and difficult terrain made it impossible to maintain continuous visual contact. Focal samples nevertheless provide quantitative data on the dynamics of muriqui spatial relations.

Because many social interactions occurred infrequently, it was necessary to rely on *ad libitum* observations during the intervals between the systematic behavior samples to supplement the records. These observations are discussed only in terms of frequencies, and are included without comment in the analyses.

6

The Development of Dominance Relations Before Puberty in Cercopithecine Societies

MICHAEL E. PEREIRA

INTRODUCTION

Many monkey species in the subfamily Cercopithecinae show broad-scale similarities in their natural histories. These are the macaques, or Asian semiterrestrial monkeys (*Macaca* spp.; also *M. sylvanus* of Africa), the savanna baboons of Africa (*Papio cynocephalus* subspp.), and an African guenon known as the vervet monkey (also grivet or green monkey, *Cercopithecus aethiops*). Social groups of these species commonly comprise 20 to 100 members, including infants, juveniles, adolescents, and adults of each sex (Figure 6-1). Males normally disperse around puberty, whereas females remain in their natal groups for their entire lives (Pusey and Packer 1987). Consequently, at the core of social groups are several distinct matrilines, or families of females accompanied by male kin that have yet to disperse.

With cercopithecine social groups, every pair of noninfants typically has a stable agonistic dominance relationship. That is, across months or even years, aggression and even nonagonistic approaches from an animal A consistently elicit species-typical signals of subordination from an animal B (e.g., grimacing, see de Waal and Luttrell 1985), whereas A never so signals toward B. Also, all dyadic dominance relationships among adults of either sex typically form a transitive linear dominance hierarchy. If A dominates B and B dominates C, then A also dominates C, and so on.

Primatologists have been criticized duly for excessive focus on agonistic conflict and dominance relations (see Bernstein 1981, and associated commentaries). This apparent narrow-mindedness, however, has been partly due to the fact that dominance asymmetries are expressed frequently in the species most often studied (vervets and papionines [macaques and baboons]), and they influence pervasively nonagonistic aspects of behavior. Dominance status has been shown to influence things as diverse as the timing and direction of dispersal (Meikle et al. 1984), priority of access to resources (e.g., Wrangham 1981; Whitten 1983), interindividual spacing relations (Pereira 1988a; see also Janson 1990), maternal style (Altmann 1980), and the distribution of visual attention (Emory 1976), grooming (Seyfarth 1980), and play initiations (Cheney 1978; Symons 1978). Because dominance

Figure 6-1   Juvenile and infant members of one study group in Amboseli National Park, Kenya (Alto's Group; Table 6-1 provides approximate ages at time of photograph). Spike received grooming from his sister Scherzo in the company of infant nephew Cymbal (biting grass corm) an unrelated young juvenile male, Putz. (Photograph by T. J. Pyer.)

contributes strongly to the structure of affinitive (mutually attractive) relations in papionine societies, and because affinitive behavior, in return, modulates agonistic relations (de Waal 1986a, b, 1989), the papionine Cercopithecinae are ideal subjects for the study of interplay between aggression, dominance, and social affinity in primates. Though this chapter does not deal in depth with affinitive behavior per se, we shall consider ways in which the organization of agonistic relations in a species influences supportive intervention during conflicts, solicitation of such support, nonagonistic social association, and mother–offspring relations.

This chapter is focused on the substantial sex differences involved in the acquisition of dominance status in cercopithecine societies. First, let us outline sex-typical patterns in adult dominance relations. After emigrating from their natal groups, males appear to depend primarily on their abilities to win dyadic fights with other males to acquire high rank in the groups into which they transfer (Hausfater 1975; Sugiyama 1976; Dittus 1977; Packer 1979a, b; Cheney 1983; Hamilton and Bulger 1990). These fights can be extremely violent, sometimes resulting in severe canine slash wounds (Hausfater 1974, but see Rowell 1972). Male dominance relations are relatively unstable, often changing over periods of months or weeks. In contrast, females, who remain in their natal groups for life, typically "inherit" dominance rank adjacent to their kin prior to reproduction (Kawai 1958; Sade 1965, 1967, 1972; Koyama 1967; Cheney 1977; de Waal 1977;

Walters 1980; Horrocks and Hunte 1983). Fights among females less commonly result in serious wounding and, most important, interfamilial dominance relations often remain stable for more than a decade (Missakian 1972; Sade 1972; Bramblett et al. 1982; Hausfater et al. 1982; see also Samuels et al. 1987).

Before going further, we must clearly define some terms. I reserve the word *status* to refer to one animal's dominance relationship with another; for example, the status of animal A1 in Figure 6-2 relative to BB is "dominant," while relative to AA it is "subordinate." Also, each matriline is dominant or subordinate with respect to each other matriline in a group (Figure 6-2). *Rank* is used to refer to a *researcher's* perception, based on the requisite data, that an animal occupies a certain position on a transitive hierarchy of dyadic dominance relations. A1, for example, would be considered third-ranking among the eight females in our hypothetical group (Figure 6-2). *Rank acquisition*, however, is used to refer to a juvenile's acquisition of dominant status over an entire set of individuals, such as all of the adult females outranked by its mother. *Highborn* animals are those born to a matriline ranking higher than that of a given subject, whereas *lowborn* refers to the opposite class of group mates.

For a specific reason, my use of *status* conflicts to some degree with the editors' recommendation (see Chapter 1). Monkeys are obviously aware of their dominance status with regard to each of their group mates: they consistently signal their submission to dominant partners, often without having received aggression or a threat. Monkeys' awareness of networks of social relations, such as matrilines or dominance hierarchies (and thereby, social ranks), however, is not as easy to demonstrate (but see Cheney and Seyfarth 1990). To begin then, we shall accept

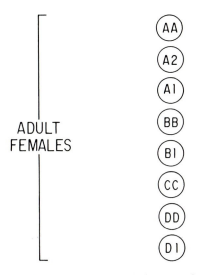

Figure 6-2 The core of a hypothetical social group of cercopithecine monkeys: eight adult females comprising four matrilines, ordered top to bottom by decreasing dominance status. Letter couplets identify matriarchs; letters followed by numbers identify matriarchs' daughters and their birth order. As females approach maturity, they acquire dominance status among adults adjacent to that of (just below) their mothers, typically above their older sisters. This latter pattern is termed "youngest ascendancy."

only that monkeys are aware of their status relative to each group mate (dominant or subordinate). Review and discussion of research on the ontogeny of cercopithecine dominance relations should convince most readers that these primates, in fact, not only discern kin groups, but also recognize the position of each on their group's matrilineal hierarchy of dominance relations.

Two additional terms requiring definition are *targeting* and *support*. During rank acquisition, juvenile baboons and rhesus macaques actually instigate agonistic conflict with the adult females they ultimately overturn in dominance status (Walters 1980; Datta 1983a; Pereira 1989). This is *targeting*. A striking pattern during my research was that challenges by juvenile baboons to older females typically began with repeated close approaches during foraging: Outside of dominance challenges, juveniles avoided approaching dominant, foraging adults because the act often invoked adult aggression (Pereira 1988a). My definition of *support* is aggression by a third party that causes or reinforces the defeat of (submissive signalling by) a supportee's opponent in an ongoing dyadic conflict. *Defense* is a different mode of intervention that plays no role in rank acquisition: it may terminate conflict, thereby shielding participants from additional trauma, but submissive signals are not elicited from the defended party's opponent.

If high rank promotes reproductive success (see Gouzoules et al. 1982; Sugiyama and Ohsawa 1982; Smuts 1985; Silk 1987; Altmann et al. 1988), we should expect immature monkeys to behave during development in ways that enhance their chances of eventually rising to high rank. Studies of females, however, have shown that juveniles do not strive for top rank, but target for status reversal only the lowborn among older females (Walters 1980; Datta 1983a; Netto and van Hooff 1986; Pereira 1988b, 1989). Do adults promote rise in rank by close kin? Females do, but, again, they rarely support juvenile kin in a manner that contravenes existing dominance relations between matrilines (Walters 1980; Datta 1983a; Horrocks and Hunte 1983; Netto and van Hooff 1986; Pereira 1989; Chapais 1991). Do adult females resist status reversals by highborn juveniles? Yes, but high-ranking females support the efforts of lowborn juveniles to attain their matrilineal status (Walters 1980; Datta 1983a; Pereira 1989; Chapais et al. 1991; Prud'homme and Chapais, n.d.).

At a glance, these results seem difficult to reconcile with theory. Why, for example, don't juveniles from low-ranking families more often cooperate with adult kin in efforts to overthrow members of higher-ranking matrilines? Walters (1980) speculated that females who contravene their hierarchy would provoke simultaneous attack by several high-ranking females (cf. Bernstein and Gordon 1974; Chapais and Schulman 1980). Also, data from macaques and vervets suggest that, prior to individuals' first competitive initiative, adult agonistic intervention is patterned so that infant monkeys are forced to assume matrilineal ranks among peers (Berman 1980, 1983a, b; Datta 1983a; Horrocks and Hunte 1983; Chapais and Gauthier, in press). Later, by supporting older juveniles against lowborn adult females, but co-attacking them during their conflicts with highborn adults, high-ranking females abbreviate the period of juvenile–adult dominance indeterminacy and minimize chances for rank overachievement (Pereira 1988b, 1989). Together with recent experimental research (Chapais 1988a; Chapais et al. 1991), these studies indicate that the top-down pattern of agonistic support among unrelated females contributes crucially to the extreme stability of dominance hierarchies among cercopithecine matrilines.

By the time of my research on savanna baboons, questions raised by the sex-specific life histories of vervet and papionine monkeys had yet to be addressed within this theoretical framework. Only preliminary and somewhat contradictory information was available on the development of dominance relations in juvenile male baboons (Cheney 1977; Lee and Oliver 1979; Walters 1980), and the possibility remained that male dominance relations were not constrained by matrilineal membership to the extent seen for developing females. If adult females establish matrilineally ordered dominance relations among immatures to ensure that such relations are maintained as juveniles mature, why should they intervene in the same pattern for and against juvenile males? Females could not similarly benefit by constraining young males' dominance relations because most males disperse around puberty. Perhaps males influence female dominance relations prior to dispersing? Male interventions had infrequently been examined apart from female interventions, though previous studies intimated that adult males tended to intervene in female conflicts less often or less systematically than adult females.

Here, I summarize three recent reports of my field data that, together, bear directly on the hypothesis that the dominance relations developed by immature male and female cercopithecine monkeys result from differential aggression and agonistic intervention received from adult females (Pereira 1988a, b, 1989). To facilitate interrelation of major patterns, several statistical analyses originally published with the data are omitted; however, only statistically significant results are emphasized. By contrasting patterns of agonistic interaction for juvenile males and females, I tested the predictions that:

1. Sex-differentiated patterns of conflict with adult females correlate with different schedules for juvenile male and female rank acquisition.
2. Different patterns of adult female intervention in the conflicts of juvenile males and females correlate with sex-typical endpoints in rank acquisition.
3. Interactions with adult males in both these areas reveal that adult males play no role in juvenile rank acquisition.
4. Juvenile male interventions show that males do not help to organize female agonistic relations prior to dispersal.

Finally, I was able fortuitously to conduct the first detailed study of a juvenile female who targeted highborn adult females for rank reversal. The outcome of her efforts to overachieve in rank acquisition was expected to depend on adult female patterns of agonistic intervention.

The normative effects of sex on the ontogeny of juvenile agonistic relations and the long-term behavioral sequelae of two females' efforts to overachieve in rank acquisition (one overachievement immediately preceded my field work) led me to elaborate a model to explain both stability and change in cercopithecine matrilineal dominance hierarchies (stabilizing dynamics originally outlined independently by Chapais and Schulman (1980) and Walters (1980)). The behavioral algorithm apparently underlying patterns of agonistic support among unrelated females is suggested to create social mechanisms for potential change in dominance relations between matrilines. I also develop a hypothesis that explains species differences in juvenile male dominance relations as a consequence of species-specific male growth trajectories and degrees of sexual dimorphism in adult body size. Differences in these growth parameters are predicted to influence female agonistic investment in offspring dominance relations. Major foci are suggested for future research on cercopithecine growth and behavioral development.

STUDY GROUPS, SUBJECTS, AND METHODOLOGY

Study Groups and Subjects

Two free-ranging groups of yellow baboons, Alto's Group and Hook's Group (*Papio c. cyanocephalus*), were studied in Amboseli National Park, Kenya, from September 1980 through December 1981 (Altmann and Altmann (1970) and Western and van Praet (1973) describe the Amboseli ecosystem). Group demographic compositions have been described elsewhere (Pereira 1988a). In Alto's Group, matrilineal kin relations among all adult females and immatures were known except for possible relationships among the group's oldest females (see Altmann 1980). In Hook's Group, all juveniles' mothers and prepubertal siblings were known as was one adult sister for each of two juveniles. A third juvenile–adult female sibling relationship was inferred (Pereira 1988a, b, 1989). Excepting this dyad, I use the term "unrelated" in reference to group members not known to be juveniles' mothers or matrilineal siblings. All adult males in each group had immigrated as adults and their kin relations were unknown.

Table 6-1 describes the juveniles studied in each group. Despite aseasonal breeding (Altmann 1980), both groups fortuitously contained discrete cohorts of young (1–2.5 years old) and old juveniles (3–5.5 years old). Only one female (Tatu) experienced menarche before the last month of the study; her data are excluded from all analyses.

Sampling Methods

Sixteen-minute focal animal samples (Altmann 1974) were conducted on the hour and the half-hour from 0700 h to 1730 h inclusive, excluding the noon hour. Comparable amounts of each subject's data were gathered during each time of day and each month it was studied. During each focal sample, I scored every noninteractive approach (see Pereira 1988a), spatial displacement, and overt agonistic interaction that involved the subject; also, the identities of all group mates within 3 m were recorded at 2-minute intervals. Immediately following each approach, the activity undertaken by the approacher and the ongoing activities of all approachees were recorded. An animal was displaced when it glanced toward an approaching group mate that was not exhibiting any communicatory behavior and immediately distanced itself from the approacher without exhibiting submissive behavior. Overt agonistic interactions began whenever one animal directed aggressive and/or submissive behavior toward another and ended when both participants discontinued their agonistic behavior. All complete interactions observed outside of focal samples were recorded *ad libitum* (Altmann 1974).

Table 6-1 Study Subjects: Names, Ages, Group Membership, Mothers' Ranks among Adolescent and Adult Females, and Hours of Sampling.

		Name	Age at beginning of study (months)	Age at end of study	Group[a]	Mother's rank among females	Hours of focal sampling
Old juveniles	Males	Hodi	45	56	A	15	56.68
		Spike	42	53	A	11	58.56
		Peanut	42	53	A	16	55.02
		Nami	34	45	H	13	49.40
	Females	Vixen	40	51	A	7	54.63
		Oreo	54	65	A	13	54.88
		Lona	39	50	H	4	49.15
		Kupima	39	50	H	6	50.42
		Lamu	36	47	H	9	50.51
Young juveniles	Males	Putz	17	28	A	16	54.78
		Sluggo	7[b]	18	A	15	28.25
		Rasta	17	28	H	5?[c]	47.55
	Females	Siku	16	27	A	1	54.83
		Pichka	17	28	A	9	54.55
		Scherzo	8[b]	19	A	11	27.52
		Sybil	16	27	H	11	49.45
		Kanga	18	. .[d]	H	6	33.69
		Poco	13	24	H	1	49.93
		Whiskey	5[b]	16	H	3	16.39

[a] There were 18 adolescent and adult females in Alto's Group (A) and 13 adolescent and adult females in Hook's Group (H).

[b] Sampling on Sluggo and Scherzo began 4 months after the start of the study, when they were 11 and 12 months old, respectively. Sampling on Whiskey began 7 months after the start of the study, when she was 12 months old. All young juvenile subjects rarely or never suckled during the day.

[c] Rasta's mother died before her dominance status could be determined precisely; however, she was known to outrank KU (mother of Kupima and Kanga) and suspected, on the basis of few observations, to be subordinate to LI (mother of Lona).

[d] Kanga disappeared, 6 months after the start of the study, at 24 months of age.

For each conflict scored, all aggressive (A), submissive (S), and agonistically neutral behavior (O) exhibited by each participant were noted using the behavioral definitions used previously at this site (Hausfater 1975; Altmann 1980; Walters 1980). Each bout was then summarized, ascribing each participant an A, an S, an AS or an O (no agonistic behavior) to denote which types of behavior it had expressed. Bouts in which one participant emitted only aggressive behavior or no agonistic behavior while its opponent emitted only submissive behavior (A-S and O-S bouts) are referred to as *decided* agonistic interactions (Hausfater 1975). All other bouts (e.g., A-O, A-AS) were *undecided*. Dyads exhibiting only unidirectional decided agonistic interactions were considered to have exhibited stable dominance relationships (Pereira 1988b).

A single, conservative criterion identified polydyadic (hereafter, polyadic or triadic) agonistic interactions: any baboon that directed submissive or aggressive behavior toward another baboon that was engaged in an ongoing agonistic interaction with a third group member was considered to have provided support to the third animal. All of the data presented here, however, involved support as defined in the Introduction: aggressive behavior contributing to the elicitation of submissive behavior from the opponent of the supported party. The identities and roles of each participant were recorded for all polyadic agonistic interactions observed during focal samples. Also, all complete polyadic interactions observed outside of focal samples were recorded on an *ad libitum* basis throughout the study. For Alto's Group, *ad libitum* data were gathered by me and three other observers during approximately 2,500 h of contact with the group; only two to three of us were present during each day spent with this group. I gathered all of the *ad libitum* data from Hook's Group during about 1,300 h of contact.

RESULTS

Dominance Relations among Juveniles

The patterning of dominance relations among juvenile baboons clearly differed from those reported for macaques and vervet monkeys. Males dominated all female peers, irrespective of their maternal rank among adult females (Figure 6-3; see Pereira (1988b) for underlying sociometric tabulations). Also, males dominated one another according to age: older males dominated younger males. Juvenile

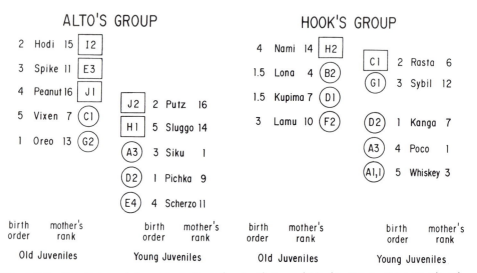

Figure 6-3 Dominance status among juveniles in Alto's and Hook's Group. Squares identify males, circles females; letters and numbers are used as in Figure 6-2. Juveniles are ordered, top to bottom, by decreasing dominance status; the young juvenile hierarchy overlapped that of the old juveniles, i.e., the young males and highest-ranking young females had unsettled rank relations or had already successfully reversed rank relations with some or all of the old juvenile females (see Pereira 1988b). Birth order is within juvenile age class. Mothers' ranks are among adolescent and adult females: 18 in Alto's Group and 13 in Hook's Group.

females dominated one another according to matrilineal status, as do juveniles of both sexes in rhesus, Japanese, and vervet monkeys. Precisely these patterns were also found among juvenile olive baboons (*P. c. anubis*) during a concurrent study conducted in Gilgil, Kenya (Johnson 1987). Finally, young males and females targeted old juvenile females for rank reversal, much as old juveniles targeted adult females (Pereira 1988b, 1989).

Dyadic Relations with Adult Females

Juveniles' agonistic relations with adult females contrasted sharply with their relations with older males (Pereira 1988b). In both juvenile age classes, female rates of submission to highborn adult females were higher than were those of males (Figure 6-4). Also, female rates of submission increased with age, whereas this was not true for males. In contrast, with increasing age, juveniles of both sexes progressively more often submitted to adult males, showing no apparent differences in rates at any age (Pereira 1988b).

Both my data and Johnson's (1987) indicate that adult female baboons are generally more aggressive toward females than males among juveniles. In my study, even young females received more aggression than did their male peers, although neither males nor females in this age class can effectively challenge or resist aggression from adult females by themselves (Pereira 1988b). A retabulation of Johnson's (1987) data indicated that juvenile females at Gilgil also had to "avoid"

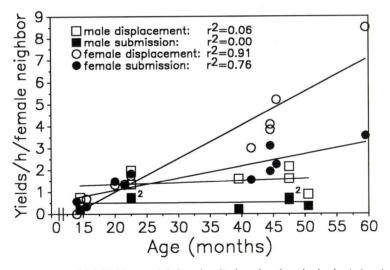

Figure 6-4 Rates at which highborn adult females displaced and evoked submissive signals from juvenile males and females per unit of time spent in proximity. The r^2 values show the proportion of variance explained by juvenile age alone. For displacements, stepwise regression selected interaction of juvenile age and sex (Age–Sex; versus Age, Sex, or Group Membership) as first variable ($F = 27.33$, $r^2 = 0.65$, $p < 0.0001$) and accepted juvenile Sex to explain significant additional variance (F-to-enter Sex = 34.47, $p < 0.004$, F for two variable model = 61.39; multiple $r^2 = 0.90$, $p < 0.00001$). For submissions, stepwise regression selects only the Age–Sex interaction variable ($F = 67.55$, multiple $r^2 = 0.82$, $p < 0.0001$).

Table 6-2   Evidence of Differential Adult Female Aggressivity toward Juvenile Male and Female Olive Baboons (*Papio c. anubis*).[a]

	Juvenile class			
	Main subjects		Secondary subjects	
	Females ($n = 8$)	Males ($n = 8$)	Females ($n = 20$)	Males ($n = 15$)
Median number of avoidances observed per unrelated adult female	0.35*	0.15*	0.08**	0.00**
Number of subjects observed to avoid >1 female from higher-ranking matrilines[b]	8	8	13***	2***
Number of subjects observed to avoid adult females from lower-ranking matrilines	3	3	2	0
Median number of avoidances of females from lower-ranking matrilines observed	4[c]	1	1	0

[a] Data retabulated from Johnson (1984, 1987); male and female main subjects, each sampled for 20 hours, matched for age, maternal rank, and presence of mother; avoidances were scored whenever one animal moved away from another shortly after the other had moved or oriented toward it.

[b] Analysis primarily to evaluate further data from secondary animals, for which relatively little focal sampling was conducted (Johnson 1984).

[c] Only subjects seen avoiding such females considered.

* Two-tailed Mann–Whitney T test; $T = 51.5$, $p < 0.09$.

** Two-tailed Mann–Whitney T test (normal approximation); $T = 183.5$, $p < 0.003$.

*** Chi-square $= 8.72$, $p < 0.01$.

adult females more frequently than did their male peers and that females were somewhat more likely than males to avoid lowborn adult females (Table 6-2).

In Amboseli, juvenile males rose in rank among adult females faster than did their female peers (Table 6-3). By the study's start, the old juvenile males had become dominant to about two-thirds of the adult females from lower-ranking families, whereas the old juvenile females had become dominant, on average, to only 11% of them. By the end, each male had become dominant to every lowborn adult female, whereas only one of the five females had accomplished this. In fact, the females had achieved dominance over smaller proportions of lowborn adults by the end than had males by the start. Remarkably, some old infant and young juvenile males were occasionally observed to elicit submissive signals from adolescent and young adult females. Finally, no female ever won a dyadic conflict with an older highborn female, whereas every old juvenile male won many such encounters.

Support and Aggression Received during Polyadic Interaction

Support Received

Soon after weaning, juveniles received more support from long-term resident adult males than from any other class of group member, whereas most old juveniles never received support from adult males (Pereira 1989). Adult male support of young juveniles was not influenced by either juvenile sex or the relative status of

Table 6-3 Sex Differences in Rates of Rank Acquisition by Juveniles among Adult Female Baboons.

Name	Age (months) at start of study	Percentage of adult females from lower-ranking families dominated		Percentage of adult females from higher-ranking families dominated	
		At start of study	At end of study	At start of study	At end of study
Old juvenile males					
Hodi	45	67	100	14	71
Spike	42	57	100	25	50
Peanut	42	100	100	0	47
Nami	34	NA	NA	9	36
Old juvenile females		*		**	
Oreo	54	0	60	0	0
Vixen	40	9	18	0	0
Lona	39	11	44	0	0
Kupima	39	43	100	0	0
Lamu	36	25	75	0	0

* Sex difference, two-tailed Mann–Whitney test; $n, m = 3, 5$, $T = 21$, $p < 0.04$.
** Sex difference, two-tailed Mann–Whitney test; $n, m = 4, 5$, $T = 31$, $p < 0.02$.

conflict participants (Figure 6-5). Finally, young females also received considerable maternal support, whereas young males did not. All maternal support versus females was against lowborn females.

With age, females' network of support broadened, whereas that of males did not. In addition to continued maternal support, females received vastly increased support from unrelated adult females: about 50% of observed support for old juvenile females came from unrelated adult females. Support from both sources against other females invariably reinforced existing rank relations among matrilines (Figure 6-5). Old juvenile males did not receive appreciable support from either related or unrelated adult females. Also, when adult female support for males did occur, it did not invariably support existing matrilineal dominance relations (Figure 6-5). Most of the males' support came from sex peers and adolescent males.

Aggression Received

With age, juveniles of both sexes became more often the recipients of third-party aggression, with unrelated adult females receiving virtually all of this support (24 of 29 supports against juveniles were against unrelated old juveniles). Comparable amounts of support against juvenile females were provided by old juveniles, adolescents, and adults of both sexes. All support by females against females ($n = 5$) reinforced dominance relations between matrilines. Remarkably, six of the seven supports by males against females contradicted dominance relations between matrilines (two each by old juvenile, adolescent, and adult males).

Support against juvenile males ($n = 14$) was provided primarily by adult males (50%) and high-ranking adult females (29%). Highborn adult females received support in every case; however, opponents were highborn in over 95% of juvenile

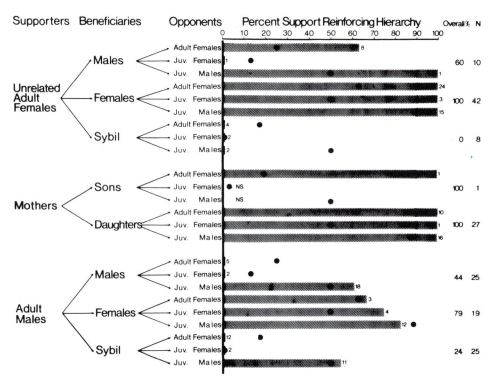

Figure 6-5   Percentages of supports received by juveniles that reinforced the existing hierarchy among families of females. Only interactions against unrelated group members are considered. Female beneficiaries do not include Sybil, whose data are represented separately (see text). Dots on bars represent the percentage of juvenile class-opponent class dyads in which juveniles' families outranked opponents' families; given comparable rates of conflict with members of higher- and lower-ranking families, that percentage of supports for juveniles would have "reinforced the hierarchy" if support had been provided without regard to fight participants' matrilineal ranks. Numbers at end of bars denote number of supports. (Figure reproduced with permission from Pereira (1989).)

male conflicts with adult females (juvenile females' adult female opponents were highborn in only 65% of conflicts; see also Figure 6-5).

Sybil: The Rare Overachiever

The behavior of Sybil, a young juvenile female, departed dramatically from the norm: whereas her mother had been among the lowest-ranking females of Hook's Group throughout Sybil's life (see Table 6-1), Sybil clearly dominated her three female peers, whose mothers ranked 1, 3, and 6, respectively (Figure 6-3). Moreover, at 18 to 24 months of age, Sybil targeted for status reversal at least two old juvenile females and five adult females from mid- to high-ranking families (Pereira 1988a, 1989).

Several patterns in agonistic interaction were associated with Sybil's efforts to overachieve in rank acquisition. Most important, Sybil was the only juvenile female to receive adult female support against highborn females during our study (Figure

6-5). All this support came from members of her group's two highest-ranking matrilines. Sybil also garnered an unusually large proportion of her support from her primary adult male associate, and an unusually large proportion of that support was directed against adult females (Pereira 1989; see also Figure 6-5).

Sex-specific Responses to the Challenge of Rank Acquisition

Spacing Behavior

Old juvenile females associated frequently with their primary supporters. For example, whereas no sex difference in time spent with adult female kin was apparent among young juveniles, old juvenile females spent significantly more time near adult kin that did their male peers (Pereira 1988a; also Pereira and Altmann 1985). Rates of juvenile but not maternal approach were correlated with time spent in proximity across dyads, indicating that the juveniles were primarily responsible for the sex difference in filial association. Females were also attracted toward highborn adult females: all nine eligible for analysis more often approached to rest near resting highborn females than they so approached resting lowborn females (Figure 6-6; two-tailed sign test: $p = 0.004$). In contrast, matrilineal status did not influence patterns of approach by juvenile males toward adult females. Notably, overachiever Sybil most strongly preferred to associate with highborn adult females (Figure 6-6).

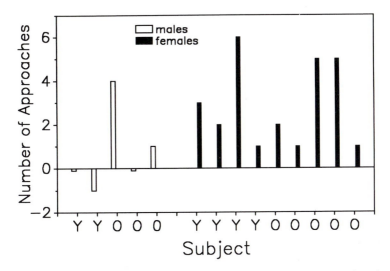

Figure 6-6   Sex difference in attraction toward highborn adult females. Approaches during group resting were analyzed (see text). For each subject, the median number of approaches made per hour toward lowborn females is subtracted from the median number made toward highborn females. Subjects are ordered within sex classes, left to right, by increasing age; Y and O distinguish young from old juveniles. Note that the strongest attraction toward high-rankers was exhibited by Sybil, the overachiever (see also text). Rasta, Nami, Siku, and Poco were ineligible for analysis due to their mothers' rank. Whiskey was omitted because she exhibited an unusually strong attraction to high-rankers that could have been due to kinship.

Very different results were obtained in feeding contexts: old juvenile females were uniformly less likely to approach highborn than lowborn adults during adult feeding (Pereira 1988a), whereas this was not true for either old juvenile males or young juveniles of either sex. After approaching feeding adult females, all old juveniles were less likely to begin feeding immediately if the adult was highborn rather than lowborn (sign test: $p = 0.004$); but, this effect was significantly stronger for females than for males, and young juveniles did not show the pattern at all (Pereira 1988a).

Solicitation of Support

Both young and old juvenile females solicited agonistic support more frequently than did their male peers (by "head-flagging" (Hausfater 1975): alternately gazing toward a potential supporter and threatening and/or screaming at the agonistic opponent). Whereas females were most likely to solicit support from adult females, either kin or highborns (61%, $n = 51$), only once was a male observed to do so ($n = 9$). The other eight male solicitations were directed toward adolescent or adult males (Pereira 1989).

Support Given

Juvenile females supported unrelated adult females more often than any other beneficiary class (15 of 20 supports observed). They intervened both for and against adult females more often than did their male peers despite the fact that every old juvenile male was reversing dominance relations with more adult females than was any juvenile female (Pereira 1988b; 1989). Females joined adult or old juvenile females during 63% of their support against adult females ($n = 32$), whereas males joined such partners for only 16% of theirs ($n = 37$), intervening most often in support of male peers and young juveniles of either sex. Also, when they intervened between adult females, juvenile females always reinforced existing matrilineal relations ($n = 15$), whereas males did so only once in three interventions. Together, these two sex differences show that females typically joined attacks upon adults already being intimidated, whereas males often joined fights to combat winning adult females.

DISCUSSION

Female Determination of Juvenile Rank and Stability of the Adult Hierarchy

Following weaning, juvenile male and female baboons experience different rules governing their development of dominance relations with peers and adult females—rules enforced by adult females. Adult males intervened in juveniles' conflicts primarily to support probable offspring (Pereira 1989), showing no bias regarding the sex or matrilineal status of conflict participants (see also Prud'homme and Chapais, n.d.). In contrast, adult females intervened primarily in the conflicts of juvenile females, invariably to reinforce existing dominance relations among matrilines (excepting Sybil). When adult female support of males did occur, its direction did not always parallel matrilineal dominance relations. Young males, not punished systematically for attacking or resisting aggression from highborn group members, appeared free from the time of weaning to assume dominance over any group mate they could intimidate independently. The one female to receive adult support against highborn females targeted these females for status reversal and was ultimately the only female to achieve adult rank above highborn females (Pereira 1989). Finally, adult females responded differentially to juvenile males and females in a second important way: they targeted females among juveniles for aggression and resistance to rank acquisition (see also Table 6-2; Dittus 1979; Silk et al. 1981; Horrocks and Hunte 1983).

I propose that the matrilineal structure of female dominance relations, Sybil's unusual efforts to overachieve in rank acquisition, and low-ranking adult females' general resistance to female rank acquisition all relate fundamentally to the primary mechanism underlying the stability of dominance relations among cercopithecine matrilines: hierarchy-reinforcing agonistic intervention by nonkin. Kin support has long been known to help stabilize female dominance relations (e.g., Marsden 1968), but the present work complements the recent experiments of Chapais and his colleagues (e.g., Chapais et al. 1991) to show that cercopithecine females discern separate matrilines and intervene agonistically between unrelated lowborn females to reinforce existing matrilineal dominance relations. By mutual-istically maintaining hierarchical stability, all females prevent their own decline in rank (Chapais et al. 1991).

In Amboseli, scores of agonistic interventions are documented annually among unrelated female baboons, and third parties almost invariably join to threaten or attack lowborn participants (e.g., Walters 1980; Pereira 1989). Macaques and vervets appear to show the same pattern (Datta 1983a, b, c; Netto and van Hooff 1986; Hunte and Horrocks 1987; Chapais et al. 1991), although their relatively high rates of *defense* and the lumping of *defense* and *support* (see Introduction) in previous studies have clouded this issue (cf. Massey 1977; de Waal 1977; Kaplan 1978; Bernstein and Ehardt 1985). Cercopithecine females, then, appear to follow a simple behavioral algorithm to intervene in fights between nonkin females at least one of which is lowborn:

Support the highborn participant.

This algorithm accounts for both major classes of female support for unrelated group mates: that for adults and that for juveniles striving to acquire matrilineal rank. The simpler "support the higher-ranking participant" fails to explain the latter.

Consider now what happens when the members of a matriline somehow become separated in the adult hierarchy: patterns of nonkin support must often become inconsistent (e.g., Walter's (1980) anecdote about juvenile Fanny and her mother). Reconsider our hypothetical group of eight females (Figure 6-7), and imagine that adult B1 has somehow declined in rank below CC. (Alternatively, imagine that pubescent B1 has yet been unable to dominate CC.) Now, if CC attacks B1, BB can intervene to support her daughter B1. While BB is attacking CC, AA might join to support BB and B1. If BB and B1 long remain split in the hierarchy, however, nonkin support may become situation-dependent or unpredictable, especially if AA or her kin begin to perceive BB as belonging at *B1*'s rank position. If AA family members begin to attack BB in support of CC, BB will decline in rank. As long as BB and B1 are recognized as members of one family, consolidation of their ranks, one way or the other, will be inevitable under the proposed algorithm for nonkin intervention. BB's support of her daughter will ensure B1's (re)acquisition of matrilineal status only if the AA females also consistently support the BB females against CC females (Chapais 1988a, b; Chapais and Larose 1988; Chapais et al. 1991). Note in addition that it will be in the best interest of the AA family to expedite consolidation of the BB females if the intervention inconsistencies generated by the split threaten the stability of the entire hierarchy.

While nonkin intervention normally stabilizes dominance hierarchies among cercopithecine females, its underlying behavioral algorithm creates social mechanisms for potential change in matrilineal dominance relations. If kin can be split in the hierarchy while they continue to be recognized as a matriline, the net balance of change in high rankers' patterns of intervention will determine whether the split matriline's rank will subsequently change. If high rankers stop interacting

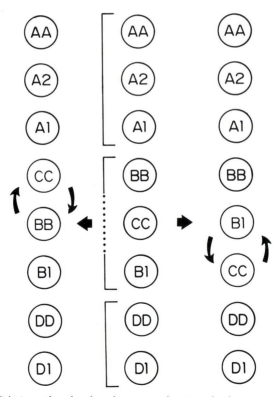

Figure 6-7   Consolidation of a family whose members' ranks become split on the female hierarchy (central column). If most high-ranking females perceived BB as a member of B1's family rank, they would attack her in support of CC, and BB would ultimately decline in rank (left arrow); alternatively, if they primarily perceived B1 as a member of BB's family rank (as during normal juvenile rank acquisition), B1 would ultimately rise in rank (right arrow).

with split kin as members of one matriline, a fallen female would be likely to recover matrilineal status only if her kin outnumber the females that overturned her (Chapais 1988a). Due to continued nonkin support, however, her kin would be unlikely to fall in rank in this circumstance.

Major features of the agonistic relations I observed between juvenile and adult female baboons are well explained by this model. By preventing a juvenile female from acquiring familial status, for example, a lowborn adult could cause the juvenile's entire matriline to fall in rank. Recently, several cases in Amboseli approximated this scenario, where a decline in rank for one adult female preceded rank decline for her female kin (Hausfater et al. 1982; Johnson 1987; Samuels et al. 1987). As with adult rank decline, juvenile failure to achieve rank should increase chances for matrilineal rank decline via changed patterns of nonkin intervention: the low rank of the recently matured female could cause highborn females to perceive her older kin as occupying inappropriately high dominance positions. Accordingly, kin support of rank acquisition likely functions, in *relation* to the standard pattern of nonkin intervention, to maintain matrilineal rank (Pereira 1988b).

During rank acquisition, high-ranking females minimize their own matrilines' chances of rank decline in several ways (Pereira 1989). First, chances of rank overachievement are reduced directly by attacking juvenile females often, both on dyadic bases and in support of higher-born females. Also, high rankers' ready support of juvenile females against lower-born adults facilitates rank acquisition, thereby minimizing the period of juvenile–adult rank indeterminacy.

Sybil's case history is the first detailed account of a naturally occurring breakdown in the cercopithecine system limiting females to inheritance of matrilineal status. Frequent adult support contradicting existing matrilineal relations ultimately allowed Sybil to exceed predicted, lifelong limitations in dominance. Most important, she was the only juvenile female ever to receive adult female support against highborn females (Figure 6-5). During the two years following my study, Sybil continued to target mid-ranking females and achieved stable adult status above two highborn matrilines (Noe, Samuels, personal communications; 1986 status summary, J. Altmann, S. Altmann, and A. Samuels, unpublished data).

The hypothesis that unrelated cercopithecine females mutualistically support one another against lowborn females predicts intense, collaborative aggression in response to "inappropriate" targeting (Walters 1980; Chapais et al. 1991). Sybil received such aggression. Despite her formidable support, she often limped severely following conflicts with her older, much stronger targets and their mid-ranking allies. She once had an eye bruised and swollen shut for over two weeks. If more high-ranking females had also punished rather than supported her, Sybil would likely have desisted in her efforts or died due to them. The potential fatality of her tactics presumably contributes to the rarity of efforts by cercopithecine females to overachieve in rank acquisition. But, what social conditions might trigger these tactics? Sybil's targeting may have been a response to the atypical adult male support she received against adult females and/or a response to unusually lax hierarchy reinforcement by the top-ranking adult females. (Such lax reinforcement is speculative, as it would have occurred before my study.) Once initiated, Sybil's persistent and unusually early targeting (Pereira 1988b, 1989) may have helped change normal patterns of support, leading top-ranking females to begin supporting her against the mid-ranking adults. In any case, Sybil's efforts were favored not only by adult support, but also by the small size of her group's mid-ranking matrilines: each of four contained only two adult or maturing females.

Unfortunately, Sybil disappeared as a young adult; thus, the prediction could not be pursued that subsequent patterns of nonkin intervention would mandate eventual rank decline for Sybil or rank rise for her mother. In Alto's Group, however, the young female Scherzo and her adult sister Summer (SC-d2 in Samuels et al. 1987) demonstrated that individual overachievement can be followed by rise in rank for an entire matriline. After Summer attained status above four highborn females (two matrilines; Hausfater et al. 1982), her sister, Scherzo (this study), targeted for rank reversal all females lower ranking than the mother (Pereira 1988b) and received nonkin support against them. Agonistic dynamics initiated by Scherzo's targeting of females ranking between her sister and mother may have catalyzed the subsequent rise in rank of Scherzo's mother (SC) and oldest sister (SC-d1). Over the five years following Summer's initial overachievement, her entire matriline rose from the bottom half to the top half of the hierarchy in a moderately large baboon group (50–60 members; Samuels et al. 1987).

Taxonomic Differences in Juvenile Male Dominance Relations

Thus far, I have suggested that adult females determine juvenile dominance relations to ensure that matrilineal relations remain unchanged as the juveniles mature. Why, then, do juvenile male as well as female rhesus, Japanese, and vervet monkeys acquire matrilineal ranks among peers and, at least initially, among adult females (Figure 6-8)? I expect that these males acquire matrilineal ranks solely in response to patterns of kin support. Unless males help to determine matrilineal dominance relations before dispersing (and there is no evidence of this), it would not "pay" high-ranking females to intervene in the agonistic interactions of unrelated juveniles one or both of which are male. The prediction remains untested because no study of rank acquisition in macaques or vervets has yet separated data by type of intervention, juvenile sex, and relatedness.

Provisionally then, the question raised by my study is "Why do female macaques and vervets promote status acquisition by all juvenile kin over lowborn group members, while female baboons promote status acquisition only for female kin among female peers?" The natural histories of macaques and vervets on the one hand and savanna baboons on the other suggest two major variables for consideration: degree of sexual dimorphism in adult body size and seasonality of breeding.

In most macaques and in vervet monkeys, adult males typically outweigh adult females by only 10 to 30%, whereas adult male savanna baboons typically weigh twice as much as adult females (Clutton-Brock and Harvey 1977; Turnquist and Kessler 1989). As a likely consequence, some adult female macaques and vervets independently dominate some adult males, these females frequently collaborate to attack adult males, and high-ranking females can even influence adult male dominance status and group membership, including that of their sons (e.g., Kawai 1958; Kawamura 1958; Koford 1963; Sade 1965, 1967, 1972;

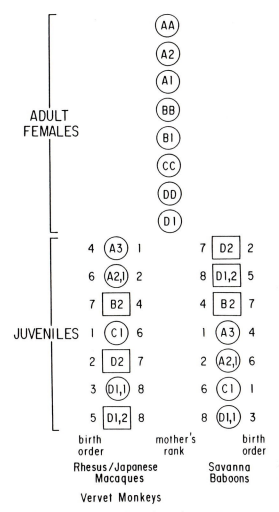

Figure 6-8 Taxonomic difference in juvenile male rank acquisition in cercopithecine societies (legends of Figures 6-2 and 6-3 explain format). In all cases, all juveniles initially rank below all adults. In rhesus, Japanese, and vervet monkeys, juveniles reportedly assume ranks among peers according to their mothers' ranks among adult females, irrespective of sex and small age differences (birth order). In savanna baboons, by contrast, juvenile males outrank all female peers and all younger males, while juvenile females dominate one another according to maternal ranks. By mid- to late juvenility, males in the former species acquire matrilineal rank among adult females, whereas male baboons outrank all but the highest-ranking adult females.

Lancaster 1971; Packer and Pusey 1979; Chapais 1983; Cheney 1983; Meikle et al. 1984; Raleigh and McGuire 1989). In contrast, adult male baboons invariably dominate adult females, female baboon coalitions against males are relatively infrequent and ineffective (Packer and Pusey 1979), and there is no known effect of maternal status on the dominance relations, migration patterns, or reproductive success of male baboons (Altmann et al. 1988). I propose that female baboons avoid structuring prepubertal male dominance relations because dramatic male growth around puberty ultimately precludes effective female use of agonistic tactics to influence male behavior (see following text).

Seasonality of breeding could also play a role: vervets and most macaques breed seasonally, whereas most savanna baboons do not (Lindberg 1987). Seasonal reproduction may exacerbate feeding competition among lactating females and among weanlings (Jolly 1984; Wasser and Starling 1988), and this might favor females that maintain as much agonistic influence over males as possible (Jolly 1984). If aseasonal breeding is associated with reduced feeding competition among mothers and among weanlings, the cost/benefit ratio for female baboons to attempt to maintain agonistic influence over maturing males, a ratio already high due to large male size, may be prohibitive.

To test the hypothesis that great adult size dimorphism alone reduces the extent to which females constrain the dominance relations of immature males, I looked for evidence of "male dominance" among juveniles in substantially dimorphic but seasonally breeding Cercopithecinae. Baker-Dittus (1985) reported that juvenile male toque macaques dominate their female peers irrespective of matrilineal rank (*M. sinica*; adult male/female weight = 1.64; Baker-Dittus 1985); Kuester and Paul (1988) recently reported the same result for Barbary macaques (*M. sylvanus*; adult male/female weight = 1.55; Fa 1986), and juvenile male longtailed macaques also typically dominate their female peers (*M. fascicularis*; adult male/female weight = 1.62; van Noordwijk and van Schaik, unpublished data). Detailed data on juvenile male–female dominance relations are yet unavailable for bonnet macaques (*M. radiata*: adult male/female weight = 1.58; Silk, unpublished data); but, preliminary data for the most dimorphic guenon, DeBrazza's monkey, also suggest that immature males may typically dominate female peers (Kirkevold and Crockett 1987; *Cercopithecus neglectus*: adult male/female weight = 1.72; Clutton-Brock and Harvey 1977).

Despite seasonal breeding, then, females in the more dimorphic macaques appear not to maintain dominance for daughters over their lowborn male peers. In each species, however, females apparently do help *sons* maintain dominance over lowborn males: while juvenile males outrank all female peers, they tend to dominate one another according to matrilineal rank (Baker-Dittus 1985; Kuester and Paul 1988; van Noordwijk, personal communication).

I suggest that, whenever feasible, cercopithecine females also promote matrilineal dominance relations for male kin as an investment in the future. In this case, however, maximizing access to nutriment during critical growth periods is the likely benefit. Maximal nutrition should enhance physical fitness, thereby promoting offspring survivability and agonistic capacity, and thus maximizing male reproductive potential (see Meikle et al. 1984; Pereira 1988b; Hamilton and Bulger 1990; and the following section Future Research). In the relatively nondimorphic species, mothers can safely maintain daughters' dominance over lowborn males and likely do so to maximize daughters' chances of surviving and of conceiving during the first possible breeding season (see Drickamer 1974; Paul and Thommen 1984).

In species with substantial adult size dimorphism, females do not attempt to maintain dominance for daughters over lowborn male peers probably because the required agonistic interventions are too risky when they would likely have their greatest effect—near the end of juvenility, when the peripubertal growth spurt begins (Watts 1985). Juvenile male primates are smaller than adult females and juvenile sexual dimorphism is negligible (van Wagenen and Catchpole 1956; Mori 1979; Sugiyama and Ohsawa 1982; Coelho 1985; Fa 1986; Altmann and Alberts 1987; Pusey 1990; Crockett and Pope, in press); but male baboons exhibit an enormous pubertal growth spurt, almost doubling body weight in just over two years (Coelho 1985). Similar trajectories characterize male growth in the dimorphic macaques (Janson and van Schaik, in press); but in the less dimorphic species, pubertal males do not increase growth so dramatically (van Wagenen and Catchpole 1956). The nutritive requirements of peripubertal male baboons, therefore, must exceed considerably those of their rhesus or Japanese macaque counterparts, relative to the needs of conspecific females. Accordingly, maturing male baboons should compete more aggressively against females and peers for access to food. Failure could jeopardize their health or reduce adult body size, compromising their ultimate reproductive potential. Even if growth can be postponed in response to stiff competition, age at first reproduction would likely be at stake for males (see Hamilton and Bulger 1990).

I propose that the great physical capacities and nutritive requirements of maturing males in the dimorphic papionines endanger females that try to maintain offspring dominance over them. In the most dimorphic species, savanna baboons, females have therefore evolved a general disinclination to control the dominance behavior of juvenile males. In the dimorphic macaques, whose degree of dimorphism is intermediate among papionines, mothers can effectively collaborate with pubertal sons, but not daughters, to maintain offspring dominance over lowborn males.

Male Acquisition of Dominance and Offspring Sex Ratios

The extent to which cercopithecine females can promote the dominance of sons may influence maternal investment in sons and daughters as a function of matrilineal rank. Consider, for example, patterns of offspring sex ratios reported for Cercopithecinae. Meikle et al. (1984) showed that high-ranking females in the rhesus groups of La Paguera had significantly more sons than daughters, while low-ranking females had more daughters. Altmann (1980) and Silk (1983) had previously found that high-ranking female baboons and bonnet macaques produced primarily daughters, while low rankers produced mostly sons (also Altmann et al. 1988). Van Schaik and Hrdy (1991) recently reanalyzed maternal rank effects on offspring sex ratios in relation to the growth rates of 11 cercopithecine populations. Barring a single outlier, they showed that nearly 90% of the variance in proportions in males born to high versus low rankers is explained by rates of population growth, which presumably represent crudely the availability of food resources. Two species studied under conditions of high and low growth rates (*M. mulatta* and *M. fascicularis*) showed the predicted sex ratio adjustments. The implications are that abundant food allows top-ranking females to produce extraordinarily viable sons (the Trivers–Willard hypothesis), while low-ranking mothers produce successful daughters; harsher conditions cause high rankers to produce daughters, who inherit the advantages of dominance, while low rankers optimize their bad situation by producing sons, who leave at least some maternal rank effects behind at emigration.

It remains of interest, however, to determine the effects of abundant food for baboons. The complete absence of maternal rank effects on the dominance relations of natal males may preclude differential production of successful sons when food is plentiful for this most dimorphic cercopithecine. The most dimorphic macaques do not provide a test of this prediction because maternal rank influences sons' ranks among male peers (citations above).

Future Research

Much remains to be discovered about the development of dominance relations in cercopithecine monkeys. The interactions of males and females and different forms of agonistic intervention (e.g., support vs. defense) will have to be examined separately for progress to be made. Also, data should be analyzed in relation to patterns of dispersal, ontogenetic and seasonal schedules of resource competition, age changes and sex differences in growth, and contexts of interactions. In addition to observational research, there is a distinct need for experimental work on semicaptive or caged social groups. While the present data, for example, provide new support for the hypothesis that adult female patterns of agonistic intervention differentially determine the dominance relations of juvenile males and females, they remain limited by their correlative nature (but see Chapais 1992).

Experiments involving cross-species cross-fostering could reveal unequivocally whether adult females determine the dominance relations of immature cerco-pithecines. Separate groups of female Barbary and Japanese macaques could be established in which low-ranking females received contraspecific male infants, while high-rankers received conspecific female infants, also cross-fostered as a control measure (Figure 6-9; see Owren and Dieter (1989) on cross-fostering of macaques). If adult females determine juvenile dominance relations, four species-atypical results should be obtained: in Japanese macaque groups, juvenile male Barbary macaques would be forced to assume status below female peers and adjacent to their mothers among adult females; in Barbary macaque groups, juvenile male Japanese macaques would be free to assume status above all female peers and would rise in status before puberty above adult females outranking their mothers (Figure 6-9). Patterns of support should show that Japanese, but not Barbary, macaque mothers support daughters consistently against their lowborn male peers.

The experiment would also allow investigation of the role of individual initiative in determining prereproductive dominance relations. How do immatures themselves contribute, for example, to the development of "male dominance" in the dimorphic species? Given that adult female baboons hardly resist status reversals with young males (Pereira 1988b), I expect that, compared to immature female rhesus or Japanese macaques, immature female baboons or Barbary macaques are relatively disinclined to persist in efforts to dominate their male peers. Appropriate observational data would allow those that conduct the proposed experiment to discover whether immature macaques differ taxonomically

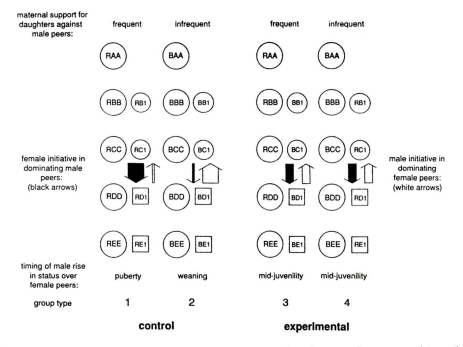

Figure 6-9 Experiment to demonstrate complementary roles of maternal support and juvenile initiative in determining dominance relations between juvenile males and females. Four sets of social groups would comprise two control types (1, 2) and two experimental types (3, 4). In every group, bottom-ranking females would receive male infants, while higher-ranking females would receive female infants (all infants cross-fostered; shown beside foster mothers). Rhesus females (acronyms begin with "R") should act to maintain daughters' dominance over male peers (socialized environment), whereas Barbary females (acronyms begin with "B") should not (nonsocialized environment; see Taxonomic Differences section in preceding text). In both socialized (1, 3) and nonsocialized environments (2, 4), Barbary males should show greater initiative than rhesus males in efforts to dominate female peers, and Barbary females should show less initiative than rhesus females to resist status reversals by males. Such results, together with differences in timing of male–female rank reversals based on maternal support (2 vs. 3, 1 vs. 4), would indicate that juvenile initiative in establishing dominance relations with peers and normative patterns of maternal support are co-adapted behavioral traits.

in their initial approach to developing dominance relations with peers of the other sex (Figure 6-9).

Field data on the contexts of dyadic conflict and third-party intervention will help evaluate further the adaptedness of species-typical ontogenetic patterns. Preliminary work, for example, showed that juvenile male baboons were aggressive to peers and adult females most often during foraging. Lower proportions of juvenile female aggression occurred during foraging, and in further contrast to males, proximate causes were not evident for large proportions of female aggression (see also Shopland 1987; Johnson 1989). These results support the idea that for males dominance functions to maximize access to nutriment, while for females acquisition of matrilineal rank is paramount.

In this context, it would be valuable to discover what kinds and timings of "poor" versus "rich" juvenile diets—variants within the range possibly determined by dominance relations within social groups—lead to consistent differences in adult body size and/or age at first reproduction (see e.g., Drickamer 1974; Sugiyama and Ohsawa 1982; Paul and Thommen 1984). To date, much research on diet and growth, especially that on potential "catch-up" growth following nutrient deficiencies (e.g., Fleagle et al. 1975; Kerr et al. 1975; Elias and Samonds 1977), has involved (1) only infant monkeys (but see Frisch 1974; Bongaarts 1980) and (2) both dietary and experiential restrictions falling well outside the range of likely dominance effects.

If, as conjectured earlier, seasonal breeding can generate greater feeding competition among juvenile macaques than occurs among juvenile baboons (see Dittus 1979; Sugiyama and Ohsawa 1982; Shopland 1987; Pereira 1988a; Johnson 1989), mother rhesus or Japanese macaques may safeguard the survival and growth potential of all offspring by helping them maintain dominance over lowborn peers. If so, sex independence in the ontogeny of juvenile initiative in feeding competition and in that of maternal support should be found. Alternatively, if access to high-quality developmental nutrition is most important for males (Meikle et al. 1984; Pereira 1988b), then this should be reflected by sex differences in the contexts of competitive aggression and receipt of maternal support. Moreover, if maternal rank in rhesus does generate greater reproductive variance among natal males than among natal females (Meikle et al. 1984), the first study to separate maternal supports by offspring sex should reveal that rhesus mothers devote more energy to maintaining matrilineal ranks for sons than for daughters, especially since support from unrelated females should facilitate female but not male inheritance of matrilineal rank.

Behavioral Development, Adult Behavior, and Social Structure

In seeking to understand primate sociality, primatologists have focused traditionally on agonistic interactions, dominance relations, and their possible evolutionary roots (see Bernstein and Gordon 1974; Bernstein 1981). More recently, researchers have begun to emphasize that conflict comprises just one component of larger, well-integrated systems of social relations, which also include conflict resolution (e.g., Judge 1982; Gouzoules et al. 1984; Cords 1988), reconciliation (de Waal and Ren 1988), tolerance (de Waal 1986b; Pereira 1988a), and mutual affinity or friendship (Altmann 1980; Smuts 1985; de Waal 1986a).

Another desirable shift in perspective would be to recognize that behavioral development not only continues across individual lifespans, but also has effects that can extend across generations within groups and populations. Too often, gross natural history features such as sex-biased dispersal, intersexual dominance relations, or rank inheritance are considered only in their modal pattern and treated as endpoints in development (Saunders and Hausfater 1978; Altmann and Altmann 1979; Gouzoules et al. 1982; Moore 1984; Pereira and Altmann 1985; Smuts 1985; Pereira 1988b). Investigation of both the variability of such grand phenomena and of potential cross-generational social and reproductive consequences will vastly improve our understanding of primate social behavior.

An important challenge will be to learn how juvenile and adult behavior mutually shape one another through both developmental and evolutionary channels (Pereira and Fairbanks, in press). Many have suggested that prereproductive experience might influence the behavioral tactics that animals use later in life (see Mason 1979; Bekoff and Byers 1985). But, having adopted particular tactics, how does the developing individual continue to affect existing networks of social relations? What aspects of juvenile and adult behavior are designed to exploit or accommodate the potential for complementation or conflict in juvenile–adult social relations in a given species? As a generation of youngsters matures and replaces the adults before it, how might its collective prior experiences and developmental adjustments change the social structure of its group and population?

As yet, virtually all detailed information on juvenile primates comes from a few cercopithecine monkeys (but see Pereira and Fairbanks, in press). Consequently, our understanding of primate development is highly restricted, and we are hardly able to begin addressing questions like those posed above. Study of juvenility in a broad range of phyletic and social contexts is needed (e.g., monogamy, fission–fusion sociality, "female dominance," predominant female dispersal). Comparative research on the ways juvenile males and females cope with adults' efforts to shape their behavior (e.g., Rosenblum and Plimpton 1979) and on the ways juveniles themselves influence the lives of peers and adults would reveal how developmental strategies shift in response to divergent socio-ecological demands. To the extent that long-term research can continue on particular populations of primates, the interplay between processes of development and their reproductive ramifications will be revealed and roles of development in the evolution of social behavior should be illuminated.

SUMMARY

Macaques, baboons, and vervets are cercopithecine monkeys that form large social groups within which each pair of individuals normally shows a decided agonistic dominance relationship. This chapter seeks to explain the substantial sex differences involved in the prereproductive acquisition of dominance status in cercopithecine societies. Previous research suggested that patterned agonistic support between unrelated females contributes importantly to the extreme stability of dominance hierarchies among cercopithecine matrilines. An important part of the phenomenon modeled was that adult females support the efforts of unrelated juvenile females to acquire matrilineal dominance rank. Predictable effects of juvenile age and sex on adult determination of juvenile dominance relations, however, had yet to be investigated.

In a study of two wild groups of savanna baboons, I contrasted patterns of adult aggression and agonistic support received by males versus females between weaning and puberty. Adult females were expected to establish matrilineally ordered dominance relations for juvenile females to ensure that existing dominance relations among matrilines would remain unchanged as the juveniles matured. Because most males disperse from natal groups around puberty, unrelated adult females were expected not to resist male rank acquisition and not to establish matrilineal relations for immature males. The data confirmed that: (1) sex-differentiated patterns of conflict with adult females correlate with different schedules of juvenile rank acquisition; (2) different patterns of adult female agonistic intervention correlate with sex-typical endpoints in rank acquisition; (3) adult males play no role in juvenile dominance acquisition; and (4) juvenile males do not help organize female agonistic relations prior to dispersal. Finally, the first study of a juvenile female who targeted highborn females for rank reversal showed that her efforts depended on patterns of intervention by the top-ranking females in her group.

Interpretation of all available data led me to propose that cercopithecine females prevent their own decline in rank by following a simple behavioral algorithm to intervene in fights between female nonkin at least one of which is lowborn: "Support the highborn participant." I suggest that this algorithm creates a particular mechanism for potential change in matrilineal rank. If the females of a matriline become separated in the dominance hierarchy, the subsequent net change of agonistic support received from high-ranking females by matriline members and their opponents will determine whether the matriline will decline in dominance as their ranks are consolidated.

From this perspective, the primary function of female rank acquisition appears to be maintenance of matrilineal rank. Mothers and adult sisters reduce the chance of decline in familial rank by supporting rank acquisition by juvenile female kin. High-ranking adult females reduce the probability of juvenile rank over-achievement by intimidating lowborn females frequently and by intervening in juvenile–adult conflicts in support of existing matrilineal status relations. Because maturing male baboons inevitably become dominant to all females, typically emigrate, and play no role in determining matrilineal dominance relations, unrelated adult females cannot benefit by either resisting their rise in rank or channeling them early into positions of matrilineal status.

This study raises the question "Why do female rhesus, Japanese, and vervet monkeys promote dominance acquisition by all juvenile kin over lowborn group members, while female baboons promote status acquisition only for female kin among female peers?" Degree of sexual dimorphism in adult body size appears critical. A survey of relatively dimorphic macaque species showed that, in each case, the dominance relations of juvenile males are relatively unconstrained by maternal rank. Interestingly, degree of dimorphism in the dimorphic macaques is intermediate among papionines, and mothers in these species apparently help sons but not daughters maintain dominance over lowborn male peers: males outrank female peers but dominate one another according to matrilineal rank. I suggest that increased adult dimorphism leads adult females to reduce their effort in maintaining offspring dominance over lowborn juvenile males, because the required agonistic support becomes too risky when it would likely be most effective—near the beginning of the peripubertal growth. The greater physical capacities and nutritive requirements of pubertal males in the more dimorphic species would endanger females trying to maintain dominance for offspring, especially daughters, over their lowborn male peers.

Much remains to be discovered about the development of dominance relations in cercopithecine monkeys. In future research, the interactions of males and females as well as different forms of agonistic intervention (e.g., "defense" vs. "support") should be examined separately. It will be most valuable to view such data in relation to patterns of dispersal, ontogenetic and seasonal schedules of resource competition, age changes and sex differences in growth, and contexts of interactions.

In addition to purely observational research, experimental work with semi-captive or caged social groups is needed. Experiments entailing cross-species cross-fostering of infants are proposed that could demonstrate unequivocally whether adult females differentially determine the dominance relations of juvenile males and females, and whether juveniles of different species show different intrinsic propensities in their approaches to dominance relations with peers of the other sex. Experimental work to discover whether certain "poor" versus "rich" juvenile diets lead to differences in adult body size and/or age at first reproduction will also be important. Such research, however, will only be valuable if both the dietary and experiential restrictions imposed on subjects fall within the range of likely dominance effects.

The social ontogeny experienced by immature primates entails potential reproductive consequences not only for the youngsters but also for the adults around them. An important challenge to deep understanding of primate social behavior is to learn how juvenile and adult behavior mutually shape one another through developmental and evolutionary channels. We have only begun to attain our first glimmerings of such understanding for vervet and papionine monkeys.

Primates occupy a broad array of socio-ecological niches, however; therefore, it will be crucial to acquire similarly detailed data on juvenile social relations in noncercopithecine species. To the extent that long-term research can continue on particular populations of primates, the interplay between processes of development and their reproductive ramifications will be revealed and roles for development in the evolution of social behavior should be illuminated.

ACKNOWLEDGMENTS

I thank J. Altmann, S. Altmann, and G. Hausfater for critical advice, field training, and use of their field station and long-term records on the Amboseli baboon population. I thank the Office of the President, the Ministry of Environment and Natural Resources of Kenya, and Amboseli National Park warden Bob Oguya for permission to work in Amboseli and J. Else, former Director, Institute of Primate Research in Kenya, for sponsorship. I am grateful to J. Friedman Mann, M. Kirega, M. Mutira, R. Mututua, S. Pilipili, C. Saunders, and D. Takacs for logistical and moral support in the field. I thank J. Silk, M. van Noordwijk, and C. van Schaik for unpublished data and J. Silverberg and P. Gray for helpful comments on the chapter's penultimate version. T.-J. Pyer receives my heartfelt gratitude for tireless, generous support of all my academic effort.

My research was supported financially by grants to J. Altmann by the National Institute of Child Health and Human Development (HD15007), the Harry Frank Guggenheim Foundation, and The University of Chicago's Spencer Foundation, to S. Altmann by the National Institute of Mental Health (19617), and to me by the Hinds Fund (University of Chicago) and the National Institute of Child Health and Human Development (R29-HD23243). Finally, I thank Section H (Anthropology) of the American Association for the Advancement of Science for the travel grant I needed to participate in the original AAAS symposium.

REFERENCES

Altmann, J. 1974. Observational study of behavior: Sampling methods. *Behaviour* 49:227–264.
———. 1980. *Baboon Mothers and Infants.* Cambridge, MA: Harvard University Press.
Altmann, J. and S. Alberts. 1987. Body mass and growth rates in a wild primate population. *Oecologia* 72:15–20.
Altmann, J., S. Altmann, and G. Hausfater. 1988. Determinants of reproductive success in savannah baboons (*Papio cynocephalus*), pp. 403–418. In *Reproductive Success*, T. H. Clutton-Brock, ed. Chicago: University of Chicago Press.
Altmann, S. and J. Altmann. 1970. *Baboon Ecology.* Chicago: University of Chicago Press.
———. 1979. Demographic constraints on behavior and social organization, pp. 47–63. In *Primate Ecology and Human Origins*, I. S. Bernstein and E. O. Smith, eds. New York: Garland Press.
Baker-Dittus, A. 1985. Infant and juvenile-directed care behaviors in adult toque macaques, *Macaca sinica.* Unpublished Ph.D. thesis, University of Maryland.
Bekoff, M. and J. A. Byers. 1985. The development of behavior from evolutionary and ecological perspectives in mammals and birds. *Evolutionary Biology* 19:215–286.
Berman, C. M. 1980. Early agonistic experience and rank acquisition among free-ranging infant rhesus monkeys. *International Journal Primatology* 1:153–170.
———. 1983a. Early differences in relationships between infants and other group members based on mother's status: Their possible relationship to peer–peer rank acquisition, pp. 154–156. In *Primate Social Relationships*, R. A. Hinde, ed. Boston: Blackwell Scientific Publications.
———. 1983b. Influence of close female relatives on peer–peer rank acquisition, pp. 157–159. In *Primate Social Relationships*, R. A. Hinde, ed. Boston: Blackwell Scientific Publications.
Bernstein, I. S. 1981. Dominance: The baby and the bathwater (and associated peer commentaries). *Behavior and Brain Sciences* 4:419–457.
Bernstein, I. S. and C. Ehardt. 1985. Agonistic aiding: Kinship, age, and sex influences. *American Journal of Primatology* 8:37–52.
Bernstein, I. S. and T. P. Gordon. 1974. The function of aggression in primate societies. *Journal of Theoretical Biology* 60:459–472.
Bongaarts, J. 1980. Does malnutrition affect fecundity? A summary of evidence. *Science* 208:564–569.
Bramblett, C. A., S. S. Bramblett, D. A. Bishop, and A. M. Coelho, Jr. 1982. Longitudinal stability in adult status hierarchies among vervet monkeys (*Cercopithecus aethiops*). *American Journal of Primatology* 2:43–52.
Chapais, B. 1983. Matriline membership and male rhesus reaching high ranks in the natal troop, pp. 171–175. In *Primate Social Relationships*, R. A. Hinde, ed. Boston: Blackwell Scientific Publications.
———. 1988a. Rank maintenance in female Japanese macaques: Experimental evidence for social dependency. *Behaviour* 104:41–59.
———. 1988b. Experimental matrilineal inheritance of rank in female Japanese macaques. *Animal Behaviour* 36:1025–1037.
———. 1992. Role of alliances in the social inheritance of rank among female primates, pp. 22–59. In *Coalitions and Alliances in Humans and Other Animals*, A. Harcourt and F. de Waal, eds. Oxford: Oxford University Press.
Chapais, B. and C. Gauthier. In press. Early agonistic experience and the onset of matrilineal rank acquisition in Japanese macaques. In *Juvenile Primates: Life History, Development, and Behavior*, M. E. Pereira and L. A. Fairbanks, eds. New York: Oxford University Press.

Chapais, B., M. Girard, and G. Primi. 1991. Nonkin alliances and the stability of matrilineal dominance relations in Japanese macaques. *Animal Behaviour* 41:481–491.

Chapais, B. and F. Larose. 1988. Experimental rank reversals among peers in *Macaca fuscata*: Rank is maintained after removal of kin support. *American Journal of Primatology* 16:31–42.

Chapais, B. and S. R. Schulman. 1980. An evolutionary model of female dominance relations in primates. *Journal of Theoretical Biology* 82:47–89.

Cheney, D. L. 1977. The acquisition of rank and the development of reciprocal alliances among free-ranging immature baboons. *Behavioral Ecology and Sociobiology* 2:303–318.

———. 1978. The play partners of immature baboons. *Animal Behaviour* 26:1038–1050.

———. 1983. Extra-familial alliances among vervet monkeys, pp. 278–286. In *Primate Social Relationships*, R. A. Hinde, ed. Boston: Blackwell Scientific Publications.

Cheney, D. L. and R. M. Seyfarth. 1990. *How Monkeys See the World*. Chicago: University of Chicago Press.

Clutton-Brock, T. and P. Harvey. 1977. Primate ecology and social organization. *Journal of Zoology, London* 183:1–39.

Coelho, A. M., Jr. 1985. Baboon dimorphism: Growth in weight, length and adiposity from birth to 8 years of age, pp. 125–159. In *Nonhuman Primate Models of Human Growth and Development*, E. S. Watts, ed. New York: Alan R. Liss.

Cord, M. 1988. Resolution of aggressive conflicts by immature long-tailed macaques, *Macaca fascicularis*. *Animal Behaviour* 36:1124–1135.

Crockett, C. and J. Pope. In press. The consequences of sex differences in dispersal for juvenile red howler monkeys. In *Juvenile Primates: Life History, Development, and Behavior*, M. E. Pereira and L. A. Fairbanks, eds. New York: Oxford University Press.

Datta, S. B. 1983a. Relative power and the acquisition of rank, pp. 93–102. In *Primate Social Relationships*, R. A. Hinde, ed. Boston: Blackwell Scientific Publications.

———. 1983b. Relative power and the maintenance of dominance, pp. 103–111. In *Primate Social Relationships*, R. A. Hinde, ed. Boston: Blackwell Scientific Publications.

———. 1983c. Patterns of agonistic interference, pp. 278–286. In *Primate Social Relationships*, R. A. Hinde, ed. Boston: Blackwell Scientific Publications.

Dittus, W. P. J. 1977. The social regulation of population density and age–sex distribution in the toque monkey. *Behaviour* 63:281–322.

———. 1979. The evolution of behaviors regulating density and age-specific sex ratios in a primate population. *Behaviour* 69:265–302.

Drickamer, L. C. 1974. A ten-year summary of reproductive data for free-ranging *Macaca mulatta*. *Folia Primatologica* 21:61–80.

Elias, M. F. and K. W. Samonds. 1977. Protein and calorie malnutrition in infant cebus monkeys. Growth and behavioral development during deprivation and rehabilitation. *American Journal of Clinical Nutrition* 28:355–366.

Emory, G. P. 1976. Aspects of attention, orientation, and status hierarchy in mandrills (*Mandrillus sphinx*) and gelada baboons (*Theropithecus gelada*). *Behaviour* 59:70–87.

Fa, J. E. 1986. *Use of Time and Resources by Provisioned Troops of Monkeys: Social Behavior, Time and Energy in the Barbary Macaque* (Macaca sylvanus L.) at Gibraltar. *Contributions to Primatology 23*. Basel: Karger.

Fleagle, J. G., K. W. Samonds, and D. M. Hegsted. 1975. Physical growth of cebus monkeys, *Cebus albifrons*, during protein or calorie deficiency. *American Journal of Clinical Nutrition* 28:246–253.

Frisch, R. E. 1974. Critical weight at menarche, initiation of the adolescent growth spurt and control of menarche, pp. 443–457. In *Control of Onset of Puberty*, M. M. Brumbach, G. D. Grove, and F. E. Mayer, eds. New York: John Wiley.

Gouzoules, H., S. Gouzoules, and L. Fedigan. 1982. Behavioural dominance and reproductive success in female Japanese monkeys (*Macaca fuscata*). *Animal Behaviour*
30:1138–1150.

Gouzoules, S., H. Gouzoules, and P. Marler. 1984. Rhesus monkey (*Macaca mulatta*)
screams: Representational signalling in the recruitment of agonistic aid. *Animal
Behaviour* 32:182–193.

Hamilton, W. J., III and J. B. Bulger. 1990. Natal male baboon rank rises and successful
challenges to resident alpha males. *Behavioral Ecology and Sociobiology* 27:357–362.

Hausfater, G. 1974. Estrous females: Their effects on the social organization of the baboon
group, pp. 117–127. In *Proceedings of the Symposia of the Fifth Congress of the
International Primatological Society*, S. Konda, M. Kawai, A. Ehona, and S.
Kawamura, eds. Tokyo: Japan Science Press.

———. 1975. *Dominance and Reproduction in Baboons: A Quantitative Analysis. Contributions to Primatology 7.* Basel: Karger.

Hausfater, G., J. Altmann, and S. A. Altmann. 1982. Long-term consistency of dominance
relations among female baboons (*Papio cynocephalus*). *Science* 217:752–755.

Horrocks, J. and W. Hunte. 1983. Maternal rank and offspring rank in vervet monkeys:
An appraisal of the mechanisms of rank acquisition. *Animal Behaviour* 31:772–782.

Hunte, W. and J. Horrocks. 1987. Kin and nonkin interventions in the aggressive disputes
of vervet monkeys. *Behavioral Ecology and Sociobiology* 20:257–263.

Janson, C. H. 1990. Social correlates of individual spatial choice in foraging groups of
brown capuchin monkeys, *Cebus apella. Animal Behaviour* 40:910–921.

Janson, C. H. and C. P. van Schaik. In press. Ecological risk aversion in juvenile primates:
Slow and steady wins the race. In *Juvenile Primates: Life History, Development, and
Behavior*, M. E. Pereira and L. A. Fairbanks, eds. New York: Oxford University Press.

Johnson, J. A. 1984. Social relationships of juvenile olive baboons. Unpublished Ph.D.
thesis, University of Edinburgh, Scotland.

———. 1987. Dominance rank in juvenile olive baboons, *Papio anubis*: The influence of
gender, size, maternal rank and orphaning. *Animal Behaviour* 35:1694–1708.

———. 1989. Supplanting by olive baboons: Dominance rank difference and resource value.
Behavioral Ecology and Sociobiology 24:277–283.

Jolly, A. 1984. The puzzle of female feeding priority, pp. 197–215. In *Studies of Female
Primates by Women Primatologists*, M. Small, ed. New York: Alan R. Liss.

Judge, P. G. 1982. Redirection of aggression based on kinship in a captive group of pigtail
macaques. *International Journal of Primatology* 3:301.

Kaplan, J. 1978. Fight interference and altruism in rhesus monkeys. *American Journal of
Physical Anthropology* 49:241–249.

Kawai, M. 1958. On the system of social ranks in a natural troop of Japanese monkeys.
I. Basic rank and dependent rank, pp. 66–86. In *Japanese Monkeys: A Collection
of Translations*, S. A. Altmann, ed. (Chicago: Published by the editor.)

Kawamura, S. 1958. Matriarchal social ranks in the Minoo-B troop: A study of the rank
system of Japanese monkeys, pp. 105–112. In *Japanese Monkeys: A Collection of
Translations*, S. A. Altmann, ed. (Chicago: Published by the editor.)

Kerr, G. R., M. El Lozy, and G. Scheffler. 1975. Malnutrition studies in *Macaca mulatta*.
IV. Energy and protein consumption during growth failure and "catchup" growth.
American Journal of Clinical Nutrition 28:1364–1376.

Kirkevold, B. C. and C. M. Crockett. 1987. Behavioral development and proximity patterns
in captive DeBrazza's monkeys, pp. 39–65. In *Comparative Behavior of African
Monkeys*, E. L. Zucker, ed. New York: Alan R. Liss.

Koford, B. 1963. Rank of mothers and sons in bands of rhesus monkeys. *Science*
141:356–357.

Koyama, N. 1967. On dominance rank and kinship of a wild Japanese monkey troop in Arashiyama. *Primates* 8:189–216.

Kuester, J. and A. Paul. 1988. Rank relations of juvenile and subadult natal males of Barbary macaques (*Macaca sylvanus*) at Affenberg Salem. *Folia Primatologica* 51:33–44.

Lancaster, J. 1971. Play-mothering: The relations between juvenile females and young infants among free-ranging vervet monkeys (*Cercopithecus aethiops*). *Folia Primatologica* 15:161–182.

Lee, P. C. and J. I. Oliver. 1979. Competition, dominance, and the acquisition of rank in juvenile yellow baboons (*Papio cynocephalus*). *Animal Behaviour* 27:576–585.

Lindberg, D. G. 1987. Seasonality of reproduction in primates, pp. 167–218. In *Comparative Primate Biology*, Vol. 2B, G. Mitchell and J. Erwin, eds. New York: Alan R. Liss.

Marsden, A. M. 1968. Agonistic behavior of young rhesus monkeys after changes induced in the social rank of their mothers. *Animal Behaviour* 16:38–44.

Mason, W. A. 1979. Ontogeny of social behavior, pp. 1–28. In *Social Behavior and Communication: Handbook of Behavioral Neurobiology 3*, P. Marler and J. G. Vandenbergh, eds. New York: Plenum Press.

Massey, A. 1977. Agonistic aids and kinship in a group of pigtailed macaques. *Behavioral Ecology and Sociobiology* 2:31–40.

Meikle, D. B., B. L. Tilford, and S. H. Vessey. 1984. Dominance rank, secondary sex ratio, and reproduction of offspring in polygynous primates. *The American Naturalist* 124:123–188.

Missakian, E. A. 1972. Genealogical and cross-genealogical dominance relations in a group of free-ranging rhesus monkeys on Cayo Santiago. *Primates* 13:169–180.

Moore, J. 1984. Female transfer in primates. *International Journal of Primatology* 5:537–589.

Mori, A. 1979. Analysis of population changes by measurement of body weight in the Koshima troop of Japanese monkeys. *Primates* 20:371–398.

Netto, W. J. and J. A. R. A. M. van Hooff. 1986. Conflict interference and the development of dominance relationships in immature *Macaca fascicularis*, pp. 291–300. In *Primate Ontogeny, Cognition and Social Behaviour*, J. G. Else and P. C. Lee, eds. New York: Cambridge University Press.

Owren, M. J. and J. A. Dieter. 1989. Infant cross-fostering between Japanese (*Macaca fuscata*) and rhesus macaques (*M. mulatta*). *American Journal of Primatology* 18:245–250.

Packer, C. 1979a. Intertroop transfer and inbreeding avoidance in *Papio anubis*. *Animal Behaviour* 27:1–36.

———. 1979b. Male dominance and reproductive activity in *Papio anubis*. *Animal Behaviour* 27:37–45.

Packer, C. and A. E. Pusey. 1979. Female aggression and male membership in troops of Japanese macaques and olive baboons. *Folia Primatologica* 31:212–218.

Paul, A. and D. Thommen. 1984. Timing of birth, female reproductive success and infant sex ratio in semifree-ranging Barbary macaques (*Macaca sylvanus*). *Folia Primatologica* 42:2–16.

Pereira, M. E. 1988a. Effects of age and sex on social association in juvenile savannah baboons (*Papio cynocephalus cynocephalus*). *Animal Behaviour* 36:184–204.

———. 1988b. Agonistic interactions of juvenile savannah baboons. I. Fundamental features. *Ethology* 79:195–217.

———. 1989. Agonistic interactions of juvenile savanna baboons. II. Agonistic support and rank acquisition. *Ethology* 80:152–171.

Pereira, M. E. and J. Altmann. 1985. Development of social behavior in free-living nonhuman primates, pp. 217–309. In *Nonhuman Primate Models of Human Growth and Development*, E. S. Watts, ed. New York: Alan R. Liss.

Pereira, M. E. and L. A. Fairbanks. In press. *Juvenile Primates: Life History, Development, and Behavior*. New York: Oxford University Press.

Prud'homme, J. and B. Chapais. n.d. Role of aggressive interventions in the dynamics of matrilineal dominance relations among female Barbary macaques (*Macaca sylvanus*). *American Journal of Primatology*.

Pusey, A. E. 1990. Behavioural changes at adolescence in chimpanzees. *Behaviour* 115:203–246.

Pusey, A. E. and C. Packer. 1987. Dispersal and philopatry, pp. 250–266. In *Primate Societies*, B. B. Smuts, D. L. Cheney, R. M. Seyfarth, R. W. Wrangham, and T. T. Struhsaker, eds. Chicago: University of Chicago Press.

Raleigh, M. J. and M. T. McGuire. 1989. Female influences on male dominance acquisition in captive vervet monkeys, *Cercopithecus aethiops sabeus*. *Animal Behaviour* 38:59–67.

Rosenblum, L. A. and E. H. Plimpton. 1979. The effects of adults on peer interactions, pp. 195–217. In *The Child and Its Family*, M. Lewis and L. A. Rosenblum, eds. New York: Plenum Press.

Rowell, T. E. 1972. *The Social Behaviour of Monkeys*. Baltimore: Penguin.

Sade, D. S. 1965. Some aspects of parent–offspring and sibling relations in a group of rhesus monkeys, with a discussion of grooming. *American Journal of Physical Anthropology* 23:1–18.

———. 1967. Determinants of dominance in a group of free-ranging rhesus monkeys, pp. 99–114. In *Social Communication among Primates*, S. A. Altmann, ed. Chicago: University of Chicago Press.

———. 1972. A longitudinal study of social behavior of rhesus monkeys, pp. 378–398. In *The Functional and Evolutionary Biology of Primates*, R. Tuttle, ed. Chicago: Aldine-Atherton.

Samuels, A., J. B. Silk, and J. Altmann. 1987. Continuity and change in dominance relations among female baboons. *Animal Behaviour* 35:785–793.

Saunders, C. D. and G. Hausfater. 1978. Sexual selection in baboons (*Papio cynocephalus*): A computer simulation of differential reproduction with respect to dominance rank in males, pp. 567–571. In *Recent Advances in Primatology*, D. Chivers and J. Herbert, eds. New York: Academic Press.

van Schaik, C. P. and S. B. Hrdy. 1991. Intensity of local resource competition shapes the relationship between maternal rank and sex ratios at birth in cercopithecine primates. *The American Naturalist* 138(6): 1555–1562.

Seyfarth, R. M. 1980. The distribution of grooming and related behavior among adult female vervet monkeys. *Animal Behaviour* 28:798–853.

Shopland, J. M. 1987. Food quality, spatial deployment, and the intensity of feeding interference in yellow baboons (*Papio cynocephalus*). *Behavioral Ecology and Sociobiology* 21:149–156.

Silk, J. B. 1983. Local resource competition and facultative adjustment of sex ratios in relation to competitive abilities. *The American Naturalist* 121:56–66.

———. 1987. Social behavior in evolutionary perspective, pp. 318–329. In *Primate Societies*, B. B. Smuts, D. L. Cheney, R. M. Seyfarth, R. W. Wrangham, and T. T. Struhsaker, eds. Chicago: University of Chicago Press.

Silk, J. B., A. Samuels, and P. Rodman. 1981. The influence of kinship, rank and sex on affiliation and aggression between adult female and immature bonnet macaques (*Macaca radiata*). *Behaviour* 78:111–137.

Smuts, B. B. 1985. *Sex and Friendship in Baboons*. New York: Aldine.

Sugiyama, Y. 1976. Life history of male Japanese macaques. *Advances in the Study of Behavior* 7:255–284.

Sugiyama, Y. and H. Ohsawa. 1982. Population dynamics of Japanese monkeys with special reference to the effect of artificial feeding. *Folia Primatologica* 39:238–263.

Symons, D. 1978. *Play and Aggression: A Study of Rhesus Monkeys*. New York: Columbia University Press.

Turnquist, J. E. and M. J. Kessler. 1989. Free-ranging Cayo Santiago rhesus monkeys (*Macaca mulatta*): I. Body size, proportions and allometry. *American Journal of Primatology* 19:1–14.

de Waal, F. B. M. 1977. The organization of agonistic relations within two captive groups of Java monkeys, *Macaca fascicularis*. *Zeitschrift für Tierpsychologie* 44:225–282.

———. 1986a. The integration of dominance and social bonding in primates. *Quarterly Review of Biology* 61:459–479.

———. 1986b. Class structure in a rhesus monkey group; the interplay between dominance and tolerance. *Animal Behaviour* 34:1033–1040.

———. 1989. Dominance "style" and primate social organization, pp. 243–263. In *Comparative Socioecology: The Behavioural Ecology of Humans and Other Mammals*, V. Standen and R. A. Foley, eds. London: Blackwell.

de Waal, F. B. M. and L. Luttrell. 1985. The formal hierarchy of rhesus monkeys: An investigation of the bared-teeth display. *American Journal of Primatology* 9:73–85.

de Waal, F. B. M. and R. Ren. 1988. Comparison of the reconciliation behavior of stumptail and rhesus macaques. *Ethology* 78:129–142.

van Wagenen, G. and H. R. Catchpole. 1956. Physical growth of the rhesus monkey (*Macaca mulatta*). *American Journal of Physical Anthropology* 19:245–273.

Walters, J. 1980. Interventions and the development of dominance relationships in female baboons. *Folia Primatologica* 34:61–89.

Wasser, S. K. and A. K. Starling. 1988. Proximate and ultimate causes of reproductive suppression among female yellow baboons at Mikumi National Park, Tanzania. *American Journal of Primatology* 16:97–122.

Watts, E. S. 1985. Adolescent growth and development of monkeys, apes and humans, pp. 41–65. In *Nonhuman Primate Models for Human Growth and Development*, E. S. Watts, ed. New York: Alan R. Liss.

Western, D. and C. van Praet. 1973. Cyclical changes in the habitat and climate of an East African ecosystem. *Nature*, London 241:104–106.

Whitten, P. L. 1983. Diet and dominance among female vervet monkeys (*Cercopithecus aethiops*). *American Journal of Primatology* 5:139–159.

Wrangham, R. W. 1981. Drinking competition in vervet monkeys. *Animal Behaviour* 29:904–910.

7

The Development of Agonistic and Affiliative Structures in Preschool Play Groups

F. F. STRAYER

INTRODUCTION

Questions about the nature and function of early social behavior in humans have preoccupied researchers in developmental psychobiology for at least 50 years. However, the empirical findings are often difficult to synthesize because they have been generated by apparently opposing theoretical or conceptual models of early socialization. A survey of the last 50 years of developmental research reveals three quite distinct approaches to the study of peer relations during early childhood.

In the 1930s, Mildred Parten proposed what was to become a classic developmental approach to the description of children's social play. Parten (1932) described children's activities during unsupervised episodes in terms of physical proximity between peers, orientation of visual attention and degree of mutual involvement. Her empirical studies led her to conclude that during the preschool period, children become progressively more sophisticated in the coordination of cooperative activity with age-mates.

A quite different approach to analysis of early social behavior dealt more directly with the social impact of observed activities. Influenced by prevailing American psychological theories of the 1940s and 1950s, this learning approach described spontaneous peer activity in terms of its presumed value as a positive or negative reinforcer for the social partners (Hartup et al. 1967). At a descriptive level, the functional preoccupation of the learning approach focused attention on the basic distinction between aggressive and cooperative social involvement. Although such a dichotomous classification of children's social activity was more general than Parten's earlier description of age-graded forms of peer play, the newer functional emphasis did not address questions about qualitative changes during the course of early childhood in the patterning of social activity.

In the 1960s, ethological critiques of such "learning-oriented studies from child psychology" stressed their lack of concern with describing basic action units, and the often arbitrary assignment of quite different activities to a single global functional category (McGrew 1972). In part as a reaction to such psychological views, the ethological approach explicitly attempted to furnish empirical justification for higher-order classifications of morphologically described social action patterns. For example, Blurton-Jones (1972) used factor analysis of the temporal association and frequency of 22 behavioral items, observed during free play, to reveal three independent classes of social activity. The first involved an opposition between "rough and tumble play" and "task-work" elements, the second subsumed a variety of aggressive actions, while the third reflected affiliative, or pro-social forms of peer involvement.

In spite of their apparently divergent interests, these three approaches to the study of early social behavior share a common perspective, that of individual differences in social adjustment. Each focuses on individual differences in the production of particular forms of social activity. Such emphasis on individual differences often leads to the premature attribution of a more or less permanent behavioral style, or social trait to each child under study. Preoccupation with identifying stable individual differences in primary social styles precludes consideration of how the individual's particular social actions are influenced or shaped by forces in the immediate social context. The influence of the social context on individual behavior is an important issue in any social analysis of individual functioning, but this issue is even more essential in studies of early social development.

Recent investigations in human ethology have stressed that social behavior must be examined at different levels of organization including the individual, the dyad and the group (Hinde and Stevenson-Hinde 1976; Strayer 1980a). This approach to the study of social adaptation, originally introduced by Crook (1970), emphasizes the importance of group processes as determinants of both individual action and social interaction. Essentially, Crook stressed that individual styles of social participation are constrained by the structured pattern of social relationships existing within stable groups. In this context, to analyze social participation in terms of individual activity profiles, or even differences in the likely consequences of socially directed acts, neglects an important source of variation in the strategic adjustment of individuals to different social partners. Social acts are not randomly distributed among group members; instead actions directed toward specific others exhibit qualitative similarity over time.

The coordinated use of particular patterns of social activity with specific social partners has already been employed as a means of classifying social behavior in studies of nonhuman primates (Strayer et al. 1975). Rather than focusing upon the individual's production of different forms of behavior, this analysis examines covariation in the dyadic allocation of social acts within the stable group. The behaviors that a single animal directs towards different social partners are treated as analytically distinct entities. They are directional dyad acts. Factor analysis of the rate of social activity for such directional dyads in studies of two captive *Saimiri* groups revealed three principal classes of social participation: aggressive, affiliative, and play behaviors. Using similar analytic techniques with a more comprehensive behavioral taxonomy, Strayer and Harris (1979) reported four forms of social participation in *Saimiri* groups which they labeled affiliation, aggression, sex, and play. More recently, Gariépy and Strayer (1983) identified two independent forms of social attention which co-varied with other forms of social participation in different ways depending upon a group's sex ratio and age distribution.

In an application of an ethological approach to the social development of young children, Strayer (1980a) suggested that the social organization of the preschool group could be discussed in terms of two major classes of activity. Drawing from the work of Kummer (1968) and McGrew (1972), he labeled these classes in terms of their "cohesive" and "dispersive" functions. Basic categories of social activity promoting group cohesion included affiliative behaviors such as orientation, approach and contact. In contrast, agonistic activity such as attack, threat and competition were described as leading to the dispersion of peer group members. Summarizing evidence from a series of independent observational studies, Strayer (1980b) showed that these two functional classes of behavioral activity could be employed to assess qualitatively different forms of social structure within the early peer group.

The systematic extension of ethological methods to the study of children's social adaptation within stable peer groups paralleled already existing trends in primate research (Bernstein 1970; Chance and Jolly 1970; Crook 1970; Alexander and Roth 1971; Kummer 1971; Soczka 1973). During the 1970s, a number of independent researchers reported empirical data stressing the importance of social dominance hierarchies as an organizational feature of preschool groups (Abramovitch 1976; Missakian 1876; Strayer and Strayer 1976; Hold 1977; Sluckin and Smith 1977; Strayer et al. 1978; Vaughn and Waters 1980). More recently, LaFrenière and Charlesworth (1983) have directly addressed the common assumption that establishing a group dominance hierarchy contributes to a reduction of intragroup aggression. Their findings suggest that organizing peer conflict in terms of stable dominance relations leads to a reduction of overt aggression during sequential periods of the school year. However since their study focused only upon a single age level, they do not provide direct information on age-related changes in the nature of peer group social organization.

Finally, ethological studies with school-aged children have begun to suggest that social dominance persists as a unifying aspect of peer group social organization through the grade school and adolescent periods (Savin-Williams 1976; Weisfeld 1980; Weisfeld et al. 1980). Following these initial efforts to document the nature of social dominance, a number of researchers have begun to explore how other, more positive forms of social activity are related to group dominance rank. Preliminary findings indicate that social dominance may be directly related to patterns of peer friendship and popularity (Strayer 1980a, b), social attention (Abramovitch and Strayer 1978), imitation and leadership (Savin-Williams 1980; Strayer 1980, 1981). However, more recent results question the central role of social dominance as an organizating principle in the early peer group (Vaughn and Waters 1981). How diverse social activities are organized and coordinated within the peer group remains an important question in current ethological research on child development.

It is apparent that the integration of individuals into a stable social unit places important limitations upon their activities. It has often been less clear how to analyze the emerging patterns of social exchange which characterize the organization of group roles and other social relationships within the collective unit. Research in social ethology suggests that the stability and organization of the social group depends upon the delicate balance struck between social activities promoting group cohesion and those leading to social dispersion (Kummer 1971;

McGrew 1972). In this view, the group dominance hierarchy formalizes dyadic roles during periods of social conflict, and thus serves as a regulatory system that minimizes dispersive aggressive exchanges between group members. In contrast, activities that more directly promote group cohesion, attracting individuals to one another and maintaining them in a coordinated social unit, have been conceptualized as an orthogonal dimension of a group's social ecology (Strayer et al. 1975; Strayer and Harris 1979).

The study of cohesive organization provides a necessary complement to analyses of dominance hierarchies within children's peer groups. The lack of a more comprehensive and balanced description of social organization in past research can be attributed to a number of methodological problems including a need to develop appropriate empirical techniques for the analysis of both cohesive and dispersive dimensions of group behavior. Primatologists were increasingly aware that standardized procedures for assessing social bonds provided reliable information, but often failed to predict social activity within the group setting (Soczka 1973; Strayer et al. 1975). This led to a greater reliance upon the direct observation of spontaneously occurring behavior as the most useful means of identifying basic dimensions of group organization. In contrast, studies in child development have continued to use indirect sociometric techniques as the principle procedure for assessing group cohesion. However, an ethological analysis of affiliative behaviors within the preschool peer group, not only permits examining social organization in preverbal children, but also facilitates direct comparisons of developmental changes in the nature and organization of early peer activity.

Although the use of direct observation has encouraged the elaboration of a more systematic conceptual approach for the inductive analysis of social relationships and group structures, a number of important differences still exist in how researchers describe naturally occurring social behavior. Our current approach stresses basic distinctions among individual behavioral profiles, interaction styles, social relationships, and group structures (see also Hinde and Stevenson-Hinde 1976). Our qualitative analysis entails examining the social action patterns of members of the different dyads in a group. Subsequently, characteristic forms of social interaction can be identified by examining recurrent sequential combinations of action patterns in social exchanges between individuals. The regularity of such interaction in different dyadic contexts suggests larger categories of social participation. These can be used as converging measures of specific dimensions in social relationships. Finally, analysis of general principles that summarize the organization of these obtained relationships provides an empirical basis for the derivation of the organization, or structure, of the stable social unit.

Although few studies on children's dominance have examined age-related changes in the nature of peer group social organization directly, some preliminary findings suggest that the organization of dispersive and cohesive activities might differ systematically in relation to age and previous social experience. For example, Missakian (1980) and her colleagues reported that patterns of social conflict differed for older and younger children in a mixed-age peer group. Correspondingly, our research has suggested that, although the dominance hierarchies of 4-year-olds are quite similar to those of 5-year-olds in both linearity and rigidity, pro-social activities relate to dominance rank in a slightly different manner at the two age levels (Strayer 1980a, 1981). Surprisingly, there is still very little empirical information concerning the age at which dyadic dominance relations and group social structures emerge as stable characteristics of a peer group. Description of the developmental processes underlying the early socialization of agonistic and affiliative behavior is a necessary prerequisite for formulating and testing intelligent hypotheses about the adaptive significance of human social behavior. The present extension of an ethological approach to the study of groups of very young children provides an initial opportunity to examine developmental changes in the organization of both cohesive and agonistic peer activities.

METHODS

The participants in the research reported on here were 134 French-speaking children who attended a community daycare center in Montreal. The children, who ranged in age from 1 to 6 years, were members of five age-stratified groups in each of two consecutive years of field study (Studies 1 and 2, Table 7-1). The daycare center provided services for a large variety of families, including tradesmen, professionals, students, and welfare recipients. About one third of the children came from single-parent homes. Daily activities for each of the groups were divided into periods of structured activity, relatively unsupervised free-play, and meal and nap-time. Most children attended the center for a full day (0900 h to 1700 h). Each class had a permanent male and female teacher, who were occasionally replaced by part-time staff of either sex.

Records of social behavior were obtained for all 10 groups using direct observation procedures during periods of free play and of structured activity (Figure 7-1). Data collection procedures involved 24 5-minute focal samples for each child in Study 1, and 16 5-minute samples for children in Study 2. Supplementary observations of dyadic conflict were collected for all groups using matrix completion procedures. These latter observations were included to facilitate analyses of social dominance relations (Altmann 1974).

For each observational record the initiator of an act, the action, the target, and the target's response were noted. If any of the required elements in this minimal syntax were not available, the social exchange was not included for data analysis.

Table 7-1   Summary of Participants.

Age level	Study 1			Study 2		
	N	Mean age (months)	S.D.	N	Mean age (months)	S.D.
One year	9	18	6.22	10	15	4.60
Two years	11	28	6.10	9	25	1.04
Three years	14	37	4.35	12	35	4.20
Four years	18	49	8.50	18	47	4.30
Five years	16	66	5.45	17	68	9.90

Figure 7-1 Doctor Strayer records the interactions of four children. (Photograph by F. de Waal.)

A change of social partners, and/or a lapse of 10 seconds between the end of one action and the onset of another was used to separate dyadic social sequences. The description of behavior required noting specific elements selected from a Social Action Inventory (Strayer 1980b). A summary of the coding categories included in the current analyses is provided in Table 7-2. All data were collected by full-time research staff with extensive training in the direct observation of preschool social behavior. Prior to the beginning of each phase of observation, interobserver reliabilities for the use of coding categories were assessed, using both correlational and agreement procedures. Reliability indices were consistently above 85% for the complete coding system, and slightly higher than 90% in the scoring of selected forms of social conflict from video records of agonistic interaction. Percentage agreement coefficients were also calculated at the midpoint of each observational phase. The values of these reliability indices ranged from 86% to 98% (mean 90.6%, S.D. = 5.08).

Initiated social activity for each group within each observational session was tabulated in dyadic matrices. These matrices summarized the distribution of observed behavior among all other group members for a complete observational session. The target's response was also tabulated as an initiated act if it entailed one of the six selected categories. Most prior studies of social participation have used marginal totals of such dyadic matrices as basic measures in the analysis of social participation. In our study, the unit of analysis is the "directional dyad". This means that, in a given dyad A–B, an initiation of A to B represents a different case from an initiation of B to A. There are N squared minus N such cases in a

Table 7-2   Principal Categories and Patterns of Social Activity.

Social initiation

I. Affiliation
   (1) Signal: glance, look-at, watch, turn-toward, beckon, point, show, wave smile, play-face
   (2) Approach: step-toward, walk-toward, run-toward, follow
   (3) Contact: touch, pat, kiss, hold-hands, shoulder-hug

II. Agonism
   (1) Attack: bite, hit, grab, kick, pull-push, throw-at, assault
   (2) Threat: fragment-hit, miss, throw, chase, facial display, body display
   (3) Competition: object struggle, steal, supplant

Social terminators

III. Affiliation
   (1) Re-orient: look-away, look to other, turn away, turn to other
   (2) Withdraw: step-away, walk away, run away, approach other

IV. Agonism
   (1) Submission: gaze-avert, crouch, cringe, flinch, cry
   (2) Retreat: step-back, flee

V. No response
   Ignore, miss

dyadic matrix. To measure the rate of activity for each directional dyad, raw data matrices were transformed into vectors representing the frequency of initiation for each social partner to the other. In order to examine the natural clustering of the observed forms of social activity, we conducted our principal component analyses on the basis of the six vectors thus obtained for each of the 10 groups. All factors were extracted according to the usual eigen threshold of 1.00 and were rotated using the Varimax option. The design of our data collection procedures permitted examining intragroup stability of obtained factor structures, as well as their replicability within and across age levels.

RESULTS

Social Activity as a Function of Age

Analyses of age differences in the hourly rate of social activity revealed a striking direct correlation in the frequency of affiliative activity. The frequency of "orientation" and "approach" more than doubled from 1 to 5 years, while "contact" also increased, although at a somewhat slower rate and with an apparent plateau at 4 years. In contrast, agonistic activity was much less frequent. The rate of "attack" and "competition" remained nearly constant until age 3, and then decreased steadily thereafter. Interestingly, the use of the least frequent form of aggressive behavior, "threat," increased between 1 and 3 years, and then decreased in conjunction with other forms of agonistic activity.

Principal Components of Dyadic Activity

Although the preliminary analyses of initiated activity showed change in behavioral rates as a function of age, they revealed little about how the allocation of different actions towards selected partners changes during the course of the preschool period. Our first set of dyadic analyses examined the convergence of allocated acts for each of the 10 peer groups. Table 7-3 provides a summary of obtained results for the 1-, 3-, and 5-year-olds observed during the first year of the project. For all three groups the principal component analyses of dyadic activity identified two orthogonal factors. In the youngest group, "attack," "threat," and "competition" had the highest loadings on the first factor. The grouping of these behaviors on the same factor readily identifies it as an agonistic dimension of social participation. The second factor was defined primarily by the category "approach," although it also had a secondary association with "competition." The dyadic variability of "orientation" and "contact" was not strongly related to either of the two principal factors in this youngest group. Affiliation in this first analysis is thus represented as an emergent dimension of social activity.

In contrast, for the other two groups in Table 7-3, the affiliative factor emerges as the first dimension of social participation, while the agonistic dimension accounts for a significant part of the residual variance in the allocation of social activity. Indeed, for both of these older groups, the variables associated with the first factor are "orientation," "approach," and "contact," while "attack," "threat," and "competition" are clustered on the second factor. Finally, although there is an age-related trend for greater independence between the behavioral indices which define the agonistic and affiliative dimensions of social participation, "competition" remains significantly correlated with both factors for each of the three ages shown in Table 7-3.

It is interesting to note that the principal dimensions of social activity generally

Table 7-3 Principal Components of Dyadic Activity.

	Age level					
	One year		Three years		Five years	
Factors	Ago.[a]	Aff.[b]	Aff.	Ago.	Aff.	Ago.
Attention	0.13	0.30	0.73*	0.20	0.81*	0.12
Approach	0.36*	0.82*	0.97*	0.19	0.75*	0.15
Contact	0.03	0.27	0.45*	0.29	0.66*	0.21
Competition	0.63*	0.40*	0.35*	0.59*	0.31*	0.34*
Threat	0.68*	0.12	0.19	0.56*	0.17	0.64*
Attack	0.97*	0.27	0.13	0.83*	0.08	0.71*
Eigenvalue	2.83	1.09	2.98	1.12	2.63	1.24
Variance	47.10	18.10	49.60	18.60	43.90	20.70

* $p < 0.01$ for correlation between behavioral category and indicated component of social participation.

[a] Ago. = agonistic.

[b] Aff. = affiliative.

discussed in the ethological and psychological literature are already evident in the 1-year-old peer group. These initial age contrasts also demonstrate that, in spite of a relatively lower frequency, agonistic activity can emerge as the main source of variation in the dyadic allocation of social behaviors. In contrast, affiliative activities become the primary source of behavioral convergence for the older groups. These initial findings suggest potentially important developmental changes between 1 and 3 years, where newly established patterns of social participation might be consolidated for the remainder of the preschool period.

Developmental Changes in Social Participation

In order to examine in greater detail the salient features of social participation at each age level, separated principal component analyses were conducted for each of the 10 social groups. The resulting number of factors, eigenvalues and explained variance were in all cases very similar to the values reported in Table 7-3. The comparison of geometrical representations obtained for our two youngest groups indicated substantial between-year differences in the communalities of "orientation," "contact," and "threat" as well as in their associations with the two principal factors. However, in spite of these differences, the general factor structures were still quite similar. In both cases, agonistic activities were more readily associated with the first factor and affiliative activities were more strongly associated with the second. Although the overall analyses for these two groups did not indicate a unique pattern of association between all six behavioral variables and the underlying factors, they suggested that the major source of variability in social participation at this age is due to differential allocation of agonistic activity, and that affiliation in groups of 1-year-olds represents a secondary form of differentiated social participation.

With the 2-year-olds, the pattern of factor loadings was mixed. In Study 1, findings were very similar to those obtained for the youngest group. In contrast, the analyses of 2-year-olds in Study 2 showed a first factor defined primarily by "contact" and associated with "approach," "orientation," and "attack," while the second factor reflected primarily "competition" and "threat." For this second group of 2-year-olds, the order of the principal factors was inverse; affiliation accounted for more of the total variance than the agonistic dimension. In spite of these between-group differences, in all four of these younger groups, there was at least some association between affiliative and agonistic activity. Closer examination of social participation among the 2-year-olds indicated that children at this age may be in a transitional phase. The behavioral ecology of their social group may be evolving away from the agonistic mode which characterized the youngest children towards an organization where more positive forms of social participation account for the greater proporton of variability in the dyadic allocation of social acts.

With the 3-year-olds, the principal component analyses provide a more clear-cut image of social participation where the usual categories defining social affiliation were tightly clustered on the first factor and those pertaining to agonistic activity are found on the second factor. With the sole exception of "competition," all categories had exclusive loadings on a single factor. Moreover, the value of these loadings were generally much higher than those obtained with the two younger age levels. This replication of the results presented in Table 7-3 suggests that the prevalence of affiliative over agonistic activity is well established in the peer group of 3-year-olds.

A very similar organization of social participation was also obtained for the groups of 4- and 5-year-olds. In each of these analyses of dyadic participation, affiliative activity emerged as the first dimension and agonistic activity as the second. At each age level, Study 1 findings were well replicated by the factor structures obtained with groups from Study 2. The relatively high loadings of most categories on a sole factor indicated that the independence of the principal components of social participation observed for the 3-year-olds is maintained throughout the rest of the preschool period. Once again, the only exception to this clear separation of agonistic and affiliative activity involved "competition." This category of activity remained significantly correlated with both dimensions of social participation throughout the latter 3 years of the preschool period.

Temporal Stability of Participation Factor Structures

The principal component analyses conducted separately for the two years of observations provided a good replication across groups of the same age and underlined consistent developmental changes. However, in order to ascertain the temporal stability of the resulting factor structures, early–late analyses were conducted with the data sets available from each of our 10 groups. These secondary analyses involved splitting the data set for each group into two equal halves (these halves roughly represented contrasting social functioning during the Winter and Spring terms of the school year). The results for the first year were in complete agreement with the global analysis for four of the five groups. The only indication of differences in factor structures was found with the 4-year-olds where the first factor reflected a more general activity dimension which regrouped five of the six categories, while the second factor corresponded to the original affiliative dimension. For the second year of observation, our stability analyses revealed identical factor structures: the general analyses replicated in both the early and late periods for four of the five groups. Interestingly, the sole exception was with the 2-year-olds where agonistic activity appeared as the first factor for the winter observations and as the second factor for the spring data. It is also important to note that for both years, the major temporal variations in the magnitude of the factor loadings were evident for the younger groups.

Peer Conflict and Social Dominance Relations

The present analysis of dyadic dominance relations is based upon three different categories of initiated conflict (aggression): attack, threat, and competition. In all cases, the critical behavior for identifying a dominance exchange entailed noting submission or retreat by the recipient. Although the frequency of such exchanges varied across groups, there was no evidence of a systematic linear trend in the number of dominance encounters as a function of age. Conflict was more frequent among children at the three younger age levels (mean of episodes per group was

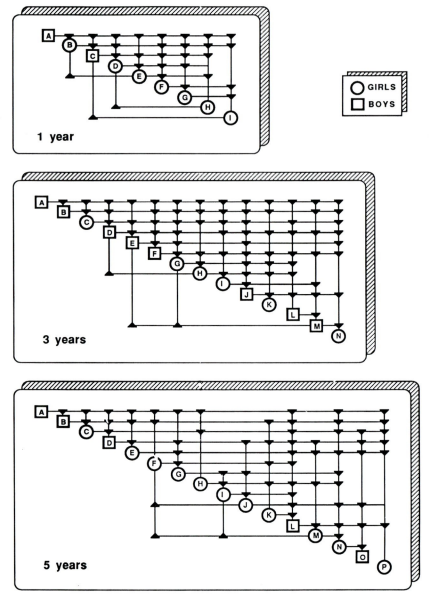

Figure 7-2   Hierarchical representation of dominance structures for three preschool groups.

321, S.D. = 66), while the 4- and 5-year olds were involved in significantly fewer dominance bouts (mean of episodes was 163, S.D. = 39).

In all ten groups, clear dominance hierarchies were evident. Figure 7-2 provides illustrations of the nature of the obtained hierarchical networks for 1-, 3-, and 5-year-olds. In each case, individuals are ordered on the diagonal according to their serial position in the group dominance hierarchy. The arrows in these social networks indicate that a dyadic relationship was established according to observed conflict outcomes. An intersecting line not marked with an arrow indicates either that no dominance relation for the dyad in question was observed, or that the child with a lower group rank dominated in that particular dyadic context. The latter case represents a nonlinear relation, and is portrayed in the diagram by an arrow under the diagonal. The frequency of such nonlinear relationships was extremely low. In each of the 10 groups, fewer than 10% of the observed relations violated predictions from the linear transitive model of social dominance.

Visual inspection of these three hierarchical networks reveals the first of two important age-related changes in the nature of the group dominance structures. For the youngest group, nearly three quarters of the possible dyadic relations were established by direct observation of aggressive exchanges. For the 3-year-olds, this proportion decreased slightly, while for the group of 5-year-olds, there was a substantial reduction in the percentage of observed dominance relations. This latter difference is especially noteworthy, since considerably more time was devoted to matrix completion sampling with the groups of 4- and 5-year-olds.

Thus, in spite of this additional sampling, the relative number of established dominance relations for the older groups remains considerably lower than the values obtained at the younger age levels. This trend toward a reduction in the number of expressed dominance relations may only reflect the more basic reduction in social conflict among the older children. However, the age-related increase in group size also suggests a reduction in the probability that any two individuals would be involved in a social exchange. Such speculations on the underpinnings of the obtained age trend should be supported by more specific information about the effects of both conflict rates and group size on the relative number of expressed dyadic dominance relationships. Regardless of the underlying process, the present finding indicates that older children have a greater likelihood of interacting with peer group members with whom they have not had an overtly expressed dominance relation.

A second age-related change in the nature of peer dominance involved the temporal stability of the obtained dominance structures. Once again, our assessment of temporal stability was assessed by dividing the agonistic data into early and late observational periods. Each subset of data was then reanalyzed to produce early and late dominance matrices for each group. The columns and rows of the resulting matrices were then reordered to maximize their fit to the linear dominance model. Finally, Spearman correlation coefficients were calculated between the resulting rank orders for each of the 10 groups. All of these correlation coefficients were positive, ranging from 0.48 to 1.00. Figure 7-3 provides a summary of four descriptive parameters of social dominance as a function of age. Although both dyadic asymmetry and linear transitivity of dominance relations increased slightly as a function of age, these first two descriptive indices of social dominance were remarkably stable throughout the period under study. In contrast, both the percentage of established dominance relations and the stability of the obtained rank orders showed substantial and systematic change as a function of age. These final results indicate that changes in the nature of peer group conflict during the first five years of life are most evident in terms of reductions in the overt agonistic expression of dominance differentials, as well as in the progressive emergence of temporally stable group dominance hierarchies.

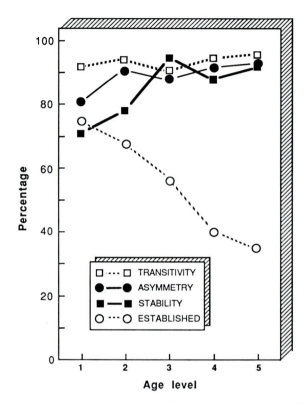

Figure 7-3   Descriptive summary of peer group dominance structure as a function of age.

Dominance and the Coordination of Affiliative Activity

In each of the 10 groups, the relative rate of affiliative activity far exceeded the rate of agonistic activity. Generally, over 80% of the total recorded behavior involved some form of socially positive initiation. However, the ratio of initiated agonistic activity to initiated affiliation varied systematically as a function of age. A substantially higher proportion (over 90%) of cohesive behaviors was evident among the oldest children, while proportionately fewer affiliative activities (just more than 60%) were evident among the 1-year-olds. Separate analyses of the total receipt of affiliative acts showed that in each of the 10 groups certain children obtained significantly more than their expected share of the group's total cohesive activity (chi-square > 6.61, $p < 0.01$) (for the details of this analysis see Soczka (1973) and Strayer (1980a)). Certain children in each group were more often chosen as preferred social partners by other group members, and thus could be identified as the more popular members of the group. Similar analyses examining individual allocations of affiliative behavior also revealed significant individual preferences within each of the 10 groups. Thus, affiliative acts were generally allocated to peer group members in a nonrandom fashion. However, social preferences were not observed for all group members. Graphic representation of all individual social choices provided sociograms of the affiliative structure of each group. Popular

Table 7-4 Spearman Correlations of Dominance Rank and Received Affiliation.

Group	Age level	1979–1980	1980–1981
Pouponnière	1 year	0.53*	0.08
Bout-de-Choux	2 years	−0.07	−0.01
Salami	3 years	0.59*	0.33
Salopette	4 years	0.28	0.17
Saltimbanque	5 years	0.59*	0.48*

* $p < 0.05$, to two significant digits, one-tail test for attraction to high rank

children appeared to be more central in these group networks, while others assumed peripheral or isolated roles (see Strayer 1980a).

Subsequently we analyzed the coordination of affiliative activity with dominance in the peer group. We examined the overall allocation of cohesive behaviors as a function of position in the group hierarchy as well as the correspondence between dominance rank and the frequency of being chosen as a significant social partner. The first set of analyses tested the hypothesis of "attraction to high rank" that has guided most earlier studies on the distribution of social attention in relation to a child's relative position in the group hierarchy (see also Seyfarth 1977, 1980). This analysis required tabulating the total affiliative activity received by each of the children and correlating this measure with their ordinal position in the group's dominance hierarchy. Table 7-4 shows the obtained results of these analyses for the 10 groups. Only four of the 10 correlations were significant. In Study 1, three groups evidenced a trend toward a positive association between the receipt of affiliative behavior and dominance rank. However, in Study 2, only the oldest group showed a similar correlation. Thus, in general, there was a consistent trend for more affiliative activity to be allocated to higher-ranking individuals only among the 5-year-old children.

A major weakness of the preceding analysis is that it fails to control for individual differences in activity levels among the members of the peer group. For example, the positive correlations between received affiliation and higher dominance rank may merely reflect a tendency for more dominant children to interact more frequently together, and thus to directly increase their receipt of all forms of social activity. The examination of individual social preferences avoids this problem because the identification of preferred social partners depends upon each child's total affiliative production, rather than upon total affiliative activity of the entire peer group. Table 7-5 shows the number of significant social choices directed to higher- and lower-ranking peers for the five age levels. It is clear that in the youngest groups there was a slight, but not significant tendency for children to choose lower-ranking group members as preferred social partners. For the 2-year-olds, affiliative choices were not coordinated with dominance differentials. However, among the three older groups, there was an increasingly evident trend for affiliative choices to be directed preferentially toward higher-ranking group members. Finally, for the 5-year-olds, this tendency attained statistical significance.

Table 7-5 Distribution of Significant Affiliative Choices as a Function of Dyadic Dominance Relation for the Two Years Combined.

Group	Higher rank	Lower rank	p level*
One year	6	12	0.88
Two years	6	5	0.50
Three years	19	15	0.25
Four years	36	27	0.13
Five years	36	23	0.05

* Binomial test $p < 0.05$, one-tail test for attraction to high rank.

The emerging trend for older children to choose higher-ranking group members as significant affiliative targets was to some extent obscured by a parallel tendency for increasing reciprocity in the choice of preferred playmates. Table 7-6 shows the distribution of asymmetrical social choices to higher- and lower-ranking peers as a function of age. The removal of reciprocal choices in the analysis of preferred social partners provides a much more vivid demonstration of how affiliative activity becomes coordinated with dominance rank during the later preschool years. At the two older age levels, there is clearly a disproportionately large number of nonreciprocated social choices that are directed toward higher-ranking group members.

The developmental shift in the coordination of asymmetrical choices with dominance rank is illustrated by Figure 7-4. For the two 1-year-old groups, the general trend is for highly ranked children selectively to choose subordinate group members as preferred affiliative partners. In fact, three quarters of the observed asymmetrical initiations were attributable to the four highest-ranking group members. In contrast, among the 3-year-olds, nearly half of the significant choices were attributable to lower-ranking group members and, with only a single exception were directed toward higher-ranking peers. Finally, in the groups of 5-year-olds, nearly all of the nonreciprocated preferences are directed by group members in the lower half of the dominance hierarchy. In all but two of these cases, the asymmetrical preferences are for peers of higher social rank. The second sample provided a solid replication of the empirical results obtained during the first year.

Table 7-6 Asymmetrical Choices toward Higher- and Lower-Ranking Peers.

Group	Higher rank	Lower rank	p level*
One year	3	9	0.93
Two years	5	4	0.50
Three years	10	6	0.23
Four years	17	8	0.05
Five years	15	2	0.00

* Binomial test $p < 0.05$, to two significant digits, one-tail test for attraction to high rank.

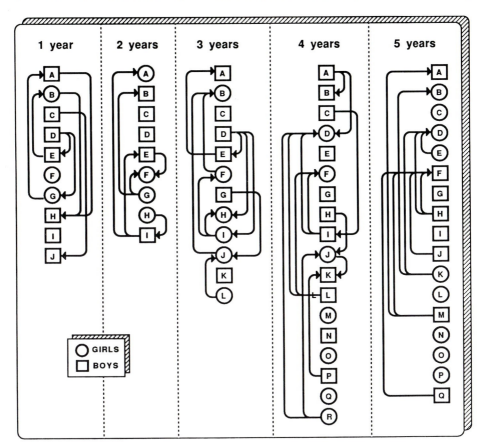

Figure 7-4   Coordination of affiliative choice and position in the group dominance structures for the first year sample.

DISCUSSION

These developmental studies were conducted from the standpoint that group processes of social regulation provide a better understanding of diversity in forms of social participation than mere individual activity profiles. Our investigation of social regulation involved an analysis of social sequences as well as of differential allocation of behavior to other members of the peer group. The examination of differences in activity level between age groups indicated that the 1- and 2-year-olds were substantially less active than the three older groups. Moreover, these older groups exhibited greater differences in the relative production of affiliative and agonistic activities, affiliation being by far their most important activity. Principal component analysis of our six categories revealed, for all age levels, two qualitatively different forms of social participation. The obtained clustering of these categories on the extracted factors suggested the labels affiliative and agonistic activity.

Although these dimensions were differentiated for all age levels, our cross-sectional analysis indicated a developmental shift in their relative importance. For the groups of 1- and 2-year-olds, the three categories of agonistic activity were the primary source of convergence in dyadic allocations. This indicates that agonistic activity is a well-established form of social participation at that age. However, an incomplete association of the positive forms of social activity with a second factor suggested that affiliation in these groups would be described best as a developmentally emerging dimension of social life. With the 3-year-olds, the most important changes concerned a greater convergence of affiliative categories and their emergence as the principal dimension. In the groups of 4- and 5-year-olds, changes consisted essentially of further differentiation between the two forms of social participation.

These findings are in agreement with results already published by Strayer (1980b, 1981): while a dominance hierarchy is well established by 1 and 2 years of age, a network of affiliative relations is not so clearly defined between group members. Individuals, at those ages, are capable of exerting their dominance over specific members of the group by attacking, threatening, or competing with them, but they still cannot successfully coordinate the multiple forms of affiliative behavior with particular play partners. At 1 year of age, for example, approached partners will eventually be attacked or contacted with equal probability.

The progressive convergence of affiliative categories, evidenced somewhat before 3 years of age, appears to parallel the formation of secondary attachment relations with same-age partners. Both same-age group analyses and intragroup factorial stability suggest that a major developmental challenge around 2 years of age is the control of synchrony and reciprocity in affiliative transactions over time. Although more positive forms of social participation are eventually established, occasional conflicts between friends over environmental resources are not precluded. As shown in our analyses, competition maintains a significant relation with affiliative categories throughout the preschool years. With age, however, the association of competition with aggression decreases, suggesting that in groups of older children competition is less likely to lead to social dispersion among interacting children.

Concerning the development of convergence between the affiliative categories two points deserve further discussion here. The first is the steady and important increase of "orientation" as a defining element of its class. Since the "orientation" category was always recorded in the context of social interactions, this finding suggests that, as children age, they increasingly rely upon visual contact to initiate, respond to, or maintain affiliative interactions. The second point concerns the ceiling effect obtained with the category contact. From 3 years of age on, this category retains the same moderate association with its class, suggesting that, in older peer groups, contact serves as a less frequent means of maintaining positive social involvement with other group members. Moreover, in one of our older groups, individuals tended also to attack those whom they contacted. Because in older groups, attackers are generally dominant over their targets, contacts recorded during these play episodes may represent attempts to control the targets' actions.

In general, the findings from these studies provide empirical support for the theoretical classification proposed over 10 years ago by Strayer (1980b).

Affiliative and agonistic activities are defined in our factor analyses by the same categories as those found in the original behavioral inventory under these two broad headings.

A possible limitation of the present research is the number and kind of behavioral categories observed. In the context of our developmental study, these categories were chosen because they were observable at all age levels. They do not represent the full complexity of social life throughout the preschool years. In a similar study, Strayer et al. (1985) included in their analyses forms of visual monitoring, nonverbal signals, and instances of object-exchanges. They reported a strong relation between these forms of social activity and other behaviors that were identified as components of the affiliative repertoire in the present study. In analyses of social involvement among 4- and 5-year-olds, "offerings" and "takings" were both related to the affiliative component. However, in subsequent analyses of 4-year-olds, taking formed an independent aspect of social involvement; for the older group, taking and offering both had their main loadings on a factor that was unrelated to the affiliative dimension. Apparently, there was greater reciprocity in object-exchanges among these older children, and these forms of interaction were relatively independent of established friendship patterns.

Answers to the questions addressed in this research will require additional studies of children functioning in other social and developmental contexts. It is well established that even at a very young age, both the interpersonal and the cultural environments are likely to have a direct impact on the production and organization of social activity (see Cairns 1979).

In daycare centers, teachers are important sources of socialization. Their conceptions of how peer interactions should be regulated have a direct bearing on the group's social life. For example, some teachers believe that children should not be allowed to claim possession of toys and instead should be encouraged to share objects with interested playmates. Another example is the belief that children should be separated when conflicts occur and/or asked to negotiate verbally and reconcile their interpersonal differences. Clearly, if these, or similar behavioral prescriptions are imposed by a majority of adults in the milieu of young children, we might expect systematic variation in the developing form and function of early peer activity.

Such issues foreshadow the more central question in ethological study: how cultural variants differentially shape the developing social skills of young children. The extent to which the social development of children can be modified by socio-cultural factors remains to be explored in future research on early peer adaptation. However, an extension of the present ethological approach to other social and cultural contexts will help sort out both the common and unique aspects of early social development. Such research would begin to trace developmental transformations in the nature of peer participation and early social competence. This information would eventually provide a more solid basis for evaluating specific developmental needs and their expression at different age levels.

Dominance relations have already received considerable attention in ethological research. The present study extends on past findings by demonstrating the existence of group dominance structures at a much earlier age, and by providing a concurrent analysis of the coordination of social dominance with affiliative behaviors. In particular, we are finding that the coordination of affiliative activity with dominance differentials is of an emerging nature, so that, toward the end of the preschool period, group dominance relations may have a number of generalized consequences in regulating a large variety of social behaviors.

Vaughn and Waters (1980) argued that if ranking were "convergent"—i.e., based on a large variety of independent behavioral variables—a broader definition of social dominance would be necessary, one encompassing a larger set of asymmetrical exchanges. Our results indicate that such an extended definition would be unlikely to apply at all age levels. Even though many behavioral indices of dyadic dominance have not been included in our developmental perspective, the present findings suggest that the significance of social dominance evolves with the increasing social skills of the peer group members. Clearly, a child's prior experience, including that with peers in a structured context, should contribute directly to his or her ability to adjust behavior strategically in order to adapt to later social situations. For example, learning to inhibit fear responses to attacks from peers might ultimately lead to a rise in the child's dominance rank.

A child who is more skillful in coordinating his or her social behavior with peers, may be better able to develop friendships and ultimately solicit allies during social conflict. Such children could enhance both their affiliative relationships and dominance rank within the peer group, simultaneously. Recent analyses of triadic conflict among 5-year-old children indicate that strategic intervention in the conflict of other group members is influenced by affiliative bonds between the various participants (Strayer and Noël 1986). Such preliminary findings suggest that Chase's (1979, 1980, 1981) recent demonstration of the importance of tripartite interaction for the emergence of linear dominance hierarchies during group formation, might also be extended to account for the developing coordination of affiliative choices and social dominance toward the end of the preschool period. Perhaps among the more sophisticated 5-year-olds, dominance rankings no longer reflect individual differences in the ability to win during dyadic conflict, but rather individual differences in the ability to identify and exploit common social resources.

Such speculation suggests that differences in peer group rank during the preschool period may contribute to individual differences in later acquisition of social skills. These secondary differences might eventually bear upon children's abilities to assure optimal control of social resources. This, in turn, could eventually influence individual reproductive success. Early peer group structures may provide concrete learning experiences which facilitate the acquisition of interactive, representational and planning skills that are universal prerequisites for successful integration into a functioning adult society. The attractiveness of dominant 5-year-olds may reflect a tendency for higher-ranking children to become more salient as affiliative partners. However, the opposite could also hold. Perhaps popular children rise in dominance rank because of their greater ability to establish "social contracts" of mutual aid with their peers. The answers to such questions can only be provided by longitudinal research which traces social adaptation across various peer groups during the course of individual development.

SUMMARY

Ethological research on children's social behavior has traditionally focused upon the identification of socially directed action patterns described in terms of observable body movements. For analytical purposes, such events are usually reclassified with respect to presumed antecedents or consequences in order to clarify processes of individual adaptation or to describe basic forms of group structure. However, few researchers have validated the internal coherence of such general functional or causal categories. None have examined age changes in the associations between behaviors subsumed in such larger analytical classes.

Our research examined the dyadic distribution of six categories of social behavior between members of 10 preschool groups ranging in age from 1 to 5 years. Principal component analyses of the dyadic allocation of social activity revealed two independent factors for all groups. Age-related changes were evident both in the importance of each factor for predicting dyadic participation, and in the convergence pattern of observed behavioral categories with respect to the identified factors.

In general, our analyses indicated that a functional classification of social activity as cohesive or dispersive was appropriate at all age levels. Agonistic exchanges ending with submission revealed linear dominance hierarchies at all age levels. In each group, certain children attracted more affiliative attention, and thus appeared as more popular individuals. The reception of affiliative gestures from peers increased as a direct function of dominance rank only at the two older age levels.

These empirical findings indicate that social dominance is developmentally the earliest stable dimension of peer group social organization and that cohesive activities are increasingly coordinated with dominance rank toward the end of the preschool years. These results are discussed in terms of ontogenetic processes which may underlie the structuring of social interaction during early peer socialization, and ultimately contribute to the patterning of social relationships later in life.

REFERENCES

Abramovitch, R. 1976. The relation of attention and proximity rank in preschool children, pp. 153–176. In *The Social Structure of Attention*, M. Chance and R. Larsen, eds. London: Wiley.

Abramovitch, R. and F. F. Strayer. 1978. Preschool social organization. Agonistic spacing and attentional behaviors, pp. 67–127. In *Recent Advances in the Study of Communication and Affect*, Vol. 6, P. Pliner, T. Kramer, and T. Alloway, eds. New York: Plenum Press.

Alexander, B. K. and E. Roth. 1971. The effect of acute crowding on aggressive behavior of Japanese monkeys. *Behaviour* 36:773–790.

Altmann, J. 1974. Observational study of behavior: Sampling methods. *Behaviour* 49:227–267.

Bernstein, I. S. 1970. Primate status hierarchies, pp. 71–109. In *Primate Behavior: Developments in Field and Laboratory Research*, L. Rosenblum, ed. New York: Academic Press.

Blurton-Jones, N. 1972. Categories of child–child interactions, pp. 97–127. In *Ethological Studies of Child Behavior*, N. Blurton-Jones, ed. Cambridge: Cambridge University Press.

Cairns, R. B. 1979. *Social Development: The Origins and Plasticity of Interchanges*. San Francisco: Freeman.

Chance, M. R. A. and C. J. Jolly. 1970. *Social Groups of Monkeys, Apes and Men*. London: Jonathan Cape.

Chase, I. D. 1979. Models of hierarchy formation in animal societies. *Behavioral Science* 19:374–382.

———. 1980. Cooperative and non-cooperative behavior in animals. *American Naturalist* 115:66.

———. 1981. Social interaction: The missing link in evolutionary models. *The Behavioral and Brain Sciences* 4:237–238.

Crook, J. H. 1970. Social organization and the environment: Aspects of contemporary social ethology. *Animal Behaviour* 18:197–209.

Gariépy, J. L. and F. F. Strayer. 1983. Relations dyadiques entre attention sociale et comportements sociaux chez *Saimiri sciureus* en captivité. *Biology of Behavior* 8:345–358.

Hartup, W. W., J. A. Glazer, and R. Charlesworth. 1967. Peer reinforcement and sociometric status. *Child Development* 38:1017–1024.

Hinde, R. A. and J. Stevenson-Hinde. 1976. Towards understanding relationships: Dynamic stability, pp. 451–479. In *Growing Points in Ethology*, P. Bateson and R. Hinde, eds. Cambridge: Cambridge University Press.

Hold, B. 1977. Rank and behavior: An ethological study of preschool children. *Homo* 28:158–188.

Kummer, H. 1968. *Social Organization of Hamadryas Baboons*. Basel: Karger.

———. 1971. *Primate Societies: Group Techniques in Ecological Adaptation*. Chicago: Aldine.

LaFrenière, P. J. and W. R. Charlesworth. 1983. Dominance, affiliation and attention in a preschool group: A nine-month longitudinal study. *Ethology and Sociobiology* 4:55–67.

McGrew, W. C. 1972. *An Ethological Study of Children's Behavior*. New York: Academic Press.

Missakian, E. A. 1976. Aggression and dominance relations in peer groups of children six to forty-five months of age. Paper presented at the Annual Conference of the Animal Behavior Society, Colorado, June.

———. 1980. Gender diferences in agonistic behavior and dominance relations of Synanon communally reared children, pp. 397–413. In *Dominance Relations: An Ethological View of Human Conflict and Social Interaction*, D. R. Omark, F. F. Strayer, and D. G. Freedman, eds. New York: Garland STPM Press.

Parten, M. B. 1932. Social participation among pre-school children. *Journal of Abnormal Psychology* 24:243–269.

Savin-Williams, R. C. 1976. An ethological study of dominance formation and maintenance in a group of human adolescents. *Child Development* 47:972–979.

———. 1980. Dominance and submission among adolescent boys, pp. 217–229. In *Dominance Relations: An Ethological View of Human Conflict and Social Interaction*, D. R. Omark, F. F. Strayer, and D. G. Freedman, eds. New York: Garland STPM Press.

Seyfarth, R. M. 1977. Social relationships among adult female monkeys. *Journal of Theoretical Biology* 65:671–698.

———. 1980. The distribution of grooming and related behaviors among adult female vervet monkeys. *Animal Behaviour* 28:798–813.

Sluckin, A. and P. Smith. 1977. Two approaches to the concept of dominance in preschool children. *Child Development* 48:917–923.

Soczka, L. 1973. Ethologie sociale et sociométrie: Analyse de la structure d'un groupe de singes crabiers (*Macaca fascicularis irus*) en captivité. *Behaviour* 50:254–269.

Strayer, F. F. 1980a. Social ecology of the preschool peer group, pp. 165–196. In *The Minnesota Symposium on Child Psychology*, Vol. 13, W. A. Collins, ed. Hillsdale, NJ: Lawrence Erlbaum Associates.

———. 1980b. Child ethology and the study of preschool social relations, pp. 235–265. In *Friendship and Social Relations in Children*, H. C. Foot, A. J. Chapman, and J. R. Smith, eds. New York: John Wiley and Sons.

———. 1981. The organization and coordination of asymmetrical relations among young children: A biological view of social power, pp. 33–49. In *Research Methods in Bio-politics*, Vol. 7, M. Watts, ed. San Francisco: Jossey-Bass.

Strayer, F. F., A. Bovenkerk, and R. F. Koopman. 1975. Social affiliation and dominance in captive squirrel monkeys (*Saimiri sciureus*). *Journal of Comparative and Physiological Psychology* 89:308–318.

Strayer, F. F., T. R. Chapeskie, and J. Strayer. 1978. The perception of preschool social dominance relations. *Aggressive Behavior* 4:183–192.

Strayer, F. F. and P. J. Harris. 1979. Social cohesion among captive squirrel monkeys (*Saimiri sciureus*). *Behavioral Ecology and Sociobiology* 5:93–110.

Strayer, F. F. and J. M. Noël. 1986. The prosocial and antisocial functions of preschool aggression: An ethological study of triadic conflict among young children, pp. 107–131. In *Altruism and Aggression: Biological and Social Origins*, C. Zahn-Waxler, E. M. Cummings, and R. Iannotti, eds. New York: Cambridge University Press.

Strayer, F. F. and J. Strayer. 1976. An ethological analysis of social agonism and dominance relations among preschool children. *Child Development* 47:980–988.

Strayer, F. F., O. Tessier, and J. L. Gariépy. 1985. L'activité affiliative et le réseau cohésif chez les enfants d'âge préscolaire, pp. 291–308. In *Ethologie et Développement de l'Enfant*, R. Tremblay, M. Provost, and F. F. Strayer, eds. Paris: Stock.

Vaughn, B. and E. Waters. 1980. Social organization among preschool peers: Dominance, attention and sociometric correlates, pp. 359–379. In *Dominance Relations: An Ethological View of Human Conflict and Social Interaction*, D. R. Omark, F. F. Strayer, and D. G. Freedman, eds. New York: Garland STPM Press.

———. 1981. Attention structure, sociometric status and dominance: Interrelations, behavioral correlates and relationships to social competence. *Developmental Psychology* 17:275–288.

Weisfeld, G. E. 1980. Social dominance and human motivation, pp. 273–286. In *Dominance Relations: An Ethological View of Human Conflict and Social Interaction*, D. R. Omark, F. F. Strayer, and D. G. Freedman, eds. New York: Garland STPM Press.

Weisfeld, G. E., D. R. Omark, and C. L. Cronin. 1980. A longitudinal and cross-sectional study of dominance in boys, pp. 205–216. In *Dominance Relations: An Ethological View of Human Conflict and Social Interaction*, D. R. Omark, F. F. Strayer, and D. G. Freedman, eds. New York: Garland STPM Press.

8

Variability in the Patterns of Agonistic Behavior of Preschool Children

CAROL LAUER

INTRODUCTION

Behavioral plasticity is a basic part of the primate adaptation. This quality is one of the reasons that our order has been so successful. Primate aggressive behaviors are among those that follow a flexible pattern varying through time and space in individuals and in populations.

Aggression has been defined as "'behavior directed toward causing physical injury to another individual,' or sometimes 'behavior where the goal is physical injury to another individual'" (Fedigan 1982:72). Knowing what is the intent or goal of an animal, however, can be impossible. Wilson has said (as noted in Chapter 1, this volume) aggression is "a physical act or threat of action by one individual that reduces the freedom or genetic fitness of another" (Wilson 1975:577). This, too, is problematic since, except in extreme instances, measuring a reduction of freedom or of fitness is difficult. Because of these problems the term agonistic activity is often used. An agonistic act is any behavior relating to conflict situations whether assertive or submissive. It can involve attack, retreat or defense (Wilson 1975; Fedigan 1982).

Primates and other animals sometimes are characterized by dominance hierarchies, based on predictable patterns of winning and losing agonistic encounters. These patterns derive from the predictable outcomes of dyadic conflicts: animal A usually wins encounters with animal B. They may also become an aspect of group structure so that all the animals in the group can be ranked in terms of who tends to win over whom. Predictable dyadic relationships, however, do not necessarily imply such a group dominance hierarchy (Hinde 1978). Winning is often defined in terms of priority access to desirable objects, but since this consequence is sometimes hard to witness in the field, researchers frequently use interaction criteria to judge dominance (Rowell 1974). If animal B cowers at animal A, animal A is judged the winner. The development of dominance relations does vary within species: for example Strum (1982) in work with olive baboons at Gilgil does not find a dominance hierarchy among males, while Smuts (1985) also working with olive baboons finds a linear (transitive) hierarchy.

The vocabulary of sociobiology suggests that a cost/benefit analysis should be useful in understanding the development of these hierarchies. A benefit to high-ranking individuals may be access to scarce resources, including mates. Low-ranking animals may accept their position as a better alternative than leaving the group.

The presence of a hierarchy appears to reduce the intensity of agonistic encounters (Hinde 1978), but there is no measurable impact on the frequency of such encounters. Indeed, in many groups much agonistic activity seems to be about maintaining dominance relationships, but these encounters usually do not involve physical contact (Walters and Seyfarth 1986). Apparently some animals learn that they are unlikely to win an encounter and they give up easily rather than risk injury (Kaufmann 1983). One could argue that such interacting in terms of cost/benefit relationship (loss or injury vs. win and possible access to resources) results in hierarchies.

Many studies exist on agonistic and dominance relationships in young children. Children are, as Blurton-Jones has noted, "a handy brand of human subject that behaves rather than talks about behaving" (1972:271). These studies imply some variability in agonistic patterns. Variability is particularly apparent in the dominance ranks of males and females. In one study of dominance hierarchies, Smith (1974) observes children ranging in age from $2\frac{1}{2}$ to 4 years. He finds no clear sex differences in dominance ranking in one group of 24 children, while in another group, also of 24 children, boys rank higher than girls. In a study of a total of 34 children in two groups, Missakian (1980) finds girls and boys at high, middle and low ranks, with girls occupying more high ranks than do boys (seven vs. four). The children range in age from 7 to 45 months. Waterhouse and Waterhouse (1973), in contrast, study 20 nursery school children, and find a dominance hierarchy for boys but cannot obtain a hierarchy for girls. The ages of the children are not given.

Rank is not necessarily related to frequency of participation in agonistic encounters. A high-ranking child may be involved in fewer encounters than a low-ranking child (Strayer and Strayer 1978). The literature consistently states that boys are more aggressive than girls, i.e., participate in more agonistic encounters (Dawe 1934; Waterhouse and Waterhouse 1973; Maccoby and Jacklin 1974; Smith and Green 1975). However, given the importance of learning in shaping human behavior, and given that boys and girls can learn different lessons about the costs and benefits of agonistic behaviors, some variability in the comparative levels of male and female aggressiveness would also be expected.

Variability in the frequency of participation in agonistic encounters is rarely seen, however, because most studies on young children involve observations on only one or two groups. Interpreting the divergent pictures of dominance hierarchies is also difficult because again most studies are based on one or two groups and because different researchers have used different definitions of dominance and different methodologies. There are a few notable exceptions to the rule of small samples, including the work of the Strayers (Strayer and Strayer 1976, 1978; Strayer 1980) on five groups of 3–6-year-old French Canadian children (see also Chapter 7, this volume) and Smith and Green's (1975) study of 15 groups of $2\frac{1}{2}$–5-year-old English nursery school children. The current study of 12 groups of children seeks to augment this literature. Its focus is first on exploring the variability in male and female participation in agonistic encounters and then on explaining variability in dominance hierarchy formation.

METHODOLOGY

Sample Subjects

The data to be discussed were collected from four groups of children in the United States at daycare centers, and eight groups in Israel at kibbutzim. The children ranged in age from 1.5 to 4 years, but in any one group the age spread was one year or less. Data were collected on Israeli kibbutz children because they become part of stable peer groups during their first year of life. These groups are ideal settings for the development of stable social relationships since members are together for many hours a day and group membership is constant for years. On a typical kibbutz, children are assigned to a children's house when they are about 2 months old. Each "house" has five to 10 children of about the same age. Although the teacher or metapelet ("house mother," pl. metapelot) of the group changes once a year, the rest of the group remains constant. In six of the eight kibbutz groups observed for this study, the children were together from 0730 h to 1600 h six days a week. At 1600 h they returned to their parents' homes. In two of the kibbutz groups the children were at the children's house from 0800 h until noon.

For comparative purposes, observations were made at four American daycare centers. Groups were selected that were relatively small in size and constant in membership, and that met five times a week for the duration of the working day. The stability of these groups never approached that seen on the kibbutz: new children joined the groups as the study progressed, others left for vacations and others only attended intermittently.

Groups ranged in size from five to 26 children, with a mean size of nine. As mentioned, the Israeli groups had five to 10 children. The American groups consisted of from 13 to 26 children, but because of intermittent attendance, no more than 14 children were present at one time.

Observational Procedures

Data were collected by six observers. Observers used pen and paper or tape recorders while sitting in full view of the children. Observers did not respond to children's approaches and after a few days these virtually ceased. Observers scanned the group continually and recorded all instances of agonistic activity. This procedure corresponds to Altmann's "sampling all occurrences of some behavior" (Altmann 1974:247) and works best with infrequently occurring events. It also requires excellent conditions for observation (Altmann 1974), which daycare centers and children's houses meet since the children are usually in one room and there are few obstructions to vision. Care is taken in constructing the space to maximize the teachers' or metapelot's ability to monitor the children's behavior.

Finally, sampling all occurrences works best when behavioral events are attention-attracting, so that the observer is unlikely to miss them (Altmann 1974). This is usually the case with agonistic encounters, but some occurrences are subtle. The probability of noticing these subtle events decreases as the group size increases, and the observer must, therefore, scan a larger population. The most subtle, and, therefore, the most easily missed interactions involve a submissive gesture made in response to no apparent threat. For example, child A walks past child B, and child B cowers before child A.

For this study, agonistic encounters were defined as interactions where one child threatened or attacked another child or elicited a submissive gesture from another child. All observers were given a list of aggressive and submissive gestures. These were culled from a review of the literature on agonistic acts among children and from preliminary observations. Aggressive behaviors listed were similar to those outlined by Strayer and Strayer (1976) and included physical attacks such as hits, hair pulls, bites, kicks, chases; threats (with no actual physical contact), and face and body postures, including lips forward, head forward or bobbed forward, chin out (Blurton-Jones 1972), and raised fist. Finally, seizing objects, usually toys, from another child was considered a class of aggressive activity as was seizing a position (Strayer and Strayer 1976). Submissive behaviors included expressions and actions such as fear grimaces (e.g., a cry face), cowering, a variety of cries, pulling away, dropping to the ground, and fleeing. A displacement, where child A approaches child B, and child B walks away was not considered an agonistic encounter unless child B made a submissive gesture before or while walking away. Figures 8-1 and 8-2 show a typical dominance interaction with an aggressive action followed by submissive behavior.

Observers did not use checklists, but wrote narrative descriptions of agonistic events. Observers were instructed to include in their descriptions identification of all participants and of initiators, a description of the actual conflict, including aggressive and submissive gestures, body contact, the subject of the interaction, and any interference by teachers. These narratives were compressed into a coded format. A child was judged the winner of an agonistic encounter if he or she elicited a submissive behavior from another child. Most interactions were dyadic, as is typical in young children (McGrew 1969; Smith 1974; Bronson 1975), but if more than two children were involved, the encounter was recorded as a series of dyadic interactions.

For error analysis, observers were shown a 45-minute videotape and asked to describe all occurrences of agonistic behavior. There was a 90% agreement between observers on what was viewed. Since the author coded all material, an independent check was done on coding error by having a naive coder review a sample of observations. There was a 91% agreement between the two samples.

RESULTS

Taking all 12 groups together, a total of approximatey 3,200 agonistic encounters were recorded over 916 hours of observation.

Turning first to an examination of the contrasts between male and female

Figure 8-1 Child on right hits child on left. (Photograph by Eva Saloman.)

Figure 8-2 Child on left cowers and makes a cry face. (Photograph by Eva Saloman.)

Table 8-1 Numbers of Boys and Girls Seen Participating in Agonistic Encounters. Data normalized to include 100 encounters in a group where number of females equals number of males.

Group	Males	Females
Israeli groups		
A*	146.8	53.2
B*	151.2	48.8
C*	154.3	45.7
D*	113.8	86.2
E	100.2	99.8
F	107.1	92.9
K	92.1	107.9
L	96.8	103.2
Mean	122.8	77.2
S.D.	26.1	26.1
American groups		
G	104.2	95.8
H	91.1	108.9
I	114.3	85.7
J*	135.1	64.9
Mean	111.2	88.8
S.D.	18.6	18.6

* Chi-square tests of goodness of fit indicate a significant difference between males and females at the 0.05 level.

agonistic patterns, Table 8-1 demonstrates that, on the average, males participate in more agonistic encounters than do females. These data have been adjusted so that they represent groups that consist of equal numbers of males and females who have perfect attendance records and who have participated in 100 agonistic encounters. Chi-square tests of goodness of fit indicate no significant differences at the 0.05 level between male and female participation in agonistic encounters in four of the Israeli groups and three of the American groups. In three groups, two Israeli and one American, girls actually participate in more encounters than do boys. The differences, however, are not significant. On the average, contrasts are greater between males and females in the Israeli groups than in the American groups. This may be due to cultural differences but 12 groups is an insufficient sample for firm generalizations. What can be said is that for more than half of these groups boys are no more frequent participants in agonistic encounters than are girls.

A related measure of aggressiveness is initiation of agonistic encounters. Even if girls and boys are involved in an equal number of agonistic encounters, it may be that boys are initiating encounters with girls forcing the girls to participate. If this is the case, the stated relative frequencies of agonistic encounters for males and females underestimate the differences between the sexes.

Table 8-2 shows initiators of male–female encounters. The table indicates that on the average males do initiate more encounters than do females, and that the

Table 8-2   Initiators of Encounters Involving Both Sexes. Data normalized
to include 100 encounters.

Group	Males	Females
Israeli groups		
A	59	41
B	53	47
C	61	39
D	61	39
E	48	52
F	60	40
K	54	46
L	62	38
Mean	57	43
S.D.	5.0	5.0
American groups		
G*	67	33
H	60	40
I*	71	29
J*	71	29
Mean	67	33
S.D.	5.2	5.2

* Chi-square tests of goodness of fit indicate a significant difference between males and
females at the 0.05 level.

contrasts are more dramatic among American groups than among Israeli groups. Chi-square goodness of fit tests indicate, however, that in nine of the groups, eight Israeli and one American, the differences are not significant. The messages of Tables 8-1 and 8-2 are the same: great intergroup variability.

The data on agonistic encounters were also used in the completion of 12 dominance matrices, one for each study group. Figure 8-3 displays a typical matrix. Winners of agonistic encounters were plotted against losers, and the children's names were arranged in the order that minimized the number of entries below the diagonal. These matrices are useful in examining dominance relationships in children because children seem to exhibit, as do many other primates, linear hierarchies. Linearity implies that, for all possible trios, if A dominates B and B dominates C, then A also dominates C. Children may also develop consistent and, therefore, predictable dominance relationships. This means that if child A is the winner of an agonistic encounter with child B today, child A is also likely to win an encounter tomorrow, or next week. This is called the rigidity of the hierarchy (Strayer and Strayer 1976). The percentage of dyadic events above the diagonal is a reflection of both linearity and rigidity. The order of the children's names alongside the matrix indicates their relative rank. The child listed at the top is the one most likely to win encounters.

These matrices can be used as a starting point in examining several factors producing variability in the dominance hierarchies of children. The first line of investigation demonstrates how variability in the sexual dichotomy of agonistic

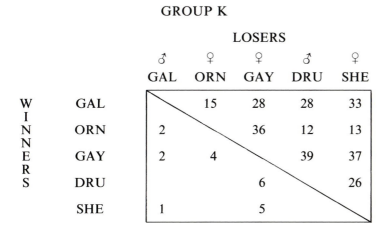

Figure 8-3 Sample dominance matrix.

behavior affects the nature of the dominance hierarchies. The second analysis shows how nonagonistic factors such as group stability and teacher interference influence the structure of the hierarchies.

As stated in this chapter's introductory section, many studies demonstrate that boys are more aggressive than girls; however, this does not mean that in every group of human children boys hold higher ranks than do girls. In the 12 study groups, while boys, on the average, rank above girls, both sexes hold high, low and intermediate ranks. As Table 8-3 indicates, in four of the groups the average ranks of males and females are virtually the same. Variability is, again, the rule.

Children's groups also vary in the rigidity and linearity of their hierarchies. Table 8-4 demonstrates this variability for the 12 study groups. Column 1 lists the percentage of encounters above the diagonal, that is the percentage explained by a linear and rigid hierarchy. In one group, Group E, a significant difference does not exist between the number of encounters above and below the diagonal. Column 2 gives the degree of linearity for each group. These percentages vary between 90 and 100% indicating moderate variability. Column 3 gives the degree of rigidity for each group and shows a wide range, from 63 to 93%. Not included in these percentages are the agonistic encounters where no winner could be determined: cases where the teacher interfered before the children concluded their encounter, cases where the threatened child did not respond, cases where the observer could not see the end of the interaction, and ties. Winners could not be determined in an average of 17% of the encounters in a group.

It was hypothesized that the linearity and rigidity of a group's hierarchy are not randomly determined. Two factors were identified as likely contributors to or at least correlates of linearity and rigidity. These factors were consistency of group composition and noninterference of teachers in encounters. The former was measured for each group by the number of hours the average child was present. This is expressed as a percentage of total observation time. A teacher's interference was measured by the number of agonistic encounters where such interference was

Table 8-3   Average Rank of Males and Females in Dominance Hierarchies.

Group	Male average rank[a]	Female average rank[a]
Israeli groups		
A	1.5	4.0
B	3.5	4.7
C	2.5	5.5
D	3.5	5.5
E	3.0	3.0
F	3.5	3.5
K	2.5	3.3
L	4.6	6.4
Mean	3.1	4.5
S.D.	0.9	1.2
American groups		
G	5.5	5.5
H	8.8	9.0
I	6.2	7.8
J	8.4	10.9
Mean	7.2	8.3
S.D.	1.6	2.3

[a] 1 is the highest rank.

Table 8-4   Linearity and Rigidity of Dominance Hierarchies.

Group	Above diagonal (%)	Linearity (%)	Rigidity (%)
Israeli groups			
A	73	100	73
B	78	95	80
C	88	93	89
D	91	100	91
E	62	90	63
F	87	100	87
K	93	100	93
L	93	100	93
Mean	83	97	84
S.D.	11.2	4.0	10.8
American groups			
G	79	93	86
H	81	97	85
I	75	94	82
J	69	96	84
Mean	76	95	84
S.D.	5.3	1.8	1.7

Table 8-5   Stability of Group Membership. Data expressed as a percentage of the total observation time during which the average child was present.

	Group	Time present (%)
Israeli groups		
	A	94
	B	88
	C	85
	D	73
	E	89
	F	98
	K	94
	L	94
Mean		89
S.D.		7.8
American groups		
	G	72
	H	48
	I	54
	J	43
Mean		54
S.D.		12.7

recorded, expressed as a percentage of the total number of agonistic encounters. Table 8-5 gives attendance figures and Table 8-6 interference figures for each group. A multiple regression formula was calculated, and Y or the percentage of entries above the diagonal in the dominance matrix was estimated to be equal to $80.7 - 0.409 X_1 + 0.223 X_2$, where $X_1 =$ percentage of teacher interference in agonistic encounters and $X_2 =$ mean percentage of attendance time. An F statistic was used to test the hypothesis that R^2, or the amount of variation explained by the regression plane, was equal to zero. $R^2 = 63.1\%$ and the hypothesis of equality to zero was rejected. An F statistic was also used to test the hypothesis that X_2 or mean attendance time does not significantly improve the fit of the multiple regression equation. That hypothesis was rejected at the 0.05 level of confidence. Attendance was tested with this statistic since it explains less variability than does X_1, the percentage having teacher interference.

A multiple regression formula was also calculated using degree of rigidity of the dominance hierarchy as Y, and interference and attendance as X_1 and X_2. The estimated formula is $Y = 89 - 0.205X_1 + 0.764X_2$ and $R^2 = 71.7\%$ and an F statistic rejected the hypothesis that $R^2 = 0$ at the 0.05 level of significance. An F statistic could not, however, reject at the 0.05 level the hypothesis that $X_2 = 0$, where $X_2 =$ mean attendance time. Distinguishing degree of rigidity from degree of linearity is clearly worthwhile but in some cases difficult to do. As the studies of many researchers have demonstrated (e.g., Missakian 1980; Strayer 1980; Vaughn and Waters 1980), children do not have absolutely rigid hierarchies. In an

Table 8-6   Interference by Teachers in Agonistic Encounters. Data expressed as a percentage of encounters in which teachers interfered.

Group	Encounters (%)
Israeli groups	
A	45
B	44
C	60
D	14
E	74
F	48
K	30
L	21
Mean	42
S.D.	19.9
American groups	
G	22
H	29
I	39
J	48
Mean	34
S.D.	11.4

absolutely rigid hierarchy, child A always receives submissive gestures from child B; the reverse never happens. The effects of linearity as opposed to those of rigidity are easily confused and can best be distinguished where a substantial number of encounters have been recorded for each dyad. Seventy-four per cent of the relationship reversals revealed in the 12 study groups involved between one and four dyadic encounters. Given the lack of rigidity in children's dominance hierarchies, these data are not sufficient for distinguishing linearity from rigidity. Indeed four of the six groups with the highest average number of encounters recorded per dyad were among the groups with the most linear hierarchies. The multiple regression formula calculated using linearity percentages and the F statistics calculated from this formula are, therefore, not reliable. The simple percentage of interactions above the diagonal in the dominance matrices is a better estimate of the predictability of the outcomes of dominance interactions.

A final set of tests was done on the dominance matrix data. In all groups, a significant majority of agonistic encounters were initiated by higher-ranking children who had sought out lower-ranking children. One possible interpretation of such an initiation pattern is that children have some perception of the existence of these hierarchies, or at least of dyadic relationships, and it influences their behavior. It was hypothesized that if children have some perception of the consistency or predictability of the hierarchy, or at least of individual dyadic conflicts, a correlation should exist between percentage of predictability (measured by the percentage of encounters above the diagonal of the dominance matrix) and the percentage of encounters begun by higher-ranking children. That is, where outcomes of agonistic encounters are less predictable, low-ranking children should initiate more of these encounters with higher-ranking children. A significant correlation does exist. The correlation coefficient was estimated to be 0.806 which is significant at the 0.05 level.

These data have not been analyzed in a way that demonstrates that child A, who ranks far above child Q will have an easier time winning an agonistic encounter with child Q than will child P, who ranks immediately above child Q (see Sade, Chapter 3, this volume). Data from other sources, however, suggest that the children themselves see the relationship of A and Q as different from the relationship of P and Q. Smith (1988) summarizes studies where preschool children are asked to rank their classmates in terms of "toughness" or "strength." The rankings done by different children correlate significantly, and these rankings, in turn, correlate with rankings made from researchers' observations of dominance encounters.

DISCUSSION

Although dominance hierarchies exist in some groups of young children, the data indicate that participation of children in agonistic interactions varies dramatically from group to group. The literature on children's behavior reveals a wide range of factors which influence participation in agonistic events. Among these factors are the prior histories of the children and the nature and history of the group itself. For example, Patterson et al. (1967) suggest that older siblings influence patterns of aggression. A child who has an older sibling is more likely to initiate agonistic encounters than is an only child. Parents also have an impact on aggressive acts by allowing or discouraging these behaviors in the home. Smith and Connolly (1972) demonstrate that the size of the group affects children's interactions. In larger groups children participate in more same-sex interactions.

An analysis of costs and benefits to the individual is useful in understanding the variability in dominance structures and in the agonistic patterns of children. From their parents, their siblings, their friends and their teachers, boys and girls learn the costs and benefits of participating in agonistic encounters. The benefits to children involve access to people, places and things. The costs of participation may include disciplining by parents or teachers as well as the risk of loss and even injury. These are costs and benefits unlikely to relate directly to inclusive fitness, but children may learn strategies of agonistic behavior that can prove adaptive in later years.

By giving attention to boys and not to girls for agonistic activity, teachers actually encourage boys to fight. Boys are, on the average, more aggressive than girls (probably in part a result of biological differences), but much room for variability exists. Boys and girls may learn different lessons about the costs and benefits of agonistic encounters. Teachers may deliver these lessons. Although Smith and Green (1975), based on a study of 15 preschool groups, find no significant difference in teachers' responses to male–male, male–female or female–female agonistic encounters, Serbin et al. (1973) and Brownlee and Bakeman (1981) show that teachers respond negatively more frequently to aggressive behavior in boys than they do to such behavior in girls. Teachers gave attention to boys and not to girls for agonistic activity, and thus actually encouraged boys to fight.

As noted earlier in this study, the contrasts between boys and girls in frequency of initiating agonistic encounters were greater in American groups than in Israeli groups (see Table 8-2). When interviewed, the Israeli metapelot said they did not consider girls to be less aggressive than boys. In one group a metapelet was frequently seen encouraging an 18-month-old girl to assert herself in agonistic encounters. In contrast, in several American groups teachers were seen telling girls that "girls do not fight." Boys and girls were taught different lessons about the costs and benefits of agonistic activity. The variability of teacher interference in the agonistic encounters of children, and their attitudes toward these encounters, may contribute to intergroup differences in the frequencies of male and female agonistic behaviors.

In looking at factors influencing the linearity and rigidity of dominance hierarchies, this study has focused on the pattern of interference by teachers and the stability of group composition. These factors also have an impact on the costs and benefits of participation in agonistic encounters. Deag (1977), in a discussion of aggression and submission in nonhuman primates, argues that there is no reason to predict linear hierarchies under all conditions. Individuals behave in ways to maximize their inclusive fitness and minimize their loss of fitness. Theoretically, all individuals may benefit from established dominance–submission relationships since these relationships save time and energy and reduce the risk of injury (Kaufmann 1983). But since submission may involve loss of a resource, willing submission—i.e., giving up without much of a fight—should depend on the quality of the resource and the probability of winning. Since these factors are not constants, dominance structures change.

There are also costs and benefits to accepting the consistent dominance relationships that suggest a rigid hierarchy. Intensity of agonistic encounters may diminish as a result of consistent dominance relationships, but low-ranking children are going readily to give up favored toys and locations to high-ranking children. If teachers interfere in a significant number of encounters, winning and losing become unpredictable, and a hierarchy does not develop. In such a situation, it is always worthwhile to fight hard, because winning is always possible. Also, if the population of the group is unstable, a hierarchy does not become apparent. In a hierarchy, children must learn their places. If they are infrequent or intermittent visitors, it is unlikely that they will do this. Those children who are constant attenders, if they are a minority of the group, are involved in frequent encounters with unknown children. This again produces circumstances where learning dyadic relationships is difficult. They could develop consistent dominance relationships with other constant attenders, but the data demonstrate that they do not. Perhaps, children do not expend the extra effort necessary to establish dominance with other constant attenders because it would have little impact on their general access to toys and favored spots. The predictable encounters might only be a small percentage of the total number of encounters in any one day.

Making inferences about the agonistic behavior of adults from the behavior of these children is difficult. As Howe (1989) states, a link is supposed to exist between child-rearing techniques, value systems and levels of violence within a society but ". . . the link between these and levels of aggression or peacefulness has not been demonstrated very convincingly, and the nature of the link has not been analyzed in detail" (Howe 1989:107). Ross (Chapter 11, this volume) and Dentan (Chapter 10, this volume) begin this analysis.

One can speculate about the links between childhood and adulthood with respect to agonistic behavior. We cannot easily examine long-term hierarchies and their consequences because children's preschool groups do not last a long time. The appropriate long-term study is certainly not possible in the United States. Kibbutz children live in a more stable environment and their groups show more continuity. One metapelet I interviewed was working with her second generation of children. Her casual observation was that children who were high-ranking at age 2 or 3 were still high-ranking in high school. In discussing her current group of children, we concurred on our identification of the highest-ranking children. This impressionistic evidence is hardly a scientific study, but it does suggest long-term consequences in a stable population.

Another connection between adults and children can be tentatively drawn. I would predict that dominance hierarchies do not exist in children's groups in "peaceable societies" (e.g., Semai, Utku, some Zapotec) because in peaceable societies the pattern seems to be that adults consistently stop children from fighting (Briggs 1978; Dentan 1978, Chapter 10, this volume; Fry 1988). This is analogous to the situation in American and Israeli groups where teachers frequently interfere in fights. The nature of the interference is no doubt different, but its effects on hierarchies should be similar.

Fry (1988) for example studied two communities of Zapotec-speaking people in Oaxaca, Mexico. One, La Paz, was a community with few homicides, and with values that supposedly discourage violence. In La Paz parents did not approve of fighting among children and discouraged it. In San Andres, violence was more prevalent, and it included wife-beating and public fighting. Here people thought "that a certain amount of fighting and play fighting was just part of the nature of children" (Fry 1988:1016). One father was even seen encouraging his daughter to hit her brother (Fry 1988).

I suspect that hierarchies can develop in cultures that resemble San Andres and, because of consistent interference, cannot and do not develop in cultures like that found in La Paz. In Israeli and American culture, where children are not consistently discouraged from fighting, hierarchies may develop. Israel and the United States also provide children with many models for aggressive behavior. In Israel even a wait in a grocery store line or at a gasoline station frequently involves agonistic encounters.

What does it do to the mentality of children when they see adult aggression frequently and are allowed to test and evaluate each other in terms of who is toughest? Although I agree with Howe (1989) that demonstrating the link convincingly is problematic, I suspect that these experiences prepare children for a life where toughness matters. While it is true that not all very young Americans or Israeli young children are involved in groups where hierarchies can develop, most will be involved in schools by age five (see Edelman and Omark 1973), and schools provide excellent circumstances for the development of hierarchies.

In peaceable societies, where agonistic encounters are not just interrupted but are diligently stopped, children must use other means to evaluate each other, and perhaps adults do so as well. In more violent societies, hierarchies are a reflection of high levels of agonistic activity, but then they reinforce the attitudes that produce those high levels. The system perpetuates itself.

SUMMARY

Data are discussed on agonistic encounters in 12 groups of children, four from daycare centers in the United States and eight from kibbutzim in Israel. These data are used to demonstrate variability in male and female participation in agonistic encounters and variability in the formation of dominance hierarchies. Information provided on participation in agonistic encounters shows that in some groups boys are more frequent participants, but in other groups girls have this distinction. The same pattern holds for initiation of male–female encounters. In actuality, in nine of the groups the differences between male and female initiation rates are not significant. Dominance matrices constructed for each of the groups show that while on the average boys rank above girls, both sexes can and do hold high, low and intermediate ranks. These dominance matrices reveal that in some groups the outcomes of agonistic encounters are more predictable than in other groups. Group instability and amount of teacher interference in encounters are among the factors that reduce the consistency of outcomes.

The variability observed in agonistic patterns and relationships demonstrates that they are shaped by personal and group history. These histories are in turn shaped by cultural differences. Boys and girls learn about the costs and benefits of aggression at home and from peers. These lessons influence their participation in agonistic encounters. Because a variety of agonistic patterns is seen, biologically shaped differences in male vs. female agonistic behavior do not seem to be great.

Children also learn that the interference of teachers can make the outcome of agonistic encounters unpredictable. Outcomes are also unpredictable if the group is unstable in composition. A basic similarity exists between the effects of frequent teacher interference and the effects of inconsistent group membership on the agonistic behavior of children. Under either condition, children do not learn dominant or subordinate roles. In the study groups marked by frequent teacher interference and/or inconsistent group membership, the outcomes are unpredictable even when teachers do not interfere or when the encounters are between children who are constant attenders. In the groups that do exhibit hierarchies either the children who become dominant are trying harder in certain agonistic encounters, or the children who become subordinate are giving up more easily. The patterns of initiation in all the groups studied also suggest learned behaviors. High-ranking children are more likely to initiate agonistic encounters with lower-ranking children than with higher-ranking children.

None of these results for agnostic encounters would have been apparent without data from a large sample of groups. Because of the importance of learning in the behavior of even young children, meaningful conclusions about agonistic patterns or the development of hierarchies are only possible with data gathered from a series of groups.

REFERENCES

Altmann, J. 1974. Observational study of behavior: Sampling methods. *Behaviour* 49:227–267.

Blurton-Jones, N. G. 1972. Non-verbal communication in children, pp. 271–296. In *Non-Verbal Communication*, R. A. Hinde, ed. London: Cambridge University Press.

Briggs, J. L. 1978. The origins of nonviolence: Inuit management of aggression (Canadian Arctic), pp. 54–93. In *Learning Non-aggression. Experience of Non-literate Societies*, A. Montagu, ed. Oxford: Oxford University Press.

Bronson, W. C. 1975. Developments in behavior with age mates during the second year of life, pp. 131–152. In *Friendship and Peer Relations*, M. Lewis and L. Rosenblum, eds. New York: John Wiley.

Brownlee, J. R. and R. Bakeman. 1981. Hitting in toddler-peer interaction. *Child Development* 52(3):1076–1079.

Dawe, H. 1934. An analysis of 200 quarrels of pre-school children. *Child Development* 5:139–157.

Deag, J. M. 1977. Aggression and submission in monkey societies. *Animal Behaviour* 25:465–474.

Dentan, R. K. 1978. Notes on childhood in a nonviolent context: the Semai case (Malaysia), pp. 94–143. In *Learning Non-aggression. Experience of Non-literate Societies*, A. Montagu, ed. Oxford: Oxford University Press.

Edelman, M. S. and D. R. Omark. 1973. Dominance hierarchies in young children. *Social Science Information* 12(1):103–110.

Fedigan, L. M. 1982. *Primate Paradigms*. Montreal: Eden Press.

Fry, D. P. 1988. Intercommunity differences in aggression among Zapotec children. *Child Development* 59:1008–1019.

Hinde, R. A. 1978. Dominance and role: Two concepts with dual meanings. *Journal of Social and Biological Structures* 1:27–38.

Howe, L. E. A. 1989. Peace and violence in Bali: culture and social organization, pp. 100–116. In *Societies at Peace*, S. Howell and R. Willis, eds. London: Routledge.

Kaufmann, J. H. 1983. On the definitions and functions of dominance and territoriality. *Biology Reviews* 58(1):1–20.

Maccoby, E. E. and C. N. Jacklin. 1974. *The Psychology of Sex Differences*. Stanford: Stanford University Press.

McGrew, W. C. 1969. An ethological study of agonistic behavior in pre-school children, pp. 146–159. In *Proceedings of the Second International Conference on Primatology*, Vol. I, C. R. Carpenter, ed. Basel: Karger.

Missakian, E. 1980. Gender differences in agonistic behavior and dominance relations of Synanon communally reared children, pp. 397–414. In *Dominance Relations*, D. R. Omark, F. F. Strayer, and D. G. Freedman, eds. New York: Garland.

Patterson, G. R., R. A. Littman, and W. Bricker. 1967. Assertive behavior in children: A step toward a theory of aggression. *Monographs of Social Research in Child Development* 32:1–43.

Rowell, T. 1974. Concept of social dominance. *Behavioral Biology* 11:131–154.

Serbin, L. A., D. K. O'Leary, R. Kent and I. Tonick. 1973. A comparison of teacher response to the pre-academic and problem behavior of boys and girls. *Child Development* 44:796–804.

Smith, P. 1974. Aggression in a pre-school playgroup: Effects of varying physical resources, pp. 97–104. In *Determinants and Origins of Aggressive Behavior*, J. deWit and W. Hartup, eds. The Hague: Mouton.

Smith, P. 1988. The cognitive demands of children's social interactions with peers, pp. 94–110. In *Machiavellian Intelligence*, R. W. Byrne and A. Whiten, eds. Oxford: Oxford University Press.

Smith, P. and K. Connolly. 1972. Patterns of play and social interaction in pre-school children, pp. 65–96. In *Ethological Studies of Child Behavior*, N. G. Blurton-Jones, ed. London: Cambridge University Press.

Smith, P. and M. Green. 1975. Aggressive behavior in English nurseries and play groups: Sex differences and response of adults. *Child Development* 46:211–214.

Smuts, B. B. 1985. *Sex and Friendship in Baboons*. New York: Aldine Publishing Company.

Strayer, F. F. 1980. Social ecology of the pre-school peer group, pp. 165–196. In *The Minnesota Symposia on Child Psychology*, Vol. 13, *Development of Cognition, Affect and Social Relations*, W. Collins, ed. Hillsdale, NJ: Lawrence Erlbaum Associates.

Strayer, F. F. and J. Strayer. 1976. An ethological analysis of social agonism and dominance relations among pre-school children. *Child Development* 47:980–989.

Strayer, J. and F. F. Strayer. 1978. Social aggression and power relations among pre-school children. *Aggressive Behavior* 4:173–182.

Strum, S. C. 1982. Agonistic dominance in male baboons: An alternative view. *International Journal of Primatology* 3:175–202.

Vaughn, B. and E. Waters. 1980. Social organization among pre-school peers, pp. 359–380. In *Dominance Relations*, D. R. Omark, F. F. Strayer, and D. G. Freedman, eds. New York: Garland.

Walters, J. R. and R. M. Seyfarth. 1986. Conflict and cooperation, pp. 306–317. In *Primate Societies*, B. B. Smuts, D. L. Cheney, R. M. Seyfarth, R. W. Wrangham, and T. T. Struhsaker, eds. Chicago: University of Chicago Press.

Waterhouse, M. and H. Waterhouse. 1973. Primate ethology and human social behavior, pp. 669–688. In *Comparative Ecology and Behavior of Primates*, R. Michael and J. Crook, eds. New York: Academic Press.

Wilson, E. O. 1975. *Sociobiology, The New Synthesis*. Cambridge: Harvard University Press.

9

Cultures of War and Peace:
A Comparative Study of Waorani and Semai

CLAYTON A. ROBARCHEK   AND   CAROLE J. ROBARCHEK

INTRODUCTION

The explanation of human violence and war has, in recent years, come increasingly to occupy the attention of social and behavioral scientists. In anthropology, the most influential of the resulting theories have offered final cause explanations that focus on factors largely external to human consciousness and purposes: on adaptations to ecological parameters and on presumed biologically based propensities of one or another sort, especially the maximization of inclusive fitness.

This chapter presents some preliminary results of a research project that was designed to address one of the limitations widely acknowledged by both critics and supporters of these ecological and sociobiological hypotheses: their difficulties in accommodating human motivations, the proximate causes of human behavior (see, for example, Orlove 1980; Johnson 1982; Barkow 1984). The field research examined the motivational context of warfare in an Amazonian society, seeking to define the psychological and sociocultural contexts of warfare—the complexes of values, beliefs, attitudes and goals that constitute the motivational context within which violence and warfare were perceived as legitimate and desirable options, and the social forms through which they are manifested.

Assessing the significance of psychological and sociocultural factors independent of ecological and biological constraints presents a methodological problem that we have addressed by employing a comparative approach and two phases of research. The first phase was an intensive ethnographic study of the Waorani (more commonly known as "Auca"), a people of the Ecuadorian Amazon who, with a homicide rate of the order of 60% over the past several generations, are the most warlike society yet described (cf. Yost 1981). The field research was conducted during the period of January through December 1987, and concentrated on documenting the psychological, social, cultural, and ecological contexts of Waorani warfare. The second phase, which is now underway, involves the qualitative and quantitative analysis of these data against the comparative background of a similar body of data on the Semai Senoi, an aboriginal people of the Malaysian rainforest, data which we had previously collected during two field studies in 1973–1974 and in 1979–1980. The Semai are apposite for this comparison because their ecological setting—the physical environment and their technological adaptation to it—and important aspects of their social organization are remarkably similar to those of the Waorani, and yet violence, either among themselves or between them and outsiders, is virtually unknown. Controlled comparison of Semai and Waorani adaptations to their tropical forest milieux thus allows us to take advantage of one of the rapidly vanishing "natural experiments" in human cultural adaptation, a strategy often advocated but seldom realized in anthropological research.

DATA COLLECTION AND ANALYSIS

The collection and analysis of the data involved the following four operations.

Construction of a Model of Waorani Cultural Activities

This was based on data derived principally from generalized participant observation and from a daily activity survey. The survey consisted of a structured interview schedule in which every resident over the age of 5 years was interviewed each evening according to a structured format that included questions on activities undertaken, assistance and commodities given and received, the participants in these activities and interactions, the kinds and amounts of goods and services exchanged, and the receipt and expenditure of money.

This survey produced a body of systematic data on the material and behavioral aspects of daily life and on social relations: patterns of cooperation, sharing, reciprocal and nonreciprocal assistance, and so on, a body of quantitative data suitable for comparison with a similar corpus of data from our earlier studies among the Semai.

Construction of a Model of Waorani Social Relations

Genealogies were collected and kin relations defined for the residents of the two primary settlements where we worked, and these were extended to include residents of most of the other communities on the Waorani Reserve as well. Data from the daily activity survey yielded patterns of cooperation, reciprocal and nonreciprocal assistance, gift giving, and so on. Focused interviews provided information on the composition of raiding parties and the relationships among raiders and victims. We also examined the relations between residence groups and between the Waorani and the cowodi—Indian and non-Indian "foreigners." This included documenting the movements of individuals and households and the development of political leadership and processes growing out of the activities of cultural "brokers"—Waorani, missionaries, and members of other indigenous groups who are intermediaries in the continuing process of acculturation. These data, together with data derived from structured and unstructured interviews, the documentation of household composition and visiting, and of patterns of marriage and residence, are being synthesized to generate a model of the organization and content of significant social relations.

Construction of a Model of Waorani World View

The objective here is to derive the cultural beliefs, values and attitudes that inform individual motivational complexes. We gathered the data necessary to this operation by the application of several techniques that we had successfully employed in our earlier research on the Semai. Focusing our observations particularly on religious rituals and beliefs, ethnomedical beliefs and behaviors, gender definitions, sex-role behaviors, childhood socialization, and conflict, we employed participant observation, informal but focused interviews with informants, and other sources (e.g., attitudes and values expressed during the activity survey) to explore the assumptions, beliefs, values, and psychological orientations that underlay the warfare complex (cf. Robarchek 1977a, b, 1979b, 1986). In investigating conflict, we also collected and tape recorded numerous firsthand accounts of specific raids that directly involved members of the study groups either as perpetrators or as victims (and in some cases, both, when we were able to interview both the attackers and the victims in a particular raid). Most of this case material still awaits transcription and translation, but the limited analysis thus far completed shows this material to be a valuable source of data on attitudes, value orientations, and motivations directly related to warfare.

Comparison of Results of Above Operations with Comparable Semai Models already Derived

The objective of the previous operations was to provide us with a holistic but structured model of the interrelationships among psychological, social, and cultural constructions which, taken together, constitute the meaningful context within which Waorani were motivated to engage in warlike and aggressive behavior, a model which can be compared with a similarly structured model of the motivational context of nonviolence among the Semai (cf. Robarchek 1977a, 1979a, b, 1986, 1988, 1989, 1990). The ultimate goal of the project is, through the comparison of these models, to reveal the similarities and differences in their organizations, structures, and internal dynamics, in order to discover how the relations among these factors eventuate in the two diametrically opposed patterns of warfare and nonviolence that are characteristic of these two, otherwise very similar, societies.

The analyses and comparisons of these data are still in a preliminary stage, but even the initial comparisons reveal that, while the ecological settings, settlement patterns, technology, subsistence practices, kinship and social organizations (and presumably biology) of these two societies are remarkably similar, the psychologically and culturally constituted realities within which they make their lives are profoundly different. This paper compares these differing constructions of reality, focusing particularly on aspects of the world views and self-images of these two groups—especially their contrasting conceptions of the nature of human beings and the relationships among them—and explores the implications of these differences for their radically divergent attitudes toward human violence, and for the behaviours that these attitudes engender.

THE SEMAI

The Semai are among the most peaceful people known. Physical violence of any sort is extremely uncommon: adults do not fight, husbands do not beat their wives nor parents their children, and homicide is so rare as to be virtually nonexistent (see Dentan 1968, 1978; Robarchek 1977b, 1979b, 1986, 1989; Robarchek and Dentan 1987).[1]

At the time of our first study in 1973–1974, there were about 13,000 Semai living in small, politically autonomous bands whose populations seldom exceeded 100, scattered along the deep rainforest-covered valleys that dissect the mountainous spine of the central Malay Peninsula. Each band occupied a well-defined territory—usually a segment of a small river valley or a segment of a larger one—with which it was identified: "they of the Sata' River," "we of the Lengkok River," and so on.

Although a great many changes have occurred in the intervening years, at that time many bands in the less accessible highland and deep forest areas still persisted in following a largely traditional way of life based on hunting and swidden gardening, although they were being increasingly drawn into the economy and politics of the Malaysian state. The ethnographic present in the description that follows refers to conditions that obtained in the Batang Padang district of Perak State in the early 1970s, when we conducted our first field study.

Subsistence is based on swidden cultivation, with dry rice and sweet manioc as the staple crops. Moving every few years to exploit mature forest, settlements cycle over their restricted territories in a 20–30 year rotation. Manioc provides the bulk of the calories, and both the leaves and tubers are eaten. Small quantities of corn, bananas, melons, eggplant and other vegetables are also grown, but these are of minor importance in the total diet. Horticultural technology is extremely simple—machetes, axes, and dibble-sticks. Native trees are also cultivated, especially *durian* and *petai*, and much of the fruit is sold to traders from the lowlands. This provides most of the cash income that is used to purchase parangs, axes, sarongs, tobacco, sugar and, ever increasingly, transistor radios, flashlights and all the other luxuries that are rapidly becoming necessities.

Animal protein comes from hunting and trapping of small game—rodents, birds, monkeys, and so on—using blowpipes and poisoned darts and a variety of small snares. Larger game such as pigs and deer are occasionally taken with spear traps or noose traps and now, more commonly, with shotguns. Game is not plentiful, so the available animal resources are intensively exploited: snakes, bats, lizards, turtles, snails, frogs, toads, all go into the cooking pots, and a variety of grubs and insects of various sorts are also gathered in season. Fishing with hooks and lines, traps, and poison is also important, especially on the larger rivers.

Aboriginally (and during our first field study) there was no use of alcohol or other drugs, and Semai traditionally feared and avoided the sensations of disorientation associated with any kind of intoxication (see Robarchek and Dentan 1987).[2]

Kinship is traced bilaterally, and the most important kin group is the ego-centered kindred, although a ramage-like unit also exists, possibly emerging as response to the development of kin-based territories as trade in durian and petai to the lowlands has become increasingly important (C. J. Robarchek 1981). The kindred is a primary reference group that should be consulted in matters of importance such as marriage and residence changes, and that has the responsibility of overseeing ego's behavior and of supporting him in disputes. Fear of censure by the kindred acts as a major constraint on the behavior of individuals (Robarchek 1979a, 1986).

Marriage within the band is common, even preferred in some groups, although it is often precluded by the small sizes of bands and the incest taboo on marriages between those who share a grandparent, thus neighboring bands are linked by ties of kinship and affinity. Polygynous marriage occurs but is not common.

Residence is ambilocal, and residence units vary from single households scattered over a band's territory to hamlets where the entire band resides. With the exception of a few large villages that have resulted mainly from government resettlement schemes, populations of these settlements seldom exceed 100, and most are in the range of 50 to 75 people. Households often consist of two or more siblings and their spouses, or parents and one or more married children, but they often include more distantly related individuals (or even unrelated friends) and their spouses and children. Settlements move every few years, as available soil, game and other nearby resources are depleted.

Bands are politically autonomous and essentially acephalous, although each has a largely hereditary (and now government certified) headman. The headmanship has been strengthened by, if it did not originate in, the occasional necessity of dealing as a unit with the politically dominant lowland peoples. Within the band, the headman exercises some moral authority as spokesman for the group but his exercise of that authority is essentially limited to his own powers of persuasion (Robarchek 1979b). On the relatively rare occasions when community-level decisions are required, they are reached through protracted discussion and consensus (Robarchek 1979b, 1990).

THE WAORANI

In a notably violent part of the world—the western Amazon basin—the Waorani, called "Auca" (savage) by their lowland Quichua neighbors, were among the most feared. Until the late 1950s, there were no regular peaceful contacts with other groups, and they and their neighbors raided each other incessantly. They numbered only about 500 people and, unlike the surrounding groups, possessed no firearms. Nevertheless, their 9 ft palmwood spears and their well-deserved reputation for ferocity allowed them to maintain control over an immense territory, some 8,000 square miles of deep valleys and dense rainforest, from which they drove out or killed all who entered or attempted to settle. Like the Semai, they are linguistically and, to some extent, culturally distinct from the surrounding peoples. Their language (Auca) is apparently unrelated to any other in the region, and their enforced isolation was so complete that, at the time of the first peaceful contacts in the late 1950s, linguists could identify only two cognates with any other language (Peeke 1973).

Scattered over their vast territory in widely dispersed settlements, each essentially an extended family band, they also raided each other almost constantly. Blood feuds and vendettas arising from past killings, quarrels over marriage arrangements or accusations of sorcery were a way of life, even among closely related bands. Based on extensive genealogies collected in the 1970s, Yost (1981) calculated that more than 60% of adult deaths over the past 5 generations were the result of warfare, 17% as a consequence of external raiding and 44% from internal feuding. The genealogies that we collected yielded comparable estimates for the precontact period. In the 1960s, after peaceful contacts had been established by a group of American Protestant missionary women, a reserve comprising less than 10% of the traditional Waorani homeland was established by the Ecuadorian government, and most of the Waorani were persuaded to resettle on it. Several bands still remain off the reserve, and at least one continues to resist all contact.[3]

Like Semai, the Waorani are swidden gardeners and hunters. They live in the dense equatorial rainforest on an uplifted and deeply dissected plateau that lies at the foot of the Andes at the headwaters of the Amazon in eastern Ecuador. Sweet manioc and plantains are the staple garden crops. The starchy fruit of the cultivated chonta palm also provides a substantial portion of the diet for several months of the year. All three of these staples are converted into liquids by boiling and mashing, and the bulk of the calories are consumed in this form. Small quantities of corn, peanuts, and other vegetables are also grown but are not of great importance in terms of the total diet.

Animal protein is provided by hunting small game—toucans, parrots, marmosets, monkeys, and the like—with blowpipes and poisoned darts. Large game such as peccary, deer, and tapir are hunted with spears and, increasingly, with shotguns. Game is relatively plentiful, even in the vastly reduced area of the reserve, and little use is made of the small animals and invertebrates that are so important for the Semai, although some large grubs and swarming leaf-cutter ants are collected as delicacies.

As was the case with the Semai, alcohol use was unknown aboriginally. Unlike surrounding groups, Waorani allow none of their drinks to ferment to alcohol. Manioc mash is allowed to sour for a day or two but is discarded when it begins to turn alcoholic. Also unlike the surrounding groups, there is no communal use of drugs, although the solitary use by sorcerers of *Banisteriopsis muricata* (a vine closely related to the *ayuhuasca* widely used in the region) is suspected and probably actually occurs. Similar use, by sorcerers, of a psychoactive fungus is also reported (Davis and Yost 1983).

Like the Semai, Waorani trace kinship bilaterally, but there is no all-encompassing kindred in the sense that it exists for the Semai: no group of kin who have significant obligations to and responsibilities for one another and who collectively constrain each other's behavior.

Bilateral cross-cousin marriage is prescribed. As with the Semai, postmarital residence is ambilocal, but prior to contact it may have been primarily uxorilocal (see Yost 1981). Polygyny was previously common but is discouraged by the missionaries and, while it still occurs, is much less common than in the recent past.

Traditionally, the Waorani lived in small hamlets, widely dispersed over their vast territory. Within this territory, there were four major, largely endogamous, regional subgroups marked by minor dialect differences, each occupying a portion of the larger territory and hostile to all the others. While bonds of kinship and affinity link the members of settlements in a particular area, for Waorani these are as likely to be sources of conflict as of unity, and the component bands were usually hostile to many of the others within the subgroup as well.

Residence units, like those of the Semai, vary from single households to hamlets of a dozen or more family groups. One very large settlement of several hundred people has grown up around the village where Rachael Saint, one of the missionaries who made the first peaceful contact in 1958, has established her residence. This settlement—with an infirmary, church, school, airstrip, and resident population of inmarrying Quichua—is a center for increasing acculturation. The rest of the population is scattered over the reserve in smaller settlements of much the same size range as those of the Semai, i.e., generally fewer than 100 people.

Household composition is also very similar to that of the Semai, typically consisting of a group of siblings and their spouses or a couple and their married children. Traditionally, all would have lived together in a single large house, and a number of these communal households still exist. Until recently, each of these settlements would have been hidden from the others, but today a network of footpaths link the dispersed communities on the reserve. Increasingly, the traditional residence pattern survives within larger settlements as extended family house clusters—married siblings or parents and married children living in a cluster of nuclear family households.

In the past, settlements moved frequently (over ranges much larger than those of Semai settlements) to exploit new hunting and gardening territories and, especially, to escape retaliatory spearing raids. As feuding and raiding have ceased, settlements have become larger and more permanent. This stability has also been the result of the construction, in several settlements, of clearings where the small, single-engine planes of the Missionary Aviation Fellowship can land. These flights transport sick and injured Waorani and other Indians to the missionary hospital located off the reserve in Shell Mera. They also bring school teachers to several settlements, bring in occasional government officials, and carry small amounts of cargo, thus providing a major link to the outside world. Households still move within these locales as old houses deteriorate and sentiments realign. Additionally, most families have at least one secondary residence with associated gardens in another valley a day or so's walk from the primary residence. Single families or entire extended family groups move to these secondary settlements for periods ranging from several weeks to several months to plant and harvest their gardens, and to fish and hunt.

The larger settlements centered on the airstrips are mostly artificial aggregations, resulting from the resettlement process. They are composed of distantly related or unrelated extended families that traditionally would have constituted separate, widely dispersed, and probably mutually antagonistic hamlets. Within these aggregated settlements, the household clusters retain their autonomy. There is little or no sharing or cooperation among them, community-wide decisions are seldom taken, and very rarely does the community act as a unit. The Sunday meetings in the Christian settlements and the periodic banana-drinking feasts are virtually the only occasions when these aggregations constitute a social unit.

The isolated extended family residence pattern is still represented in the smaller hamlets, but even there autonomy is the norm and family elders have but limited influence over the actions of their adult or adolescent kin.

Waorani settlements, like those of the Semai, are politically autonomous and essentially acephalous. There is no headmanship, even in the restricted sense of that institution among the Semai, although political leaders, many of them women, are emerging in the larger settlements where they act as "cultural brokers" in transactions with surrounding groups (see Yost 1981).

THE HISTORICAL CONTEXTS OF WARFARE AND NONVIOLENCE

As Spiro (1967) has shown, the explanation of any sociocultural phenomenon, and this includes warfare and nonviolence, must be at least in part historical, an explanation of the social and cultural contexts within which the phenomenon originally arose in the social group under investigation. In this case, that would require specification of the historical conditions that gave rise to these two patterns of peacefulness and violence. Unfortunately, and as is often the case, the historical data that would be necessary to explicate these origins simply do not exist for these two societies (but see Dentan (Chapter 10, this volume), for the kind of explanation that would be required and for a hypothesis persuasive in the Semai case).

In the case of Waorani warfare, we cannot say with any confidence how, when or why it came into being, since no reference to a group that can be unambiguously identified as Waorani occur before the turn of this century. Nevertheless, even though the historical record with specific regard to the Waorani is virtually blank, the history of the region provides some understanding of the context within which Waorani warfare must have arisen.

The Regional Culture of War

Raiding and warfare have long been endemic in the western fringe of the Amazon basin, and we can only speculate about the ultimate origins of this widespread culture of war. The earliest accounts, from the beginning of the Spanish colonial era and even before, describe the bellicosity of the inhabitants of the region. Inca attempts at colonization were repelled by the Jivaros and others, as were the early incursions by the Spanish. In 1599, many indigenous groups united to drive all Spanish colonists from the region, sacking their cities and killing the inhabitants (cf. Harner 1972).

In the nineteenth century, the rubber boom brought major dislocations and disruptions to the native peoples. Large numbers of Indians were enslaved to work as rubber collectors and were subjected to brutal mistreatment by the Europeans and their local henchmen. Epidemics of introduced diseases swept through the indigenous populations and the mortality was enormous. The haciendas established on the major rivers at the foot of the Andes utilized what amounted to Indian slave labor to exploit the region's resources, including the alluvial gold deposits in the Andean foothills, and the hacendados supported and encouraged intertribal slave raiding.

While it is clear that warfare in the region predated large-scale European contact, the level of violence was almost certainly greatly intensified by the exploitation of the region and its inhabitants during (and following) the colonial period.[4] Moreover, differential access to the technology, especially firearms, introduced by the Europeans further exacerbated the conflicts and altered the power relationships among the various groups, encouraging some to press their advantage at the expense of others. It also presented additional incentives for raiding by the disadvantaged groups as they fought to obtain the new tools and weapons.[5] At the same time, the physical environment counterbalanced, to some extent, the advantages provided by the new technologies. The dense forests and swamps, the difficulty of the terrain, the impossibility of maintaining supply lines, all worked to resist long-term incursions into hostile territory.

In such a situation, where warfare is endemic, a people's options are rather limited: they can either flee, fight back, or be overwhelmed. Given the sociocultural environment of the region (and with no safe refuge available), engaging in at least defensive warfare becomes a functional necessity for group survival. Warfare, under these conditions, is contagious; once one group adopts it as a tactic for advancing its ends, others must either take it up or be destroyed.

Thus, while the specific conditions that underlay the origins of the regional culture of war are largely lost in time, once begun, it took on a life of its own. In such a situation, where groups seldom had the absolute superiority in technological or other resources to defeat conclusively both the forest and their enemies—to kill their men, kidnap their women, capture their children, and occupy their territory—the result is predictable: a more or less stable balance of terror with constant raiding among the various social groups.

The Waorani Culture of War

Even in this violent milieu, the Waorani were legendary. Although vastly outnumbered, they regularly attacked neighboring groups to steal machetes, axes, and, occasionally, women. The surrounding groups also raided them for women, and for children who were taken to work on the haciendas that persisted in the Andean foothills until the middle of this century.[6]

Among related Waorani bands, hostilities frequently were precipitated by disagreements arising from the Waorani practice of bilateral cross-cousin marriage. These marriages were arranged by parents, often by one parent without the knowledge or consent of the other. Thus a father, who may have agreed to marry his daughter to his sister's son, might return to his house during a banana-drinking feast to find that, in his absence, the girl had been married to his wife's brother's son. In the absence of any institutionalized mechanisms for dealing with conflicts or resolving disputes, the anger and animosities generated often led to spearing raids.[7]

Witchcraft accusations and their aftermath were another common source of lethal hostilities. Since serious illnesses were infrequent, and since most of those bitten by snakes survived, a death from either of these causes was an abnormal event that required an explanation. The explanation that was almost certain to be offered was witchcraft, probably by a relative or a member of a related band who had a grudge against the victim or his kin. The typical response was a retaliatory raid on the suspected sorcerer's household, the raiders bursting into the house at night and spearing the sorcerer and as many of his housemates—men, women, and children—as possible.

These killings, in turn, generated their own momentum, and long-term blood feuds developed between groups, motivated by the desire to avenge past killings. Following an attack, the raiders and their families would abandon their houses and fields and retreat into the forest to avoid retaliation. They would establish a new hamlet many miles away and several years might pass before a tell-tale footprint betrayed the location of the settlement to hunters from another band and led to a new cycle of killing.

The Motivational Context of Waorani Warfare

As we have seen, the historical record is insufficient to allow us to draw more than the most general conclusions concerning the origins of the Waorani warfare pattern. Even if that record were complete, however, accounting for the origin of Waorani violence would not be sufficient to explain its continued existence. We know that cultural patterns are far from immutable so, regardless of how a cultural complex came into being, any explanation of a perduring behavioral pattern must also account for how and why it persists through time. It is here that a motivational explanation is required, one that explores the cultural constructions of reality, the beliefs and values, and the psychological orientations that define the context of action within which individuals are motivated to engage in warfare.

This is the culturally constituted reality into which each new generation is born and which, through culturally patterned experience, penetrates to the very core of individual psychology. At the most fundamental levels, those of the perceptions of external reality and the attachment of meanings and significance to those perceptions, the processes are culturally informed. These systems of meanings, of values and beliefs, of symbols and significations, and the purposes that they define, constitute the definitions of reality within which human goals are generated and realized, and within which violence or nonviolence are seen as legitimate behavioral options in service of these goals.

Our objective here, by examining the similarities and differences in these two societies and exploring the relations of these to peacefulness and warfare, is to arrive at an understanding of the motivational context of Waorani warfare, its proximate cause.

COMPARATIVE ANALYSIS

In brief summary, the comparative analysis shows two societies strikingly similar in terms of their physical environments, their technological adaptations to them, and many aspects of their social organizations. But they are worlds apart in their cultural constructions of these realities—their fundamental conceptions of the nature of the world, and of human beings and their relationships to one another, and to their environments—and in the attitudes, values and behaviors generated within these psychological and cultural contexts.

Similarities

Environments, Subsistence and Technologies

Both groups are interriverine swidden gardeners, hunters and gatherers, living at similar altitudes in equatorial tropical rainforest environments. For both, sweet manioc is one of their two staple crops. Both also cultivate plantains, bananas and a number of minor crops, including corn, and both cultivate forest trees for fruit. Gardening technologies—machetes, axes, and digging sticks—are virtually identical. Protein in both societies is derived from the hunting of small and large game. Hunters in both societies take the former with blowpipes and poisoned darts and the latter with spears and, increasingly, with shotguns. Fishing with lines, nets and poisons is also important to both.

Social Organizations

Social organizations, including political organizations, descent, and residence patterns, are also strikingly similar. Both are band-level societies consisting of largely kin-based residence groups of generally fewer than 100 people. These bands, in both societies, are politically autonomous and essentially acephalous. Among both groups a previous pattern of dispersed extended family households is now being replaced, as a result of external contacts, by nuclear family households and nucleated settlements. In both societies, however, the households were, and are, the basic economic units.

Descent in both societies is bilateral, with a resulting lack of "fraternal interest groups" (as defined by Otterbein 1980) in both. In neither are there significant structural features that cross-cut kin ties to bind individuals into interdependent groups.

Both societies are highly egalitarian, with few rank differentials of any sort. In neither society does gender entail a significant distinction in rank, nor are gender roles highly differentiated in either. With no strong sex dichotomies, there are no puberty rites, men's clubs, or other associations in either society.

Polygyny is permitted but infrequent in both. Socialization in both societies is indulgent and nonpunishing; both husbands and wives tend children, and children's relations with both parents are warm and affectionate.

Differences

Environment

In general, and contrary to the predictions of ecological theories of warfare that hold resource scarcity—especially protein—to be the crucial determinant (e.g., Harris 1974, 1979; Gross 1975; E. Ross 1978, 1979; Bennett Ross 1980), the Waorani environment is much more productive than that of the Semai. In the areas of the reserve where we worked, soils are more fertile, allowing longer use of fields and shorter fallow periods. Game is also much more plentiful, even though the human population is increasing, and the reserve where most of the Waorani now live comprises less than $\frac{1}{10}$ of their traditional range (cf. Yost and Kelley 1983). The rivers are also, in general, larger and more productive. While our data on hunting and fishing productivity are as yet incompletely analyzed, it is already apparent that Waorani intake of animal protein exceeds that of the Semai by several orders of magnitude (and substantial quantities of smoked meat and fish are now exported to surrounding groups). As a consequence, Waorani do not bother to trap small animals nor do they utilize the snakes, frogs, lizards, and invertebrates that form a significant portion of Semai protein intake. Population density is also much lower among the Waorani; prior to the creation of the Waorani Reserve, Semai population density (4.1 per square mile) was approximately 68 times that of the Waorani (0.06 per square mile). Even now, on the reserve, Waorani population density is only about 1.1 per square mile, approximately one quarter that of the Semai.[8]

Semai also suffer from disease to a much greater extent than do the Waorani. Typhoid, cholera, tuberculosis, and a great many other diseases are all endemic in Southeast Asia and periodic local epidemics can literally decimate Semai settlements (one tenth of the band that my wife and I lived with died in a series of epidemics that swept through the band in the six years between our first and second field studies). Additionally, people are commonly confined for days or weeks at a time by less severe or chronic illnesses. Waorani, in contrast, are remarkably healthy. With the exception of dental problems, from which they (and the Semai) suffer terribly, they are seldom incapacitated by sickness.

The one exception to this picture of robust good health among the Waorani is snakebite. The Waorani have what may be the highest rate of snakebite mortality in the world—on the order of 5% (Larrick et al. 1978). Virtually every adult has been bitten at least once, and many two, three, or more times. Two serious snakebites occurred during our residence in the settlement where we did the bulk of our research.[9] Both victims were given antivenin and survived (although one had to be evacuated by air to the missionary hospital). Recovery time for those who survive ranges from a few days to many weeks, and scarcely a day passes in any settlement without at least one close call with a poisonous snake.

The truly fundamental differences between Semai and Waorani worlds, however, are not to be found in the material realm of animals and plants, proteins and carbohydrates, soil fertility and pathogenic organisms; they lie rather in the cultural constructions of these realities and the social, psychological and behavioral implications of those constructions. Of special concern to us is the relationship of these constructions to the motivational contexts of violence and nonviolence.

World Views

The world views of these two societies, their cultural constructions of themselves and their environments could hardly be more different. Semai see themselves as essentially helpless in a hostile and malevolent universe that is almost entirely beyond their control. Their world is populated by a vast variety of supernatural beings, the great majority of which are actively hostile to human beings. The forest world surrounding a Semai settlement is a world of unremitting danger, of violently malevolent beings and forces virtually all of which prey on humans. People are reluctant to venture alone into the deep forest away from the settlements, and no one in his right mind would spend a night alone there (sleeping alone in the forest is, in fact, seen as a primary symptom of psychosis). Nearly every element or activity, no matter how seemingly mundane or innocuous, has the potential to bring disaster and death. Imitating a bird call may bring an attack from a forest spirit who shoots illness-causing projectiles with his blowpipe; a child playing with a blackened pot may bring an attack by a thunder-spirit; discarding an empty bottle can cause a child's belly to swell. Even children playing with or laughing at the most harmless creatures—dragonflies and butterflies—will provoke an attack by Ngku, a thunder spirit who attacks with wind, torrential rain, and landslides. In this world of ubiquitous dangers, even the most ordinary activities—gardening, firewood gathering, hunting, eating, even children's play—are hedged by taboos and circumscribed by rituals in an inevitably vain attempt to ward off the dangers that constantly menace without (Robarchek 1977b; 1979a, b; 1986, 1988).

Waorani, on the other hand, live in a very different world, one which carries little danger beyond the human threats of witchcraft or a spearing raid. The surrounding forest itself holds no terrors; it is a world to be exploited. Lone individuals go off for days at a time to hunt and fish, or just to wander. There are few animistic beliefs, little concern with "supernatural" beings, and few taboos or rituals designed to ward off danger. The taboos that do exist seem to be rather lightly held; there were, for example, taboos on the eating of certain animals, most notably deer, tapir, and collared peccary, but these were quickly abandoned when the acquisition of dogs and shotguns made it possible to hunt them effectively. Taboos on giant catfish and other large river fish have similarly been abandoned as utilization of the larger rivers has increased since contact (cf. Yost and Kelley 1983). Compared with Semai, there is little emphasis on magic; there is little need for it since they see their knowledge as fully adequate to their tasks. They are, in general, a thoroughly confident and pragmatic people living in a world that they feel fully equipped to deal with and control.

Semai and Waorani perceptions of themselves and their relationships to the world and to their kin and community are similarly divergent. Semai see themselves as helpless in a malevolent world entirely beyond their control. The only protection from this danger, the only source of security and nurturance lies in the band, that group of a hundred or so human beings with whom one's life is bound up from birth to death. Without the support and nurturance of this group, no individual can survive. Anything that jeopardizes its cohesion is intolerably threatening to individuals, calling into question the only force that holds the world's malevolence at bay. Paramount cultural values stress sharing and non-aggressiveness; dependency and nurturance are major cultural and psychological themes and individual values. To be given nurturance by the community is to be given life itself; to have it denied is to be left exposed to the dangers that menace from without, a message that is constantly stressed and reaffirmed, both directly and symbolically (Robarchek 1979a, b, 1986, 1988; Robarchek and Robarchek 1988).

Waorani self-image, in contrast, is highly individualistic and autonomous; both men and women are expected to be self-reliant and independent, and they see themselves as such. While there is sharing among close kin, especially parents and children and real and classificatory siblings (parallel cousins), every person's survival and well-being is ultimately his own responsibility. Women give birth alone and unattended, and snakebite victims are sometimes left in the forest to fend for themselves. Until recently, the elderly were not infrequently speared to death by their own kin when they became a burden (we have several accounts of the spearings of old people by their own grandchildren) (cf. Yost 1981). In the event of a raid, all fled for their lives, men often abandoning their wives, and women their children (Robarchek and Robarchek 1988).

Social Relations

These differences in the cultural conceptions of the relationships of individuals to one another are clearly reflected in the content of social relations in these two societies. Although kinship is traced bilaterally in both, there are important differences in the ways that kin are classified, and in the social implications of those classifications. Thus, despite the many similarities in kinship and social organization, the psychological and behavioral contexts that these define are profoundly different.

Semai terminology is of the Hawaiian type; thus terminologically—and to some degree socially—both cross and parallel cousins are classed with siblings (and the incest taboo forbids marriage between any of these people). This creates, for any individual, a large and symmetrical kindred, with the relations of all those in the same generation conceived (ideally, at least) in terms of the obligations and responsibilities of siblingship (see Robarchek (1979a, b, 1989) for examples of this cultural ideal). Coupled with the Semai perception of the group as the sole locus of nurturance and security, the result is a strong sense of group consciousness on two levels: the kindred and the band.

The primary group orientation is toward the bilateral kindred. These are the people who have primary responsibility for one's well-being, for providing assistance in case of illness or injury, for summoning the spirit familiars in times of illness, and for coming to one's defense in disputes. Since these kindreds are ego-centered, any individual is a member of many different kindreds; obligations and responsibilities are diffuse and cross-cutting, and these ramify to encompass the entire band and beyond, since the taboo on cousin marriage forces inter-marriage between bands, expanding kindreds into neighboring bands as well.

In any conflict, either within or between bands, the kindreds of any two opposed individuals will likely include people who are members of each other's kindreds. Given the powerful affective salience of kindred and band, this minimizes the possibility of the band splitting into antagonistic mutually exclusive factions, and it provides a powerful motive for resolving disputes in ways that are as equitable as possible for all concerned (Robarchek 1979b). It also makes the prospect of open conflict within the band extremely threatening for all involved, both because it disrupts the relations of individuals to their kin and because it thus threatens the unity of the group, the sole source of security in a hostile world. Thus any individual who becomes embroiled in a dispute can expect to be reprimanded by his own kindred if he is found to have any fault in the matter, a prospect that is threatening in the extreme to most people (cf. Robarchek 1986). Kinship terminology reinforces siblingship as the central metaphor for relations within the band. "We are all siblings here and we take care of one another" is a constantly reiterated ideal (see Robarchek 1979b, 1986, 1989).

The analogues, in the supernatural world, of these protective kinsmen are the *gunik*, the familiar spirits who have come in dreams and asked to become members of the dreamer's family. They can be called upon in times of sickness and danger, to ward off the attacks of *mara'*, the malevolent spirits that cause sickness and death. These *gunik* are incorporated into the kinship system, becoming siblings of the dreamer's children, the uncles and aunts of his grandchildren, and so on. The songs that summon the *gunik* are passed from generation to generation until, after several generations, parents' and grandparents' *gunik* become, in the generational terminology of the Semai, grandparents to most of the people in the band. They become *mai mana*, "the old ones," responsible for the welfare of the entire community, protecting it from the attacking *mara'*.

Every year or so, the ties between the entire band and its spirit protectors should be reaffirmed in a three-night ceremony to which all the *gunik* are called, and during which individuals dance into trance as they are possessed by the returning *gunik*. These spirit kin symbolize and express the unity and interdependence of the band, and any human discord at this time, or at any other time when they have been called into the settlement, will offend and anger them, leading them to abandon their human kin to the malevolent forces without.

Thus, although the formal features of social organization provide little basis for group integration, Semai world view motivates a powerful affective concern with interdependence and group cohesion. This is evidenced in the extreme reluctance of individuals to become involved in disputes, and in the formal dispute-settlement procedures that are immediately called into action when any conflict emerges into general awareness, a process whose objective is less the attribution of fault than the restoration of amicable relations between the disputants and within the band as a whole (Robarchek 1979b, 1990).

Waorani social structure, like that of the Semai, provides little support for group orientation but, in contrast to the Semai, Waorani culture also provides few bases for social solidarity, little sense of group-consciousness and little concern with group cohesiveness beyond the extended family.

In many societies where there is intense external warfare, internal solidarity is promoted and mechanisms exist to restrain conflict within the group so that a united front can be presented to the outside (e.g., Murphy 1957). Among the Waorani, however, no such social or cultural mechanisms exist. With bilateral kinship, there are no lineages or clans to provide a framework for mutual obligations and support. Even the kindred is attenuated; Dravidian kinship classification and cross-cousin marriage split the kindred into classificatory parents and siblings on the one hand, and potential spouses and affines on the other, the latter being those with whom conflict is likely to occur. With no strong sexual dichotomy, there are none of the men's clubs or men's houses, so important in many other Amazonian societies, to bind individuals into interdependent groups. For the Waorani, every kindred, and in the final analysis, every individual, is an independent entity (Robarchek and Robarchek 1988).[10]

As is true for the Semai, the human world is mirrored in Waorani conceptions of and relations with the supernatural, but the image reflected and sustained is a very different one. No spirit familiars come in dreams to offer protection or assistance to their human kin. *Wengongi*, the creator who set the world in motion, has no significant role in human affairs, and human actions are thus not contingent upon or constrained by more powerful beings or forces.[11] With no tutelary spirits and few animistic beliefs, there are no communal rituals or responsibilities linking people together. With the exception of witchcraft, there is little concern given to the "supernatural." Even here, although the witch may use magical animal familiars to work his evil, the active malevolence is individual and human, and the response to it is likewise individualistic, pragmatic, and violent.

Social Control

The possibility of violent behavior by individual Semai is heavily constrained by individual and cultural values that stress nonviolence, and by the internalized need to avoid any disruption in relations within the kindred and band. When conflict does occur, social mechanisms are immediately brought into play to defuse it (Robarchek 1979b).

Among the Waorani, there are no such cultural or individual values nor is there a concern with group cohesion, and thus there are no comparable internalized controls on conflict and violence. Moreover, no institutionalized mechanisms exist for the resolution of disputes and the restoration of amity. Nothing comparable to the Semai kindred exists, in the sense of a primary reference group that acts to constrain individual behavior. There are thus few constraints, social, cultural, or psychological, on the actions of individuals.

Individual autonomy is the norm and, even within the extended family, elders have but limited influence over the actions of their kin. All this is well illustrated by a case—not atypical—described to us by an eye-witness, in which three young men—brothers and classificatory brothers—killed their paternal grandmother, bursting into her house and spearing the old woman in her hammock. Their father was furious at the killing of his mother, but did nothing. "What could he do?" our informant observed, "they are his sons."

In such a cultural, social, and psychological context—with no emphasis on nonagressiveness, with no social bases for the creation of mutual-interest groups or the suppression of self-interests, with few obligations among individuals, few integrating social mechanisms, little expectation of or interest in group cohesiveness, and no mechanisms for resolving disputes—the conflicts that are inevitable in any society, and the anger and hostility that they can engender, were given free rein. Given the pre-existing culture of violence into which each generation was born and enculturated, any dispute was likely to escalate into a killing which, in turn, called for endless retaliation.

The End of Warfare

Occasional spearings, although very infrequent, still occur among those Waorani living on the reserve, but the large-scale raiding within and without has ended. Understanding how this came about provides some important additional insights into the dynamics of warfare in this society and argues strongly against the ecological and biological theories that have dominated recent discussions of warfare in these kinds of societies.

When the first missionaries appeared as mediators between hostile groups, most Waorani were suprisingly willing to cease raiding, once they were convinced that the other groups would do the same. This transition is even more remarkable in that it occurred, at least in its initial phases, in the absence of other major changes, either inside or outside of Waorani society. There was no military conquest, social organization had not changed, and the ecological situation had not been altered. The killing stopped because the people themselves made a conscious decision to end it.

It is important to emphasize that the Waorani were not conquered, nor were they coerced into giving up warfare. The missionaries (and there were never more than a half-dozen in residence, all but one of whom were women) made the ending of warfare their highest priority, but they had no way of enforcing this goal, since they were completely without coercive authority. No troops or police were on call; the region was and is essentially beyond Ecuadorian political and military control. For the missionaries to succeed in their objective, the Waorani had to be persuaded to give up internal feuding and external raiding.

Our informants recounted how, on many occasions, Waorani themselves had tried to reduce the intragroup feuding. Individual bands had sought to make peace with their enemies, only to see their efforts fail when some long-standing grudge or newly aroused suspicion led one or another individual or group to violate the truce. Lacking were any social mechanisms either to allow initial peaceful contacts between enemies or to permit the growth of trust. There were also no social mechanisms for dealing with conflict in the service of social cohesion, nor were there cultural values promoting peacefulness. Instead, there was a world view and a value system that promoted autonomy and individualism, and that demanded blood vengeance.

What the missionaries provided were a means for establishing peaceful contacts (mediated by their technology), a new view of a world in which not all outsiders were implacable enemies and cannibals, an alternative value system that stressed nonviolence and, perhaps most important, a glimpse of a world without constant fear of violent death. One by one, over a period of several years, new groups were located from the air and, for several months, flights dropped gifts—tools, food, clothes and so on. Through loudspeakers, Waorani from contacted groups spoke to their hostile kinsmen, promising an end to the vendettas until, finally, contact could safely be made on the ground. (This was not always successful, however; the first Waorani who attempted such a contact was killed almost immediately (cf. Wallis 1973)). Still, once bands became convinced that the feuding could stop, their commitment to ending the killing (buttressed among most, but not all, individuals and groups by some of the Christian values stressed by the missionaries) became a goal in its own right, one which superseded the desire for revenge (cf. Yost, in Anonymous 1980).[12]

Social mechanisms for resolving disputes are still largely lacking, but the commitment to avoiding a return to the old pattern has become so strong a value in its own right that even when a spearing does occur there is no retaliation. When a group of young men speared an old woman to death several years ago, the woman's daughter, the politically most powerful woman on the reserve, refused even to acknowledge that her mother had been murdered. The old woman's brother, himself a renowned killer, said recently "In the old days, I would have killed them all by now, but we don't spear any more."[13] Our informants unanimously stressed their relief that the cycle of killing has come to an end. This commitment, for its own sake and on the part of the Waorani themselves, to end the killing is also evidenced in the fact that several bands on and off the reserve, whose members do not see themselves as Christians, have also given up raiding.

Once the initial peaceful contacts were established, of course, many other inducements quickly came into play. As raiding declined and peaceful contacts with the missionaries and with surrounding indigenous peoples increased, Waorani began to acquire the material goods and other products of the outside world—iron tools, shotguns, flashlights, new foods, snakebite antivenins, medical care, and so on—that their long isolation had denied them. Also, the intensity of the hostilities had left many bands without access to potential spouses of the proper kin type, and peaceful contacts with formerly hostile bands provided new marriage possibilities with former enemies (cf. Yost 1981). Increasing desire for continued access to new marriage partners and to trade goods and services certainly reinforced their commitment to ending the violence, but the speed with which the transformation from violence to peacefulness occurred, as each new group was contacted, can only be explained as a consequence of the Waorani consciously striving to achieve what they themselves wanted to do: end the killing. When the opportunity presented itself, they seized and implemented it.

DISCUSSION

This brief comparison of Semai and Waorani, provisional and incomplete as it is, nevertheless casts serious doubts on the adequacy of the most prominent current anthropological theories of violence and warfare.

Regarding the ecological-functional approaches, the "techno-environmental" (Harris 1968) circumstances of these two societies are virtually identical, and where they differ in terms of variables proposed as significant by ecological hypotheses—e.g., resource (especially protein) availability or population densities—the differences are precisely the reverse of the predictions of these hypotheses.

Sociobiological explanations fare little better. In proposing a sociobiological "theory of tribal violence," Chagnon argues that "reproductive variables must be included in explanations of tribal violence and warfare" (1988:985). In the Waorani case, however, it is difficult to see how any functional explanation, sociobiological or ecological, could be advanced, since the level of the violence—the functional dependent variable in all of these hypotheses—was so intense that it threatened the very survival of the society (with a 60% homicide rate, there were only about 500 Waorani left alive at the time of contact; since then, the population has grown dramatically). The Waorani themselves clearly recognize the effects of the warfare pattern: "We were down to almost two people," one veteran of many raids told us. "If it hadn't been for Nimo and Dayume (Rachael Saint and her first Waorani convert) we would all be dead by now."[14]

A more fundamental problem with these and many other of the current approaches to the explanation of warfare (and of human behavior in general), is that they entail a conception of human beings not as active, but as *reactive*, responding mechanically to biological or environmental (or sociological, cultural, or psychological) determinants (cf. Robarchek 1989, 1990). The comparison of Semai and Waorani, so strikingly similar in terms of their ecological situations and, presumably, their biological propensities, but so different in their behaviors, argues that human behavior is not a determined response to an "objective" reality, either ecological or biological.

Biology and the environment are most certainly relevant; they impose constraints upon and provide opportunities for the generation and realization of individual and social goals, but those constraints and opportunities are heavily conditioned by other levels. The worlds with which human beings interact are cognized worlds. Psychological and cultural information structures mediate between biological and environmental constraints and opportunities, and individual and collective behavior; they construct the realities within which purposive action takes place. The motivations of individuals and groups are not the self-evident stimulus–response reactions of a universal human psychobiology to an objective external reality but, rather, are generated in the appraisals and interpretations of situations, largely in terms of culturally given meanings (cf. Ross 1986a).

Understanding human behavior, including violence and nonviolence, requires putting the material "facts" into psychological, social, and cultural contexts, and attempting to comprehend how situations are conceptualized by the people involved. Semai and Waorani decisions, and the actions that flow from them are not incidental epiphenomena; rather, in the aggregate they *constitute* these diametrically opposed patterns of nonviolence and violence.

To return to Spiro's observation that causal explanations must account for both the origin and the persistence of sociocultural phenomena, the Waorani case shows that, whatever the historical origins of warfare in societies such as these, neither ecological adaptation nor inclusive fitness maximization is, in itself, sufficient to account for the persistence of warfare in Waorani society since, in the absence of changes in these areas, individual bands of Waorani abandoned warfare in a matter of months after contact, and virtually the entire society changed, in little more than a decade, from the most warlike yet described, to one that is essentially peaceful.

The fact that, after generations of warfare and raiding, they were persuaded almost overnight to abandon it suggests that an internal psychocultural dynamic was crucial to the maintenance and continuation of the pattern of endemic warfare. The pattern changed when new cultural knowledge—new information and new perceptions of reality—allowed the formulation of new individual and cultural values and goals. People responded by choosing courses of action based on what they wanted from this new reality.

This study thus argues for a perspective that sees people not as passive ciphers pushed this way and that by determinants external to their own consciousness, but as active participants in their own destinies, as purposeful decision-makers in pursuit of particular goals and objectives. They pick their ways through fields of options and constraints in pursuit of individually and culturally defined goals within culturally constituted realities that they themselves are actively constructing and reconstructing.

SUMMARY

This chapter presents preliminary results of a comparative study of peacefulness and warfare in two tropical forest societies. The Semai of West Malaysia are perhaps the most peaceful society known, and the Waorani of the Ecuadorian Amazon, with a homicide rate on the order of 60% over at least the past five generations, are the most warlike people yet described. While these two societies are at opposite extremes on a continuum of violence, they are nevertheless very similar in a great many other regards. Their ecological settings and their technological adaptations to them are virtually identical. Both live at similar altitudes in upland interriverine territories covered by dense equatorial rainforest, and subsist by swidden gardening of manioc and bananas supplemented by hunting, fishing, and gathering. Subsistence technologies are virtually identical: blowpipes and poisoned darts, spears, machetes (and, increasingly, shotguns), axes, digging sticks, nets, lines, and fish poisons.

The ecological differences that do exist are the opposite of those predicted by current ecological theories of warfare that see resource scarcity, especially of protein, or the need to limit populations as the crucial determinants. The Waorani environment is much more productive than that of the Semai: soils are more fertile, fish and game are much more plentiful, and Waorani population density in the precontact period was roughly $\frac{1}{68}$ that of the Semai.

Social organizations are also remarkably similar. Both are band-level societies, politically acephalous, with no significant distinctions in rank. Both are sexually egalitarian and neither has men's clubs or other associations. Both trace kinship bilaterally, and bilateral kindreds are the central structural elements in both. In neither are there significant social structural features that cross-cut kin ties to unite kindreds into interdependent groups. In both, polygyny is permitted but infrequent, the nuclear family is the minimal political and economic unit, and socialization is indulgent and nonpunishing. Biological differences, presumably, are insignificant.

There are, however, truly fundamental differences between these two societies, but they lie not in the material realm of biological propensities or proteins and calories. Rather, they are in the cultural constructions of these realities and in the social, psychological, and behavioral implications of those constructions.

The world views of these two societies, their cultural constructions of themselves and their realities, could hardly be more divergent. Semai see themselves as essentially powerless, helpless in a world of overwhelming malevolence over which they have little control. Keeping the infinite numbers of malevolent supernaturals at bay is a constant concern, and even the most mundane activities are hedged by rituals and surrounded by taboos in an effort to ward off the dangers that constantly threaten human survival.

Waorani look out on a very different world, one that holds few dangers beyond the human threats of witchcraft and raiding. There are few taboos, little magic, and little concern with the supernatural in general. People see themselves as independent and autonomous, and the world around as a place to be exploited. They are confident and pragmatic, feeling fully capable of dealing with the world on their own terms.

While social structures and organization are quite similar, the tenor and content of social relations, premised as they are on these two differing views of the world, are dramatically different. For Semai, the only source of security in an overwhelmingly malevolent world lies in the nurturance and protection of kin and community. Anything that threatens the solidarity of this group of about 100 people is intensely threatening to individuals. The prospect of open conflict is extremely threatening, disrupting social relationships and calling into question the unity of the band. When conflict emerges, institutionalized mechanisms are immediately called into play to resolve the dispute and repair the social fabric, lest individuals be left alone and defenseless against the dangers that constantly menace without.

Similarly, lacking lineages, clans, clubs, or other associations, Waorani social structure, like that of the Semai, provides little framework for constructing social solidarity. Unlike the Semai, however, Waorani culture provides little basis for group integration or group consciousness and little concern with group cohesiveness beyond the extended family. With no communal rituals or responsibilities and little expectation of giving or receiving aid and assistance, every kindred and, ultimately every individual, is a self-sufficient and independent entity.

For the Semai, the possibility of violence is further limited by individual and cultural values that stress nonviolence and affiliation. These are an important part of the motivational context of all social interaction and an important component of self-image as well, exerting a powerful constraining influence on conflict and violence and helping to constitute a reality where violence is not perceived as an option in human relations.

For the Waorani, no such individual or social values exist. There are no comparable internalized controls on conflict and violence and no institutionalized mechanisms for resolving disputes and restraining conflict. Self-reliance is an ideal and individual autonomy a norm, and there are, thus, few constraints—psychological, social, or cultural—on the actions of individuals. In such a setting, the conflicts that are inevitable in any society were, until recently, given free rein, and any dispute was likely to escalate into a killing, which called for endless retaliation.

While the Waorani culture of war is undoubtedly the historical precipitate of a violent past, most of whose details are lost to us, the maintenance and continuation of Waorani warfare depended not on biological propensities or ecological relationships, but on an internal psychocultural dynamic. This is evidenced by the fact that, in the absence of substantive changes in the material realm, Waorani society transformed itself, almost overnight, from the most warlike known into one that is essentially peaceful. The catalyst was the return of several Waorani women and girls who had previously fled to other Indian groups to escape the killing, accompanied by two American missionary women. What they provided to their society was new cultural knowledge—new information and new perceptions of reality—and the Waorani responded by formulating new goals and choosing courses of action based on them. The result was that individual bands, in a matter of months, abandoned a pattern of internal and external war that had persisted for generations.

When the perceptions of a new reality presented the opportunity to escape from the cycle of vendettas, the Waorani seized and implemented it, suggesting that human action, far from being the determined product of forces and factors external to human beings and human consciousness, is rather the result of people striving to realize their objectives within the context of realities that they themselves are constructing and reconstructing.

ACKNOWLEDGMENTS

Field research among the Waorani and the continuing comparative analysis of the Semai and Waorani data were made possible by Research Grants from the H. F. Guggenheim Foundation, whose support is gratefully acknowledged. We also wish to thank those in Ecuador who contributed to the successful completion of the field research, especially Sra. Josephina Torres de Penahererra, for her many kindnesses and her invaluable assistance, Katherine Peeke and Rosie Jung, the pilots and staff of the Missionary Aviation Fellowship, The Summer Institute of Linguistics, and the Instituto de Patrimonio Cultural.

NOTES

1. The "nonviolent" characterization of the Semai has recently been questioned by Knauft (1987), using his estimate of a Semai homicide rate. That estimate was based on reports of two killings cited by Dentan (1978) (one of which was the abandonment of a terminally ill person), and a population of 300, the size of Dentan's study community. The two cases that Dentan reported, however, represented the only known homicides in the total Semai population of some 15,000 people over nearly a generation (see also Robarchek and Dentan 1987; Dentan 1988; Robarchek 1989).

2. Now, however, with increasing acculturation, alcohol use is on the rise, especially in heavily acculturated lowland villages and among young men who have left their home settlements for wage labor, usually on plantations.

3. In 1987, while we were conducting our fieldwork, two Catholic missionaries—a bishop and a nun—were speared to death after an oil company helicopter ferried them into this group in an attempt to make contact. We also heard unconfirmed rumors of the spearings of several Indian oil exploration workers. (Also rumored are the killings of Waorani by oil workers shooting from helicopters.)

4. For a discussion of the impact of European penetration of Amazonia on indigenous warfare, see Ferguson (1990).

5. This was clearly illustrated by our Waorani informants who recounted stories of raids that they launched against neighboring Quichua for the purpose of acquiring machetes and axes.

6. With little resistance to introduced diseases, it is unlikely that many of these Waorani children survived for long. An elderly Ecuadorian woman, who spent her youth on haciendas near Tena owned by her grandfather, father, and husband, clearly remembered the capture of Waorani children "but," she recalled, "those Auca children always died from colds very soon."

7. This was so common that Yost (personal communication) recalls that he assumed

at first that the expression of rage by one or another of the fathers was simply a part of the marriage ritual.

8. For a critical discussion of the "scarce resource" argument, see Otterbein (1985).

9. Actually, there were three. One of us (C.J.R.) was also bitten, but we did not recognize it as a snakebite until much later, since the bite apparently occurred inside our house, she did not see the snake, and the fang marks were very small. Fortunately, envenomization was apparently light, but she was nevertheless delirious for several days and incapacitated for more than a week.

10. These differing perceptions of and attitudes toward kin and community are clearly expressed in other cultural beliefs and modes of social interaction, for example, in Semai and Waorani beliefs about ghosts and witches, and in differing patterns of economic exchange (see Robarchek 1988; Robarchek and Robarchek 1988).

11. Among Christian Waorani, *Wengongi* has now been largely assimilated to the Christian God, and he can now be called upon to intervene in human affairs. This is most commonly seen at the conclusion of the weekly church meetings, in prayers asking him to prevent individuals who are involved in conflicts from spearing one another.

12. We thank Katherine Peeke and Rosie Jung for sharing with us their recollections of the period of contact.

13. Our thanks to James Yost for making available to us the unpublished interview from which this quote is taken.

14. These two societies are also virtually identical in terms of other variables such as social structure, gender roles, and socialization, that have been central to recent discussions of violence and warfare (e.g., Munroe et al. 1981; Segall 1983; Ross 1985, 1986a, b). They are also strikingly similar to the Gebusi described by Knauft (1985, 1987), who argues that the lack of culturally recognized distinctions in rank among adult men predisposes societies to a particular pattern of violence, but with "variations ... influenced by interactions between ecological and culture-historical factors as well as by sociopolitical and psychological dynamics." The issue raised by these authors is beyond the scope of this paper, but they will be addressed elsewhere.

REFERENCES

Anonymous. 1980. Jungle identity crisis: Auca country revisited. *Christianity Today* 4 January: 48–50.

Barkow, J. H. 1984. The distance between genes and culture. *Journal of Anthropological Research* 40(3):367–379.

Bennett Ross, J. 1980. Ecology and the problem of the tribe: A critique of the Hobbesian model of preindustrial warfare, pp. 33–60. In *Beyond the Myths of Culture*, E. B. Ross, ed. New York: Academic Press.

Chagnon, N. 1988. Life histories, blood revenge, and warfare in a tribal society. *Science* 239:985–992.

Davis, W. E. and J. A. Yost. 1983. The ethnobotany of the Waorani of Eastern Ecuador. *Botanical Museum Leaflets, Harvard University* 29(3):159–217.

Dentan, R. K. 1968. *The Semai: A Nonviolent People of Malaysia*. New York: Holt, Rinehart and Winston.

———. 1978. Notes on childhood in a nonviolent context: The Semai case, pp. 94–143. In *Learning Non-aggression. The Experience of Non-literate Societies*, A. Montague, ed. Oxford: Oxford University Press.

———. 1988. On reconsidering violence in simple societies. *Current Anthropology* 29(4):625–629.

Ferguson, R. B. 1990. Blood of the Leviathan: Western contact and warfare in Amazonia. *American Ethnologist* 17(2):237–257.

Gross, D. R. 1975. Protein capture and cultural development in the Amazon Basin. *American Anthropologist* 77(3):526–549.

Harner, M. J. 1972. *The Jivaro: People of the Sacred Waterfalls.* Garden City, NY: Doubleday.

Harris, M. 1968. *The Rise of Anthropological Theory.* New York: Thomas Y. Crowell Company.

———. 1974. *Cows, Pigs, Wars and Witches: The Riddles of Culture.* New York: Random House.

———. 1979. The Yanomamo and the causes of war in band and village societies, pp. 121–133. In *Brazil: Anthropological Perspectives,* M. L. Margolis and W. E. Carter, eds. New York: Colombia University Press.

Johnson, A. 1982. Reductionism in cultural ecology: The Amazon case. *Current Anthropology* 23(4):413–428.

Knauft, B. M. 1985. *Good Company and Violence: Sorcery and Social Action in a Lowland New Guinea Society.* Berkeley: University of California Press.

———. 1987. Reconsidering violence in simple human societies. *Current Anthropology* 28(4):457–500.

Larrick, J. W., J. A. Yost, and J. Kaplan. 1978. Snakebite among the Waorani Indians of Eastern Ecuador. *Transactions of the Royal Society of Tropical Medicine and Hygiene* 72(5):542–543.

Munroe, R. L., R. H. Munroe, and J. W. M. Whiting. 1981. Male sex-role resolutions, pp. 611–632. In *Handbook of Cross-Cultural Human Development,* R. H. Munroe, R. L. Munroe, and B. B. Whiting, eds. New York: Garland STPM Press.

Murphy, R. 1957. Intergroup hostility and social cohesion. *American Anthropologist* 59:1018–1035.

Orlove, B. S. 1980. Ecological anthropology. *Annual Review of Anthropology* 9:325–373.

Otterbein, K. F. 1980. Internal war: A cross-cultural study, pp. 204–223. In *The War System: An Interdisciplinary Approach,* R. A. Falk and S.S. Kim, eds. Boulder: Westview Press.

———. 1985. *The Evolution of War: a Cross-Cultural Study* (2nd edn.). New Haven: HRAF.

Peeke, C. 1973. *Preliminary Grammar of Auca.* Norman, Oklahoma: Summer Institute of Linguistics.

Robarchek, C. A. 1977a. Semai nonviolence: A systems approach to understanding. Unpublished Ph.D. dissertation, Department of Anthropology, University of California, Riverside.

———. 1977b. Frustration, aggression, and the nonviolent Semai. *American Ethnologist* 4(4):762–779.

———. 1979a. Learning to fear: A case study in emotional conditioning. *American Ethnologist* 6(3):555–567.

———. 1979b. Conflict, emotion and abreaction: Resolution of conflict among the Semai Senoi. *Ethos* 7(2):104–123.

———. 1986. Helplessness, fearfulness and peacefulness: The emotional and motivational context of Semai social relations. *Anthropological Quarterly* 59(4):177–183.

———. 1988. Ghosts, witches and the psychodynamics of Semai peacefulness. Paper presented at the 87th Annual Meetings of the American Anthropological Association, 16–20 November 1988, Phoenix, Arizona.

———. 1989. Primitive warfare and the ratomorphic image of mankind. *American Anthropologist* 91(4):903–920.

Robarchek, C. A. 1990. Motivations and material causes: On the explanation of conflict and war, pp. 56–76. In *The Anthropology of War*, J. Hass, ed. Cambridge: Cambridge University Press.

Robarchek, C. A. and R. K. Dentan. 1987. Blood drunkenness and the bloodthirsty Semai: Unmaking another anthropological myth. *American Anthropologist* 89(2):356–365.

Robarchek, C. J. 1981. Cash economy and the evolution of ambilineal ramages among the Semai Senoi. Paper delivered before the Southwestern Anthropological Association Annual Meetings, 2–6 December 1981, Los Angeles, California.

Robarchek, C. J. and C. A. Robarchek. 1988. Reciprocities and realities: World views, peacefulness and violence among Semai and Waorani. Paper delivered before the 87th Annual Meetings of the American Anthropological Association, 16–20 November 1988, Phoenix, Arizona.

Ross, E. B. 1978. Food taboos, diet and hunting strategy: The adaptation to animals in Amazonian cultural ecology. *Current Anthropology* 19(1):1–36.

———. 1979. Reply to Lizot. C.A. comment. *Current Anthropology* 20(1):51–55.

Ross, M. H. 1985. Internal and external conflict and violence: Cross-cultural evidence and a new analysis. *Journal of Conflict Resolution* 29:547–579.

———. 1986a. The limits to social structure: Social structural and psychocultural explanations for political conflict and violence. *Anthropological Quarterly* 59(4):171–176.

———. 1986b. A cross-cultural theory of political conflict and violence. *Political Psychology* 7:427–469.

Segall, M. H. 1983. Aggression in global perspective, pp. 1–43. In *Aggression in Global Perspective*, A. P. Goldstein and M. H. Segall, eds. New York: Pergamon Press.

Spiro, M. E. 1967. *Burmese Supernaturalism*. Englewood Cliffs, NJ: Prentice-Hall.

Wallis, E. G. 1973. *Aucas Downriver*. New York: Harper and Row.

Yost, J. A. 1981. Twenty years of contact: The mechanisms of change in Wao (Auca) culture, pp. 677–704. In *Cultural Transformations and Ethnicity in Modern Ecuador*, N. A. Whitten, ed. Urbana: University of Illinois Press.

Yost, J. A. and P. M. Kelley. 1983. Shotguns, blowguns, and spears: The analysis of technological efficiency, pp. 189–224. In *Adaptive Responses of Native Amazonians*, R. B. Hames and W. Vickers, eds. New York: Academic Press.

10

The Rise, Maintenance, and Destruction of Peaceable Polity: A Preliminary Essay in Political Ecology

ROBERT KNOX DENTAN

Natural selection designs different kinds of animals and plants so that they *avoid* competition. A fit animal is not one that fights well, but one that avoids fighting all together [sic] (Colinvaux 1978:144).

The colonial relationship which I had tried to define chained the colonizer and the colonized into an implacable dependence, molded their respective characters and dictated their conduct (Memmi 1965:ix).

It is our principle to feed the hungry and give the thirsty drink; we have dedicated ourselves to serve all men in everything that can be helpful to the preservation of men's lives, but we find no freedom in giving, or doing, or assisting in anything by which men's lives are destroyed or hurt (Mennonite Memorial to the Pennsylvania Assembly (1775)).

Defeat tamed them... those that survived did so by learning virtues of political accommodation or withdrawal from temporal affairs. The bellicose Taborites merged into the Moravian Brethren, the once feared Anabaptists... became Mennonites, and the anti-Cromwellian Fifth Monarchists dissolved into Quakerism (Barkun 1986:68–69).

One uses Chinese culture to transform barbarians. It is unthinkable to use barbarian culture to transform Chinese (Mencius; cf. Lau 1970:103).

INTRODUCTION

Topic

This chapter sketches a political ecological model for the origin, persistence and demise of peaceable societies. The model fleshes out the familiar suggestion that nonviolence is a way less powerful societies respond to violence by stronger ones (Dollard 1941:8–9; Gardner 1966; Sipes 1973; Dentan 1978:97, 129, 133–134,

214

1979:2; Endicott 1983:238; Donald 1987; but cf. Fabbro 1980:181; Knauft 1987b:489–490). As Robarchek (1986:183) notes with typical insight, models like this serve to contextualize, supplement, or integrate more purely psychic, evolutionary, or environmental models (e.g., Miller and Dollard 1941:8–9; Paul 1978; O'Nell 1979, 1986a; Denich 1987; Fry 1987, 1988a, b, 1990, n.d.; Knauft 1988; Simon 1990). The first section discusses nonviolent peoples in geographic refuges. The second discusses their probable history and the fate of nonviolence in nation-states.

In a recent letter to the *New York Times* Carl Senna remarks that "I suspect that wars have many causes, that peace has only one . . ." (1990). Personally, I suspect that the roots of peace are as complex as those which predispose people to violence or agonistic behavior. This chapter concerns just one way to be peaceable, a way perhaps characteristic only of people on the margins of the world system. Aspects of their adaptation, however, may show up among other peaceable peoples. Moreover, the described invader–refugee pattern of relationships was more common in the past, when human populations were generally thinner on the ground (Boserup 1988:24–25). Space limitations prevent detailed examination of violent situations.

Definitions of Peaceability

"Peaceable"

A few terms need preliminary definition, with the understanding that preliminary definitions are tools, not straitjackets. The definitions refer to Weberian ideals or prototypes to which patterns in the real world more or less closely conform (cf. Gibson 1986a). Since recent studies (e.g., Pratt 1986; Knauft 1987a, b; Cadelina 1988; Headland 1989:65–66, 69; 1990) indicate that some peoples once classified as peaceful may actually have high rates of violence and even homicide, precision about "peace" is important.[1] "Peaceable" in this essay refers only to shunning physical violence. The presence or absence of psychic or symbolic aggression is not at issue here, nor is there any implication that peaceable people are incapable of violence under altered circumstances (cf. Dentan 1978:97–98; O'Nell 1979:301–302; Lee 1984:150; Robarchek and Dentan 1987).

For peaceability is not disability, not a cultural essence unrelated to a people's actual circumstances. It should not be surprising that nonviolent peoples can become violent or vice versa. Nor does violence in a particular time and place necessarily indicate that peaceability in a different time or place is illusory. To the degree that peaceability grows out of particular historical and geographical situations, aggregated statistics—collected over long periods of time or throughout a population which lives in several political ecological niches—may be misleading (cf. Lee 1984:90–97, 150; Knauft 1987a; Albert 1989).

For example, the historical moment of !Kung San peaceability seems to have been between the mid-1950s and the mid-1970s: the heyday of their equestrian cattle raiding was long over, their refuge still intact, and their homicide rate low (Lee 1984:90–91, 147–150). Later, as armed recruits for a hierarchical society which richly rewards violence, protected from their enemies by their comrades in arms, dealing with traditional enemies with whom they have no social ties, San, like some nonviolent Malaysian indigenes in similar circumstances, again became violent enough to earn their keep (Lee and Hurlich 1982; Lee 1984:147–149; Robarchek and Dentan 1987:359–361; Leary 1989:8, 11, 12, 16, 20; Nicholas et al. 1989; Hood 1990:142–144; cf. von Graeve 1989:20).

Conversely, the Penan peoples of east Malaysia—their territories completely penetrated and occupied by swiddeners who occasionally raided them for slaves and heads—traditionally retaliated with violence and even hunted heads like their neighbors (Rousseau 1990:241–244, 272–275). In the 1980s, however, a Swiss botanist introduced them to the tactics of nonviolent protest pioneered by Henry David Thoreau and perfected by Gandhi and the American civil rights movement (Anonymous 1989a, c, 1990a; Genam et al. 1989; Jalong Apoi 1989). By adopting these tactics, Penan and their neighbors won the attention and support of local scientists (e.g., Chin 1989) as well as of foreign environmentalists and opportunists like the US Congress and the Grateful Dead (Anonymous 1989b, 1990b; European Parliament 1989; Hashim 1989; Carothers 1990). By contrast, the indigenous nonviolent tactics of peninsular Malaysian peoples like Semai attracted little local and almost no international interest, let alone support, although their situation was, if anything, more grave (Anonymous 1989d; Gomes 1990; Hood 1990; Nicholas 1990; Todd 1990). Perhaps techniques of nonviolent confrontation come more easily to peoples with a tradition of violent confrontation than to peoples with a tradition of avoiding confrontation; the former certainly get more air time in the West.

Finally, the Brazilian peoples of the Pacaa Nova River seem to have alternated between flight and counterviolence as a response to the penetration of their area by settlers (von Graeve 1989:10, 26). Their traditions refer to some feuding among themselves before contact (von Graeve 60, 62). Early on, they staged revenge raids against slavers, and in 1724 the government armed and trained them to resist (von Graeve 16–20). Later, as rubber tappers moved in, they began simply to flee settler violence (von Graeve 25–26, 46, 49, 61), until finally increasing numbers of settlers made flight almost impossible, and a brief final phase of violent resistance began, only to end in final regroupment and coercive pacification (von Graeve 50–59; cf. Albert 1989).

Therefore this paper treats peaceability as a tactical cultural adaptation to particular situations rather than as a Platonic essence which disables people from committing violence. Peaceability in some circumstances is a response reasonable and intelligent people can adopt, as Penan have done. When it fails to be adaptive, the same people may abandon it, at least temporarily, as !Kung San seem to have done. Peaceable people need not be pacificists. All peoples have histories and ecologies which affect their behavior, peaceable peoples no less than others.

Types of Peaceability

Many nonanthropological students of peaceability focus on pacifism, the conscious choice of a nonviolent way of life. Pacifism is indeed a genre of peaceability, and as such gets some attention in the second section of this paper. To concentrate on pacifism to the exclusion of other forms of peaceability, however, stultifies understanding by narrowing it to a few world-religious sects. Moreover, even sectarian pacificism seems easier at some times and places than others. Perhaps, then, sometimes such ideals come neither from God nor from dispassionate philosophizing but from the humdrum, often difficult reality of people's daily lives. If so, understanding peaceable ways of life requires examining the contexts within which they occur, as this paper tries to do, rather than focusing on ideological constructs which rationalize, justify and mystify them.

"Behavioral peaceability" or "nonviolence" shows up in relatively low rates of interpersonal violence and warfare, for example, among Semai and other Orang Asli of west Malaysia or among Buid and what Gibson (1986a) calls "Type 1" societies of the Philippines. It may occur among isolated peoples simply because there is not much to fight about rather than because of an ideological or enculturating stress on nonviolence. That situation, once thought to typify foragers' lives, seems relatively rare (Dentan 1988d).

Nonviolence often occurs in association with "attitudinal peaceability" or "peace-loving," the

> absence of any social situation in which acts of aggression are assigned a positive value. That is not to say that acts which we, or the Buid, would interpret as aggressive never occur, but that such acts are viewed as deviations from the ideals of Buid political culture. The fact that acts of violence . . . are consistently condemned; and the lack of any positive evaluation of acts of "bravery" or "courage", probably does result in a lower rate of intentional maiming and homicide among the Buid than among populations which attach positive evaluations to such acts (Gibson 1986b; cf. Dentan 1978:97–98).

Attitudinal peaceability can be an explicit code, as in Quaker or Hutterite pacifism. It can, however, be inexplicit, as among peaceable Zapotec who remain nonviolent "despite the absence of any explicitly stated ideal system (religious or ethical) which unequivocally can be called antiviolent" (O'Nell 1979:318).

Attitudinal peaceability often reflects and buttresses relationships of mutual dependency and support. Studies of foraging and swiddening peoples since the 1960s have stressed the positive peaceability which comes from sharing and exchanging goods and personnel (e.g., Price 1975; Woodburn 1982; Gibson 1986b, 1989; Dentan 1988d; Howell 1988; Robarchek and Robarchek 1988; Roseman 1988). The relationships between behavioral peaceability, dependency and social support are so complex, however, that the correlation of nonviolence with positive attitudinal peaceability is low. Many peoples who value peace positively still have relatively high rates of violence, e.g., Gebusi of New Guinea (Knauft 1985a, b, 1987a, b, c), the Pacaa Nova peoples (von Graeve 1989:69–70, 73, 98, 111, 116) and San foragers ("Bushmen") of southern and eastern Africa (Knauft 1987a). Thus a cultural emphasis on dependence and nurturance does not by itself account for nonviolence. Social support networks themselves involve costs and conflicts (Kursh 1971; Tilden and Galyen 1987). Besides, the social cohesion which stems from external stress (see Chapter 1, this volume) can be pathogenic (Schaffer 1964). In other words, people are not nonviolent unless they feel nonviolence is good or at least that violence is bad; but peace-loving people on occasion may commit acts of violence, and those occasions may come often.

Positive and Negative Attitudinal Peaceability

The distinction between positive and negative peaceability implicit in the last sentence can also be useful (Sponsel 1989:29–30; Stephenson 1990:5). It may well be that nonviolence comes more from hating or fearing violence (negative peaceability) than from loving peace (Briggs 1978:64–68; Gibson 1986a). This hate or fear can show up as denial, so that people even deny feeling the anger their body language seems to show (Dentan 1979; Gregor 1988; Howell 1988). This essay emphasizes how people come to hate and fear violence, i.e., negative peaceability.

Internal and External Peaceability

Finally, people everywhere tend to value peace within the group more positively than peace with outsiders (e.g., von Graeve 1989:106, 111–112, 116, 118). Among the traditionally nonviolent Senoi peoples of Malaysia there has been only one case of unequivocally internecine (intra-Senoi) murder between 1930 and 1990. As reported to Clayton Robarchek, it involved a Semai man's killing another Semai man over a woman. Aside from the abandonment of the terminally sick and the assassination of people targeted by outsiders during the Malaysian insurgency, there are only four relatively well-documented murders, all involving love troubles. Except for the case cited above, none seems to have involved a Semai victim. In one, an old "aborigine" woman killed her husband, who had a Malay name and may have been Malay (Nicholas et al. 1989:229). The other two victims were a British anthropologist and a Chinese shopkeeper, killed by a Temiar and Semai man, respectively (Noone and Holman 1972; Dentan 1988c:627).

People are also more likely to fear violence from outsiders than from intimates (Knauft 1988). The interworking of these two ethnocentrisms is complex. For example, Okiek foragers of east Africa feuded internally but fled from Maasai warriors (Blackburn 1982:291, 293); Hadza, east Africans of San origin but in a political ecological situation like that of Okiek, seem similar in this respect (Siedentopf 1946:335; Woodburn 1982).

One threat to internal nonviolence is a belief in witches. Many nonviolent peoples assert that some people, usually not in one's own community or kindred, are secretly violent. Witchcraft accusations, for instance, seem to account for most internal violence among Gebusi of New Guinea and the peoples of the Upper Xingu River (Gregor 1988; Knauft 1987a, b, c). In most of these societies witches seem to be among the "key symbols" (Ortner 1973) that represent, dramatize and intensify an abhorrence of violence: thundersqualls, for instance, also seem to serve that function among most indigenous foragers and horticulturalists of Malaysia and the upper Xingu (Dentan 1979:22–23, 1988f:860, 868; Gregor 1988). Among some Malaysian peoples ghosts seem to serve the symbolic functions witches serve elsewhere, so that witchcraft accusations and the often associated violence are rare or nonexistent (Dentan 1988b:54–55; Robarchek 1988).

A stereotype of horrible outsiders may fill some of the functions of witches but also rationalize, justify, and mystify the choice of flight over fighting as a response to aggression by outsiders (Lee 1984:103, 116–117; Dentan 1988f:868; Gomes 1988a:102–104; Gregor 1988; von Graeve 1989:4).

Peoples Discussed

Malaysian Peaceable Peoples (Orang Asli)

The people always at the back of my mind when I think of peaceable peoples are Semai, central Malaysian swiddeners with whom I lived for a couple of years in the early 1960s and mid-1970s. They are peaceable in all the senses discussed above. They also are in this regard representative of Orang Asli, the indigenous Austroasiatic peoples of west Malaysia, although even among them, Semai peaceability is striking. Aslians comprise swidden horticulturalists, sometimes generically called "Senoi," and foragers, sometimes generically called "Semang." Nonviolence is so salient in Aslian everyday life that all the ethnographers who have worked there—whatever their nationality, gender, theoretical biases, or original scientific "problem"—have wound up grappling with peaceability and its relationship with Aslian egalitarianism, ethnopsychology, and religious ideology (Howell 1988). I spent about six months with Btsisi', littoral Aslians, in 1976.

Other Peaceable Peoples

The other peoples I discuss as peaceable are those with whose lives I have become somewhat familiar through reading. Rather than attempting sampling or statistical techniques too sophisticated for the data available, "the best principle of selection has seemed to me to be that of looking at what I know best, partial and uncertain though that very often is" (Gilsenan 1982:22). Among those are Buid, Philippine swiddeners who seem peaceable in all the senses discussed here. They represent a number of highland Philippine peoples whose political ecology resembles that of Aslians (e.g., Gibson 1985, 1986a). Other peaceable peoples mentioned include Pacaa Nova (at some times) and Xinguanos of central Brazil; "pygmies" of central Africa (Mbuti, Twa, Aka); San of south and east Africa (especially !Kung during their peaceable era, 1955–1975); Paliyan of South India; modern Onge of the Andaman Islands and Siriono of Bolivia. Limitations of time and space make comparisons with particularly violent people outside the scope of this study, but I will refer to the two most promising ongoing comparative studies, the work of the Robarcheks with Semai and the Ecuadorian Waorani (Robarchek and Robarchek 1988, Chapter 9, this volume; cf. Collins 1983) and of O'Nell and Fry with violent and nonviolent Zapotec of Mexico (O'Nell 1979, 1981, 1986a, b; Fry 1987, 1988a, b, 1990).[2]

Peaceable "Intentional Groups"

Within nation states, some peaceable peoples are "intentional groups" (Erasmus 1981), i.e., they have a conscious program which justifies maintaining their identity. Part of this program is to love peace, a positive attitude which they act out in nonviolent lives. Some of these groups are "cenobites," people living communitarian religious lives, e.g., the pacifist Hutterites, Amish, and Shakers. Others are therapeutic groups like Alcoholics Anonymous. Although the programs of AA and its offspring are not primarily to foster peace, they tend to do so. Indeed, M. Scott Peck, author of *The Different Drum*, urges modelling peace groups after AA (Brooks 1987:38). I have been a member of AA for over a decade, talk with my

Amish neighbors in Allegany County, NY, and read about ideal communities (e.g., Whitson 1983).

Pastoralists

Since pastoralism correlates with violence, pastoralist peoples in refuge areas, Mongols or Uzbeks, for example, are beyond the scope of this study. So are violent pastoralist variants of generally nonviolent nonpastoralist cultures, e.g., equestrian nineteenth-century San rustlers (Wright 1971; Guenther 1980, 1986). It should be noted, however, that such instances confirm the points made above: (1) that ideology by itself does not determine peacefulness, (2) that nonviolence is not due to a psychic or cultural inability to be violent, and (3) that static interpretations of dynamic adaptations are unlikely to be helpful.

POLITICAL ECOLOGY

Introduction

In the model I am presenting, relatively powerful people, "invaders," force themselves into the milieu of relatively powerless people, "refugees." The terms refer to poles of a relationship across a frontier (cf. Wilmsen and Denbow 1990). A "frontier" in Turner's classic sense (1894:200) marks "the hither edge of free land," i.e., land on the margin of an expanding invader population but still occupied by weaker people with relatively low population density. It usually follows "natural boundary lines which have served to mark and to affect the characteristics of the frontiers" (Turner 1894:205; cf. Gardner 1985:420), e.g., between desert San and bush Bantu in southern Africa or between hill and valley people in Southeast Asia. That is, it is often a natural as well as a cultural ecotone.

For any of several reasons the invaders lack the capacity or the will to extend political control over the relatively unattractive region the refugees occupy, but content themselves with sporadic raids ("razzias"), typically to collect slaves. As frontiersmen, "that line of scum that the waves of advancing civilization bore before them" (Turner 1894:223n), invaders rarely represent the gentlest of their people: "dominantly male . . . characterized by large-scale drunkenness and violence" (von Graeve 1989:25). Razzias are brutal by any standards.

Thus, within the refuge, refugees are fairly secure most of the time from attack by invaders; but they are always aware that invaders may at any time unpredictably and brutally irrupt into their world.

Niche Specializations

The general principle is that, given the availability of underpopulated refuge areas, the more devastating the military superiority of the invaders, the more successful the refugee adaptation of flight. When successful, slaving and slaughter reduce the fitness of the refugees. Death puts an end to reproduction, and traditional slave populations do not reproduce themselves (Manning 1990:27–28). The result is a niche specialization: the slavers' search and destroy strategy evokes a run and scatter response. The analogy is with the sort of relationship found between insect predators and prey. In any encounter, the former could exterminate the latter, but in fact

> Locally the prey is wiped out as the model of efficient hunting says it must be, but the game has been started all over again somewhere else by refugees from the first game. The result is a scattered population of prey ... living many generations in security, but occasionally faced with local annihilation (Colinvaux 1978:160).

The resulting insecurity, "fear," leads refugees to enculturate children in ways that foster nonviolence and to maintain or initiate a flexible band organization which (1) permits flight and regrouping in response to marauding invaders, and (2) both fosters and requires the nonviolence children learn. Maintaining nonviolence within nation-states takes conscious effort, both to strive towards a nonviolent ideal and to maintain social constructs functionally equivalent to refuges, xenophobia, and bands.

The rest of this section fleshes out this simple model, but first a word of caution about ecological explanations (Ellen 1982:64):

> Simple one-way cause-and-effect sequences are rare ... it is therefore important to take into account possible circular or reticulate relations between causes and effects ... because certain cultural traits have effects which make them ecologically adaptive, this in itself is insufficient to make them inevitable ....

"Refuge"

Definition

In ecology, a "refuge" is a niche in which a species can survive the predation and competition that wipe out its populations elsewhere, although even within the niche some populations may die out (Clapham 1973:86, 122–123). Often the niche is a geographical region in which conditions, particularly of movement, are so unattractive to, or access so difficult for, invaders that, at least for a while, they do not bring their full force to bear upon or occupy the territory (e.g., Gomes 1988a:105). Even with modern technology, exploiting available resources entails more effort and expense than the returns justify. The limits of invader transportation possibilities are crucial in preserving a refuge: "Every river valley and Indian trail became a fissure in Indian society, and so that society became honeycombed" (Turner 1894:209). In Malaysia, "roads are a boon to the outsiders, a great help to middlemen and thus work less in favour of Orang Asli" (Hood 1990:146; cf. Nicholas 1990:73, 76, 80).

Therefore refugees may oppose roads. For instance, Waorani, whose territory is accessible only by helicopter or foot, protested plans to build a road into the area (Orville 1988). As long as access is difficult, industrial societies keep refuges in reserve until the desire for their resources is great enough, or technology improved enough, to warrant their exploitation (Aguirre Beltran 1979:23). In this sense, refuges can exist in any type of social system, including the most repressive nation-states, as long as the law of diminishing returns makes it economically or politically unprofitable for the invaders to occupy the enclaves in force, to exterminate refugees or to integrate them into invader society as an underclass or bottom caste.[3]

A refuge is a demographic "region" with (1) a topology, (2) an internal homogeneity, and (3) a systematic structure (Zubrow 1976:254–256).

1. Regional geographers discuss regions not merely as places but also as fields of action, "functional regions" (cf. Aguirre Beltran 1979:30). Thus, for Amish their enclaves are functional refuges; for Alcoholics Anonymous, church basements; and so on. In other words, a refuge needs some physical space but need not monopolize that space nor occupy it continuously. A church basement can, at other times, be the locus of a rummage sale.

2. Demographic homogeneity stems from the exclusion of invaders, which also leaves refugees free from surveillance and lets them keep some independence and self-respect (e.g., Memmi 1965:xii; Gomes 1987). By this criterion, many Indian reservations and Socialist countries' "autonomous regions," beset by BIA officials or apparatchiks, are not refuges.

   On both sides of a Turneresque frontier population density is low (Turner 1894:207, 221–223; Paxon 1924:95–96); e.g., in Malaysia, for Temiar and Semai about 5 per square mile; for the surrounding Malays and Thais, less than 50 per square mile (Ooi 1963:129; Benjamin 1987:9; cf. Peterson 1990:56). While invader metropolises may be densely populated, invaders are too few along the frontier to colonize the relatively inaccessible refuge and thus transform it into a reserve or colony. Conversely, there are so few refugees that there is always a place for them to flee to within the reserve without overburdening the carrying capacity of the land under their traditional ecology.

3. A refuge is a system in the sense that many of its cultural features come from being a place where refugees can temporarily find some degree of safety from supervision by invaders and from such social predation as enslavement, massacre, genocide, or forced assimilation. Specifically, nonviolence seems to be one of several features which refugee ways of life share. These features, discussed below, are not random but interconnected in complex patterns of causation, function, and feedback.

Refuge Subtypes

Subtyping refuges along a continuum can be useful.

1. A "sanctuary" is a region whose inhabitants can and do repel invaders by force. People within a sanctuary may behave in an aggressive and fearless way quite different from the way they act outside (Aguirre Beltran 1979:27). Contact with the outside is at least partially under the control of the people inside. Thus in the nineteenth century, "!Kung San traded when they could, defended themselves when they had to, and during the long intervals between trading expeditions went about their business" (Lee 1990:512).

2. A refuge proper (hereafter simply "refuge") occupies a position on the continuum between a virtually impregnable "sanctuary" and a "ghetto."

3. A reserve is economically and politically subject to outsiders, but within its borders limited autonomy, "beggar's democracy" (Wittfogel 1957), may prevail in matters of no interest to the invaders.

4. At the far end of the continuum is a ghetto, in which invaders are settlers, daily contact with whom is a lesson in humiliation and impotence (Memmi 1965).

An "enclave" of people surrounded by others with a different culture is a type of frontier which can fall into any of these categories (Castile and Kushner 1981), although this paper concentrates on enclaves which function as refuges. Of all these types, nonviolence characterizes only refuges.

For example, "Montagnards" occupied Southeast Asian hill sanctuaries, Asli West Malaysian refuges. Many foragers lived in sanctuaries or refuges until this century. Until recently deserts of southern Africa and central Australia were refuges for San and their Native Australian counterparts, as the Bangweulu swamps were for Twa in central Africa until the 1920s (Brelsford 1946). The Sea Islands off the coast of Georgia and South Carolina apparently were a refuge for Gullah-speakers until recently (Rosengarten 1987). As noted above, the area occupied by Penan foragers of Borneo was more reserve than refuge, although Penan were prone to resist attacks by force (Rousseau 1990:241–244, 272–275). The life of west Semang on reserves differs greatly from that of other Semang peoples in interior refuges and involves considerably more violence (Ngata 1990). Less precisely bordered refuges occur in industrialized societies, often as enclaves, e.g., of American cenobites.

Transience of This Adaptation

Frontiers Are Imaginary

A "frontier," as Turner (1894) shows, is not so much a geographical area as a social and intellectual construct arising from dualistic social relations which, at any given historical moment, tend to occur in a particular space (Ver Steeg 1964:153–156). The differentiation of the trans-frontier population into invader and refugee is analogous to the "character displacement" which can occur among sympatric races of the same species precisely where their ranges overlap (Colinvaux 1978:144, 185–188). On the frontier, timid or gentle invaders and rash or aggressive refugees are in trouble. For the latter, "quitting can be a 'fit' thing to do" (Colinvaux 1978:174).

People along the frontier, or outside observers, may gloss the resulting differentiation as "ethnic." The connection between frontiers and ethnicity is marked enough to have led some students to speculate that ethnic identity, at least in Southeast Asia, is simply a matter or different ecological adaptations (e.g., Rambo et al. 1988; Rousseau 1990). But frontiers move or vanish entirely as invaders establish permanent settlements or complete political control in former refuges. Refuges are also transitional (Eder 1988). Hinterland refuges, once beyond the frontier of an expanding population, may vanish or become enclaves.

Thus, until this century, mangrove swamps along the western Malay peninsula were a hinterland refuge for Semang foragers and Btsisi' fisher-horticulturalists, among others; nowadays the coastal Semang Wila (Bila) are extinct, the remaining Semang live in the hills, and the surviving Btsisi', under heavy assimilationist pressure, are being forced into enclaves, which themselves are subject to expropriation (Nowak 1984, 1985; cf. Eder 1988). A similar transition is occurring among Semai (Gomes 1990; Nicholas 1990). The recurrent "termination" movement to abolish reservations threatens to wipe out such enclaves in the United States. Therefore, to the degree that nonviolence stems from having a geographic refuge, nonviolence must also be a transitory phase in a people's history. (So, of course, is violence.) The second section of this paper deals further with this transience.

Cultural Adaptation Is a Variable

Although this chapter stresses the two extremes of fight and flight as adaptive responses, the band social organization of refugees reflects a basic strategy which includes not just foraging but an "economic flexibility, which has allowed rapid alteration of strategy with ecological and/or social conditions" (Casimir 1990:551; cf. Wilmsen and Denbow 1990). People who are refugees at one time and place may try different tactics in other circumstances. Other options include trade and submission as slaves, serfs, or rural proletarians. For example, Hadza foragers of Tanzania recognize a number of strategic options they can take in response to their agropastoralist neighbors. Their tactics are in part in response to contact, which may vary "yearly, seasonally, microenvironmentally, and, most relevant to this discussion, in degree of intrusion" (Bicchieri 1990:507; cf. Lee 1990:512).

Cultural Oscillation

Since the political ecological context of refugee societies is variable, not constant, refugee culture may fluctuate in response. Paliyan and other peoples considered for this chapter live under conditions which permit "cultural oscillation" between the refugee culture outlined below and the modified invader low-stratum culture which forms in response to the unequal conditions just described (e.g., von Graeve 1989; Wilmsen and Denbow 1990). Ecological conditions for such oscillation require that (Gardner 1985:428):

> (1) there be only one major neighboring social system . . . , (2) ecological relations permit life both at the frontier and away from it, and (3) the two systems be spatially discrete so that frontier life is an option, not a requirement.

Dualism: Invaders, Refugees, Frontiers
Ethnicity

In this chapter, and, as I hope to show, in the minds of refugees, "invader" and "refugee" are mutually symmetric opposites (e.g., Gomes 1988a). This dualism pervades refugee thinking, so that, for example, Aslian refugees rarely talk about their own lives without instancing how Malay invaders do the opposite (Dentan 1976a; Hood 1990:144–145; Robarchek and Robarchek 1990:5, 9). The distinction between invader and refugee is structural rather than "ethnic" in the sense of being based on differentially shared descent (Dentan 1975, 1976a, b; Rousseau 1990; Wilmsen and Denbow 1990).

East African forager castes may consist, at least in part, of "disenfranchised pastoralists and farmers, rather than being descendants of ancient populations who have hunted since 'time immemorial'" (Chang 1982:271; but cf. Blackburn 1982:295). Many Malays are descendants of aborigine slaves kidnapped as children (Endicott 1983; Reid 1988:133; Rousseau 1990:286, 299). Conversely, impoverished Malays may live among Asli, although Semai and Btsisi' say that only "ugly" and "stupid" Malays do so (cf. Headland 1978; Peterson 1978:90–94; Couillard 1986).

Such frontiers may override other political economic similarities. For instance, toponyms, etymologies, oral histories, and certain details of social structure suggest that some of the ancestors of Malaysian Orang Asli were peasants cut off from their urban centers when the shadowy Mon-Khmer kingdom of Tambralingga III fell to the thirteenth century Thai armies from a civilization much like their own (e.g., Endicott 1990). Wilmsen and Denbow (1990:494–496) argue that Kalahari people had ties to Great Zimbabwe. Paliyan, Semang, and Orang Kubu of Sumatra seem to oscillate between foraging and horticulture, crossing the economic frontier but not the political ecological one. The dual opposition invader–refugee that frontiers generate seems particularly marked when Moslems are on one side of the frontier and infidels on the other (Pipes 1983:165–167) or when one party, like American Shakers, has an ideology that stems in part from ancient dualistic religions.

On both sides of the frontier people often talk about invader–refugee dualism in ethnic terms but typically stereotype everyone across the frontier as if they were undifferentiated (Dentan 1976a, b). All hill people are "moi" to Vietnamese (cf. Mabbett 1983:44–45). Invaders may class refugees with apes. Thus Bantu class central African "pygmies" with chimpanzees (e.g., Bahuchet and Guillaume 1982:193). Likewise, Malay orang hutan, "jungle people," refers to Asli and apes alike. Semang headmen and Malay patrons of Asli clients were "gembala Sakai" (Endicott 1983:226); "gembala," from a Sanskrit word for "herdsmen," e.g., of goats or sheep, is insulting when applied to Malays (Wilkinson n.d., I:346, II:368). "Sakai," the obsolescent derogatory word for Asli, implies subjection and inability to speak Malay and thus to be cultured or intelligent (Nowak and Dentan 1984:58–62). This sort of derogation rationalizes and justifies taking refugee land. People who wander like wild animals can have no land rights (Hitchcock 1990:53).[4]

Reciprocally, refugees fear, detest, and admire invaders. Btsisi' and Semai tend to talk about generic "Malay" invaders rather than to distinguish invaders from local Malay peasants with whom relations were sometimes amicable. Accusations of cannibalism may reflect the predatory relationships involved (Singh 1989; [Williams-Hunt] 1989a). Refugees may fear that razzias are to provide food for cannibals. Reciprocally, invader ethnonyms for refugees may imply cannibalism, e.g., "Batak" in Sumatra and Palawan, "Bateq" in west Malaysia.

Invader Power and Attitudes towards Refuges

Power

The invaders' greater power involves one or more of several factors.

1. Their economic activities are often more energy-intensive than those of the

refugees, thus requiring and supporting a denser and significantly larger population than refugees can muster. Invaders may, e.g., be pastoralists invading forager territory or irrigation agriculturalists invading horti-culturalist areas.

2. Invader military technology is more efficient (e.g., Gomes 1988a:105).

3. For invaders, wealth is often a more important determinant of rank than it is for refugees; they may also have a class system based on wealth or military might. In Southeast Asia, unfortunately for refugees, traditional invader hierarchies rested largely on how many slaves a person possessed; one way to get slaves was to raid the refuges (Dove 1983; Reid 1983, 1988).

Savage Wilderness

Invaders usually treat geographical refuges as wilderness. Thus Malays and Maasai fear the forest and the supposed sorcery of its Asli or Okiek inhabitants (Skeat and Blagden 1906, II:199, 233–234, 539; Blackburn 1982:293). Invaders associate refugees with this "undeveloped" wilderness, "wild people," (Malay "orang liar"), closer to animals than to real people like the invaders. In some Austronesian languages the term "hill people" (e.g., Orang Bukit, Ebukid), referring to refugees, has the connotations of American "hillbilly" (Headland 1978:135). Invaders deny refugee territorial claims and denigrate the ways refugees use their environments. Thus, neither British nor Malay laws recognize traditional Aslian claims to land (Chee 1990; Gomes 1990:21–26; Nicholas 1990:71–76; Rachagan 1990). The general ideological claim that refugees are "savages" rationalizes dominating them politically and exploiting them economically, much like ruling class or caste ideologies elsewhere (e.g., Ryan 1971:3–60).

Invaders who inherit a state apparatus from departing European colonialists, like the colonialists themselves, treat refuges as unowned land to which they can help themselves (Nietschmann 1987). Ironically, traditional attempts by refugees to find a sanctuary from invader razzias may prevent their establishing long-term relationships with particular tracts of land, as in the case of Bateq Semang. The invader state anyway lays claim to all land within its borders. The mobility of foragers or swiddeners, once their salvation, is a constant irritation to the new state's bureaucrats. Settlement programs, often irrational in economic or ecological terms, serve the political purposes of (1) dispossessing refugees of land on which they are not actually living, (2) opening that land to invaders and (3) destroying the refuge so that refugees come under the control of the invader state (e.g., Dove 1983, 1985, 1988). Former refugees like Asli naturally distrust such schemes (Endicott 1982; Jimin 1983:57–63; Endicott 1984; Nowak 1985; Anonymous 1987b; Catmandu and Sivashanmugam 1987; Gomes 1987, 1990; Man and Hoh 1987; Nicholas 1990; Todd 1990).

Exploiting Refugees: Unequal Trade

Few invaders intrude physically into refugees' lives; most settle on a frontier. Trade may flourish across the frontier, since the invaders, by definition, are not much concerned with conquest or coercive incorporation of refugees except as slaves. Thus slaving and trading often coexist (Skeat and Blagden 1906, I:528; Endicott 1983; Reid 1983, 1988; Gibson 1986a; Wilmsen and Denbow 1990). Some invaders may set up what they think are patron–client relationships with some refugees, since clientage makes sense in their own stratified society, while the more egalitarian-minded refugees themselves retain, or think they retain, a good deal of independence. Trade can let invaders get by on relatively sparse agricultural acreage, thus minimizing the effects of their permanent settlement on refuge borders (Peterson 1990:58).

The power differential between invaders and refugees, however, ensures that, although both sides may benefit at particular times and places (e.g., Peterson 1978), in the long term, frontier exchanges benefit invaders and harm refugees (Headland 1988a). Labor relations are asymmetric in the sense that invaders hire refugees or take their land, not vice versa (cf. Rousseau 1990:234–245). Indeed, the distinction between patron–client relationships and slaver–refugee ones may be a bit picky and ethnocentric. In Malay, "sakai" refers indiscriminately to clients and slaves of Aslian origin; and Malay traders used razzias and the associated massacres to discipline their Bateq Semang "trading partners" just as American managers create unemployment to discipline the labor force (Endicott 1990:6–8). Conversely, refugees may regard invaders as simultaneously aggressors and protectors (e.g., Robarchek and Robarchek 1990).

Refuge life may attract invaders, particularly those in the lowest strata of their society, and people may pass back and forth across the frontier. Ultimately, the patron–client relationships may simply destroy refugee society (e.g., Bodley 1982:37–39; Eder 1988; Headland 1988a) or collectively crystallize into the sort of caste relationship between refugees and invaders which seems widespread in Northeast Africa. Another classic case involves "pygmies" and Bantu or Oubangui (Turnbull 1962, 1965, 1978:163–164, 194–195; Bahuchet and Guillaume 1982). The related Twa may have had similar relations with Bemba, Huta and Tutsi (Brelsford 1946:12–14; d'Hertefelt 1966). Before European colonization, patron–client ties occurred between settled Malays or Thais and Asli (Benjamin 1968; Dunn 1975; Endicott 1983; Couillard 1986) and between San and invading Bantu pastoralists (Denbow and Wilmsen 1986). The first Boer frontiersmen became patrons to Bantu clients, while the latter were still too numerous and powerful to subjugate. Similarly, where Boer farmers were poor and Bantu workers unavailable, San sometimes more or less volunteered to become serfs (Guenther 1976, 1977:196, 201; Giliomee 1981:82–87; cf. Eder 1988).

Exploiting Refugees: Razzias

People within the refuge but away from the frontier may be useless as clients. To an expanding hierarchical people, such "wild" refugees themselves may become an exploitable resource, potential slaves (e.g., Goody 1980:24; Turton 1980:257–258; Bodley 1982:32, 36–37; Rousseau 1990:175–178, 242, 284–285). In an area like traditional Southeast Asia, where slaves constituted the fundamental basis of wealth and power, slaving by lowlanders was almost universal (Morris 1980; Turton 1980; Reid 1983, 1988; Gibson 1986a; Rousseau 1990:165–179, 284). Turner (1894:207–212) distinguishes several types of frontiers according to the economic interests of the invaders: traders, farmers, ranchers, and soldiers. The focus of this chapter is on how a slavers' frontier affects life on the slave side.

Slaving is arduous and dangerous in a refuge which, from the invader viewpoint, is "wild." Transportation is difficult for invaders. Adult refugee men tend to be intractable, hard to catch and capable of resistance, however futile (Goody 1980:20–21). Children are easier to catch, transport and break to a life of servitude (Duncan 1982:96). Therefore, unlike their counterparts in the European slavery business, traditional slavers prefer to take women and children (Manning 1990:22–23, 98). Noncommercial European razzias follow the same pattern. A missionary in colonial South Carolina remarks that razzias by European invaders and their Indian allies took only "poor women and children; for the men taken prisoners are burnt most barbarously" and the goal of punitive expeditions was to "kill the Men and make the women and children Slaves" (LeJau, quoted in Duncan 1982:94, 95); the ratio of women and children enslaved to men was between two and five to one (Duncan 1982:92, 94).

Among peoples this chapter discusses, Ge- and Carib-speakers killed Xinguano men and took only women and children as slaves (Gregor 1988). Bantu and Europeans enslaving San, and Southeast Asian lowlanders enslaving refugees, normally massacred adults of both sexes and took only children less than 10 or 12 years old. For example, Tswana hunters raided San camps, killing men and taking women and children as "serfs" (Guenther 1976). European farmers enslaved San and Khoikhoi, particularly children, and terrorized or slaughtered adults (Giliomee 1981:82–87; R. Ross 1981:223–224).

> On the Eastern frontier, where commandos were raised to exterminate the San, frontiersmen brought back San children and indentured them on the grounds that their parents had been killed and that this would prevent them from starving.... In Natal... in the late 1830s, the slightly more than three hundred burgers who participated in the so-called Cattle Commando received permission beforehand to capture four native children each (Giliomee 1981:86).

One justification for the raids was that San treated children badly (Guenther 1981:115n10).

Slaving is not ancient history. Semai and Btsisi' still talk about Malay razzias against Asli, which continued into the 1920s or 1930s, although slavery was outlawed in 1884 (Cerruti 1904:113; Wheeler 1928:69; Endicott 1983; Gomes 1990:12; Nicholas 1990:68). I have talked with people who said they had survived such razzias. European slave raids on indigenes continue in parts of South America.

Razzias, like colonialist punitive raids, probably (Bodley 1982:45):

> caused loss of life, which was a significant disruption of tribal society in itself, and they seriously disturbed the subsistence economy when stored food or gardens were destroyed. The psychological impact of such displays of overwhelming force would also do much to undermine native morale and the self-confidence necessary for tribal autonomy..

Flexibility of Exploitation and Response

Classifying the flexible political relationships between invaders and refugees is useful for analysis but often plays no important role in the thinking or behavior of the actors. Being serfs did not protect San from "tribute payment, forced labor, kidnapping, murder, rape, and other instruments of oppression" (Wilmsen and

Denbow 1990:493). Nor did the serfdom of some San keep others from trading and yet others from flight to semidesert refuges. Trading and slaving often go together (e.g., Headland 1988b:94–95; Wilmsen and Denbow 1990:492–493, 497). Indeed, invaders can run a sort of "protection racket," promising clients security from attacks by other invaders or by themselves (e.g., von Graeve 1989:111–116; Endicott 1990; Hitchcock 1990:52; Rousseau 1990:242). As noted, the Malay word "Sakai" covers "Orang Asli" indiscriminately, as an ethnic group, as slaves, as bestial infidels, as serfs, as dependants, as clients, and as trading partners, i.e., the whole gamut of possible relationships.

Thus, despite the Great Kalahari Debate (e.g., Solway and Lee 1990; Wilmsen and Denbow 1990), there is no empirical inconsistency between (1) a situation in which refugees are killed, enslaved or otherwise exploited and (2) a situation in which other refugees, or the same refugees at other times and places, live a relatively carefree life in refuges. Indeed, the concept of "refuge" implies the presence of the first situation outside the refuge. Flight is most adaptive when the alternative is death before reproduction. The adaptation is cultural rather than a matter of "hereditary docility" (Simon 1990), however, and therefore can change rapidly. The dichotomizing question of whether San are traditionally free or oppressed implies a "spurious uniformity" (Lee 1990:512; Solway and Lee 1990:109–110), although their way of life, even in "freedom" is at least partly an adaptation to their more powerful neighbors (Wilmsen and Denbow 1990). In a lifetime, individuals and groups of invaders and refugees can move through several patterns of relationships.

Refugee Responses: Personal

"Fear"

However optimal the slaving tactics described above are in terms of invader risk/benefit ratios, however "open" the system of slavery (Watson 1980), razzias tend to horrify refugees who have learned that they lack sanctuaries. The security of everyday life becomes fragile. What seems safe is not. At any moment, irresistible raiders may smash into the settlements to loot, burn, rape, murder, and enslave. The refugee response is fear. This fear underlies the attitude which this chapter calls "negative peaceability" (Gregor 1988; Sponsel 1989:29–30).

For this Hobbesian situation, I use the word "fear" as Hobbes does in "Philosophical Rudiments concerning Government and Society" (1966 [1651]:216n), rather then as psychologists might, who

> presume ... that to fear is nothing else than to be affrighted. I comprehend in this word fear, a certain foresight of future evil; neither do I conceive flight the sole property of fear, but to distrust, suspect, take heed, provide so that they may not fear, is also incident to the fearful. .... It is through fear that men secure themselves by flight indeed, and in corners, if they think that they cannot escape otherwise; but for the most part, by arms ...

Since social pessimists often misconstrue Hobbes, a brief exegesis may be useful (cf. Hobbes 1968[1651]).

1. The word "fear" in Hobbes's time covered a wider semantic range than nowadays, embracing awe, respect, and anxiety.
2. Hobbes stresses that "fear" means not just the emotion (being "affrighted") but the commonsensical or ritual precautions people take to avoid running afoul of frightening situations. If these precautions work, people are no longer "affrighted."
3. He also explicitly includes the mindsets appropriate to the situation which produced the fear and the resulting, anxiety-reducing precautions: caution, circumspection, and wariness, for example. Simple fear of invaders may initially create the precautionary behaviors and cautious mindsets; but they reciprocally reduce the fear to manageable proportions, so that the daily routine of refugee life is not noticeably fearful. "Hobbesian fear" is a useful shorthand for this complex, in which, I think, negative peaceability flowers.

The Semai word -sng^h seems to refer to fear in a Hobbesian sense (Dentan 1978:128–129; Means and Means 1986:89). Asli express their objection to violence in commonsensical rather than fearful (or moral) ways: if you hit people, they'll hit you back; if they've already hit you, hitting them back still means they'll hit you again; violence cannot win. Similarly, a !Kung San headman explained, one should shun fighting because "fighting is very dangerous; 'someone might get killed'" (Marshall 1967:17). The objection is to the consequences that may ensue for the perpetrator. For people who see themselves as powerless to resist violence, the idea of starting a cycle of violence seems stupid. Immunity to retaliation can change that attitude, of course, as discussed below.

Outside the refuge, the first impression refugees make on outsiders is of a people who seem timid or surly, suspicious or mistrustful, evasive or dishonest. Watching their behavior inside the refuge, however, observers may reach completely different conclusions about what refugees are "really like," finding them gentle, friendly, forthcoming, humorous, gossipy, and so on. The seeming incongruity comes from attributing to personality, and to personality alone, behaviors which make sense in mutually contrastive social contexts. Similarly divergent impressions of a people's personality occur when people from upper classes or castes encounter children from lower ones (Ryan 1971:40–42). The mistake is to think that refugees or lower-class children are radically different from other people in their essences or personalities, so that they are, say, incapable of violence (Robarchek and Dentan 1987). To repeat: Peaceability is not disability. Refugees' peacefulness lies as much in their circumstances as in themselves.

Flight

For flight to work as an alternative to fighting, there must be a place to flee to. Otherwise, as Hobbes says, violent resistance is the only recourse. Penan foragers used to live in fear but had no recourse but fighting back (Rousseau 1990:235, 271–273).

> For settled groups, nomads are a resource to be exploited. The nomads must always have felt surrounded: wherever they go, there are swiddeners, and even if they can flee one oppressive group, they have to come terms with another....
> It has been said that nomads have been exploited because they are timid. While

this is true, it is not an explanation. The nomads are timid because they are surrounded by the more numerous agriculturalists.... The only effective action would be withdrawal and this is not feasible in Borneo (Rousseau 1990:241–242).

Letting-Go

Refugees' constant fear may generate a couple of psychological adjustments that differ both from the defiance of people in sanctuaries and the humiliated despair of the conquered. The first involves psychologically giving up the struggle and with it the attempt to control external events. I know no English or psychologese label for the resulting attitude. AAs call it "letting-go;" Hutterites, "Gelassenheit" (see following text). In Daoism, which dates from the Warring States period when armies of thugs roamed China, killing, enslaving, and brutalizing Chinese peasants much as invaders treat refugees, the term for a similar attitude is "wu wei," not striving (Creel 1970; for further references and discussion, see Dentan 1988f:876–877n).

The other adjustment is to avoid direct conflict when possible. Flight is one tactic. "Passive aggression" (Parsons and Wicks 1983) is another. In the ideal behavior, told to me as personal autobiography by three different east Semai men in 1962 on three separate occasions, enraged "Malays" are chasing the hero's friend, screaming obscenities. The hero seizes one Malay's wrist in one hand, the other's in the other and says firmly, "Kill me if you want to. But let my friend go." Abashed, the Malays fall silent, and the Semai escape harm.

On a practical level, the way the same people deal with government officials is a lesson in passive aggression as Parsons defines it (1983:175–176):

> individuals perceive themselves to be abused by those in control and thus view authority figures as unjust and tyrannical. Having a low sense of self-esteem and an inordinate fear of retaliation, the person is unable to directly express anger and aggressive feelings towards authority. Consequently, he or she relies on passive procedures which provide a "safe," somewhat "hidden" avenue for ventilation. Anger and hostility find expression in stubbornness, procrastination, dawdling, intentional inefficiencies, and "forgetfulness."

When abuse or injustice is real, such tactics are adaptive rather than symptoms of "mental illness." In other words, refugee nonviolence does not stem primarily from a personality defect rooted in individual ontogeny. It is a "status personality" appropriate to the invader–refugee situation, which can change as the situation changes (cf. Sargent and Beardsley 1960).[5]

Teaching Fear

The other response to the fear razzias cause is to teach children that external events are uncontrollable and that flight is the proper reaction to danger. Adults may inculcate xenophobia as Orang Asli, Hutterites, and peaceable Zapotec do (Dentan 1976a, 1978:128–130, 1979:59–64; Robarchek 1977, 1979a, b; O'Nell 1979:312–313; Peter 1987:64). Semai and Pacaa Nova use amiably visiting strangers as bogey men to make children fear outsiders (Dentan 1978:128; von Graeve 1989:4) (see Figure 10-1). !Kung San call strangers *zhu dole*, "dangerous people." Non-San are *zo si*, hoofless beasts, "because, they say, non-Bushmen are

Figure 10-1 From behind a housepost nine-year-old Wa' Prankuup grins at the photographer while her father trims rattan in the background. The flirtatious pose expresses an ambiguity common in east Semai social relations: her grin is chummy, but she keeps herself hidden. (Photograph by R. Dentan, 1962.)

angry and dangerous like lions and hyenas" (Thomas 1959:24). Even when adults do not preach xenophobia, simply hearing them describe invaders or watching their reactions to actual encounters must teach children that fleeing violence is more sensible than meeting it with counterforce.

Conversely, refugee adults rarely provide models for violence. In most cases, since their population density is low, refugees can simply move away when internecine quarrels move towards violence, just as they move away from invaders (e.g., von Graeve 1989:106, 112, 116, 118). Thus San "are extremely wary of persons known to have violent tempers or unpredictable behavior" and shun them (Draper 1978:40; cf. von Graeve 1989:111–112). Otherwise, Aslians or peaceable Zapotec, who have cause to be angry, fall into named states of "soul loss" which is said to make them liable to sickness or injury unless the offender assuages their hurt feeling, a syndrome resembling passive aggression. Refugee adults fend off a child's attack with laughter; but they immediately, without laughter, cart away any child who seems about to attack its playmates (Draper 1978:36–39; Turnbull 1978:184–186; Dentan 1979:61). The child gets no practice in fighting as opposed to fleeing. As a result, at least among Semai, San, and peaceable Zapotec (but not among violent Zapotec), children learn such self-control that their spontaneous games may involve seeming to strike at each other without ever actually landing a blow (for photograph, see Alland 1980:433–434; cf. Dentan 1979:59; Guenther 1981:111; Robarchek and Dentan 1987:362; Fry 1988a, 1990). Such self-control is required in the absence of external control (cf. Robbins 1973:101).

The situation appears different among Mbuti, who seem rarely to have suffered slave raids. "For children, life is one long frolic, interspersed with a healthy sprinkle of spankings and slappings. Sometimes these seem unduly severe, but it is all part of their training" (Turnbull 1962:129). Such training may help prepare Mbuti children for the physically painful initiation rites their non-Pygmy neighbors impose on them. For Semai, particularly east Semai, who almost never strike children ("Suppose you hit it and it DIED?"), such discipline would seem invaderish. Moreover, many peaceable intentional communities discipline children harshly (see below), so that enculturating nonaggression may be a relatively minor factor in the creation of peaceability compared with the "status personality" discussed above, which varies according to circumstances.

Discontinuity Between Infancy and Childhood

Another factor in enculturation which may have the unintended consequence of teaching children insecurity is the discontinuity between the way people treat young children and older ones, characterized by O'Nell (1979) for the peaceable Zapotec as "affective nurturance" followed by "affective neutrality" (cf. Dentan 1979; Peter 1987:63–64). For east Semai, Hutterites, and peaceable Zapotec, the result seems to be people who are fully engaged in their social system but "expected to be reserved, aloof and not affectively involved in their relations with others" (O'Nell 1979:308; cf. Dentan 1978).

Nurturance

For flight to work as an adaptation to invader violence requires people to shelter refugees as well as places to go. Almost all peaceable people stress sharing as an objective correlative of such nurturance (e.g., Thomas 1959:22; Turnbull 1962:102, 107, 134, 274; Dowling 1968; Robbins 1973:101; Price 1975; Robarchek 1977; Dentan 1979:48–50). Sharing expresses mutual dependence; failure to share portends the physical danger selfish people pose to the group (Gibson 1985, 1986b, 1989).

The Semai and Btsisi' trope for sharing and nurture is "feeding;" a foster child is a "fed child." They stress that individual survival depends on sharing. Any formal public assembly includes a recitation of past aid given and received, with the explicit assertion that everyone depends on others, that no one can survive alone and that band members are all siblings. Not sharing food when one can afford to is "taboo," *phunan*, and increases the risk that rejected people will fall sick or have an accident (Robarchek 1977; Dentan 1979:55–56). Not to share is thus to do violence. Similarly, the peaceable Siriono express aggression almost entirely through food (Holmberg 1950:61–62, 98), and Gebusi sharing works against aggression (Knauft 1987c).[6]

Depending on people, however, entails the chance that they may let one down. The tension becomes obvious when large game is to be shared, and may account for the prevalence of joking and respect relationships, which relieve or prevent tension, among peaceable peoples (for the complex relationships between !Kung sharing and joking, see Marshall (1961) and Lee (1984:64–66, 76, 92, 151–157); cf. Dentan (1979:48–50, 74–75) and Knauft (1987a:478)). Cross-culturally, joking and avoidance tend to flourish in relationships where tensions are potentially greatest (Radcliffe-Brown 1965:90–116).

On the one hand, a Semai "ego" is the center of a set of neighbors and kinsmen variably "distant" from ego and proportionally dangerous, Malays being only the most distant and most dangerous (Dentan 1975, 1976a, b). By the same token, neighbors and kinsmen are variably "close" to ego and proportionally nurturant. Mbuti seem to structure their social world similarly (Mosko 1987). Thus all human relationships are ambivalent: potentially dangerous, potentially nurturant. The farther from ego, the more dangerous, with invaders the ultimate in frightfulness.

Generalization of Xenophobia

As Americans who warn children about child molesters have learned, teaching xenophobia teaches that the whole world is threatening, not just strangers. The fear "generalizes," as psychologists say. Similarly, teaching letting-go and its complementary self-control teaches both that the world is uncontrollable and that uncontrolled emotions are dangerous. Thus peaceable Zapotec stress emotional reserve (O'Nell 1979). Asli in refuges deny ever being angry (cf. Howell 1988; Nagata 1990) while those being incorporated into Malaysia's rural proletariat do not. A Semai anthropologist (Juli 1987) writes

> Semai that lived deep in the forest . . . fear their own strong feelings . . . But for Semai who lived near town, this concept isn't true, even though they depend on each other most of the time (example: wedding, death) because they do show their feelings somehow, whether in front or at the back of the person. Anyway, we believe it is very rude to show out your anger or laugh at others because this attitude might threaten the good relationships among us.

Thus, the xenophobia which creates "negative peaceability" ultimately creates behavior conducive to "positive peaceability;" conversely the erosion of xenophobia by contact may subvert both sorts of peaceability.

As noted above, invader–refugee dualism pervades refugee cognitive systems. Stereotyped, the invader stands for the inverse of human decency, and in several refugee ideologies plays the same function that witches play in others. The stereotype impels refugees to turn to their own people for comfort and security (Dentan 1976a). Robarchek (1988) (see Figure 10-2) suggests that, since believing that one's own people might be witches would threaten social solidarity and positive peaceability, beliefs in evil spirits or demonic invaders may substitute for the witchcraft beliefs found among other peoples like the peaceable Zapotec (e.g., O'Nell 1979:317; Dentan 1988f; Gregor 1988; Robarchek 1988). The invader bogeyman promotes both sorts of peace: negative, by showing how fearful aggression can be; and positive, by making people value warm social relations

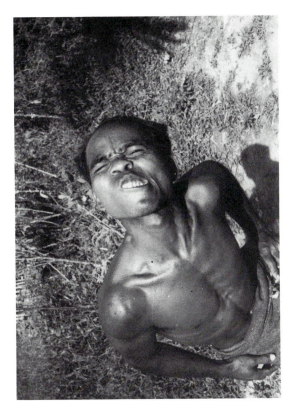

Figure 10-2   Risaw, the father of Prankuup in Figure 10-1, gives a humorous demonstration of an evil spirit's agonistic grimace. Other Asli (Jah Hut and Btsisi') make masks and sculptures of evil spirits with similarly twisted features. (Photograph by R. Dentan, 1962.)

within the refugee community. In other words, the social invader–refugee dualism shows up in an ideological dualism of demonic rule outside refugee society and nurturant security within.

Refugee Responses: Social

Band-style Organization

The phenomena just described are common, although not universal, among foraging bands, leading some students to lament that "peacefulness is found only in simple band societies" and must be reinvented by people higher on the evolutionary totem pole (Denich 1987:1). Therefore, it is worth remarking that, although some foragers manage to continue hunting and gathering after being incorporated as dependent traders or as a low caste into invader societies, they do not seem especially peaceable there (e.g., Siedentopf 1946; Queeny 1952; Huntingford 1954; Sheldrick 1957; Simon and Treichel 1959; Peterson 1978; Gamst 1979; Blackburn 1982; Dentan 1988f; Rousseau 1990:272–273). The association between foraging and nonviolence is not that the former causes the latter. Rather, the flexibility of band social organization suits it both to foragers and to refugees. Refugees must scatter in flight; absorb their losses, often of leaders; and join together again, perhaps with new people in a "fission–fusion" model which, as noted in the brief description of the refuge model, recalls the demographic pattern of prey subjected to extremely efficient predation (e.g., Marshall 1967:34–36; Fix and Lie-Injo 1975; Endicott 1983; Gibson 1986a; von Graeve 1989:60, 106, 112, 116, 118; Gomes 1990:22–23). The ability to disperse and regroup, an important part of the foraging band adaptation to environmental variability, is thus a "preadaptation" to razzias.

This "preadaptation" to refuge life, plus the relatively low population density of foragers compared with more powerful peoples, may account for the former's prominence in the literature on peaceful people. Nonhunters need not despair of peaceful life because of "some mystic, archaetypal estrangement from nomadic hunting societies" (Guenther 1977:203; cf. Dentan 1988a, d; Wilmsen and Denbow 1990). Aslian, Philippine, and Xinguano swiddeners, Amish and Hutterite farmers, and many enclaved peoples with band-like social organization also lead peaceful lives.

Other characteristics of bands may be adaptive in invader–refugee situations (e.g., Service 1962, 1966; Fried 1967:28–35; Keesing and Keesing 1971:133–138; Fabbro 1980:181). By definition, this "simplest, most rudimentary form of social organization" (Service 1962:107) is a homogeneous primary group. That is, any member interacts face-to-face with all other members, and does so oftener than she interacts with outsiders. Sharing ("generalized reciprocity") is the dominant mode of exchange, with the results noted above. Band autonomy and autarky (e.g., Marshall 1967:19–20) let people survive even if razzias decimate their neighbors.

The ultimate basis for band membership is territorial, although initial affiliation is by birth or marriage (e.g., Marshall 1967:33–34). The territory is a tract of land with whose specific resources people are familiar and which they routinely exploit. The relation between band and territory is economic, historic, and sentimental, so that a territory is not alienable, not defended, and not clearly demarcated. Thus there is no jural reason to exclude fellow refugees fleeing invaders (cf. Gibson 1986a).

Most political, economic, or religious activities other than marriage recruit participants only from within the band. Decision making is usually egalitarian (Sponsel 1989:36), reflecting people's uneasiness about external control, and leadership rests on locally recognized persuasive talent (e.g., hunting prowess, verbal facility, spiritual contacts). In many nonhierarchical societies, including bands, "[l]ong meetings are held to discuss issues of community concern and much time and energy are devoted to these events. But in many cases, either no decision is reached in meetings or a decision is made but later ignored and seemingly forgotten" (Brison 1989:97; for examples, see Brenneis and Myers 1984). Such meetings: (1) bore people into resolving their conflicts just so they can get on with their lives (Robarchek 1979b); (2) let everyone ventilate grievances; and (3) reinforce a system which "discourages disruptive action and allows individuals to influence events in relatively cost-free ways" (Brison 1989:99). Though any faculty member knows that long inconclusive meetings occur in other contexts, the relevant link here is to egalitarian politics in small isolated communities, where coercion is almost impossible (Brison 1989:98).

Noneconomic distinctions based on age and sex are informal and unelaborate (e.g., Marshall 1967:38–39; Endicott 1984). Since newcomers fleeing other areas would have to learn their place and the places of others, a constant influx of newcomers makes a consistent hierarchy hard to maintain. Acephaly minimizes the consequences, if not the likelihood, of the murder by invaders of particular leaders (Gibson 1986a). In the absence of authority, cosmologies tend to be flexible, amorphous and individualistic (Gardner 1966; Guenther 1979; Dentan 1988f).

Still, nonviolence is no more universal among bands than among foragers (Marshall 1967:25, 39, 41; Dentan 1988a, d). Indeed, killing people who threaten group survival may occur most often in foraging bands (Otterbein 1986:49–60). Moreover, although in band societies peaceable living seems congenial with egalitarianism by age and gender, it does not necessitate age or gender equality. Stratification in peaceable societies, when it occurs, usually involves ostensible patriarchy or "power-empty hierarchies (such as age–respect hierarchies), which do not reflect social prestige or social power beyond that which comes with age to all people" (Colby 1967:424).

On the other hand, there is some evidence that otherwise egalitarian societies in which men seek to control women's sexuality, sexual rivalries generate a lot of violence (e.g., Knauft 1987a). Even among Semai the frustrations of love increase the chance of violence, although it may take the form of suicide rather than the murder of rivals or the beloved. The sociobiological tenet that success in violent rivalry increases a man's access to women works only if women are attracted to violent men or if the victor is willing and able to subdue women by force. For many refugees, like Semai, neither condition holds (Dentan 1988b, c, e).

CONJECTURAL HISTORY OF THIS ADAPTATION

Introduction

To the degree that nonviolence stems from having a geographic refuge, nonviolence must also be a transitory phase in a people's history. So, of course, is violence. It seems worthwhile to add a temporal dimension to the model by sketching where refuges seem to fit in the processes of cultural contact and acculturation.

Origins

Beginnings

Accounts of "first contact" are speculative. Still, the history of native Australians and European invaders suggests a preliminary scheme (Elkin 1967). First contacts are probably tentative, and it is pointless to speculate whether or not they are peaceful. If only because invaders are too few at first to menace natives, one might expect the invaders to be cautious about starting violence. However, the first account of Europeans (Vikings) meeting native North Americans (Thordharson 1938 [1387]:12) suggests that people traditionally violent will remain so:

> They . . . discovered on the sands, in beyond the headland, three mounds: they went up to these, and saw that they were three skin canoes with three men under each. They thereupon divided their party, and succeeded in seizing all the men but one, who escaped with his canoe. They killed the eight men . . . .

In response to the Vikings' unprovoked attack, the locals raided the Viking camp. The following year, however, they tried to set up trade relations, a pattern of alternate or simultaneous trade and violence which, as noted above, is characteristic of frontier situations and which presumably characterizes most early contact situations (Thordharson 1938 [1387]:12–13, 15–16). The last recorded skirmish between Vikings and "Skrellings," i.e., indigenous Americans (Thordharson 1938 [1387]:16), suggests one way nonviolence and flight as a tactic might originate in the realization of invader military superiority. During the skirmish

> [o]ne of the Skrellings picked up an [iron Viking] axe; and, having looked at it for a time, he brandished it about one of his companions, and hewed at him, and on the instant the man fell dead. Thereupon the big man [who led the Skrelling forces] seized the axe; and, after examining it for a moment, he hurled it as far as he could out into the sea. Then they fled helter skelter into the woods, and thus their intercourse [with Vikings] came to an end.

Similarly, the fact that Columbus began contact by kidnapping natives to act as interpreters (Columbus 1938 [1493]:24) may partly account for the striking "timidity" he attributes to them (Columbus 1938 [1493]:21, 23, 26). On the other hand, their propensity to flee may have stemmed from fear of the "ferocious" cannibals they told him about (Columbus 1938 [1493]:25–26).

Resistance by Force

As the number of invaders increases and competition for frontier resources pushes them further and further into the refuge, refugees may turn increasingly to countervailing violence. As long as refugees retain sanctuaries where they can do serious damage to invaders in local engagements, violent resistance may continue. The violence attributed to some band societies may be due to their being at this second stage of contact, retaining sanctuaries in some places invaders rarely penetrate, e.g., the upper part of river basins, where "the Pacaa Nova were concentrated and where they were relatively safe from intruders, who would not risk an ambush on these narrow streams" (von Graeve 1989:10).

     The standard account of the Andamanese (Radcliffe-Brown 1964:6–7) paints them as foragers, entirely isolated from others because of their penchant for killing and devouring anyone who landed on their shores. This picture rests on a ninth century Arab account and an excerpt from Marco Polo's "*Travels.*" The rapacity of Moslem slavers in Southeast Asia makes indigenous ferocity superfluous to understanding Andamanese inhospitality to Arab voyagers (Cipriani 1966:3–4; Endicott 1983; Reid 1988). Radcliffe-Brown ignores reports of peaceful contact (Cipriani 1966:4) and dismisses the part of Polo's account (1934:377) which does not fit his preconceptions, without suggesting why it is less reliable than the part he accepts:

> They have abundance and variety of drugs. Their food is rice and milk, and flesh of every description. They have Indian nuts, apples, and many other fruits different from those which grow in our country (Polo 1934:377).

Isolated foragers would not live on rice, milk, and coconuts. Moreover, most foragers do not as adults produce the enzyme lactase necessary to digest lactose (milk sugar). The "commonly accepted view" is that, as an adaptation to animal husbandry during the last 10,000 years or so, human adults became able to produce lactase; San foragers produce it as a result of their long association with pastoralists (Casimir 1990:552).

Therefore, Polo's Andamanese either (1) were invaders, in which case there is no reason to think that they treated the indigenes better than later invaders did, or (2) were at one time not foragers and able to resist invasions successfully. The North Sentenelese and Jarawa, who continued to fight off invaders and their native allies (Radcliffe-Brown 1964:12–19; Cipriani 1966:2–4; Venkatesan 1990:50), were "surrounded by seas so stormy that they are frequently impassable" and "well sheltered by an unbelievably dense forest" (Cipriani 1966:2), i.e., in a sanctuary. The Onge, in a refuge on Little Andaman, became peaceable (Cipriani 1966) after a period of violent resistance (Venkatesan 1990:49).

Violent San resistance to European, Bantu, and Khoikhoi encroachment is well documented (e.g., Wright 1971; Marks 1972; Guenther 1977:199n8; Giliomee 1981:83, 97; Saunders 1981:151). Asli history is murkier. The oldest Malay history, the Hikayat Marong Mahawangsa (ʿAbdul-Hadi 1925:16–23), describes how invading Malays defeated Asli armies (cf. de Morgan 1886:58–61). In 1976 Btsisi', who used tree houses to escape Malay slavers (Skeat and Blagden 1906, I:180–183), recalled with relish letting slavers part way up the rope ladders before cutting the ropes so that the invaders crashed to the ground. Semai tell similar stories of a war with Malays (Robarchek and Robarchek 1990:1–2). Endicott (1983, 1990) gives other examples of violent resistance by Asli into whose sanctuaries slavers penetrated only rarely (cf. Mikluho-Maclay 1878:206). As noted above, most Aslian homicide involves non-Asli.

Other currently peaceful peoples may have violently resisted invasion in the past. For example, although the Siriono of Bolivia normally fled from more powerful invader tribes who killed the men and enslaved the women and children (Holmberg 1950:8–10, 62–63), they may have sporadically resisted European invasion (Fabbro 1980:181, 185; cf. von Graeve 1989). Robarchek (1987) has seen Waorani

> change from an extremely violent society to an essentially nonviolent one (although there are still bands that have not made the change, and an occasional relapse among those that have) . . . [T]he crucial initial changes were social (the creation of a structural level that permitted mediation between hostile bands) and cultural (the conscious and explicit adoption of a new value system).

Meanwhile, trade relations take on a patron–client structure which becomes serfdom as local invader power increases. When invaders become able to penetrate refuges at will and their military superiority becomes overwhelming, they may exterminate refugees, assimilate them to an underclass or exploit them as subhuman natural resources.

Destruction of Refuge

To the degree that nonviolence stems from refuge life, destroying a refuge opens the door to violence. The native Australian experience (Elkin 1967) suggests possible futures. When invasion of the refuge is complete, or exploitation ("development") has destroyed the refuge ecology, then geographic flight is impossible, and erstwhile refugees must seek alternatives.

Violent resistance is always possible, particularly as invader traders peddle alcohol and advanced weapons to former refugees. Moreover, since invaders generally see refugees as an undifferentiated subhuman mass, invader state agencies for dealing with them may treat all alike. This treatment may overcome the mutual distrust that refuge life can generate to the point that refugees form themselves into ethnic groups which reflect the invaders' categories, e.g., "Abos," "Indians," or "Orang Asli" (Gomes 1988a; Hood 1990:141; [Williams-Hunt] 1989b).

This chapter, however, examines only nonviolent alternatives. At first, surrender may seem like one nonviolent possibility. For refugees to submit to assimilative pressures, however, not only ultimately leads to their destruction as a distinct people but proximately most often assures the transfer of their traditional land to invader "development" or "resettlement" schemes (Nietschmann 1987). They become landless peasants or reservation aborigines, dependants of the invader state, "parasites" (Elkin 1967; Gomes 1987, 1990; Peterson 1990:61). Australian and South African experience suggests that "relocation is detrimental to people even if land supposedly equivalent in ecological terms is provided" (Hitchcock 1990:54). Deprivation makes them prey to despair, alcohol, self-hatred, suicide, and violence (Gomes 1987; Nagata 1990). For example, the San present (Guenther 1976, 1977; Lee 1984:147–150; Ritchie 1988) seems like the future that Asli most fear. Dispossessed of their hunting grounds, many San entered the South African, Namibian, or Botswanan rural underclass as de facto serfs to Bantu or as often unemployed, landless farm laborers:

> They are severely impoverished, malnurtured, exploited and a large percentage are unemployed. They are totally dependant [sic] on whites: for employment, residential and grazing rights and water. . . . [Wages are] much below the legal minimum . . . only about a half or a third of what black farm labourers are paid (Guenther 1977:197).

Like many other former refugees they recognized that they needed a land base to survive (Nietschmann 1987). The first demand of politically active San was for a reservation (Guenther 1976, 1977:201), but San "homelands," ostensibly kept in trust for the people, are up for grabs as far as their powerful neighbors are concerned (e.g., Marshall 1984; Hitchcock 1988, 1990). Similarly, the Orang Asli union founded in 1977 lists secure land tenure as its first priority ([Williams-Hunt] 1989b:1), although the experience of other infidel peoples under Muslim rule is not hopeful (Pipes 1983:164–167), and over 80% of the land recognized as "Orang Asli areas" has not been gazetted as Orang Asli property ([Williams-Hunt] 1989b:1).

Destroying the Peace

Alcohol

To the degree that (1) nonviolence stems from anxiety and (2) alcohol reduces anxiety, introducing alcohol to a people may erode negative peaceability. My impression is that many peaceable peoples, including Orang Asli and native North Americans outside the southwest, have no indigenous alcoholic beverages (e.g., Cipriani 1966:5, 46; MacAndrew and Edgerton 1969; Shostak 1981:216, 347) or at least no tradition of heavy drinking. Conversely, a number of foraging band peoples who are not particularly peaceable, e.g. Okiek and Agta, seem to use alcohol often (Blackburn 1982:295; Headland, cited in Knauft 1987b:490). Cross-culturally the statistical association between drinking and violence is overwhelming. Among Alaskan natives, for example, "alcohol-related accidental death, murder, and suicide are the leading killers" (Wohlforth 1990:9).

Within this nexus, however, causal connections are unclear (Mangin 1957; MacAndrew and Edgerton 1969; Wilson 1983:233; Wilson and Herrnstein 1985:356–363). Drunken violence is not random but culturally patterned, so that, for instance, Native American onlookers may say that a Native American whose drunken violence does not fit the normal acculturated Indian pattern is "drinking like a white man" (e.g., Holmberg 1950:62; Lemert 1958:101). Part of the violence which sometimes follows heavy drinking may be due to conforming to invader stereotypes or imitating the invaders themselves. In the life of Euroamerican frontiersmen, drunken violence is commonplace (e.g., von Graeve 1989:25, 44). People who do not normally shun aggression may simply integrate drinking into previous patterns of violence, as Northwest Coast Indians integrated it into potlatch feasting (Lemert 1958).

In short, while drinking may not be sufficient to produce drunken violence, it facilitates the expression of violence along stress lines already present even in a peaceable society (e.g., Lee 1984:140, 144, 147, 148; Shostak 1981:204, 251; Knauft 1987b:490). Thus introducing alcohol works against peaceability.

Firearms

To the degree that (1) nonviolence stems from a disparity in power and resultant Hobbesian fear, and (2) a gun is a practical and psychic "equalizer" (Silberman 1978:36–37, 58), the ready availability of firearms potentiates violence (Zimring 1967, 1972; Schur 1969:143, 237; Wilson 1983:261–264). Guns make it easy to kill; that is why gunshot wounds are the eighth leading cause of death in the U.S., accounting for 60% of the 20,000 or so homicides annually (Malcolm 1990).

> The trading post left the unarmed tribes at the mercy of those that had purchased fire-arms—a truth which the Iroquois Indians wrote in blood.... The trading frontier,

while steadily undermining Indian power by making the tribes dependent on the whites, yet, through its sale of guns, gave to the Indians increased power of resistance to the farming frontier (Turner 1894:209).

Invaders do not always agree among themselves. To further their own interests, they may arm indigenous people and urge them to kill other invaders, as in the "French and Indian War" (e.g., von Graeve 1989:20). Since the invader state is often occupied with repressing insurrections by its own people, erstwhile refugees may gain military skills and confidence in dealing with armed invaders or indigenous rebels; conversely, they may join the rebels and gain the same experience (Kolata 1981; Nietschmann 1987; Robarchek and Dentan 1987; Robarchek and Robarchek 1990). Soldiering typically pays more than work on the reserves (e.g., Marshall 1984). Returning soldiers may introduce heavy drinking into their home communities (e.g., Ahmad Tajuddin, quoted in Nagata 1990:9; Lee 1984:140–145).

Since one of the few marketable skills former refugees have is familiarity with the refuge area, men may join the invader state's army or paramilitary forces as trackers. San and Orang Asli have obtained weapons and skills this way. As noted in the introduction to this paper, they have become violent enough to earn their keep; conversely, for Penan, once relatively violent, the nonviolent tactics they learned from Western environmentalists have been successful enough to win wide adoption. Since peaceability is not disability, such intelligent adaptations to political ecology merit less astonishment or gloating than they seem to incur (e.g., Leary 1989). Hobbesian fear is not a psychic essence but an intelligent emotional and attitudinal response to disproportionate power; change the power relations, and the response will change.

In short, invader states arm and unify former refugees. Also, although individual invaders may despise refugees, they sell them both alcohol, which melts constraints against rage, and weaponry, which facilitates expressing that rage. Thus invader state policies and individual bigotry work to foster violent resistance.

Rise of New Ethnic Identities

As already noted, however heterogeneous the peoples on one side of a frontier, they share the characteristic of being opposed in several senses to peoples on the other. Thus a frontier is a "consolidating agent" (Turner 1894:210, 219–221). Treating mutually distinct refugees as a single category potentiates the development of a "refugee" social identity like "Asli" or even "Semai" (Dentan 1979:1–4; Gomes 1988a; Hood 1990).

In the 1970s the sense of "Asli" as an ethnic identity remained elusive for the people the term covers (Dentan 1975, 1976a, b). Arabic supplies the "educated" and genteel words in Malay as Greek and Latin do in English, and the word "Asli" is of Arabic origin, designed to replace the English "Aborigine" as that term had replaced the even more derogatory word "Sakai." Early attempts to form an Asli "union" foundered on mistrust between the Temiar, heirs of British favoritism, and the more numerous and better educated Semai. When the union (POASM) took form, it began cautiously to argue against assimilationist policies.

In 1987 the leadership resigned to avoid conflict with more militant "progressives," who apparently sought a better deal for Asli within the framework of assimilation ([Williams-Hunt] 1989b; cf. Memmi 1965:x, xiv). Asli seemed to be gaining sympathizers among Malaysian liberals, e.g., environmentalists who feared the ecological consequences of destroying Asli refuges, civil rights activists who worried about the implications of Asli dispossession and dependency, as evidenced in articles in environmentalist publications (e.g., Catmandu and Sivashanmugam 1987; Todd 1990) and in *The Star*, a Penang newspaper associated both with the Malaysian Chinese Association and the first Malaysian Prime Minister, Tunku Abdul Rahman (e.g., Ambimathe 1987; Anonymous 1987a, b, c, d; Gomes 1987; Hoh and Matthews 1987; Man and Hoh 1987; Nicholas 1987; Paul 1987; Selva 1987). The mass arrest of environmentalists, Chinese politicians, feminists, civil rights activists, and spokesmen for non-Malay indigenes in October 1987, has muted Asli ethnic self-assertion (e.g., Anonymous 1987e; Crossette 1987a, b, c; Suhaini 1987; Tan 1990).

Dispossessed San, like dispossessed Asli, are coming to have a sense of themselves as a people with a common ethnic identity that transcends language (Guenther 1976, 1977:201). Indigenous leadership for this emergent people seems to be arising (Guenther 1975, 1975/76). Pariah status helps enclaved peoples maintain their identity, as in Northeast Africa.

At first glance, these new identities seem to have the potential of maintaining peaceful ways of life within the violence and coercion of modern nation-states. It may be useful therefore to look at intentional groups that seek more or less consciously and diligently to construct a society in many ways like the one that occurs naturally among refugees (Holloway 1951:21–22, see note 13; Castile 1981:xviii). This conscious effort produces a lifestyle that merits comparison with that of people like the Gullah, peaceable descendants of slaves who have a refuge on the Sea Islands (Jones-Jackson 1987; Rosengarten 1987).

PEACEABLE INTENTIONAL SOCIETIES

Introduction

A similar evolution through violent resistance to peace-loving seems to mark the birth of self-consciously nonviolent intentional groups in modern Western societies. The persistence of nonviolent groups inside nation-states may shed light on whether refugee nonviolence can outlive the refuge. Many such groups are "cenobitic," i.e., seek to establish a community which follows an explicit code in which positive peaceable attitudes are salient, i.e., pacifism. The following account summarizes a discussion which is to appear elsewhere (Dentan n.d.).

Cenobites

Both the Camisards who influenced Shakerism and the Anabaptist forerunners of American Hutterites and Amish instigated violence and suffered defeat (Holloway 1951:29; Hostetler 1974:6–27; Johnson 1976:260; McKay et al. 1984:636, 646).

The Anabaptists were violent revolutionaries, "the left wing of the Reformation" (Holloway 1951:29; Hostetler 1974:7; McKay et al. 1984:645; Chodorow et al. 1986:446). Their leader

> signed his letters with the Sword of Gideon and the phrase "Thomas Muntzer the Hammer...." "Let not the sword of the saint get cold" was his motto; and his heraldic sign was a red cross and a naked sword ... (Johnson 1976:261; cf. Mayer 1954:132).

Revolutionary Anabaptist communities were authoritarian and violent (Mayer 1954:392; Hostetler 1974:6, 21; Johnson 1976:262–263; McKay et al. 1984:646), becoming peaceable and egalitarian only after their bloody repression (Ahlstrom 1972:231). Pacificism seems to have begun to spread rapidly in the years after the crushing of the main rebellion in 1525, perhaps as a conscious reaction to military defeat (Hostetler 1974:6; Peter 1987:10, 27–28). Persecution continued, of course (e.g., Holloway 1951; Hostetler 1974:11–12), but the sects which survived were pacifist, while resisters "died out" (Hostetler 1974:26).

Shakerism seems partly an outgrowth of proselytizing by refugee "French prophets," Huguenot revolutionaries called Camisards in France (Holloway 1951:56; Mayer 1954:422; Ahlstrom 1972:494; Foster 1981:23–24; but see Foster 1981:267n9). The long vicious persecution of Protestants after the revocation of the Edict of Nantes in 1688 spawned the Camisard movement, whose revolutionary counterviolence led to incredible brutality on both sides and drove hundreds of thousands of Huguenot refugees to England, Holland, and Prussia (Schwartz 1980:11–27; McKay et al. 1984:727; Chodorow et al. 1986:586).

Though alcohol addiction brings recruits to AA, an explicit sense of defeat underlies their acceptance of the AA "program." Inability to play one's part in ordinary or even in alcoholic society is a major factor in convincing people to join. As long as life outside AA seems "manageable," heavy drinkers opt to continue (e.g., Kessel and Walton 1967:143, 153–155; Schur 1969:212; Spradley 1970:12–64; Weppner 1973, 1983:8–17). Their "deviant" pattern of living may "preadapt" them for membership in the relatively closed society of AA, which recruits most successfully among those who have "hit bottom," i.e., those whose suffering far outweighs pleasure (e.g., Kessel and Walton 1967:87, 105–106; Anonymous 1972; Alcoholics Anonymous 1976:171–561).

Shared Characteristics

North American nonviolent groups share several traits (Hardman 1924; Ahlstrom 1972:231). They have a Malinowskian charter derived from a notion of primitive Christianity which stresses asceticism, equality, mutual aid, sharing (communalism or communism), and regular face-to-face meeting in primary groups (e.g., Kessel and Walton 1967; Hostetler 1974; Brewer 1986:21). All involve conversion, which begins with fear or pain and includes an element of surrender and acceptance which brings those feelings within tolerable limits.

Gelassenheit and "Letting-Go"

"Gelassenheit," roughly equivalent to "letting-go," is a central tenet for Hutterites and Amish. In this sort of "self-surrender," one "lets go" of worldly concerns and turns one's life over to God's will, making one's own will one with God's, serenely detached from property and sexual love (Hostetler and Huntington 1967:15; Hostetler 1974:144–145, 201–202; Peter 1987:11–12, 40–41). Although Hutterites stress that "personal suffering [is] a necessary condition for following Christ" (Hostetler 1974:11), the intrinsic trope of Gelassenheit is of relaxing, not stress or effort. It solves suffering; it is a "state of mind," not an emotion or feeling (Peter 1987:29).

The first step of the 12-step AA program consciously draws on the same Christian roots as Gelassenheit (Kessel and Walton 1967:140, 141, 153; Anonymous 1972:165; Alcoholics Anonymous 1976:59): "We admitted we were powerless over alcohol—that our lives had become unmanageable." The fear of admitting personal powerlessness (Kessel and Walton 1967:105–106) is like the Hobbesian fear of refugees faced with overwhelmingly powerful invaders. The traditional public admission of being "sick and tired of being sick and tired" as the sole criterion of membership resembles the Shaker requirement (Ahlstrom 1972:492).

Band-like Organization

These groups attribute band-like social organization to the early Christians they emulate. In fact, of course, whatever their mythic charter, such revitalization movements recur throughout European history. In the 1960s alienated youngsters adopted idealized "primitives" instead of primitive Christians as models for quasi-cenobitic communities or "alternative" psychotherapies. New Agers and Jungians in the 1980s continued to expound supposed "primitive spirituality" (McGlashan 1987; Dentan 1988a; cf. Holloway 1951:21–22). For example, American "Senoi dream therapy" mimics a fictitious communitarian Temiar and Semai praxis (e.g., Leonard 1968:165–168; Dentan 1983a, b, c, 1984, 1987; Domhoff 1985; Strunz 1985; McGlashan 1987, 1988).

Affiliation with a particular local group usually depends on proximity or birth. Membership is flexible, following a fission–fusion pattern like that of bands (Barkun 1986:135–137; Hostetler 1974:370–372; Peter 1987:61, 81). Leadership often rests on persuasion. Age and sex distinctions within the group may be subordinate to the principle of egalitarianism. Members should share resources and often "feelings," e.g. in confession. Many social activities, e.g., dances and picnics, involve only group members, and so on.

Still, differences of degree and kind exist between intentional nonviolent groups and peaceable refugees. Where refugee egalitarianism and nonviolence often seem unselfconscious, equality and nonviolence are explicit central values for the intentional groups, with an authoritative mythic charter of their own (Sponsel 1989:41–43). For example, the communism of Shakers and Hutterites comes from Acts 2:44–45 and 5:1–11. Both are rigorous communists, with group ownership of property. Amish and other Mennonites are communalists, who mandate nurturance and sharing within the community. All refer to Acts 4:32–37, in which God kills Ananias and Ananias' wife, who had tried to avoid giving all they had to the Church by underreporting how much money they earned from selling their property. Cenobitic sharing is thus quite different from the informal sharing that occurs in peaceable refugee bands.

Maintaining Identity

Group identity is not a problem for people hiding in a geographic refuge. Most intentional groups, however, live in enclaved reserves. They need special tactics to remain unique (Castile 1981:xix).

Although cenobites live in close-knit communities, maintaining geographical isolation in North America is hard. Still, despite depending on the outside world for technology, Hutterites remain socially isolated from it (Holloway 1951:212–213; Hostetler 1974). AA and other therapeutic "fellowships," especially those focused on obsessive–compulsive behavior or shared traumas, isolate themselves structurally by preserving anonymity, refusing or limiting outside funding and publicity, limiting at least some meetings to members, neither endorsing nor opposing causes which engage the attention of the wider society, using a patois partly unintelligible to outsiders, and in other ways fostering a "we-group" ethos. Although groups modelled on AA are growing and diversifying, their insulation seems successful enough to have kept them relatively immune to social science (but see, e.g., Weppner 1983; Gartner 1984; Suler 1984).

Neither Hutterites nor Amish stress shared descent. Although one major schism was about language, being of German origin seems unimportant (Turner 1894:216–217; Hawgood 1940; Nowak 1972:46–48). The British origins of Shakerism did not slow its rapid growth in the North during the Civil War. Although disproportionately few African Americans join AA, "race" is of no ideological importance. Ethnic or "racial" slurs are signs of "not working the program."

Common icons often outweigh shared orthodoxy in preserving group identity (Schwartz 1975). Unlike avowing a belief, flaunting a group-specific icon actually demonstrates membership, so that quarrels about such apparent minutiae are far more likely to lead to fission than quarrels about dogma (Mayer 1954:393; Knauft 1985a:327–328). Similarly, though ideology may oppose group members to outsiders, it is ritual which reflects and maintains a separate identity (e.g., Hostetler 1974:169–177, 257–260). The 12 steps of AA are explicitly "suggestions" (Alcoholics Anonymous 1976:59), though group pressure to conform is heavy. Individual cenobites may have "weird" or "radical" ideas (Mayer 1954:391) as long as they participate in group meetings and rituals (Holloway 1951:73; Peter 1987:30–31, 67–68; cf. Peter 1987:30–31). Agreeing on the meaning of such icons is supererogatory. Insisting on agreement might undermine solidarity (e.g., Gilsenan 1982:20, 33; Knauft 1985a:328–329; cf. Castile 1981:xix; Dentan 1988f).

AAs, for instance, maintain their identity in part by a "memorable, technical language" (Kessel and Walton 1967:141) in which outsiders are "normal people" or "earth people" and drinkers "wet people" whom "AAs" should avoid (cf. Peter 1987:64). AA slogans imply identity, e.g., bumperstickers proclaim "Easy does it" or "One day at a time." The program stresses the need to maintain the gregariousness and solidarity characteristic of band societies while hiding members' true identities as alcoholics from nonmembers who might react with prejudice (Kessell and Walton 1967:141, 143; Alcoholics Anonymous 1976:565).

All these intentional groups stress confession, sharing feelings, and solidarity (e.g., Weigle 1928:243; Holloway 1951:68–69; Schwartz 1980:215; Foster 1981:75;

Brewer 1986:13, 20, 50–51). For example, "confessions provided much of the cement that kept the [Shaker] Family system from falling apart" (Brewer 1986:71). The fourth and fifth "steps" of the basic 12-step AA program involve revealing intimate secrets. AA "speaker's meetings" usually involve confession by a single person; members call such confessions "drunkalogs." "Closed meetings" may involve joint confessions. Confession formalizes the informal social control which intimacy and absence of privacy produce among naturally peaceable peoples. Moreover, like the long debates discussed above, it vents and reduces resentments against group members and binds them together. Indeed, the French Prophets' failure may have been due in part to their failure to develop a system of confession (Schwartz 1980:214–215).

Practices which foster group identity often clash with outsider norms. Confession is congenial to American pop psychotherapy but not to the love of privacy and individualism which provides its patients. The asceticism of Amish and Hutterites (Hostetler 1974:255–284), Shakers (Emlen 1987) and AA (cf. Hardman 1924) runs counter to the fusillade of consumerist messages which target ordinary Americans. Conflict with locally hegemonic values leads members to lapse, e.g., from Amish to mainline Mennonite (Hostetler 1964), or "slip," e.g., back into alcoholic drinking, or die out like Shakers. One result is that, to escape outsider individualism and consumerism, endogamy is preferential (AA) or prescribed (Old Order Amish). For the same reasons, Amish discourage fraternizing with outsiders (Hostetler 1964), and AA encourages socializing with other members.

Controlling Emotions

Though originating in the violent defeat of violent revolution, Amish, Hutterite, and Shaker refusals to retaliate with violence or to bear arms has a religious rationale which mandates suppressing anger (e.g., Hostetler 1964:186). In AA theory, "resentment" is a main cause of relapse. The official commentary on the "tenth step" focuses on handling anger. Different local AA groups have differential success in muting intragroup hostilities, but all stress the need to "let go of" anger (Kessel and Walton 1967:142). Without a conscious and overriding commitment to nonviolence, groups otherwise quite similar to the cenobites and AA can be extremely violent. The armed American "survivalist right," for example, has a "primitive Christian" charter, seeks a refuge area, stresses face-to-face involvement, creates group identity out of ethnicity, etc. but remains murderous (Coates 1987).

Cenobites control in-group conflicts over sex in various ways, though all of them, and AA, stress self-control (e.g., Foster 1981:234–235; Peter 1987:11, 78). In some cases, following European tradition, they equate controlling sexuality with suppressing women. Since cenobitic Christians, like Christians in general, are selective about their beliefs, Saint Paul's endorsement of patriarchy does not explain why Hutterites and Amish accept patriarchy (e.g., Holloway 1951:212; Hostetler 1974:143, 145–146, 165); why AAs are neutral to negative about patriarchy; and why Shakers explicitly put absolute equality of genders at the center of their belief system. The Shaker founder, Mother Ann Lee, represents the Second Coming of an androgynous deity whose First Coming, as Christ, was necessarily imperfect because He was merely male (Holloway 1951:53–59, 64–79; Foster 1981:41–42).

Such diversity of Christian opinion about ranking the sexes is ancient. At least some German Anabaptists oppressed women more rigorously than do the most patriarchal modern Amish or Hutterites (Johnson 1976:262–263; Mayer 1954:392; McKay et al. 1984:646). Opponents of Pauline patriarchy can cite Matthew 22:30: "For in the resurrection they neither marry nor are given in marriage but are like angels in heaven." This Christian tradition, endemic in southern France into the time of Huguenot Camisard forerunners of the Shakers, united gender equality with the ideal of Platonic love, i.e., chastity for both genders, practiced by Shakers and other American cenobites (Holloway 1951:34–35, 39, 44, 50, 53–78, 88, 117, 132, 159; Foster 1981). Before the Camisard revolt, women were important in Huguenot revitalization movements; during the revolt, men took control; afterwards women became important again, but often felt forced into schisms due to the patriarchal "French prophet" authority structure (Schwartz 1980:32–36, 80, 134–141, 210–214).

If violence among "band-level" peoples stems in large part from male sexual rivalry, as sociobiologists claim (Knauft 1987a; Chagnon 1988, 1990; Dentan 1988c, e), then mandatory chastity, besides maintaining gender equality, works against violence. Indeed, Shaker authors explicitly say that controlling sexual conflict is fundamental to avoiding social disorder (Foster 1981:46–47). It should be remembered that the Shakers are among the most successful American cenobites in terms of endurance and prosperity. Patriarchy, which also ostensibly controls sexuality, seems connected to the difficulty all the cenobitic converts had transmitting their faith to their children (see following text).

Coercion

Without the confrontational frontier processes that characterize sanctuaries or refuges, the outside world is always a lure to members of peaceable enclaved intentional groups, even on reserves where members can exercise a "beggar's freedom" of religion.

1. In the dominant North American macho ethic, peaceability and refusal to compete reveal weakness or impractical idealism.
2. Capitalist advertising relentlessly touts the joy of secular consumerism.
3. Like its counterparts in ancient Rome and medieval China, traditional American religious tolerance entails the insidious assumption that all religions are equivalent and to be respected—but only as long as their devotees do not assert any exclusive claim to truth which might provoke reciprocal intolerance.

Accordingly, the passions which motivate cenobites are at best harmless idiosyncrasies, so that Amish, for example, seem merely colorful and folkloric. Thus, outside media assure members of peaceable intentional groups that their way of life is wimpy or quaint, entails great sacrifice and, after all, is no better than some other, less taxing lifestyle (what AA dismisses as "an easier, softer way"). That message is hard to combat.

In response, direct coercion is common among Christian cenobites, although AA relies on "attraction," and the Amish rely on the same ostracism ("shunning") that precipitated their own fissiparous separation from their parent group. Since an intrarefuge class structure seems incompatible with nonviolence (e.g., Hostetler 1964:185; Dentan 1978:134), the coercive authority structure follows age and gender lines, ostensibly on the Biblical model. Cenobitic nonviolence can coexist with gender equality or patriarchy (e.g., Peter 1987:61–62, 68, 70, 78–81). Authoritarianism may originate in the legitimate fear that the outside world will seduce members away (Hostetler 1964, 1974:162–165), but AA and sometime Shaker practice shows that it is not a necessary consequence of such fears.

Still, the authoritative and explicit peace-loving mythos may lead to authoritarian educational policies alien to the practice of refuge bands. As noted, the rationalization of these policies by reference to Western Christian ideology (Fabbro 1980:199) does not account for its occurrence, since AA transmits its "primitive Christian" code while rejecting overt authority structures, and Christians have always been selective in the beliefs they emphasize. Familial authoritarianism is common among Amish, Hutterites, and sometimes Shakers (Holloway 1951:19, 212; Hostetler 1964, 1974:145, 203–206; Hostetler and Huntington 1967:61). Among Hutterites, communal educational structures are even more authoritarian than familial ones (Hostetler 1974:145, 210–220, 321–328; Peter 1987:12–13, 62–67, 83–102).

In fact, the continuation of groups like these, based on ideology, may require coercive enculturation. Schwartz (1980:279–282) blames the Camisard French prophets' decline after their flight to London on a failure to inculcate their values in their children. Similarly, Hutterite periods of decline seem to coincide with periods of less strict enculturation of children, particularly with respect to Gelassenheit (Peter 1987:12–14, 40–41); and the Shakers' ambivalence about discipline may have been a factor in their decline (Brewer 1986:13–14, 74–78, 147–148). The groups with less authoritarian techniques of enculturation, like Shakers and AA, depend for survival on recruiting nonmembers.

Authoritarianism poses problems for the conventional attribution of positive peace to gentle child rearing (M. H. Ross 1981; Knauft 1987a:457, 473–475; Fry n.d.).

Summary

In brief, band-style social and psychological organization seems to help keep the peace within peaceable intentional groups. These preliminary findings are consistent with the evidence from unselfconsciously peaceable peoples. On the other hand, the gender equality characteristic of many band societies does not seem to be a necessary correlate of peaceability among intentional groups, although the two phenomena can co-occur, and the permissive child-rearing characteristic of most peaceable peoples seems to work against the survival of peaceable intentional groups enclaved in Western society.

CONCLUSION

Perils of Essentialism

Cultural Essentialism

The adaptation just sketched is delicate and often transitory. It is not an "essence" of the people or their culture. I suspect that nonviolent groups, other than cenobites, are temperamentally neither for nor against violence in the abstract. During the heyday of razzias some peoples worked out a strategy which allowed them to survive and which included nonviolence. It is possible to imagine any number of ways in which this adaptation would become less effective. If, for example, invaders move into their refuges in force and refuse to leave, some other adaptation becomes necessary. Alcohol reduces the fear on which refugee psychological adaptation depends. Organizing refugees into trained, paid military units with advanced weaponry and a mission against outsiders upsets the balance of power which makes refuges necessary. AAs do fight in national wars.

This model gives no reason to expect that a people with a history of nonviolence will remain nonviolent no matter what happens to their world; the San, Semai, and Pacaa Nova cases show that such a change can occur in a short period of time. Nor does it suggest that a people with a history of violence need remain violent; the Anabaptist and Waorani cases demonstrate that they need not. For that reason, it is hard to get a useful idea of the variables that affect violence and nonviolence by examining statistics aggregated over long periods of time or by conflating populations confronted with different political ecologies in different areas (Albert 1989, 1990). Such data can neither confirm nor deny the incidence of violence or nonviolence at particular places and times. Essentialism about violence may result from analysts' stances for or against utopia rather than from their attention to the complexities of history.

Psychological Essentialism

The individualism which characterizes the societies from which analysts come is conducive to quasi-essentialist explanations based on individual psychology, patterns of child rearing, and so on. It also supports explanations based on "human nature," e.g., that people are "naturally aggressive," so that peaceability always involves repressed aggression; and, if peaceability is striking, "reaction-formation."

For this reason, I want to reiterate that the Hobbesian fear and letting-go in question are as much intellectual and social phenomena as "deep psychological" ones. Flight rather than fighting is a sensible option when the enemy is invincible and there is a place to flee to; but, to make that choice, you need to be afraid. Americans' fears of the Greenhouse effect, carcinogens, nuclear winter, or violence in the streets are similarly Hobbesian, in the sense that:

1. they stem from realities which would be terrifying if people thought much about them;
2. they rarely take the form of obsessive emotions or conscious terrors and indeed, for most people most of the time, do not enter consciousness;

3. but, conscious or not, they do lead Americans to take routine precautions, some of which are rational and many of which relieve whatever anxiety people would otherwise feel (cf. Ryan 1971:185–210).

One such precaution for Americans is to inculcate these fears in their children through TV violence, school sessions on ecology, pictures of kidnapped children on milk cartons, and so on. For similar reasons, refugees inculcate xenophobia. What most Americans do not have, because their political ecological situation is different, is a way of dealing with these fears other than by denial, drugs, despair, or trying to reduce the threat. They do not and, because they are much more powerful than the peoples this paper considers, need not "let go."

A similar sort of psychological essentialism might ethnocentrically conceptualize the self-control found among people who live in egalitarian bands in terms of the repression which emerged in Western society as a result of the rationalizing forces of the industrial revolution. The former is a product and expression of internalized communal sentiment. The latter is the internalized individualist equivalent of the clerical and aristocratic oppression which preceded it (see, e.g., Lears 1981:12–15).

An Adaptive Model of Peaceability

The discussion of human violence and nonviolence has suffered from ahistorical essentialism, treating particular historical moments as if they represented universal evolutionary trends or deep-rooted manifestations of quasi-national characters (Sponsel 1989:33–35). This essentialism is congenial to Euroamerican crypto-Platonism and intolerance of ambiguity. Applied to the peoples this chapter covers, it is ethnographically misleading and always ultimately disappointing (Sponsel 1990). Applied to Euroamerican societies, it generates either hopeless dystopias or hopelessly fanciful utopias.[7]

A Darwinian approach, which takes nonviolence as an adaptation to particular political ecological circumstances, seems more viable. In place of the sexual selection favored by current sociobiological explanations of warfare (e.g., Chagnon 1988, 1990; Lieberman 1989), this approach stresses natural selection. Under some circumstances, opting for warfare is fatal. Death decreases one's fitness to zero. Under those circumstances, a population which fights to the death is likely to leave fewer offspring, at least in the short run, than one which flees. The choice of flight, however, has complex social and psychological consequences, some of which this paper has tried to sketch.

The Future of Negative Peaceability

Among Traditional Refugees

By this model the prospects for transforming one-time peaceable refugees into peaceable people enclaved in an invader nation-state are not good, if only because such a transformation is not high among the priorities of the people themselves or of the peoples who rule them. Refugees are not ardent proponents of positive nonviolence the way Amish, Hutterites, or AAs are; their peaceable attitudes are primarily negative. In general, it is an ethnographic error to see them as more moved by a love of peace than people everywhere are or can be. Their "conservatives" (sometimes called "radicals") want sanctuaries, not functional refuges. Their "progressives" are less opposed to assimilation than to assimilation into an underclass. Moreover, the sort of identity created by a frontier is less stable than one created by ethnic myths or cenobitic dogma. By 1976 little Semai boys were playing at karate kicks they learned from "kung-fu" movies (cf. Nagata 1990). Refuges from the mass media are hard to find.

In Nation-States

One epigraph to this paper is Mencius's smug remark that it is unimaginable to suppose that Han Chinese could learn anything from primitives. We who live in nation-states, beset within and without by violence, may feel less smug but equally pessimistic about our ability to use other people's solutions to our problems. Apparently, negative peaceability works better than positive peaceability under ordinary conditions. But American values, and the psychotherapeutic apparat which enforces them, deny the validity of the vague anxiety associated with the Hobbesian fear which underlies negative peaceability. Also the "ordinary conditions" of negative peaceability seem to include both a defeat, which it is difficult to imagine a nation-state arranging for itself, and a refuge, which present-day world communications and trading networks make almost impossible. As it seems suicidal to abandon a nation-state as long as other nation-states exist, so in the absence of refuges a commitment to peaceability runs the risk of inviting attack by peoples not so committed.

Moreover, the cenobitic experience seems to testify to the difficulty of transmitting a conscious desire for peace to children who have not experienced the pain that precedes letting-go. Advertising tempts them, and the bland religiosity associated with religious tolerance undercuts their parents' claims to have a way of life better than other people's. Without that vapid tolerance, however, cenobitic sects have little chance of surviving, let alone transforming the society in which they remain undigested lumps.

Finally, the hope for peace is utopian in the strict sense. Utopians prefer positive peaceability to peaceability based on fear. They want it to be associated with gentle sexuality, kindness to children, and equality between the genders; with "equity," "social justice," and "human rights" (Sponsel 1989:30; Stephenson 1990:3, 5, 6–7, 12). Nonviolence is often associated with intimacy, sharing, and equality outside nation-states. But within nation-states, for the reasons given, successful pacifist cenobites tend to favor patriarchy, repressive child training, and even celibacy as a solution to sexual conflict. There may be a need to set priorities here, which utopians tend to shun.

Conclusion

Still, the psychotherapeutic cults which pervade America reflect a yearning which includes a sense of powerlessness and a desire for peace. The co-dependency movement and many "support groups" model themselves on AA. Others, like Senoi dream therapy or neoshamanist groups, model themselves on dimly understood "primitive" praxis, which devotees often think of as including a peaceability wildly divergent from ethnographic fact. The fact that the intellectual content of these movements is often laughable should not lead anthropologists to treat them any less respectfully than similar movements among non-Western peoples. Anthropologists know little about these movements and need to know more.

It is also encouraging to note a recent development among Semai. The model this paper presents suggests that by now Semai should be ripe for violence: they are increasingly dispossessed and subject to heavy assimilative pressures (Todd 1990); alcohol and firearms are available to them. Nevertheless, Batin Yan Ibor, headman of a besieged settlement that is threatened with expropriation, still says:

> The outsiders may force us to do anything; but if they do we will not fight; but instead [we are] willing to be killed here (Catmandu and Sivashanmugam 1987:2).

SUMMARY

This paper deals with one set of political ecological circumstances which seems conducive to peaceability. Often negative peaceability seems to originate when two peoples encounter each other in a region where population density is generally low enough that useable tracts of land remain unoccupied. The more powerful people, "invaders," decisively defeat less powerful ones, "refugees." The latter respond first with Hobbesian fear, which manifests itself in flight to areas the invaders cannot easily penetrate (refuges). The fear is initially a painful sentiment with which they deal by "letting-go," accepting the fact of their own inability to control the forces that threaten them, an acceptance which seems to bring them some relief and to allow them to lead fairly serene and autonomous lives most of the time, albeit with a sense that the cosmos is unstable and threatening. The stress on flight and fear of invader violence, introjected, comes to include a fear of one's own violence, so that all acts of violence become too frightening to countenance. Thus negative internal peaceability develops historically as an unintended consequence of negative external peaceability.

To perpetuate this adaptation people need to be able to maintain places of refuge, usually geographic, where invaders for whatever reason normally leave them alone. If these places were completely secure, the psychological adaptation of fear and letting-go would be superfluous. If the refuges were completely penetrated, people would lose their autonomy and sink into the apathy and despair characteristic of dominated communities. Band-style social organization of the sort described can be a "preadaptation" to a reliance on flight into refuges. The positive peaceability often found in band societies can predispose people to the negative peaceability that the contact situation fosters. Similarly, negative peaceability may reinforce positive peaceability, e.g., by affording an ideological contrast between "peaceable us" and "violent them." When underpopulated geographical refuges of the sort described are unavailable, refugees depend on the tolerance of the group that has defeated them in order to maintain places which can serve them as functional refuges.

As long as this adaptation is successful, people will more or less consciously try to transmit it to their children. For example, most will teach children to fear strangers, and few will celebrate violence-entailing heroics. Societies not enclaved in nation-states seem most successful at enculturating peaceability when they neither expect nor violently punish childish aggression. Enclaved peaceable societies, however, apparently must resort to authoritarian and punitive measures to survive more than a couple of generations. The authority in such cases is often patriarchal.

As an adaptation, however, peaceability of all kinds is dynamic. Refugees can import weapons or acquire military sponsors to offset their initial military weakness. Alcohol and other drugs can reduce or cloud Hobbesian fears. Invasion, occupation, and "development" can destroy the refuge. The evidence currently available suggests that, given long enough, many people who seem currently peaceable have been violent in the past and vice versa.

Essentialist models distort this dynamic adaptation. They generate facile optimism or despair. Because each adaptation grows out of a particular reality, Euroamericans cannot simply decontextualize it and insert it into their own society. On the other hand, the rise and survival of peaceful societies suggests that human peaceability is not an impossible, anti-Darwinian fantasy but instead an adaptive response (in the Darwinian sense) to particular political ecologies.

ACKNOWLEDGMENTS

The editors of this volume express gratitude to three of Dr. Dentan's students, past and present—Drs. Christine E. Eber of SUNY/Albany and Barbara Nowak of Grinnell College, and doctoral candidate at SUNY/Buffalo, Zoe Zacharek—for their kind cooperation in responding to editorial questions that arose after Dentan left for fieldwork.

NOTES

1. Bohannon's collaborators (1960), Otterbein (1986, 1987) and Knauft (1987a, b) suggest other nosological refinements.

The definition of violence is also problematic. Leary (1989) feels that Orang Asli killings during counterinsurgency operations show that Asli are not especially nonviolent. Yet state-supported killing within or between nation-states does not appear in national homicide statistics. Although Gebusi or Yanomamo homicide rates include what Bohannon and his collaborators would call "altruistic" homicides ("executions" or "wars" in nation-states), they are compared only with murders in, usually, Detroit or Houston. Moreover, in industrialized countries, corporate managers and bureaucratic regulators know that the failure to adopt particular remedial measures will cause a statistically calculable number of deaths, although the identity of the particular individuals to be killed is unknown. On the basis of cost/benefit analyses these decision makers often opt to "accept" a certain number of such deaths. A case can be made for calling these deaths "homicides," although they too rarely figure in comparative studies or national homicide rates. The omission of nation-state and corporate homicides paints "primitive" peoples as relatively more murderous than "civilized" ones, just as within the statisticians' own societies it makes the lower classes and castes seem more criminal than higher ones (Ryan 1971:194–198). But surely, to behaviorist statisticians, killing ought to be just killing, whatever the killer's supposed motive.

2. For Aslians, see, e.g. Skeat and Blagden (1906); Evans (1920, 1923); Noone (1936); Stewart (1948, 1954, 1972); [Williams-Hunt] (1952); Anonymous (1961); Benjamin (1968, 1976, 1986); Schebesta (1973); Dentan (1975, 1976a, 1978, 1979, 1983a, b, 1988b, f, n.d.); Fix (1977); Robarchek (1977, 1979a, b); Hood (1979); Rambo (1979); Couillard (1980, 1986); Howell (1981, 1983); Endicott (1982, 1983, 1988); Nowak (1984, 1985, 1988); Bock (1985 [1881]); Gomes (1987, 1988a, b); Gianno (1988, 1989); Nicholas et al. (1989).

Gibson's (1986a) Type 1 includes hill peoples of Palawan (Palawan, Tagbanuwa, Batak), Mindoro (Hanunoo, Taubuid, Alangan, Iraya), and Mindanao (Subanun, Tiruray); Wana of Sulawesi and Sulod of Panay. Bajau Laut, also on his list, seem in some ways inappropriate.

The 10 single-village tribes of the Upper Xingu River speak four different languages (Trumai, Tupi, Carib, and Arawak) and three mutually unintelligible dialects but have a fairly homogeneous culture (Gregor 1988); the peoples of the Pacaa Nova River seem to present a similar case (von Graeve 1989). Turnbull's work (e.g., 1962, 1965, 1978; cf. Bailey 1982) has made Mbuti famous as gentle people.

3. The Okiek–Maasai case (Blackburn 1982:293, 295) is in some ways exemplary:

Maasai fear the forest and harbour all sorts of unfounded suspicions about the dangers of the forest and of the Okiek, to whom they impute certain malevolent supernatural powers. An aggressive people, the Maasai tended to want to treat the Okiek as they have treated other tribes ... [but Okiek] do not hold the things Maasai covet most: cattle, sheep and goats. Furthermore, the Okiek, with nothing to lose or gain, would not stand and fight. The Okiek were and are wisely passive and slip back into the shadows of the forest when confronted by Maasai warriors. ... The fundamental reason the Okiek, as a people, have survived the waves of pastoral invasions in central Kenya, when all previous groups have been decimated, scattered, or merged with their conquerors, is that pastoralists have no use for forests.

The quasi-caste relationship between Okiek and Maasai, however, resembles that between the dominant people of Rwanda and Burundi on the one hand and the "Twa" pygmies on the other. The rarity of razzias by Nilotic pastoralists on foragers and the omnipresence of mead in the Okiek area may partly account for the fact that Okiek are not especially nonviolent (see also text discussion of alcohol).

4. Han Chinese traditionally transform "raw" (unsinicized) tribespeople into "cooked" peasants and eventually digest them into Han society. In the process, Han acquire their land, especially valley land (Speidel 1976:457; Sangren 1985:537, 538). Still, writes the liberal Tang poet Bai Juyi of his "digested" neighbors (Waley 1941:222)

Among such as these I cannot hope for friends
And am pleased with anyone who is even remotely human..

5. Observers have harsh words for Asli whom they met for the first time or on the frontier: "sullen reserve" and "appalling bad manners" of the "nervous," "timid," "reticent," "stupid," "weak," "wretched," on the one hand (Evans, quoted in Schebesta 1926:88; Wheeler 1928:33, 278; Porteus 1937:263–265; Slimming 1958:41). By contrast, describing Asli at home, they use words like: "disarmingly jolly, laughing curiosity" (Westwood 1962:194), "jolly" (Wavell 1958:38), "strong-looking, loud voice [sic], witty, authoritative"

(Stacey 1953:110). Dentan (1975, 1976a, b) and Slimming (1958:127–130) describe some of the dynamics of this shift in Asli status personality. Even within the refuge, however, traditional Asli are not especially forthcoming (e.g., Westwood 1962:190–195).

European observers of Aka "pygmies" give similarly discordant accounts of refugee personality (Bachuchet and Guillaume 1982:203). These discordances are significant insofar as they indicate that nonviolence is not so much a personal as a social attribute. To that degree peaceable living has not "robbed them of the ability to respond to the intruders with equal and opposite force" (Jones-Jackson, quoted in Rosengarten 1987:66; cf. Aguirre Beltran 1979:27, Robarchek and Dentan 1987).

6. See, e.g., Wrong, who also comments on the connection between power-hunger and aggression (1980:218–237). Semai voice similar connections. Bah Juli Edo, a west Semai anthropologist at the Universiti Malaya, writes (1987):

We agreed with your definition of phunan ... [see Evans 1920; 1923:39, 237–239, 294–296; Bock 1985 [1881]:112; Howell 1981:135–137, 140–141], that it is mostly caused by frustrated desire. But ... we don't agree that coercion produces phunan because you only suffer phunan if you couldn't get something that you want badly. And doing something that you don't want to do produces "mnuur" (example: say your parents asked you to get some food from the jungle but you insist on not doing it. And if you go without your own wish, you might have an accident or [be] bit[t]en by [a] snake.... [People usually talk about mnuur] when there is loss of life on that day.).

That is, trying to coerce someone, or refusing to share and thus frustrating someone's desires, both have the same results as overt violence (cf. Turner 1894:222, 227).

7. An earlier reference to these two essentialist stances as "liberal" and "conservative" (Robarchek and Dentan 1987) provoked outrage. In the utopian view human nature is good and society is perfectible. Dystopians and social pessimists posit some secular version of Original Sin like "innate aggression" which requires discipline by external agencies, often manned by people who resemble the theorists. Karl Mannheim (1946) provides a useful analysis of the dynamics of this sort of thinking.

REFERENCES

ꞏAbdul-Hadi bin Haji Hasan. 1925. *Sejarah ꞏAlam Melayu*. The Malay School Series #7.

Aguirre Beltran, G. 1979. *Regions of Refuge*. Society for Applied Anthropology Monograph #12. Washington, DC: SAA.

Ahlstrom, S. E. 1972. *A Religious History of the American People*. New Haven: Yale University Press.

Albert, B. 1989. Yanomami "violence": Inclusive fitness or ethnographer's representation. *Current Anthropology* 30:637–640.

———. 1990. On Yanomami warfare: Rejoinder. *Current Anthropology* 31:558–563.

Alcoholics Anonymous. 1976. *Alcoholics Anonymous. The Story of How Many Thousands of Men and Women Have Recovered from Alcoholism*, 3rd edn. New York: Alcoholics Anonymous World Services.

Alland, A. 1980. *To Be Human: An Introduction to Anthropology*. New York: John Wiley and Sons.

Ambimathe, K. 1987. Saving the Asli link to our past. [*Penang*] *Star* 6 July.

Anonymous. 1961. *Statement of Policy Regarding the Long Term Administration of the Aboriginal Peoples in the Federation of Malaya.* Kuala Lumpur: Ministry of the Interior. [Updated version of 1977 contains few significant changes].

———. 1972. An alcoholic's story, pp. 156–166. In *Readings in Criminology and Penology*, D. Dressler, ed. New York: Columbia University Press.

———. 1987a. Sarawak Govt. plan won't work: Experts. [*Penang*] *Star* 13 July.

———. 1987b. Orang Asli: Department not giving us much help. [*Penang*] *Star* 16 July.

———. 1987c. JOA: We can't provide all. [*Penang*] *Star* 17 July.

———. 1987d. JOA allocated $3.8m this year: Director. [*Penang*] *Star* 18 July.

———. 1987e. Genuine Orang Asli wedding at Selangor tourism week. [*Penang*] *Star* 24 September.

———. 1989a. Manser's family appeals for his return. *New Straits Times* 4 August.

———. 1989b. Taking on the conservationists. *Tapol Bulletin*, August.

———. 1989c. Situation update: Sarawak. Asian-Pacific environment. *Newsletter of the Asia Pacific People's Environment Network* 6(1):2–3.

———. 1989d. The Rampage Worsens. *Suara Sahabat ꞌAlam* [*Voice of Friends of the Earth*] *Malaysia* 5(3):2.

———. 1990a. 24 Penans discharged. *Sarawak Tribune* 10 January.

———. 1990b. Joint efforts vital to counter drive against Malaysia-Indon timber. *Sarawak Tribune* 1 February.

Bahuchet, S. and H. Guillaume. 1982. Aka-Farmer relations in the Northwest Congo Basin, pp. 189–211. In *Politics and History in Band Societies*, E. Leacock and R. Lee, eds. (S. M. Van Eyck, tr.). Cambridge: Cambridge University Press.

Bailey, R. 1982. Development in the Ituri Forest of Zaire. *Cultural Survival Quarterly* 6:23–25.

Barkun, M. 1986. *Crucible of the Millennium. The Burned-Over District of New York in the 1840s.* Syracuse: Syracuse University Press.

Benjamin, G. 1968. Headmanship and leadership in Temiar society. *Federation Museums Journal* 13 (n.s.):1–43.

———. 1976. Austroasiatic subgroupings and prehistory in the Malay Peninsula, pp. 37–128. In *Austroasiatic Studies, Part I*, P. N. Jenner, L. C. Thompson and S. Starosta, eds. Honolulu: University Press of Hawaii.

———. 1986. Achievements and gaps in Orang Asli research. Paper Presented at the Orang Asli Symposium (Universiti Kebangsaan Malaysia, 22–23 September).

———. 1987. Process and structure in Temiar social organization. Department of Sociology, University of Singapore, Working Paper #82.

Bicchieri, M. G. 1990. Comment [on Wilmsen and Denbow 1990]. *Current Anthropology* 31:507.

Blackburn, R. H. 1982. In the land of milk and honey: Okiek adaptations to their forests and neighbours, pp. 283–305. In *Politics and History in Band Societies*, E. Leacock and R. Lee, eds. Cambridge: Cambridge University Press.

Bock, C. 1985 [1881]. *The Head-Hunters of Borneo: A Narrative of Travels up the Mahakkam and down the Barito; also Journeyings in Sumatra.* Singapore: Oxford University Press.

Bodley, J. H. 1982. *Victims of Progress*, 2nd edn. Menlo Park, CA: Cummings.

Bohannon, P., ed. 1960. *African Homicide and Suicide.* Princeton: Princeton University Press.

Boserup, E. 1988. Environment, population, and technology in primitive societies, pp. 23–38. In *The Ends of the Earth: Perspectives on Modern Environmental History*, D. Worster, ed. Cambridge: Cambridge University Press.

Brelsford, W. V. 1946. *Fishermen of the Bangweulu Swamps. A Study of the Fishing Activities of the Unga Tribe.* Livingstone, Northern Rhodesia: Rhodes-Livingstone Institute.

Brenneis, D. L. and F. R. Myers, eds. 1984. *Dangerous Words. Language and Politics in the Pacific.* New York, London: New York University Press.

Brewer, P. J. 1986. *Shaker Communities, Shaker Lives.* Hanover: University Press of New England.

Briggs, J. L. 1978. The origins of nonviolence: Inuit management of aggression (Canadian Arctic), pp. 54–93. In *Learning Non-aggression. The Experience of Non-literate Societies*, A. Montagu, ed. New York: Oxford University Press.

Brison, K. J. 1989. All talk and no action? Saying and doing in Kwanga meetings. *Ethnology* 28:97–116.

Brooks, D. 1987. Good vibrations: The new peace offensive. *National Review* 39 (21):36–39.

Cadelina, R. V. 1988. A comparison of Batak and Ata subsistence styles in two different social and physical environments, pp. 59–81. In *Ethnic Diversity and the Control of Natural Resources in Southeast Asia*, A. T. Rambo, K. Gillogly and K. L. Hutterer, eds. Michigan Paper on South and Southeast Asia #32, Ann Arbor: Center for South and Southeast Asian Studies, University of Michigan.

Carothers, A. 1990. Defenders of the rainforest. *Greenpeace* 15(4):8–12.

Casimir, M. J. 1990. On milk-drinking San and the "primitive isolate." *Current Anthropology* 31:551–554.

Castile, G. P. 1981. Issues in the analysis of enduring cultural systems, pp. xv–xxii. In *Persistent Peoples. Cultural Enclaves in Perspective*, G. P. Castile and G. Kushner, eds. Tucson: University of Arizona Press.

Castile, G. P. and G. Kushner, eds. 1981. *Persistent Peoples. Cultural Enclaves in Perspective.* Tucson: University of Arizona Press.

Catmandu and Sivashanmugam. 1987. Semais living in fear of eviction ... but willing to be killed. *Suara Sahabat ꞌAlam* [*Voice of Friends of the Earth*] *Malaysia* 4 (#4):2–5.

Cerruti, G. B. 1904. The Sakais of Batang Padang, Perak. *Journal of the Straits Branch of the Royal Asiatic Society* 41:113–117.

Chagnon, N. A. 1988. Life histories, blood revenge, and warfare in a tribal society. *Science* 239:985–992.

———. 1990. On Yanomamo violence: reply to Albert. *Current Anthropology* 31:49–53.

Chang, C. 1982. Nomads without cattle: East Africa foragers in historical perspective, pp. 269–282. In *Politics and History in Band Societies*, E. Leacock and R. Lee, eds. Cambridge: Cambridge University Press.

Chee Yoke Ling. 1990. Land and forest rights of natives. *Suara Sahabat ꞌAlam* [*Voice of Friends of the Earth*] *Malaysia* 5(5):14.

Chin, S. C. 1989. Penan survival bound to health of forest. [*Penang*] *The Star.*

Chodorow, S., H. W. Gatzke, and C. Schirokauer. 1986. *A History of the World.* New York: Harcourt Brace Jovanovich.

Cipriani, L. 1966. *The Andaman Islanders.* D. T. Cox and L. Cole, eds. and trs. London: Weidenfeld and Nicholson.

Clapham, W. B. 1973. *Natural Ecosystems.* New York: Macmillan.

Coates, J. 1987. *Armed and Dangerous. The Rise of the Survivalist Right.* New York: Hill and Wang.

Colby, B. N. 1967. Psychological orientations, pp. 416–431. In *Social Anthropology, Handbook of Middle American Indians*, Volume 6, M. Nash, ed. Austin: University of Texas Press.

Colinvaux, P. 1978. *Why Big Fierce Animals Are Rare. An Ecologist's Perspective.* Princeton, NJ: Princeton University Press.

Collins, G. 1983. Tribe where harmony rules. *New York Times* 19 September:B12.

Columbus, C. 1938 [1493]. The letter of Columbus to Luis de Sant Angel announcing his discovery, pp. 21–27. In *American Historical Documents 1000–1904. The Harvard Classics*, C. W. Eliot, ed. New York: Collier.

Couillard, M.-A. 1980. *Tradition in Tension: Carving in a Jah Hut Community*. Penang: Universiti Sains Malaysia.

———. 1986. Les rapports sociaux dans la Société malaise pre-coloniale. Hypothèses et commentaires. *Anthropologie et Sociétés* 10:145–162.

Creel, H. 1970. On the origin of wu-wei, pp. 48–79. In *What is Taoism? and Other Essays in Chinese Cultural History*. Chicago: University of Chicago Press.

Crossette, B. 1987a. Malaysia shuts down three papers. *New York Times* 29 October:A8.

———. 1987b. Malaysia stages wave of arrests of opposition and civic leaders. *New York Times* 30 October:A8.

———. 1987c. Malaysian crackdown shatters a bright image. *New York Times* 2 November:A8.

Denbow, J. R. and E. N. Wilmsen. 1986. Advent and course of Kalahari pastoralism. *Science* 234:1509–1514.

de Morgan, J. 1886. *Exploration dans le Presqu'ile Malaise: Royaumes de Perak et de Patani*. Paris: A. Lahure.

Denich, B. S. 1987. As war has evolved, can also peace? *Newsletter, Commission on the Study of Peace, International Union of Anthropological and Ethnological Sciences* 5 (2)—Supplement.

Dentan, R. K. 1975. If there were no Malays, who would the Semai be? *Contributions to Asian Studies* 7:50–64.

———. 1976a. Identity and ethnic contact: Perak, Malaysia, 1963. *Journal of Asian Affairs* 1 (1):79–86.

———. 1976b. Ethnics and ethics in Southeast Asia, pp. 71–82. In *Changing Identities in Modern Southeast Asia*, D. J. Banks, ed. The Hague: Mouton.

———. 1978. Notes on childhood in a nonviolent context: The Semai case. pp. 94–143. In *Learning Non-aggression. The Experience of Non-literate Societies*, A. Montagu, ed. London: Oxford University Press.

———. 1979. *The Semai: A Nonviolent People of Malaysia*, Fieldwork edition, New York: Holt, Rinehart and Winston.

———. 1983a. *A Dream of Senoi*. Council on International Studies, State University of New York at Buffalo, Special Study 150.

———. 1983b. Senoi dream praxis. *Dream Network Bulletin* 2 (5):1–3, 12.

———. 1983c. Hit and run ethnograph[y]. *Dream Network Bulletin* 2(8):11–12.

———. 1984. Techniques and antecedents: A response to Gieseler. *Lucidity Letter* 3 (2 and 3):5–7.

———. 1987. You can never find a cop when you need one: A response to Faraday. *Association for the Study of Dreams Newsletter* 4(2):14–16.

———. 1988a. Response [to McGlashan 1987]. *Parabola* 13 (1):4–6.

———. 1988b. Lucidity, sex and horror in Senoi dreamwork, pp. 37–63. In *Conscious Mind, Sleeping Brain: New Perspectives on Lucid Dreaming*, J. L. Gackenbach and S. LaBerge, eds. New York: Plenum.

———. 1988c. On reconsidering violence in simple societies. *Current Anthropology* 29:624–629.

———. 1988d. Band-level Eden: A mystifying chimera. *Cultural Anthropology* 3:276–284.

———. 1988e. On violence. *Checkpoint* 1 (1):3.

———. 1988f. Ambiguity, synecdoche and affect in Semai medicine. *Social Science and Medicine* 27:857–877.

Dentan, R. K. n.d. "Surrendered men:" Peaceable enclaves in the postenlightenment West. In *Nonviolence and Peace: Anthropological Insights*, T. Gregor and L. Sponsel eds.

D'Hertefelt, M. 1966. The Rwanda of Rwanda, pp. 403–440. In *Peoples of Africa*, J. L. Gibbs, Jr., ed. New York: Holt, Rinehart and Winston.

Domhoff, G. W. 1985. *The Mystique of Dreams. A Search for Utopia through Senoi Dream Theory*. Berkeley: University of California Press.

Donald, L. 1987. Comment [on Knauft 1987a]. *Current Anthropology* 28:483.

Dove, M. R. 1983. Theories of swidden agriculture and the political economy of ignorance. *Agroforestry Systems* 1:85–99.

———. 1985. The agroecological mythology of the Javanese and the political economy of Indonesia. *Indonesia* #39 (April):1–36.

———. 1988. Introduction: Traditional culture and development in contemporary Indonesia, pp. 1–37. In *The Real and Imagined Role of Culture in Development: Case Studies from Indonesia*, M. R. Dove, ed. Honolulu: University of Hawaii.

Dowling, J. H. 1968. Individual ownership and the sharing of game in hunting societies. *American Anthropologist* 70:502–507.

Draper, P. 1978. The learning environment for aggression and anti-social behavior among the !Kung, pp. 31–53. In *Learning Non-Aggression. The Experience of Non-literate Societies*, A. Montagu, ed. New York: Oxford University Press.

Duncan, J. D. 1982. Indian slavery, pp. 85–106. In *Race Relations in British North America, 1607–1783*, B. A. Glasrud and A. M. Smith, eds. Chicago: Nelson-Hall.

Dunn, F. 1975. Rain-forest collectors and traders. A study of resource utilization in modern and ancient Malaya. *Monograph of the Malaysian Branch of the Royal Asiatic Society* #5.

Eder, J. F. 1988. Hunter-gatherer/farmer exchange in the Philippines: Some implications for ethnic identity and adaptive well-being, pp. 37–57. In *Ethnic Diversity and the Control of Natural Resources in Southeast Asia*, A. T. Rambo, K. Gillogly and K. L. Hutterer, eds. Michigan Paper on South and Southeast Asia #32. Ann Arbor: Center for South and Southeast Asian Studies, University of Michigan.

Elkin, A. P. 1967. Reaction and interaction: A food gathering people and European settlement in Australia, pp. 44–70. In *Beyond the Frontier: Social Process and Cultural Change*, P. Bohannon and F. Plog, eds. Garden City, NY: Natural History Press.

Ellen, J. F. 1982. *Environment, Subsistence and System. The Ecology of Small-scale Social Formations*. Cambridge: Cambridge University Press.

Emlen, R. P. 1987. Shaker village views. *Natural History* 96 (9):48–57.

Endicott, K. L. 1984. The Batek De' of Malaysia. *Cultural Survival Quarterly* 8 (2):6–8.

Endicott, K. M. 1982. The effects of logging on the Batek De' of Malaysia. *Cultural Survival Quarterly* 6 (2):19–20.

———. 1983. The effects of slave raiding on the aborigines of the Malay Peninsula, pp. 216–245. In *Slavery, Bondage, and Dependency in Southeast Asia*, A. Reid and J. Brewster, eds. Brisbane: University of Queensland Press.

———. 1988. The basis of egalitarian social relations among the Batek foragers of Malaysia. Paper presented at the 87th Annual Meetings of the American Anthropological Association, 16–20 November, Phoenix, Arizona.

———. 1990. Batek ethnohistory and ethnogenesis. Paper presented at the 89th Annual Meeting of the American Anthropological Association 28 November–2 December, Washington, DC.

Erasmus, C. J. 1981. Anarchy, enclavement, and syntropy in intentional and traditional communities, pp. 192–211. In *Persistent Peoples. Cultural Enclaves in Perspective*, G. P. Castile and G. Kushner, eds. Tucson: University of Arizona Press.

European Parliament. 1989. Resolution. Asian-Pacific Environment. *Newsletter of the Asia-Pacific People's Environment Network* 6(1):7–8.

Evans, I. H. N. 1920. Kempunan. *Man* 38:69–70.

———. 1923. *Studies in Religion, Folk-lore, & Custom in British North Borneo and the Malay Peninsula.* London: Frank Cass & Co.

Fabbro, D. 1980. Peaceful societies, pp. 180–203. In *The War System. An Interdisciplinary Approach*, R. A. Falk and S. S. Kim, eds. Boulder, CO: Westview Press.

Fix, A. G. 1977. *The demography of the Semai Senoi.* Anthropological Papers, Museum of Anthropology, University of Michigan #62.

Fix, A. G. and Luan Eng Lie-Injo. 1975. Genetic microdifferentiation in the Semai Senoi of Malaysia. *American Journal of Physical Anthropology* 43:47–55.

Foster, L. 1981. *Religion and Sexuality. Three American Communal Experiments of the Nineteenth Century.* New York: Oxford University Press.

Fried, M. H. 1967. *The Evolution of Political Society: An Essay in Political Anthropology.* New York: Random House.

Fry, D. P. 1987. Differences between playfighting and serious fighting among Zapotec school children. *Ethology and Sociobiology* 8:285–306.

———. 1988a. Intercommunity differences in aggression among Zapotec children. *Child Development* 59:1008–1019.

———. 1988b. Intergenerational transmission of conflict resolution styles in two Zapotec communities. Paper presented at the 87th Annual Meetings of the American Anthropological Association, 16–20 November, Phoenix, Arizona.

———. 1990. Play aggression among Zapotec children: Implications for the practice hypothesis. *Aggressive Behavior* 16:321–340.

———. n.d. Social learning theory and intra-cultural variation in aggression and child discipline among the valley Zapotec.

Gamst, F. C. 1979. Wayto ways: Change from hunting to peasant life, pp. 233–238. In *Proceedings of the Fifth International Conference on Ethiopian Studies*, Session B, R. L. Hess, ed. Chicago: University of Chicago, Illinois.

Gardner, P. M. 1966. Symmetric respect and memorate knowledge: The structure and ecology of individualist culture. *Southwestern Journal of Anthropology* 22:389–415.

———. 1985. Bicultural oscillation as a long-term adaptation of cultural frontiers: Cases and questions. *Human Ecology* 13:411–432.

Gartner, A. 1984. Widower self-help groups: A preventive approach. *Social Policy* 15 (Winter):37–38.

Genam anak Bangau, Janging Jambilong, Juwin Lihan and Anjeng Kiew. 1989. Logging in Sarawak. *Suara Sahabat ʾAlam [Voice of Friends of the Earth] Malaysia* 5(3):2.

Gianno, R. 1988. Orang Asli strategies of forest adaptation. Paper presented at the 87th Annual Meetings of the American Anthropological Association, 16–20 November, Phoenix, Arizona.

———. 1989. *Semelai Culture and Resin Technology.* Memoir of the Connecticut Academy of Arts and Sciences #22.

Gibson, T. 1985. The sharing of substance versus the sharing of activity among the Buid. *Man* (n.s.) 20:391–411.

———. 1986a. Raiding, trading and tribal autonomy in insular Southeast Asia. Paper presented at the Conference on 'The Anthropology of War' (Harry Frank Guggenheim Foundation, 24–28 March).

———. 1986b. Symbolic representations of tranquillity and aggression among the Buid. Paper presented at the Conference on 'Peace, Action and the Concept of Self', 19–22 June, Edinburgh.

Gibson, T. 1989. Meat sharing as a political ritual: Forms of transaction versus modes of subsistence, pp. 165–179. In *Hunting and Gathering Societies*, J. Woodburn, T. Ingald, and D. Riches, eds. London: Berg Publishers.

Giliomee, H. 1981. Processes in development of the Southern African frontier, pp. 76–119. In *The Frontier in History. North America and Southern Africa Compared*, H. Lamar and L. Thompson, eds. New Haven: Yale University Press.

Gilsenan, M. 1982. *Recognizing Islam. Religion and Society in the Modern Arab World*. New York: Pantheon.

Gomes, A. 1987. Dependence on the Govt. will hurt Orang asli. [*Penang*] *Star* 22 July.

———. 1988a. The Semai: The making of an ethnic group in Malaysia, pp. 99–105. In *Ethnic Diversity and the Control of Natural Resources in Southeast Asia*, A. T. Rambo, K. Gillogly, and K. L. Hutterer, eds. Michigan Paper on South and Southeast Asia #32. Ann Arbor: Center for South and Southeast Asian Studies, University of Michigan.

———. 1988b. Demographic implications of villagisation among the Semang of Malaysia. Paper presented at the Fifth International Conference on Hunting and Gathering Societies, 29 August–2 September, Darwin, Australia.

———. 1990. Confrontation and continuity: Simple commodity production among the Orang Asli, pp. 12–36. In *Tribal Peoples and Development in Southeast Asia, Manusia dan Masyarakat* special issue, Lim Teck Ghee and A. G. Gomes, eds. Kuala Lumpur: Jabatan Antropologi dan Sosiologi, Universiti Malaya.

Goody, J. 1980. Slavery in time and space, pp. 16–42. In *Asian and African Systems of Slavery*, J. L. Watson, ed. Berkeley: University of California Press.

Gregor, T. 1988. Intertribal relations among the tribes of the Upper Xingu River and "negative peace." Paper presented at the 87th Annual Meetings of the American Anthropological Association, 16–20 November, Phoenix, Arizona.

Guenther, M. G. 1975. The trance dancer as an agent of social change among the farm Bushmen of the Ghanzi District. *Botswana Notes and Records* 7:161–166.

———. 1975/76. The San trance dance: Ritual and revitalization among the farm Bushmen of the Ghanzi District, Republic of Botswana. *Journal of the South West African Scientific Society* 30:45–53.

———. 1976. From hunters to squatters: Social and cultural change among the farm San of Ghanzi, Botswana, pp. 120–133. In *Kalahari Hunter-Gatherers*, R. B. Lee and I. DeVore, eds. Cambridge: Harvard University Press.

———. 1977. Bushman hunters as farm labourers. *Revue Canadienne des Etudes Africaines* 11:195–203.

———. 1979. Bushmen religion and the (non)sense of anthropological theory of religion. *Sociologus* 29:102–132.

———. 1980. From "brutal savages" to "harmless people." Notes on the changing Western image of the Bushmen. *Paideuma* 26:123–140.

———. 1981. Bushman and hunter-gatherer territoriality. *Zeitschrift für Ethnologie* 106:109–120.

———. 1986. From foragers to miners and bands to bandits: On the flexibility and adaptability of Bushman band societies. *Sprache und Geschichte in Afrika* 7:133–159.

Hardman, O. 1924. *The Ideals of Asceticism: An Essay in the Comparative Study of Religion*. New York: Macmillan.

Hashim, S. 1989. Panel criticizes Sarawak but admits to US deficiency. *New Straits Times* 13 July.

Hawgood, J. A. 1940. *The Tragedy of German-America*. New York: Putnam.

Headland, T. N. 1978. Cultural ecology, ethnicity, and the Negritos of Northeastern Luzon. *Asian Perspectives* 21:127–139.

Headland, T. N. 1988a. Ecosystemic change in a Philippine tropical rainforest and its effects on a Negrito foraging society. *Tropical Ecology* 29:121–135.

———. 1988b. Review of James F. Eder, *On the Road to Tribal Extinction. Journal of Asian History* 22:93–95.

———. 1989. Population decline in a Philippine hunter-gatherer society. *American Journal of Human Biology* 1:59–72.

———. 1990. Time allocation, demography, and original affluence in a Philippine Negrito hunter-gatherer society. Paper presented at the 6th International Conference on Hunting and Gathering Societies, 28 May–1 June, University of Alaska, Fairbanks.

Hitchcock, R. K. 1988. Decentralization and development among the Ju/Wasi, Namibia. *Cultural Survival Quarterly* 12(3):30–32.

———. 1990. Land reform, ethnicity, and compensation in Botswana. *Cultural Survival Quarterly* 14(4):52–55.

Hobbes, T. 1966 [1651]. The state of nature, pp. 214–219. In *Value and Man. Readings in Philosophy*, L. Z. Hammer, ed. New York: McGraw-Hill.

———. 1968 [1651]. *Leviathan*, C. B. Macpherson, ed. Harmondsworth: Penguin.

Hoh, A. and J. Matthews. 1987. Don: Orang Asli status will worsen Penan woes. [*Penang*] *Sunday Star* 5 July.

Holloway, M. 1951. *Heavens on Earth. Utopian Communities in America 1680–1880*. London: Turnstile Press.

Holmberg, A. R. 1950. *Nomads of the long bow. The Siriono of Eastern Bolivia*. Smithsonian Institution, Institute of Social Anthropology Publication #10.

Hood, H. M. S. 1979. The cultural context of Semelai trance. *Federation Museums Journal* 24:107–124.

———. 1990. Orang Asli of Malaysia: An overview of recent development policy and its impact, pp. 141–149. In *Tribal Peoples and Development in Southeast Asia, Manusia dan Masyarakat* special issue, Lim Tec Ghee and A. G. Gomes, eds. Kuala Lumpur: Jabatan Sosiologi dan Antropologi, Universiti Malaya.

Hostetler, J. A. 1964. Persistence and change patterns in Amish society. *Ethnology* 3:185–198.

———. 1974. *Hutterite Society*. Baltimore: Johns Hopkins University Press.

Hostetler, J. A. and G. E. Huntington. 1967. *The Hutterites of North America*. New York: Holt, Rinehart and Winston.

Howell, S. 1981. Rules not words, pp. 133–143. In *Indigenous Psychologies*, P. Heelas and A. Lock, eds. London: Academic Press.

———. 1983. *Our People: Chewong Society and Cosmos*. Oxford: Oxford University Press.

———. 1988. Total prestations as the life-giving acts among the Chewong. Paper presented at the 87th Annual Meetings of the American Anthropological Association, 16–20 November, Phoenix, Arizona.

Huntingford, G. W. B. 1954. The political organization of the Dorobo. *Anthropos* 49:123–148.

Jalong Apoi, T. 1989. Penans call for rattan ban. *Suara Sahabat ꜣAlam* [*Voice of Friends of the Earth*] *Malaysia* 5(3):2.

Jimin bin Idris, Mohd. Tap Salleh, Jailani M. Dom, Abu. Halim Haji Jawi and Md. Razim Shafie. 1983. Planning and administration of development programs for tribal peoples (the Malaysian setting). Committee on Integrated Rural Development for Asia and the Pacific. Planning and Administration of Development Programmes for Tribal Peoples, CIRDAP Country Report: Malaysia (mimeograph).

Johnson, P. 1976. *A History of Christianity*. New York: Atheneum.

Jones-Jackson, P. 1987. *When Roots Die: Endangered Traditions on the Sea Islands*. Atlanta: University of Georgia Press.

Juli Edo. 1987. Personal communication in author's files.

Keesing, R. M. and F. M. Keesing. 1971. *New Perspectives in Cultural Anthropology.* New York: Holt, Rinehart and Winston.

Kessel, N. and H. Walton. 1967. *Alcoholism,* revised edn. Harmondsworth: Pelican.

Knauft, B. M. 1985a. Ritual form and permutation in New Guinea: Implications of symbolic process for socio-political evolution. *American Ethnologist* 12:321–340.

———. 1985b. *Good Company and Violence. Sorcery and Social Action in a Lowland New Guinea Society.* Berkeley: University of California.

———. 1987a. Reconsidering violence in simple human societies: Homicide among the Gebusi of New Guinea. *Current Anthropology* 28:457–482.

———. 1987b. Reply. *Current Anthropology* 28:489–493.

———. 1987c. Managing sex and anger: Tobacco and kava use among the Gebusi of Papua New Guinea, pp. 273–289. In *Drugs in Western Pacific Societies,* L. Lindstrom, ed. ASAO Monograph #11. Lanham, MD: University Press of America.

———. 1988. Culture and cooperative affiliation: The evolutionary emergence of simple human societies. Paper presented at the 87th Annual Meetings of the American Anthropological Association, 16–20 November, Phoenix, Arizona.

Kolata, G. B. 1981. Bushmen join South African army. *Science* 211:562–564.

Kursh, C. O. 1971. The benefits of poor communication. *The Psychoanalytic Review* 58:189–208.

Lau, D. C., ed. and tr. 1970. *Mencius.* Harmondsworth: Penguin.

Lears, J. T. J. 1981. *No Place of Grace. Antimodernism and the Transformation of American Culture 1880–1920.* New York: Pantheon.

Leary, J. 1989. The importance of the Orang Asli in the Malayan Emergency 1948–1960. Centre of Southeast Asian Studies, Monash University, Working Paper 56.

Lee, R. B. 1984. *The Dobe !Kung.* New York: Holt, Rinehart and Winston.

———. 1990. Comment [on Wilmsen and Denbow 1990]. *Current Anthropology* 31:510–512.

Lee, R. B. and S. Hurlich. 1982. From foragers to fighters: South Africa's militarization of the Namibian San, pp. 327–345. In *Politics and History in Band Societies,* E. Leacock and R. Lee, eds. Cambridge: Cambridge University Press.

Lemert, E. M. 1958. The use of alcohol in three Salish Indian tribes. *Quarterly Journal of Studies on Alcohol* 19:90–107.

Leonard, G. B. 1968. *Education and Ecstasy.* New York: Delacourte Press.

Lieberman, L. 1989. A discipline divided: Acceptance of human sociobiological concepts in anthropology. *Current Anthropology* 30:676–682.

Mabbett, I. W. 1983. Some remarks on the present state of knowledge about slavery in Angkor, pp. 44–63. In *Slavery, Bondage and Dependency in Southeast Asia,* A. Reid, ed. New York: St. Martin's Press.

MacAndrew, C. and R. B. Edgerton. 1969. *Drunken Comportment. A Social Explanation.* New York: Aldine.

Malcolm, A. H. 1990. Gun control groups adjust their aim. *New York Times* 20 May:E22.

Man Yuke Foong and A. Hoh. 1987. Living in fear of 'outsiders.' [*Penang*] *Sunday Star* 5 July.

Mangin, W. 1957. Drinking among Andean Indians. *Quarterly Journal of Studies on Alcohol* 18:55–66.

Mannheim, K. 1946. *Ideology and Utopia. An Introduction to the Sociology of Knowledge.* New York: Harcourt, Brace and Company.

Manning, P. 1990. *Slavery and African Life. Occidental, Oriental and African Slave Trades.* Cambridge: Cambridge University Press.

Marks, S. 1972. Khoisan resistance to the Dutch in the seventeenth and eighteenth centuries. *Journal of African History* 13:55–80.

Marshall, J. 1984. Death blow to the Bushmen. With an update by Claire Ritchie. *Cultural Survival Quarterly* 8(3):13–17.

Marshall, L. 1961. Sharing, talking, and giving: Relief of social tensions among !Kung Bushmen. *Africa* 31:231–249.

———. 1967. !Kung Bushman bands, pp. 15–43. In *Comparative Political Systems*, R. Cohen and J. Middleton, eds. Studies in the Politics of Pre-industrial Societies. Garden City, NY: Natural History Press.

Mayer, F. E. 1954. *The Religious Bodies of America.* St. Louis, MO: Concordia Publishing.

McGlashan, A. 1987. The dream people. *Parabola* 12(3):11–15.

———. 1988. Response [to Dentan 1988a]. *Parabola* 13(1):6–7, 132–133.

McKay, J. P., B. D. Hill, and J. Buckler. 1984. *A History of World Societies.* Boston: Houghton Mifflin.

Means, N. and P. B. Means. 1986. *Sengoi–English and English–Sengoi Dictionary*, G. P. Means, ed., with Balahu Hassan, Wah Alang Busu, Bah War Rantau, and Wah Long Tangoi. Toronto: Joint Centre on Modern East Asia.

Memmi, A. 1965. *The Colonizer and the Colonized.* Boston: Beacon Press.

Mikluho-Maclay, N. V. 1878. Ethnological excursions in the Malay Peninsula—November 1874 to October 1875 (preliminary communication). *Journal of the Straits Branch of the Royal Asiatic Society* 2:205–221.

Miller, N. E. and J. Dollard. 1941. *Social Learning and Imitation.* New Haven: Yale University Press.

Morris, H. S. 1980. Slaves, aristocrats and export of sago in Sarawak, pp. 293–308. In *Asian and African Systems of Slavery*, J. L. Watson, ed. Berkeley: University of California Press.

Mosko, M. S. 1987. The symbols of "forest": A structural analysis of Mbuti culture and social organization. *American Anthropologist* 89:896–913.

Nagata, S. 1990. The origin of an Orang Asli Reserve in Kedah, Malaysia. Paper presented at the 89th Annual Meeting of the American Anthropological Association, 28 November–2 December, Washington, DC.

Nicholas, C. 1987. When will Orang Asli enjoy their rights? [*Penang*] *Star* 9 October.

———. 1990. In the name of the Semai? The state and society in peninsular Malaysia, pp. 68–88. In *Tribal Peoples and Development in Southeast Asia, Manusia dan Masyarakat* special issue, Lim Teck Ghee and A. G. Gomes, eds. Kuala Lumpur: Jabatan Sosiologi dan Antropologi, Universiti Malaya.

Nicholas, C., A. [Bah Tony] Williams-Hunt, and Tiah Sabak, eds. 1989. Orang Asli in the news. The emergency years: 1950–58. Kuala Lumpur: photocopy.

Nietschmann, B. 1987. The third world war. *Cultured Survival Quarterly* 11(3):1–16.

Noone, H. D. 1936. Report on the settlements and welfare of the Ple-Temiar Senoi of the Perak-Kelantan watershed. *Journal of the Federated Malay States Museums* 19:1–85.

Noone, R. with D. Holman. 1972. *In Search of the Dream People.* New York: William Morrow.

Nowak, B. S. 1984. Can the partnership last? Btsisi' marital partners and development. *Cultural Survival Quarterly* 8(2):9–11.

———. 1985. The formation of aboriginal reserves: The effects of land loss and development on the Btsisi' of Peninsular Malaysia, pp. 85–110. In *Modernization and the Emergence of a Landless Peasantry. Essays on the Integration of Peripheries to Socioeconomic Centers*, G. N. Appell, ed. Studies in Third World Societies Publication #23. Williamsburg, VA: Anthropology Department, College of William and Mary.

Nowak, B. S. 1988. The cooperative nature of women's and men's roles in Btsisi' marine activities, pp. 51–72. In *To Work and to Weep: Women in Fishing Economies*, J. Nadel-Klein and D. Davis, eds. Social and Economic Papers #18. St. John's: Institute of Social and Economic Research, Memorial University of Newfoundland.

Nowak, B. S. and R. K. Dentan. 1984. Problems and tactics in the transcultural study of intelligence: An archival report. *Behavior Science Research* 18(1):45–99.

Nowak, M. 1972. *The Rise of the Unmeltable Ethnics. Politics and Culture in the Seventies.* New York: Macmillan.

O'Nell, C. W. 1979. Nonviolence and personality dispositions among the Zapotec: Paradox and enigma. *Journal of Psychological Anthropology* 2:301–322.

———. 1981. Hostility management and the control of aggression in a Zapotec community. *Aggressive Behavior* 7:351–366.

———. 1986a. The nonviolent Zapotec: The phenomenon and some explanatory factors derived from research. Paper presented at the Conference on Peace, Nonviolent Action and the Concept of Self, 19–22 June, Edinburgh.

———. 1986b. Primary and secondary effects of violence control among the nonviolent Zapotec. *Anthropological Quarterly* 59:184–190.

Ooi Jin-Bee. 1963. *Land, People and Economy in Malaya.* London: Longmans, Green.

Ortner, S. B. 1973. On key symbols. *American Anthropologist* 75:1338–1346.

Orville, N. 1988. Road construction threatens Huaorini in Ecuador. *Cultural Survival Quarterly* 12(3):43–46.

Otterbein, K. F. 1986. *The Ultimate Coercive Sanction.* New Haven: Human Relations Area Files.

———. 1987. Comment [on Knauft 1987a]. *Current Anthropology* 28:484–485.

Parsons, R. D. 1983. The educational setting: A cultural milieu fostering passive-aggressiveness, pp. 174–193. In *Passive-Aggressiveness. Theory and Practice*, R. D. Parsons and R. J. Wicks, eds. New York: Brunner/Mazel.

Parsons, R. D. and R. J. Wicks. 1983. *Passive-Aggressiveness. Theory and Practice.* New York: Brunner/Mazel.

Paul, D. 1987. Carving up a debate. Is the spirit of change 'ruining' Asli carvings? [*Penang*] *Star* 13 September.

Paul, R. 1978. Instinctive aggression in man: The Semai case. *Journal of Psychological Anthropology* 1:65–79.

Paxon, F. L. 1924. *History of the American Frontier 1763–1893.* New York: Houghton Mifflin.

Peter, K. A. 1987. *The Dynamics of Hutterite Society. An Analytical Approach.* Edmonton: University of Alberta Press.

Peterson, J. T. 1978. The ecology of social boundaries. Agta foragers of the Philippines. Illinois Studies in Anthropology #11.

Peterson, R. B. 1990. Searching for life on Zaire's Ituri Forest frontier. *Cultural Survival Quarterly* 14(4):56–61.

Pipes, D. 1983. *In the Path of God. Islam and Political Power.* New York: Basic Books/Harper Colophon.

Polo, M. 1934. *The Travels of Marco Polo*, M. Komroff, ed. New York: Heritage Press.

Porteus, S. D. 1937. *Primitive Intelligence and Environment.* New York: Macmillan.

Pratt, M. L. 1986. Fieldwork in common places, pp. 27–50. In *Writing Culture. The Poetics and Politics of Ethnography*, J. Clifford and G. E. Marcus, eds. Berkeley: University of California Press.

Price, J. A. 1975. Sharing: The Integration of Intimate Economies. *Anthropologica* 71:3–26.

Queeny, E. M. 1952. The Wanderobo and the honey guide. *Natural History* 61:392–396.

Rachagan, S. S. 1990. Constitutional and statutory provisions governing Orang Asli, pp. 101–111. In *Tribal Peoples and Development in Southeast Asia, Manusia dan Masyarakat* special issue, Lim Teck Ghee and A. G. Gomes, eds. Kuala Lumpur: Jabatan Sosiologi dan Antropologi, Universiti Malaya.

Radcliffe-Brown, A. R. 1964. *The Andaman Islanders*. New York: Free Press.

Radcliffe-Brown, A. R. 1965. *Structure and Function in Primitive Society*. New York: Free Press.

Rambo, A. T. 1979. Human ecology of the Orang Asli: A review of research on the environmental relations of the aborigines of peninsular Malaysia. *Federation Museums Journal* 24:41–71.

Rambo, A. T., K. Gillogly, and K. L. Hutterer, eds. 1988. Ethnic diversity and the control of natural resources in Southeast Asia. Michigan Paper on South and Southeast Asia #32. Ann Arbor: Center for South and Southeast Asian Studies, University of Michigan.

Reid, A. 1983. *Slavery, Bondage and Dependency in Southeast Asia*. New York: St. Martin's Press.

———. 1988. *Southeast Asia in the Age of Commerce 1450–1680. Volume One: The Lands below the Winds*. New Haven: Yale University Press.

Ritchie, C. 1988. Update on the status of Bushmanland. *Cultural Survival Quarterly* 12(3):34–35.

Robarchek, C. A. 1977. Frustration, aggression and the nonviolent Semai. *American Ethnologist* 4:762–779.

———. 1979a. Learning to fear: A case study in emotional conditioning. *American Ethnologist* 6:555–567.

———. 1979b. Conflict, emotion and abreaction: Resolution of conflict among the Senoi Semai. *Ethos* 7:104–123.

———. 1986. Helplessness, fearfulness, and peacefulness: The emotional and motivational contexts of Semai social relations. *Anthropological Quarterly* 59:177–184.

———. 1987. Personal communication, 9 November.

———. 1988. Ghosts and witches: The psychocultural dynamics of Semai peacefulness. Paper presented at the 87th Annual Meetings of the American Anthropological Association, 16–20 November, Phoenix, Arizona.

Robarchek, C. A. and R. K. Dentan. 1987. "Blood drunkenness" and the bloodthirsty Semai: Unmaking another anthropological myth. *American Anthropologist* 89:356–365.

Robarchek, C. J. and C. A. Robarchek. 1988. Reciprocities and realities: World views, peacefulness and violence among Semai and Waorani. Paper presented at the 87th Annual Meetings of the American Anthropological Association, 16–20 November, Phoenix, Arizona.

———. 1990. Semai ethnopolitics: Images of the self and the state. Paper presented at the 89th Annual Meetings of the American Anthropological Association, 28 November–2 December, Washington, DC).

Robbins, R. H. 1973. Alcohol and the identity struggle: Some effects of economic change on interpersonal relations. *American Anthropologist* 75:99–122.

Roseman, M. 1988. Self, other and land: Temiar rainforest dwellers (or "good exchange is good health"). Paper presented at the 87th Annual Meetings of the American Anthropological Association, 16–20 November, Phoenix, Arizona.

Rosengarten, T. 1987. The reckless advance of the modern world. [Review of Jones-Jackson 1987]. *Natural History* 96(9):66–71.

Ross, M. H. 1981. Socioeconomic complexity, socialization, and political differentiation. *Ethos* 9:217–247.

Ross, R. 1981. Capitalism, expansion, and incorporation on the Southern African frontier, pp. 209–233. In *The Frontier in History. North America and Southern Africa Compared*, H. Lamar and L. Thompson, eds. New Haven: Yale University Press.

Rousseau, J. 1990. *Central Borneo. Ethnic Identity and Social Life in a Stratified Society*. Oxford: Clarendon Press.

Ryan, W. 1971. *Blaming the Victim*. New York: Pantheon.

Sangren, P. S. 1985. Social space and the periodization of economic history: A case from Taiwan. *Comparative Studies in Society and History* 27:531–561.

Sargent, S. S. and K. Pease Beardsley. 1960. Social roles and personality traits. *International Journal of Social Psychiatry* 6:66–70.

Saunders, C. 1981. Political processes in the Southern African frontier zones, pp. 149–171. In *The Frontier in History. North America and Southern Africa Compared*, H. Lamar and L. Thompson, eds. New Haven: Yale University Press.

Schaffer, H. R. 1964. The too-cohesive family: A form of group pathology. *International Journal of Social Psychiatry* 10:266–275.

Schebesta, P. 1926. Sakai in Malakka. *Archiv für Rassenbilder* 9:81–90.

———. 1973 [1928]. *Among the Forest Dwarfs of Malaya*. London: Oxford University Press.

Schwartz, H. 1980. *The French Prophets. The History of a Millenarian Group in Eighteenth-century England*. Berkeley: University of California Press.

Schwartz, T. 1975. Cultural totemism: Ethnic identity, primitive and modern, pp. 106–131. In *Ethnic Identity: Cultural Continuities and Change*, G. De Vos and L. Romanucci-Ross, eds. Palo Alto: Mayfield.

Schur, E. M. 1969. *Our Criminal Society. The Social and Legal Sources of Crime in America*. Englewood Cliffs, NJ: Prentice-Hall.

Selva, T. 1987. Penans may get same benefits as Orang Asli. [*Penang*] *Star* 3 July.

Senna, C. 1990. Letter to the editor. *New York Times* 28 October:18E.

Service, E. R. 1962. *Primitive Social Organization: An Evolutionary Perspective*. New York: Random House.

———. 1966. *The Hunters*. Englewood Cliffs, NJ: Prentice-Hall.

Sheldrick, D. 1957. [Suggestions]. *Annual Report of the Kenya Wild Life Society* 2:43–45.

Shostak, M. 1981. *Nisa. The Life and Words of a !Kung Woman*. Cambridge: Harvard University Press.

Siedentopf, A. R. 1946. Africa's cave folk on a new trail. *Natural History* 55:332–336.

Silberman, C. E. 1978. *Criminal Violence, Criminal Justice*. New York: Random House.

Simon, H. A. 1990. A mechanism for social selection and successful altruism. *Science* 250:1665–1668.

Simon, N. and G. Treichel. 1959. Only a decade to save our wildlife? *Wild Life* 1 (2):41–46.

Singh, H. 1989. Orang Asli shot by hunters. [*Penang*] *Star* 10 January.

Sipes, R. G. 1973. War, sports and aggression: An empirical test of two rival theories. *American Anthropologist* 75:64–86.

Skeat, W. W. and C. O. Blagden. 1906. *Pagan Races of the Malay Peninsula*. 2 vv., London: Macmillan.

Slimming, J. 1958. *Temiar Jungle. A Malayan Journey*. London: John Murray.

Solway, J. S. and R. Lee. 1990. Foragers, genuine or spurious? Situating the Kalahari San in history. *Current Anthropology* 31:109–146.

Speidel, W. H. 1976. The administrative and fiscal reforms of Liu Ming-ch'uan in Taiwan, 1884–1891: Foundations for self-strengthening. *Journal of Asian Studies* 35:441–459.

Sponsel, L. E. 1989. An anthropologist's perspective on peace and quality of life, pp. 29–48. In *Peace and Development: An Interdisciplinary Perspective*, D. S. Sanders and J. K. Matsuoka, eds. Honolulu: University of Hawaii School of Social Work.

Sponsel, L. E. 1990. Ultraprimitive pacifists: The Tasaday as a symbol of peace. *Anthropology Today* 6(1):3–5.

Spradley, J. P. 1970. *You Owe Yourself a Drunk. An Ethnography of Urban Nomads.* Boston: Little, Brown.

Stacey, T. 1953. *The Hostile Sun. A Malayan Journey.* London: Duckworth.

Stephenson, C. 1990. Peace studies: The evolution of peace research and peace education. University of Hawaii Institute for Peace Occasional Paper #1.

Stewart, K. R. 1948. Magico-religious beliefs and practises [sic] in primitive society—a sociological interpretation of their therapeutic aspects. Doctoral thesis, London School of Economics.

———. 1954. *Pygmies and Dream Giants.* New York: W. W. Norton.

———. 1972. Dream theory in Malaya, pp. 161–170. In *Altered States of Consciousness,* C. T. Tart, ed. Garden City, NY: Anchor.

Strunz, F. 1985. Die Legende vom Wundervolk des Traums und die Wirklichkeit einer neuen Therapie. *Gestalt Theory* 7:182–200.

Suhaini Azam. 1987. Mahathir cracks down. *Far Eastern Economic Review* 5 November:14.

Suler, J. 1984. The role of ideology in self-help groups. *Social Policy* 15 (Winter):29–36.

Tan, S. 1990. The rise of state authoritarianism in Malaysia. *Bulletin of Concerned Asian Scholars* 22(3):32–42.

Thomas, E. M. 1959. *The Harmless People.* New York: Alfred A. Knopf.

Thordharson, J. 1938 [1387]. The Voyages to VinLand, A. M. Reeves tr., pp. 5–20. In *American Historical Documents 1000–1904. The Harvard Classics,* C. W. Eliot, ed. New York: Collier.

Tilden, V. P. and R. D. Galyen. 1987. Cost and conflict: The darker side of social support. *Western Journal of Nursing Research* 9:9–18.

Todd, H. 1990. Dispossessed. Orang Asli rapidly losing land. *Utusan Konsumer* (mid-April):1, 9–12.

Turnbull, C. M. 1962. *The Forest People. A Study of the Pygmies of the Congo.* New York: Simon and Schuster.

———. 1965. *Wayward Servants: The Two Worlds of the African Pygmies.* Garden City, NY: Natural History Press.

———. 1978. The politics of non-aggression, pp. 161–221. In *Learning Non-aggression. The Experience of Non-literate Societies,* A. Montagu, ed. London: Oxford University Press.

Turner, F. J. 1894. The significance of the frontier in American history. *Annual Report of the American Historical Association for 1893*:199–227.

Turton, A. 1980. Thai institutions of slavery, pp. 251–292. In *Asian and African Systems of Slavery,* J. L. Watson, ed. Berkeley: University of California Press.

Venkatesan, D. 1990. Ecocide or genocide? The Onge in the Andaman Islands. *Cultural Survival Quarterly* 14:49–51.

Ver Steeg, C. L. 1964. *The Formative Years 1607–1763.* New York: Hill and Wang.

von Graeve, B. 1989. *The Pacaa Nova. Clash of Cultures on the Brazilian Frontier.* Peterborough, Ontario: Broadview Press.

Waley, A. 1941. *Translations from the Chinese.* New York: Knopf.

Watson, J. L. 1980. Slavery as an institution, open and closed systems, pp. 1–15. In *Asian and African Systems of Slavery,* J. L. Watson, ed. Berkeley: University of California Press.

Wavell, S. 1958. *The Lost World of the East. An Adventurous Quest in the Malayan Hinter Land.* London: Souvenir Press.

Weigle, L. A. 1928. *American Idealism.* New Haven: Yale University Press.

Weppner, R. S. 1973. An anthropological view of the street addict's world. *Human Organization* 32:111–121.

———. 1983. *The Untherapeutic Community. Organizational Behavior in a Failed Treatment Program.* Lincoln: University of Nebraska Press.

Westwood. T. 1962. *The Face of the Beloved.* London: Allen & Unwin.

Wheeler, L. R. 1928. *The Modern Malay.* London: Allen & Unwin.

Whitson, R. E., ed. 1983. *The Shakers. Two Centuries of Spiritual Reflection.* New York: Paulist Press.

Wilkinson, R. J., n.d., A Malay-English Dictionary. Tokyo: Armed Forces.

[Williams-Hunt] Bah Tony. 1989a. Orang Asli are not cannibals. [*Penang*] *Star* 16 January.

———. 1989b. Sepatahkata dari Presiden. *Berita POASM* 1:1–2.

Williams-Hunt, P. D. R. 1952. *An Introduction to the Malayan Aborigines.* Kuala Lumpur: Government Press.

Wilmsen, E. N. and J. R. Denbow. 1990. Paradigmatic history of San-speaking peoples and current attempts at revision. *Current Anthropology* 31:489–507.

Wilson, J. Q. 1983. *Thinking about Crime*, revised edn. New York: Vintage.

Wilson, J. Q. and R. J. Herrnstein. 1985. *Crime and Human Nature.* New York: Simon and Schuster.

Wittfogel, K. A. 1957. *Oriental Despotism. A Comparative Study of Total Power.* New Haven: Yale University Press.

Wohlforth, C. P. 1990. Off the pot. *The New Republic* 203 (3 December):9–10.

Woodburn, J. 1982. Egalitarian societies. *Man* 17:431–451.

Wright, J. B. 1971. *Bushman Raiders of the Drakensberg, 1840–1870: A Study of their Conflict with Stock-Keeping Peoples in Natal.* Pietermaritzburg: University of Natal Press.

Wrong, D. 1980. *Power: Its Forms, Bases and Uses.* New York: Harper Colophon.

Zimring, F. E. 1967. Is gun control likely to reduce violent killings? *University of Chicago Law Review* 35:721–737.

———. 1972. The medium is the message: Firearm caliber as a determinant of death from assault. *Journal of Legal Studies* 1:97–123.

Zubrow, E. B. W. 1976. Stability and instability: A problem in long-term regional growth, pp. 245–274. In *Demographic Anthropology. Quantitative Approaches*, E. B. W. Zubrow, ed. Albuquerque: University of New Mexico.

11

Social Structure, Psychocultural Dispositions, and Violent Conflict: Extensions from a Cross-cultural Study[1]

MARC HOWARD ROSS

INTRODUCTION

It is difficult to conceive of a human community where there is no conflict among its members or between persons in the community and outsiders. At the same time, the degree to which conflict is physically violent varies widely. There are cases such as the Yanomamo (Chagnon 1967), where feuding and warfare are an ongoing condition of daily life in contrast to the Semai of Malaysia where open physical expressions of differences is rare and strongly discouraged (Dentan 1968; see also Chapters 9 and 10 of this volume). How can we best understand such variation?

The research reported here summarizes and extends a series of studies contrasting two broad societal level explanations for within society (internal) and between society (external) conflict and violence (Ross 1985, 1986a, b, forthcoming). One view is structural, accounting for patterns of conflict in terms of competing interests that develop in particular forms of social and economic organization. The other is psychocultural, explaining violent conflict as a result of both culturally learned dispositions and interpretations of the world typical in a society.

Hypotheses from each perspective are tested using data from a worldwide sample of 90 preindustrial societies. The statistical results are consistent with both explanations for internal and external conflict. More interesting, the analysis integrates the two to form a general theory of conflict behavior. My argument is that psychocultural dispositions, rooted in early learning experiences and crucial in creating commonly held images of the self and others, determine a society's overall level of conflict. But if psychocultural interpretations of the world lead to a certain propensity for disputing, they do not tell us very precisely who argues, contests, and fights with whom. Here the structural features of the social, economic, and political system are crucial in determining the people with whom one cooperates and with whom one fights, meaning whether they are within one's society, in another society, or both.

One test of the utility of a theory is its application in settings very different from those in which it was developed. To what extent can a theory of conflict behavior, developed with data from small preindustrial societies, usefully help us understand high versus low levels of conflict within and between contemporary nations? In the final section of this paper, the general theory offered here is applied to Northern Ireland, a political community wracked by especially high levels of violence, and Norway, a society where political conflict and aggression levels are quite low. It is argued that the psychocultural interpretations and interests rooted in social structural factors and identified in the cross-cultural analysis provide important insights into the dynamics of these two, very different, cases.

The framework adopted is highly consistent with, but does not spell out here, an evolutionary argument for the development of human conflict and violence. This argument would draw attention to biologically evolved capacities but especially to social and cultural evolution as it has shaped human institutions and behavior. My argument about the importance of interests and interpretations in conflict and in cooperation suggests that human conflict behavior is rooted in an evolved capacity for group living. Yet, at the same time, cultural innovations and responses to different environmental settings have meant that the specific institutional forms of group living and the nature of behavior within communities show great variability. For this reason cultural evolution is likely to be particularly significant in understanding human conflict, while individual level biosocial models such as sociobiology are not so much wrong as they are incomplete (Campbell 1983; Boyd and Richerson 1985; Ross 1991).

THE CONCEPT OF CONFLICT

The conflict behavior of interest here is group behavior, not that of individuals acting alone. While the formation of groups seems to be a universal human phenomenon, there is much variation in the extent to which groups develop in-group solidarity and out-group hostility (LeVine and Campbell 1972). A good deal of group behavior is highly cooperative and group attachment contributes to well-being in a variety of ways (Lancaster 1987). In-group cooperation makes groups more effective in intergroup conflict, conferring distinct long-term advantages over groups which are incapable of coordinated action (Bigelow 1973; van der Dennen 1987; Ike 1987; Lancaster 1987). Data show that groups that develop the capacity to achieve internal coordination and the technology to wage external conflict are at higher levels of social, economic, and political complexity (Wright 1942; Broch and Galtung 1966; Otterbein 1970). High internal cooperation, however, does not necessarily mean that groups are more aggressive externally (Deutsch 1973).

Conflict is an integral aspect of political life. It involves efforts of two or more mutually opposed parties to obtain scarce resources, either material or symbolic, at each other's expense. Each does so through destroying, injuring, thwarting, or otherwise controlling the other party or parties (Mack and Snyder 1957; Ross forthcoming).[2] Conflicts vary in severity from hostile verbal exchanges to armed battles. A convenient way to evaluate a conflict's severity is in terms of its costs, both material and psychic, to the parties as they prepare for and engage in it.[3] In this paper I use the term conflict to refer to all forms of group disputing, while violence is reserved for those conflicts in which physical force is used. Although particular conflicts may be without violence, no society is. Aggression, defined as effort to injure or thwart another party, generally overlaps with violence, although some verbal behavior which is best described as aggressive stops short of physical force.

Societies differ greatly in their levels of conflict behavior, meaning the amount and severity of conflict and violence in which they are involved. My goal is to explain this variation. This analysis does not seek to explain the outbreak of any particular conflict; rather, it directs attention to factors which make a society more or less prone than another to engage in certain levels of conflict and violence. From this perspective, the same sorts of precipitating incidents—such as livestock theft, economic tension, or adultery—occur in many settings, but in some cases they unleash an escalating pattern of violent conflict, while in other cases such intensification is severely limited.

Measuring Political Violence

This study is part of a larger cross-cultural investigation of political life in preindustrial societies (Ross forthcoming).[4] To consider the broad pattern of worldwide variation in political life, 44 variables were coded for 90 preindustrial societies, half the cases in Murdock and White's (1969) Standard Cross-Cultural Sample (SCCS).[5] Factor analysis of the political variables was then used to develop five scales (Ross 1983). Two of these describe the organization of political power and authority, one describes patterns of multiple (overlapping) loyalties, and two, which are the focus of attention here, group together variables measuring internal conflict and violence and external conflict and warfare (Table 11-1).[6]

Table 11-1 shows the variables used in constructing the internal and external conflict scales from the factor analysis.[7] The internal conflict and violence dimension distinguishes societies in terms of their level of disputing, the legitimation and use of physical violence, feuding, strong factionalism, and compliance with local community norms. The seven variables in the internal conflict scale, in descending order of importance, are: the severity of conflict between residents of different communities in the same society, the acceptability of using violence against members of the same society but outside the local community, the frequency of internal warfare, the severity of conflict within local communities in the society, the degree to which physical force is used as a mechanism for dispute settlement, the acceptability of violence against members of the community, and the variability of compliance with norms and decisions on the part of members of the local community.

Societies on the high end of this scale, such as the Jivaro or Somali, have frequent violent conflict and internal warfare both within and between communities of the same society. Societies at the middle of the scale, such as the Kikuyu have regular conflict, but internal warfare and the use of physical violence in local disputes is less common. At the low point are societies where conflict itself is milder and physical violence infrequent. The Mbuti Pygmies, Semang, and Papago fall here.

Three variables make up the external warfare and conflict scale: the frequency

Table 11-1 Variable and Factor Loadings for Internal and External Conflict and Violence Measures.[a]

Variable	Factor loading
Internal violence and conflict	
1. The severity of conflict between different communities of the same society (four-point measure)	0.94
2. The acceptability of violence when directed against members of the same society outside the local community (four-point measure)	0.90
3. Frequency of internal warfare (four-point measure)	0.81
4. The severity of conflict within the local community (four-point measure)	0.68
5. The extent to which physical force is used as a mechanism for dispute settlement (three-point measure)	0.67
6. The acceptability of violence when directed against members of the local community (four-point measure)	0.55
7. Degree of compliance with community norms and decisions by members of local communities (three-point measure)	0.52
External warfare and conflict	
1. Frequency of external warfare (four-point scale)	0.86
2. Degree of hostility—not just warfare—expressed towards other societies (four-point scale)	0.69
3. Acceptability of violence when directed towards persons in other societies (four-point measure)	0.64

[a] Complete definitions and raw data for these measures are presented in Ross (1983).

of external warfare, the degree of hostility expressed to other societies (not just in war), and the acceptability of violence directed against people in other societies. Organized intergroup fighting, warfare, is more central to this dimension than it is in the internal conflict scale, and this is reflected in the slightly different label given to each dimension.[8] Societies such as the Buganda, Maori, Comanche, and Jivaro are high on this dimension, while low external conflict societies are the !Kung Bushmen, the Lepcha, and the Trobriand Islanders.[9]

HYPOTHESES ABOUT SOCIETAL DIFFERENCES IN CONFLICT BEHAVIOR

The extensive literature on international violence and conflict offers at least three major explanations for observed variations in violence. Some theorists argue that nations which differ in terms of internal or external conflict are not necessarily very different in terms of their internal characteristics (Zinnes 1980). In Midlarsky's (1975) view, for example, international warfare is better understood as a function of alliances, constraints in the international system and status inconsistency than as the outcome of national characteristics (see also Waltz 1959).[10]

In contrast, the two other explanations agree that internal differences exist between polities that are high versus low on violence, but disagree about what the differences are. Some explain violence and warfare in terms of the interests associated with structural features of particular societies (e.g. Otterbein 1968, 1970;

Hibbs 1973), linking aspects of the social, economic, or political system with patterns of conflict. In contrast, others emphasize psychocultural dispositions associated with interpretations of the social world as key factors in understanding the behavioral expression of aggression and violence (e.g. Durbin and Bowlby 1939; Gurr 1970; Montagu 1978; Huyghe 1986).

While it is relatively easy to find highly partisan supporters for either position—that social structural interests or psychocultural interpretations are of primary importance—it is a good deal more difficult to find clear-cut empirical evidence for one side or the other. Of course, another possible view is that there may be ways in which the psychocultural and structural explanations for conflict behavior are compatible with each other, as a number of authors have suggested (Edgerton 1971; Harrington and Whiting 1972). In fact, Greenstein (1967) and Whiting (1980) warn against expecting either theory to hold across all behaviors or situations. We hope to determine ways in which each set of forces has an independent effect on conflict and how they interact.

Social Structural Hypotheses

Structural hypotheses link conflict to the interests associated with particular forms of social and economic organization and suggest ways in which the structure of a society creates interests directing conflict in particular directions (cf, Evans-Pritchard 1940; Colson 1953; Coleman 1957; Gluckman 1963; Beals and Siegel 1966; Fried 1967). Different theories, which I place in two major groups, identify a wide range of social structural elements as central. *Cross-cutting ties* theories explain conflict and conflict management in terms of the nature of links between different members of a society. *Complexity* theories, in contrast, give a primary role to the competing (group) interests associated with a society's level of socioeconomic and/or political organization in accounting for conflict behavior. Whereas cross-cutting theories focus on the common interests formed through interaction and exchange, complexity theories emphasize competing and incompatible interests and the tensions that result from them. If the former stresses the benefits of interdependence, the latter draws our attention to ways in which group-based inequalities of power and resources characterize exchanges and sow the seeds of conflict.

Cross-Cutting Ties Theories

The hypothesis that the existence of cross-cutting ties—linking different members of the same community and different communities in the same society—limit the existence, or at least the severity, of conflict, and promote dispute settlement through shared interests, is probably the most widely cited structural hypothesis about conflict (Colson 1953; Coleman 1957; Gluckman 1963; LeVine and Campbell 1972: Chapter 4). At the same time, while cross-cutting ties limit the severity of conflict within a society by unifying it, it is argued that they can increase the severity of conflict with outsiders (LeVine and Campbell 1972). But what produces strong cross-cutting ties? Many different possibilities can be cited.

Overlapping reference groups.[11] In some societies there are important attachments, formal or informal, material or psychic, that link members of different residential and kinship groups. For example, among the Ndembu, Turner (1957) describes cult groups which unite individuals who might otherwise be opposed to one another on other structural grounds such as kinship or residence. Other forms this might take include age organizations, religious solidarities, or even more diffuse political identities. Where such groups are present, linkages can have political relevance in enhancing the internal unity of society, inhibiting internal conflict, and facilitating defense against perceived outside enemies.

Marriage. Much of anthropological theory begins, not surprisingly, by looking at kinship and marriage alliances. In an exchange view, such as Lévi-Strauss's, kinship bonds create mutual obligation and solidarity, while the absence of these ties is accompanied by potentially hostile relationships. Preference for marriage outside the local community inhibits conflict among different communities of the same society because people will not want to fight against those with whom they share kinship and other affective bonds.

Residence. Knowing whether a society favors internal community marriage or not only tells us part of what we want to know about who is marrying whom. Several anthropologists have focused particular attention on the impact that the dispersion versus concentration of males has on a society's violence and conflict since it is the males who are almost universally predominant in overt fighting and warfare (LeVine and Campbell 1972:52). Murphy (1957) and LeVine (1965) both argue that matrilocal or uxorilocal residence disperses related males thereby inhibiting conflict between communities of the same society while promoting external fighting. Using cross-cultural samples, Ember and Ember (1971) and Divale (1974) also find that matrilocality is associated with external warfare, with patrilocality more common when internal fighting is high. Exactly why residence and warfare are associated is the subject of disagreement, however.

Intercommunity trade. The functionalist school in international relations advocates the exchange of persons and goods as crucial to inhibiting warfare among nations (Haas 1964). Developing interdependencies among communities will, in this view, inhibit overt fighting between them and encourage the development of peaceful mechanisms for resolving disputes when they do arise.

Fraternal interest groups. Fraternal interest group theory connects internal conflict to the actions of localized, male kinship groups protecting common interests (van Velzen and van Wetering 1960). In several tests of this hypothesis, Otterbein (1968) and Otterbein and Otterbein (1965) found that in politically uncentralized societies the levels of feuding and internal warfare (armed conflict between different communities of the same society) are related positively to the presence of fraternal interest groups, operationally measured by the presence of patrilocality and polygyny. Paige and Paige (1981) propose a more refined version of this theory, suggesting that fraternal interest groups will be particularly strong when the resources males protect are significant, non-mobile and stable. Strong fraternal interest groups are a structural arrangement making possible the rapid mobilization of related males into fighting groups.

Complexity Theories

Socioeconomic and political complexity. Although the popular image holds that simple societies are characterized by violence and anarchy, studies demonstrate that societies at the simplest level of technological complexity are no more violence prone than those which are more complex. Some theorists have argued that social and economic differentiation creates competing interests which produce more disputing in complex societies. More frequent disputes may not result in an increase in internal warfare, however, because more complex societies exhibit higher levels of political coordination and control (Fried 1967; Ross 1981; Bates 1983).

The case of external conflict seems more straightforward. Bigelow (1973) argues that groups which engage in external conflict also successfully evolve more sophisticated mechanisms of internal social coordination. Other theorists who discuss the positive relation between external warfare and social complexity include Wright (1942), Broch and Galtung (1966), LeVine and Campbell (1972), and Otterbein (1970).

Psychocultural Hypotheses

If structural explanations for conflict, violence, and warfare focus on how the organization of society shapes action, psychocultural explanations look to a very different place: the actors themselves. Psychocultural explanations emphasize conflict behavior as a consequence of actor interpretations arising from their internal images and perceptions of their external social worlds. Psychocultural theorists draw attention to culturally shared notions about trust, self-esteem, and identity, and how people define and defend each of these in light of specific events. They are concerned with the ways people process events, and the feelings (emotions), perceptions, and cognitions they evoke. The term psychocultural is used, as opposed to psychological, to emphasize assumptions, perceptions, and images about the world that are widely shared by participants in the same sociocultural system. Drawing on the work of students of child development and post-Freudian psychoanalysis, such explanations see conflict behavior as a function of both developmental and social processes (Volkan 1988).

In light of the many quantitative cross-cultural studies linking child-rearing practices to other cultural domains, the lack of attention to associations of political life generally, and conflict behavior in particular, with childhood socialization is surprising as Harrington and Whiting (1972) suggest. Here I spell out what such a link between socialization practices and conflict behavior might be.

Early socialization influences adult behavior by shaping the personality of the individual (Whiting and Child 1953; Harrington and Whiting 1972) as well as the cognitions that prepare individuals for patterns of conflict and cooperation in their society. Psychodynamic theories, beginning with Freud's *Civilization and its Discontents* (1930), provide several key hypotheses relevant to internal violence and external warfare. Perspectives that are more social-psychological also attribute a role to social, economic, and political conditions while identifying different underlying mechanisms (e.g. Horkheimer 1950).

Harsh Socialization

Several psychological approaches—psychoanalytic theory (and the authoritarian personality work derived from it), social learning theory, and frustration–aggression theory—associate harsh and severe child-training practices with later aggressivity. Although the mechanisms underlying each of the theories are different, the predictions are similar (Zigler and Child 1969). For example, where psychoanalytic and frustration–aggression theory relate severe physical punishment of children to adult aggression through the mechanisms of externalization, projection and displacement of hostile feelings onto outgroups (Volkan 1988), social learning theory explains the connection more in terms of imitation, modelling, and reinforcement. Several cross-cultural studies find a positive association between harsh socialization practices and physical aggression, bellicosity, or warfare (Levinson and Malone 1980:249).

Warmth and Affection

A second perspective emphasizes that love-oriented socialization practices involving high affection and warmth are associated with low violence and conflict in adulthood. Both conceptually and empirically there is good reason to see this dimension as independent of harsh child-training, not its inverse.[12] Conceptually the distinction is perhaps parallel to the differences between permissiveness and punishment that Sears et al. (1958) find to have independent effects in the socialization of aggression. Greater expression of affection towards children, greater emphasis on values such as trust, honesty, and generosity, and closer father–child ties, for example, are all factors which lead individuals towards cooperation, rather than animosity and aggressiveness.

Healthy psychosocial development of the individual, in terms of early "object relations" (internalized images of others based on early experiences) and of secure ties to parental figures, prepares the way for socially cooperative behavior later in life (Fairbairn 1954; Winnicott 1965; Guntrip 1971; Stern 1985). The profiles of seven small-scale societies low on internal conflict and aggression present some good ethnographic examples of this pattern (Montagu 1978). In these societies, great affection is frequently directed towards the child, whose overall feelings of security are high. Overt expression of aggression is discouraged, but not through physical punishment. Finally, these societies lack highly aggressive persons whom the child can imitate.

Male Gender Identity Conflict

The Whitings use the term "protest masculinity" to refer to the pattern which links uncertainty concerning gender identity to overt aggression (Whiting 1965; Whiting and Whiting 1975). In male-dominated cultures, where fathers are distant and aloof from their children, young boys develop especially strong bonds with their mothers. Intense psychological conflict may occur when boys later need to forsake such identifications to meet societal expectations of adult male behavior (Herdt 1987). Males in such cultures may develop very ambivalent feelings towards females and tend to exhibit narcissistic personalities marked by a preoccupation with early developmental tasks, pride, and a desire for self-enhancement that frequently lead to aggressive actions (Slater and Slater 1965; also see Kernberg 1975; and Spotnitz 1976).

RESULTS

Procedures

The data used in testing these hypotheses were coded, as previously noted, from ethnographic reports on 90 societies located throughout the world.[13] Multiple regression is used in the analysis. Because there are many moderate correlations among the independent variables, it is especially useful in showing how each of the independent variables is related to the dependent variables after the effects of the other independent variables are removed.[14] With this procedure, we arrive at results which are different from, and more straightforward than, those we get from simply looking at the bivariate correlation matrix.

The regression results presented in Table 11-2 were selected from several different specifications. Because a number of reseachers have suggested important differences between politically centralized and uncentralized societies in their conflict behavior (e.g., LeVine and Campbell 1972), in addition to the substantive variables, earlier versions included sets of interaction terms for each variable to test for systematically different effects in uncentralized and centralized societies.[15]

Table 11-2 shows that both structural and psychocultural variables are significantly related to internal and external conflict and in combination they explain conflict better than either set of variables alone. A closer look shows that low affection, harsh socialization, and male gender identity conflict increase internal and external conflict and violence, but the specific structural factors which are associated with internal and external conflict differ. These results suggest a dispositional basis for aggression and violence rooted in early learning, while the selection of targets for aggression is shaped by the structural features of a society (Ross 1986a, b). In some cases the targets will be outside one's society, in some they will be inside it, while in many situations targets will be in both locations. Before elaborating on the general argument, it is useful, first, quickly to examine the specific results.

Analysis
Structural Hypotheses

The results show that the specific structural factors associated with internal and external conflict differ. Internal conflict is higher in societies with few overlapping reference groups, and in uncentralized societies with strong fraternal interest groups. External conflict increases with socioeconomic complexity, and in uncentralized societies is higher where there are numerous overlapping reference groups and where there is a higher level of intracommunity marriage. If cross-cutting ties theory does better in explaining internal conflict and violence, complexity theory is stronger in the case of external conflict and warfare.[16]

The results, however, are only partially supportive of the specific hypotheses

Table 11-2   Multiple Regressions: Internal and External Conflict.

	Standardized regression coefficient (beta)	Standard error of beta	Pearson correlation[a,b]	
Internal violence and conflict				
Overlapping reference group scale	−0.29**	0.11	−0.24**	(90)
Fraternal interest group strength in uncentralized societies	0.22**	0.10	0.26**	(90)
Affectionate socialization practices	−0.31**	0.10	−0.35***	(89)
Harsh socialization practices	0.22*	0.10	0.33***	(82)
Political power concentration	−0.11	0.14	−0.03	(90)
Polygyny	0.12	0.10	0.20*	(90)
Male gender identity conflict	0.13	0.10	0.05	(68)
Intercommunity trade	0.04	0.11	0.03	(89)
Socioeconomic complexity	0.09	0.14	0.08	(90)
Matrilocality[c]	−0.07	0.10	0.05	(90)
Marital endogamy	0.01	0.10	0.04	(90)
Multiple $R = 0.60$; R square $= 0.36$				
External violence and conflict				
Overlapping reference groups in uncentralized societies	0.21*	0.10	0.20*	(90)
Fraternal interest group strength	0.07	0.12	0.24**	(87)
Affectionate socialization practices	−0.39***	0.09	−0.41***	(89)
Harsh socialization practices	0.19*	0.09	0.30**	(82)
Political power concentration	−0.12	0.12	0.11	(90)
Polygyny	−0.12	0.09	0.03	(90)
Male gender identity conflict	0.32***	0.08	0.29**	(68)
Socioeconomic complexity	0.27*	0.13	0.24**	(90)
Matrilocality[c]	0.11	0.09	0.14	(90)
Marital endogamy in uncentralized societies	0.43***	0.11	0.28**	(90)
Multiple $R = 0.69$; R square $= 0.47$				

Sample size $= 90$ in the regressions.

Means have been substituted for missing data in the regressions.

[a] Sample size are given in parentheses.

[b] Correlations are for all cases, not just uncentralized societies.

[c] Results are the same when matrilocality is substituted for patilocality; but the sign is reversed.

*** Statistically significant at the 0.001 level.

** Statistically significant at the 0.01 level.

* Statistically significant at the 0.05 level.

concerning residence, marriage, and trade which have been found in earlier work. Marital endogamy, not exogamy as expected, is associated with higher external warfare in uncentralized societies, but I did not find any connection between endogamy and internal conflict. Matrilocality, which a large number of previous studies identify as a crucial predictor of external warfare, is only weakly related to external conflict once the effect of the other variables in the model is taken into account. Similarly, partilocality is not particularly related to internal violence and conflict in the multivariate model. The point is not so much that these residence variables are irrelevant to understanding patterns of violence and conflict, but rather that they do not operate in isolation and their effects need to be considered within the context of other structural and psychocultural variables. My argument is not that the earlier models are invalid—the bivariate correlations are more or less consistent with their findings—but that those models are *incompletely* specified and therefore biased.

The literature on societal complexity and violent conflict is confusing, but perhaps the results are less so. *Socioeconomic* complexity is positively associated with both forms of conflict, but only in the case of external warfare is the association statistically significant. *Political* complexity, measured as the concentration of political power, is weakly and negatively associated with both internal and external conflict, despite the fact that socioeconomic and political complexity are themselves strongly and positively related. This suggests that perhaps, socioeconomic development unleashes forces that enhance the likelihood of conflict while political complexity provides opportunities to control it. The results also support the contention that an adequate explanation for conflict will be different in uncentralized and centralized societies (LeVine and Campbell 1972; Otterbein 1977). Because there is no authority exerted beyond the local level in uncentralized societies, the organization of fraternal interest groups, exogamous marriage, and cross-cutting ties among local communities of the same society are all important in shaping the level and targets of violence in these societies, whereas these same variables are not important in the centralized cases.

Psychocultural Hypotheses

The regression analysis provides support for each of the three psychocultural hypotheses. When early socialization is harsh, when it is low in affection and warmth, and when male gender identity conflict is high, the levels of both internal and external violence are high. It should be underlined that while these three dimensions of socialization are conceptually related, the results show that each makes a statistically independent contribution to explaining the level of conflict, for the regression coefficient gives the effect of each variable when the others are controlled.

Identifying psychocultural dispositions related to conflict and violence also requires the specification of mechanisms linking socialization to personality formation and adult behavior. In an earlier explication of my results (Ross 1986a) I spelled out what such linkages might be, drawing heavily on psychoanalytic theory with an emphasis on the role of mechanisms central in object relations theory (Greenberg and Mitchell 1983; Volkan 1988): attachment, identification, repression, externalization, projection, and displacement.

Early relationships with the environment provide a template for dealing with conflict later in life (Fornari 1975:101; Stern 1985). It is this notion of a framework for the interpretation of events which provides the crucial linkages between culture and dispositions, and places the concepts of perception and interpretation at the center of a cross-cultural theory of conflict and cooperation. *Dispositional* patterns build on *cultural* constructions of the world and human relationships. For example, Volkan describes how members of ethnic communities share objects of externalization. For this reason, dispositions are more than individual personality configurations;

they are also culturally learned and approved methods for dealing with others. Although participants have little trouble in citing "objective" bases for conflict— "She[he] took my toy[land, water, women, cows]"—what is striking to the outsider is the number of times when the same supposedly provocative action occurs and is not followed by aggressive action. This point is crucial. It means that the origins of conflict reside in *interpretations* of such situations, not the objective situations themselves.

A frequent criticism of theories emphasizing dispositional variables is that socialization should be analyzed as a social process. This argument means that we should look further for the *social* variables required to explain the results. Have I failed to look hard enough for social variables to explain the results? I do not suggest that socialization patterns develop *sui generis*, for the data show a modest relationship (similar to that which Barry et al. (1959) found in their earlier study) between social and economic organization and child rearing. But the magnitudes of most of their correlations are low, although they are statistically significant (Hendrix 1985). The data show that socialization variables are at least *as* good predictors of conflict as the social or economic variables are. For the criticism of those who reject dispositional explanations to be sustained there must be a closer fit between the needs of social and economic systems and psychocultural processes than I found. But there is another point as well. Psychocultural interpretations are built from dispositions which are more than personality configurations; they are also culturally learned and approved methods for dealing with others, both inside and outside one's community. They are guides to behavior, providing models for behavior in different situations.

It is probably useful to think of a *range* of dispositional configurations which might be adaptive in particular settings, rather than personality traits which are simply present or absent. Because of social, technical, economic, and political change, there are certainly situations where social organization and socialization practices have evolved in different directions and at different rates. Thus, a clear correspondence between the two which once may have existed in a society may have gradually disappeared. In addition, we should not expect an exact isomorphism between socialization practices and socioeconomic characteristics because each domain is subject to different forces of continuity and change.

Situations of great importance to people's lives, or which are central to their self-concept, or which are ambiguous, unstructured situations, are all likely to engage the interpretive and projective systems of individuals, more than situations without these characteristics. Cruciality produces engagement and emotional investment while ambiguity leaves room for interpretation and the projection of individual inner worlds on a hazy, but important situation. For Whiting (1980) areas such as religion and the interpretation of illness are best understood as psychological products, as projective behaviors. My argument is that conflict and violence should frequently be seen in this same framework. Conflict situations are often high in cruciality and ambiguity which require that individuals interpret them in terms of their own psychological needs. The social dynamics within groups which begin with perhaps accurate, but scanty, information concerning a sup-posedly objective situation provide great room for interpretive processes to manifest themselves in collective behavior (Janis 1972).

EXTENSIONS OF THE MODEL

If the models developed here are to be useful they need to be examined in other contexts.[17] Where might it be easiest to test the models in the case of contemporary nations? Probably less at the national and more at local levels; probably more in homogeneous settings than in heterogeneous ones; probably more in relatively isolated settings such as peer or work groups in semi-autonomous settings, or in voluntary organizations.

Here I have tried to apply insights from my cross-cultural investigations to two small political units. Northern Ireland and Norway, with very different levels of overt conflict. Preliminary observations suggest that those insights help us understand the differences in internal conflict patterns between these two cases.[18]

Northern Ireland

Why does the violence persist? The standard explanations attribute severe communal distrust and fears to historically rooted religious differences, key historical events, social divisions, economic inequality, or the personalities involved. While these are certainly involved, many seem as much like effects as causes to me. After all, often people use history by weaving selected elements into narratives that rationalize action, while Catholics and Protestants do live in peace in other places. Even the physical and social separation of the two communities is relative and seems to increase after outbursts of violence and not necessarily to precede them.

These explanations are all interest-based, emphasizing the weak cross-cutting ties between Protestants and Catholics and the strong fraternal interest groups within each community. Without denying their role, I suggest that they are incomplete by themselves. Again, I would suggest the importance of thinking about the psychocultural context in which such feelings are nurtured. Why is it that other settings with similar events, inequalities or permanent social divisions do not have the long-term severe violence that the people in Northern Ireland have had? Why is it that countries such as Nigeria, which have experienced extremely severe internal conflict, have apparently achieved far more ethnic reconciliation than have the Catholics and Protestants of Ulster?

Messenger (1971) and Scheper-Hughes' (1979) work in rural areas in the Republic of Ireland suggest a strong Irish fear of intimacy, extremely low social trust, low sociability, high emotional distance between fathers and children. While these variables cannot explain the outbreak of violence, the modeling behavior of terrorist groups and youth gangs in the extremely divided social world of the cities in the North in the past 20 years has offered ample opportunity for members of each sectarian community to learn both aggressive behavior and acceptable targets for their violence. All of these are predispositions which make it hard to deal with political differences peacefully. Their analysis suggests a strong emphasis on social and emotional withdrawal from cooperative collective action, similar to, but weaker than that described by Briggs (1975) for the Eskimo. The Irish have the highest rates of schizophrenia in the world; there are powerful sexual fears on the part of both men and women (Scheper-Hughes 1979). We can suggest that too often, among the Irish, high latent aggression is variously turned inward (schizo-phrenia and alcohol) or outward toward acceptable targets when they are available as in the North.[19] Of the dispositional elements identified in the cross-cultural study, high male gender identity conflict, low affection and warmth, are clearly present in both Catholic and Protestant cultures in Ulster, and are more important than harsh early childhood socialization.

Focusing on the psychocultural dimension of the Irish conflict encourages us to consider the role of perceptions and ideas about what each party to the conflict is seeking.[20] It turns our attention to an important source of the *intensity* and persistence of insecure social and personal identities and profound distrust relevant to the conflict which many of the historical analyses only address in a circular fashion (Horowitz 1985). Within this perspective, deep-seated fears result in projective aggression, which provides a motivation for one's own action as a function of the aggressive motive attributed to the other side (Fornari 1975; White 1984). O'Malley's (1983) in-depth analysis of key political actors in Northern Ireland shows how important such perceptions are in this highly divided world. However, there are limits to this dispositional argument and my point is that the psychocultural dimension provides a broader context to understand the force of social and political divisions in Northern Ireland, not an alternative explanation by itself.

In Northern Ireland the level of psychic or political trust across sectarian lines is minimal; my analysis suggests important ways in which the issue of mistrust can be seen within the communities as well. The underlying world view makes attachments—both those of a personal psychic and those of a larger political nature—difficult to achieve. Basic identity issues produce high levels of insecurity which are then reinforced by a political world in which capricious and arbitrary violence easily becomes a way of life, where factions take on excessively contrasting black and white images, and where the choice becomes extreme action or withdrawal.

Norway

In contrast, why is there relatively little overt violence and conflict in Norway today?[21] In cross-national studies the country is rated low on internal violence, strikes, homicide, and suicide (Galtung 1974; Naroll 1983). Of course, there is some conflict and internal violence: mobbing among children, mistreatment of non-white immigrants, and disputes, sometimes bitter, about language.

It is not hard to identify the structural factors associated with Norway's low level of conflict. The society is ethnically homogeneous, and class divisions are not prominent. Norwegians have an extended family life with what Naroll (1983) calls large moralnets, which can provide extensive support to individuals (Eckstein 1966). Norwegian values de-emphasize competition and achievement. Egalitarianism is emphasized even in sports and the economy (Castberg 1954; Bolton 1984); safety and health are stressed. Extensive involvement in voluntary associations and overlapping networks is widespread making it difficult for communities to divide into permanent factions. Family roles are highly structured to separate individuals when tensions might develop (Hollos 1974).

There is also interesting evidence in support of the psychocultural hypotheses. Norwegian child-rearing practices use low physical punishment. Hollos's (1974) profile of an isolated rural community describes a very high level of maternal nurturance and supervision, with little emphasis on discipline or control. Not much is demanded of young children and they engage in a great deal of self-initiated play and exploration of their immediate environment. Bolton (1984) describes a more urban setting as one in which there is often high involvement of fathers, a strong emphasis on peer culture, and low performance pressure on children. Interestingly, for adults emotional *self-control*, especially over negative feelings, is stressed (Hollos 1974; Bolton 1984), and much adult interaction is highly stylized and emotionally disengaged.

The expressive culture provides a few aggressive models. There is low television violence, no boxing, and films are controlled. For example, *ET* was banned as too violent for children under 12. Newspapers do not emphasize crime. Other than the police, few people have guns. Finally, the daily life of most people produces little stress. There is low noise, low population density, and the use of nature, such as hiking in the woods, to relieve stress. Some research links the typical diet—high fat, low carbohydrate, 4–5 meals/day—to low levels of stress and violence (Bolton 1984).

The emphasis on low overt aggression and high self-control, which both Bolton and Hollos report, is consistent with the findings of Sears et al (1958) that low aggression is promoted in children by both low punishment and high structuring of their social environment. It is clear to Norwegians that overt aggression or even direct confrontation of others is unacceptable. Social conformity pressure seems to make strong punishment unnecessary as individuals and groups often monitor themselves.

In Norway the strong egalitarian nature of society is accompanied by a reluctance to be highly directive towards others; self-control and avoidance are important mechanisms used in both primary groups and local communities to limit the expression of possible differences. At the same time, the nurturance and support for children in the early years, combined with almost constant but not intrusive surveillance, seems to produce adults who are self-reliant, and able to develop linkages to each other which are highly supportive in times of need.

CONCLUSION

The general approach to conflict taken here suggests some final theoretical, methodological, and substantive conclusions. Theoretically, the argument that dispositions and structures best explain distinctive features of conflict behavior—levels and targets respectively—is very different from the view that they offer competing explanations. It says we need to identify more carefully *when* each is important rather than think of one theory as necessarily more correct than the other.[22] Methodologically, the analysis showed that the complexity of conflict behavior needs to be matched by the complexity of models used to study it. Looking at single variable explanations produces misleading results. The integration of both psychocultural and social structural elements into an explanation for conflict is far more useful than reliance on either alone. Substantively, the analysis focused on societal level differences in conflict behavior, and identified two powerful ways collective processes affect conflict. Cultures provide their members with, and reinforce, world views rooted in early socialization and manifest in the interpretive frameworks people share for understanding their own actions and those of others. They also institutionalize behaviors in social structures which direct fears, expectations and hopes towards particular groups or individuals. Although a sample of preindustrial societies provided the data base to reach these conclusions, there is good reason to see the argument as applying to conflict in other settings as well. Finally, understanding the roots of human conflict is important to increase our possibilities for managing it more successfully than we have to date.

SUMMARY

While conflict and aggression are found in all human societies, there is a wide range of variation in their manifestation. A cross-cultural investigation of 90 small-scale, preindustrial societies showed that psychocultural factors are particularly crucial in shaping the *level* of conflict and violence associated with a society while social structural determinants are crucial in the selection of social *targets*. This explanation points to the critical role of interpretive frameworks which cultures develop to understand and explain the social behavior of individuals and groups.

Two contrasting case studies showed important implications of this theory for understanding conflict behavior in social and political units beyond the pre-industrial societies in the cross-cultural sample. This was illustrated in a comparison of Northern Ireland, where overt aggression is especially high, and Norway, a small nation where the quality of life is generally seen as especially high and where manifest conflict is low. The analysis shows that, while the levels of internal conflict in both societies are consistent with the predictions a structural theory would make, consideration of psychocultural factors as well offers a more complete explanation, not only for the levels of aggression each society manifests, but especially for understanding possible reasons why these differences persist over time. Psychocultural factors emphasizing culturally shared interpretations of the social world seem particularly useful in explaining the persistence of violence in Northern Ireland and of constructive, low violence, conflict management procedures in Norway.

NOTES

1. Parts of this chapter appeared in Ross (1986a). Support for the research was provided by the National Science Foundation (BNS82-03381) and the Harry Frank Guggenheim Foundation.

2. While most definitions of conflict focus on incompatible behaviors of two or more parties, some emphasize differences in goals and perceptions. For example, Pruitt and Rubin (1986:4) say that "conflict means perceived divergence of interest, or a belief that the parties' current aspirations cannot be achieved simultaneously." While their point about perceptions

is certainly important, it seems crucial to me to include behaviors in any definition of conflict which they do not do.

3. Although in practical terms this is extremely hard to measure precisely, rank orders are often far easier to describe both for conflicts within any society and ones between it and outsiders.

4. My more general interest also includes societal differences in the ways conflicts are played out, and the mechanisms for dispute settlement which are utilized to control or direct conflicts when they occur but these are not the focus of attention here.

5. For more on the sampling and coding procedures used, detailed description of the variables, and the scores for each society on each variable, see Ross (1983, 1988).

6. Greater discussion of the individual components of these scales, the actual measures involved, the sampling procedures and questions of reliability is found in Ross (1983, 1986a). While internal and external conflict and violence produce separate dimensions in the factor analysis, there is still a moderate correlation between them ($r = 0.39$, $N = 90$). Note how this provides little support for the general idea that societies use external conflict to displace internal problems. Only sometimes is this the case. The important question of the conditions under which societies are likely to have high levels of either form of conflict or both is addressed at length in Ross (1985).

7. The variables which load on each factor are used to form two scales which are the sum of the scores of the variables on each dimension after they have been standardized and weighted by their squared factor loadings. The raw scores for each of the component variables as well as the scores for each society on these composite scales are found in Ross (1983: Table 4).

8. For convenience I often use the labels internal or external conflict, but in the data analysis I am nonetheless referring to each of these scales, internal conflict and violence and external conflict and warfare.

9. The scores for each society in the sample on each dimension are given in Ross (1983).

10. Waltz's (1959) influential work on international warfare is organized around three kinds of explanations: those which focus on individuals (psychology), those which focus on the structure of individual states, and those which focus on the international system itself rather than its component parts. He offers a number of appropriate criticisms of the first two viewpoints and advocates the third as the most useful. While I find fault with few of his criticisms of either of the first two positions, it is the underlying assumption that he makes here and elsewhere that it is necessary to choose among the positions, rather than integrate them, that I find simplistic.

11. The Appendix to this chapter explains the operationalization of each of the variables discussed in this section.

12. In several factor analyses, including one I did which is cited in the Appendix to this chapter, variables measuring harsh socialization practices load on different factors from indicators of warmth and affection (Russell 1972; Steward and Jones 1972), which means that these two dimensions are not simply opposite poles on the same continuum.

13. The codes for the political variables used below are found in Ross (1983), while the socioeconomic and child-training variables are found in Barry and Schlegel (1980), a collection of codes originally published in *Ethnology*. These sources also consider problems of sampling and reliability that may be of interest to certain readers. The Appendix to this chapter lists the independent variables used in the data analysis in the following text and the way each is operationally defined.

14. Multicollinearity is not a problem here. First, the correlations among the independent variables can, but did not here, produce large standard errors of the regression coefficients. Second, of course, multicollinearity does not bias the regression coefficient, it only increases the standard errors.

15. Interaction terms were specified as the original variable multiplied by a dummy variable (1 = uncentralized, and 0 = centralized). If the regression coefficient for an interactive term is large, the original variable has a different impact in the two groups of societies. Societies were coded as centralized only if Tuden and Marshall (1972) scored them as having political authority exercised beyond the level of the local community. In cases where the interaction terms produced small regression coefficients, the variable was dropped from the model presented here.

16. The importance of structural variables in predicting internal and external conflict is further demonstrated in an examination of different ways internal and external conflict are related to each other cross-culturally. It shows that while the psychocultural variables best predict the amount of total conflict (internal plus external) a society has, the structural factors are much better at accounting for the contrasts between differentiating societies (those cases where one kind of conflict is dominant) and generalizing societies (those which have both kinds of conflict at roughly the same levels).

17. For an application of the argument to a single preindustrial society, the Mae Enga of highland New Guinea, see Ross (1986b).

18. Although the cross-cultural study is interested in both internal and external conflict, in the two cases examined here my focus is only internal conflict. External conflict for Northern Ireland and Norway would have to consider such factors as Northern Ireland's attachment to the United Kingdom and the behavior of neighboring states, such as Germany in the twentieth century. For a more extended description of the Northern Ireland case, see Mulvihill and Ross (1989).

19. Because Scheper-Hughes's data on schizophrenia suggests important continuities in the psychocultural setting between the Republic of Ireland and Ulster, it seems plausible to assume that this is, in fact, the case.

20. In a short but very effective piece McLachlan (1987) points out crucial consequences for peacemaking that follow from the separate cultural assumptions about authority and conflict dominant in each community.

21. A question I have yet to address is an explanation for the evolution from the high aggression society of the Vikings.

22. Rule (1988) makes the same very important point in his evaluation of theories of civil violence. The challenge to proponents of particular theories is, from his point of view, not just to identify the cases where their theories fit best, but also to attempt to falsify them in a larger range of perhaps not so congenial cases as well.

REFERENCES

Barry, H. III, I. L. Child, and M. K. Bacon. 1959. Relations of child training to subsistence economy. *American Anthropologist* 61:51–63.

Barry, H. III, L. Josephson, E. Lauer, and C. Marshall. 1976. Traits inculcated in childhood: Cross-cultural codes 5. *Ethnology* 15:83–114.

———. 1977. Agents and techniques for child training: Cross-cultural codes 6. *Ethnology* 16:191–230.

Barry, H. III and L. M. Paxson. 1971. Infancy and early childhood: Cross-cultural codes 2. *Ethnology* 10:466–508.

Barry, H. III, and A. Schlegel, eds. 1980. *Cross-Cultural Samples and Codes*. Pittsburgh: University of Pittsburgh Press.

Bates, R. 1983. The centralization of African societies, pp. 21–58. In *Essays on the Political Economy of Rural Africa*, R. Bates, ed. New York: Cambridge University Press.

Beals, A. R. and B. J. Siegel. 1966. *Divisiveness and Social Conflict*. Stanford: Stanford University Press.

Bigelow, R. 1973. The evolution of cooperation, aggression, and self-control, pp. 1–57. In *Nebraska Symposium on Motivation 1972*, J. K. Cole and D. D. Jensen, eds. Lincoln: University of Nebraska Press.

Bolton, R. 1984. Notes on Norwegian nonviolence. Paper presented to the Annual Meeting of the Society for Cross-cultural Research, Boulder Colorado.

Boyd, R. and P. J. Richerson. 1985. *Culture and the Evolutionary Process*. Chicago: University of Chicago Press.

Briggs, J. L. 1975. The origins of nonviolence: Aggression in two Canadian Eskimo groups, pp. 134–203. In *The Psychoanalytic Study of Society*, Volume 6, W. Muensterberger and A. Esman, eds. New York: International Universities Press.

Broch. T. and J. Galtung. 1966. Belligerence among the primitives. *Journal of Peace Research* 3:33–45.

Campbell, D. T. 1983. The two distinct routes beyond kin selection to ultrasociality: Implications for the humanities and social sciences, pp. 11–39. In *The Nature of Prosocial Development: Theories and Strategies*, D. Bridgeman, ed. New York: Academic Press.

Castberg, F. 1954. *The Norwegian Way of Life*. London: William Heinemann.

Chagnon, N. 1967. Yanomamo social organization and warfare, pp. 109–159. In *War: The Anthropology of Armed Conflict and Aggression*, M. Fried, M. Harris, and R. Murphy, eds. Garden City, NY: Natural History Press.

Coleman, J. S. 1957. *Community Conflict*. New York: Free Press.

Colson, E. 1953. Social control and vengeance in plateau Tonga society. *Africa* 23:199–211.

van der Dennen, J. M. G. 1987. Ethnocentrism and in-group/out-group differentiation: A review and interpretation of the literature, pp. 1–47. In *The Sociobiology of Ethnocentrism: Evolutionary Dimensions of Xenophobia, Discrimination, Racism and Nationalism*, V. Reynolds, V. Falger, and I. Vine, eds. Athens: University of Georgia Press.

Denton, R. K. 1968. *The Semai: A Nonviolent People of Malaya*. New York: Holt, Rinehart and Winston.

Deutsch, M. 1973. *The Resolution of Conflict: Constructive and Destructive Processes*. New Haven: Yale University Press.

Divale, W. T. 1974. Migration, external warfare and matrilocal residence. *Behavior Science Research* 9:75–133.

Durbin, E. F. M. and J. Bowlby. 1939. *Personal Aggressiveness and War*. New York: Columbia University Press.

Eckstein, H. 1966. *Division and Cohesion in a Democracy: A Study of Norway*. Princeton: Princeton University Press.

Edgerton, R. 1971. *The Individual in Cultural Adaptation*. Berkeley: University of California Press.

Ember, M. and C. R. Ember. 1971. The conditions favoring matrilocal versus patrilocal residence. *American Anthropologist* 73:571–594.

Evans-Pritchard, E. E. 1940. *The Nuer*. Oxford: Oxford University Press.

Fairbairn, W. R. D. 1954. *An Object-Relations Theory of Personality*. New York: Basic Books.

Fornari, F. 1975. *The Psychoanalysis of War*. Bloomington: Indiana University Press.

Freud, S. 1930 [1962]. *Civilization and its Discontents*. New York: Norton.

Fried, M. H. 1967. *The Evolution of Political Society*. New York: Random House.

Galtung, J. 1974. Norway in the world community, pp. 325–427. In *Norwegian Society*, N. Rogoff Ramsøy, ed. New York: Humanities Press.

Gluckman, M. 1963. *Order and Rebellion in Tribal Africa.* New York: Free Press.

Greenberg, J. R. and S. A. Mitchell. 1983. *Object Relations in Psychoanalytic Theory.* Cambridge: Harvard University Press.

Greenstein, F. 1967. The impact of personality and politics: An attempt to clear away the underbrush. *American Political Science Review* 61:629–641.

Guntrip, H. 1971. *Psychoanalytic Theory, Therapy, and the Self.* New York: Harper Torchbooks.

Gurr, T. R. 1970. *Why Men Rebel.* Princeton: Princeton University Press.

Haas, E. 1964. *The Uniting of Europe.* Stanford: Stanford University Press.

Harrington, C. and J. W. M. Whiting. 1972. Socialization processes and personality, pp. 469–507. In *Psychological Anthropology*, 2nd edn, F. L. K. Hsu, ed. Cambridge, MA: Schenkman.

Hendrix, L. 1985. Economy and child training reexamined. *Ethos* 13:246–261.

Herdt, G. 1987. *The Sambia: Ritual and Gender in New Guinea.* New York: Holt, Rinehart and Winston.

Hibbs, D. 1973. *Mass Political Violence: Cross-National Causal Analysis.* New York: John Wiley.

Hollos, M. 1974. *Growing Up in Flathill.* Oslo: Universitetsforlaget.

Horkheimer, M. 1950. The lessons of fascism, pp. 209–242. In *Tensions that Cause Wars*, H. Cantril, ed. Urbana: University of Illinois Press.

Horowitz, D. L. 1985. *Ethnic Groups in Conflict.* Berkeley, Los Angeles: University of California Press.

Huyghe, B. 1986. Toward a structural model of violence: Male initiation rituals and tribal warfare, pp. 25–48. In *Peace and War: Cross-Cultural Perspectives*, M. LeCron Foster and R. A. Rubinstein, eds. New Brunswick, NJ: Transaction Books.

Ike, B. W. 1987. Man's limited sympathy as a consequence of his evolution in small kin groups, pp. 216–234. In *The Sociobiology of Ethnocentrism: Evolutionary Dimensions of Xenophobia, Discrimination, Racism and Nationalism*, V. Reynolds, V. Falger, and I. Vine, eds. Athens: University of Georgia Press.

Janis, I. L. 1972. *Victims of Groupthink.* New York: Houghton Mifflin.

Kernberg, O. 1975. *Borderline Conditions and Pathological Narcissism.* New York: Jason Aronson.

Lancaster, C. 1987. The evolution of violence and aggression, pp. 216–222. In *Dominance, Aggression and War*, D. McGuinness, ed. New York: Paragon House.

LeVine, R. A. 1965. Socialization, social structure, and intersocietal images, pp. 43–69. In *International Behavior: A Social Psychological Analysis*, H. Kelman, ed. New York: Holt, Rinehart and Winston.

LeVine, R. A. and D. Campbell. 1972. *Ethnocentrism: Theories of Conflict, Ethnic Attitudes and Group Behavior.* New York: John Wiley.

Levinson, D. and M. J. Malone. 1980. *Toward Explaining Human Culture: A Critique of the Findings of Worldwide Cross-Cultural Research.* New Haven: HRAF Press.

Mack, R. W. and R. Snyder. 1957. The analysis of social conflict: Toward an overview and synthesis. *Journal of Conflict Resolution* 1:212–248.

McLachlan, P. 1987. Northern Ireland: The cultural bases of the conflict. *Conflict Resolution Notes* 4:21–23.

Messenger, J. 1971. Sex and repression in an Irish folk community, pp. 2–37. In *Human Sexual Behavior: Variations in the Ethnographic Spectrum*, D. S. Marshall and R. C. Suggs, eds. New York: Basic Books.

Midlarsky, M. 1975. *On War: Political Violence in the International System.* New York: Free Press.

Montagu, A., ed. 1978. *Learning Non-aggression. The Experience of Non-literate Societies.* New York. Oxford University Press.

Mulvihill, R. and M. H. Ross. 1989. Theories of conflict and conflict management and peacemaking in Northern Ireland. Paper presented to the National Conference on Peacemaking and Conflict Resolution, March, Montreal, Canada.

Murdock, G. P. 1967. *Ethnographic Atlas.* Pittsburgh: University of Pittsburgh Press.

Murdock G. P. and D. O. Morrow. 1970. Subsistence economy and support practices: Cross-cultural codes 1. *Ethnology* 9:302–330.

Murdock, G. P. and C. Provost. 1973. Measurement of cultural complexity. *Ethnology* 12:379–392.

Murdock, G. P. and D. R. White. 1969. Standard cross-cultural sample. *Ethnology* 8:329–369.

Murdock, G. P. and S. F. Wilson. 1972. Settlement patterns and community organization: Cross-cultural codes 3. *Ethnology* 11:254–295.

Murphy, R. F. 1957. Intergroup hostility and social cohesion. *American Anthropologist* 59:1018–1035.

Naroll, R. 1983. *The Moral Order: An Introduction to the Human Situation.* Beverly Hills: Sage Publications.

O'Malley, P. 1983. *The Uncivil Wars: Ireland Today.* New York: Houghton-Mifflin.

Otterbein, K. 1968. Internal war: A cross-cultural comparison. *American Anthropologist* 70:277–289.

———. *The Evolution of War.* New Haven: HRAF Press.

———. 1977. Warfare as a hitherto unrecognized critical variable. *American Behavioral Scientist* 20:693–710.

Otterbein, K. F. and C. S. Otterbein. 1965. An eye for an eye, a tooth for a tooth: A cross-cultural study of feuding. *American Anthropologist* 67:1470–1482.

Paige, K. E. and J. M. Paige. 1981. *The Politics of Reproductive Ritual.* Berkeley: University of California Press.

Pruitt, D. G. and J. Z. Rubin. 1986. *Social Conflict: Escalation, Stalemate, and Settlement.* New York: Random House.

Ross, M. H. 1981. Socioeconomic complexity, socialization, and political differentiation: A cross-cultural study. *Ethos* 9:217–247.

———. 1983. Political decision making and conflict: Additional cross-cultural codes and scales. *Ethnology* 22:169–192.

———. 1985. Internal and external violence and conflict: Cross-cultural evidence and a new analysis. *Journal of Conflict Resolution* 29:547–579.

———. 1986a. A cross-cultural theory of political conflict and violence. *Political Psychology* 7:427–469.

———. 1986b. The limits to social structure: Social structural and psychological explanations for political conflict and violence. *Anthropological Quarterly* 59:171–176.

———. 1988. Some comments on the quality and reliability of political decision making and conflict codes and scales. *World Cultures: Electronic Journal and Data Base* 5:1.

———. 1991. The role of evolution in ethnocentric conflict and its management. *Journal of Social Issues* 47(5):167–185.

———. Forthcoming. *The Culture of Conflict: Interpretations, Interests, and Disputing in Comparative Perspective.*

Rule, J. B. 1988. *Theories of Civil Violence.* Berkeley, Los Angeles: University of California Press.

Russell, E. W. 1972. Factors of human aggression: A cross-cultural factor analysis of characteristics related to warfare and crimes. *Behavior Science Research* 7:275–312.

Scheper-Hughes, N. 1979. *Saints, Scholars and Schizophrenics: Mental Illness in Rural Ireland.* Berkeley: University of California Press.

Sears, R. R., E. E. Maccoby, and H. Levin. 1958. The socialization of aggression, pp. 350–358. In *Readings in Social Psychology*, 2nd edn, E. Maccoby, T. Newcomb, and E. L. Hartley, eds. New York: Holt, Rinehart and Winston.

Slater, P. E. and D. A. Slater. 1965. Maternal ambivalence and narcissism: A cross-cultural study. *Merrill-Palmer Quarterly* 11:241–259.

Spotnitz, H. 1976. *Psychotherapy of Preoedipal Conditions.* New York: Jason Aronson.

Stern, D. N. 1985. *The Interpersonal World of the Infant.* New York: Basic Books.

Steward, R. A. C. and K. J. Jones. 1972. Cultural dimensions: A factor analysis of Textor's "A Cross-Cultural Summary". *Behavior Science Research* 7:37–81.

Tuden, A. and C. Marshall. 1972. Political organization: Cross-cultural codes 4. *Ethnology* 11:436–464.

Turner, V. 1957. *Schism and Continuity in an African Society.* Manchester: Manchester University Press.

van Velzen, H. U. E. Thoden, and W. van Wetering. 1960. Residence, power groups and intra-societal aggression. *International Archives of Ethnography* 49:169–200.

Volkan, V. 1988. *The Need to Have Enemies and Allies: From Clinical Practice to International Relationships.* Northvale, NJ: Jason Aronson.

Waltz, K. 1959. *Man, the State, and War.* New York: Columbia University Press.

White, R. K. 1984. *Fearful Warriors: A Psychological Profile of U.S.–Soviet Relations.* New York: Free Press.

Whiting, B. B. 1965. Sex identity conflict and physical violence: A comparative study. *American Anthropologist* 67 (2):123–140.

———. 1980. Culture and social behavior: A model for the development of social behavior. *Ethos* 8:95–116.

Whiting, B. B. and J. W. M. Whiting. 1975. *Children of Six Cultures: A Psycho-Cultural Analysis.* Cambridge: Harvard University Press.

Whiting, J. W. M. and I. L. Child. 1953. *Child Training and Personality.* New Haven: Yale University Press.

Winnicott, D. W. 1965. *The Maturational Process and the Facilitating Environment.* New York: International Universities Press.

Wright, Q. 1942. *A Study of War.* 2 vols. Chicago: University of Chicago Press.

Zigler, E. and I. L. Child. 1969. Socialization, pp. 450–589. In *Handbook of Social Psychology*, Vol. 3, 2nd edn, G. Lindzey and E. Aronson, eds., Reading, MA: Addison-Wesley.

Zinnes, D. A. 1980. Why war? Evidence on the outbreak of international conflict, pp. 331–360. In *Handbook of Political Conflict*, T. R. Gurr, ed. New York: Free Press.

APPENDIX: MEASURES AND SOURCES FOR THE INDEPENDENT VARIABLES

In all cases the specific measures used begin with published data for the societies in the Standard Cross-Cultural Sample (Murdock and White 1969). The measurement of the two dependent variables is explained in the text. The measures for each of the independent variables are as follows.

Overlapping reference groups is a scale developed from factor analysis of 36 political variables for the societies in the sample as explained in the text and details of which are given in Ross (1983). Scale scores are the sum of each society's score on each variable after it has been standardized and weighted by its squared factor loading. The raw scores for each variable as well as the scale scores are presented in Ross (1983). The variables used were (with their factor loadings in parentheses): the extent to which individuals living in different communities of the same society are linked together in politically relevant ways (0.64); the strength of in-group or we-feelings directed towards the wider society—i.e., beyond the local community (0.62); the number of different areas of life in which community decision making (either formal or informal) occurs (0.58); the strength of in-group or we-feelings directed towards the local community (0.56); the extent to which kinship organizations linking different communities are present and politically important (0.53); the extent to which ritual groups exist linking different communities are present and politically important (0.50); and the extent to which there is intervention in disputes as they develop and community pressures work towards settlement (0.42).

Intercommunity marriage. The extent of local exogamy vs. endogamy is a five-point variable taken from Murdock and Wilson (1972).

Matrilocality and *patrilocality* are coded from Murdock and Wilson (1972). Societies are coded as patrilocal if Murdock and Wilson said they were patrilocal or virilocal, otherwise patrilocality is absent; similarly, matrilocality is scored as present if the society is matrilocal or uxorilocal, absent if it is not.

Intercommunity trade is a seven-point measure of the extent to which a community in the society trades for foodstuffs (Murdock and Morrow 1970).

Fraternal interest group strength is taken from Paige and Paige (1981). It is based on the presence of brideprice, patrilineality and a trichotomized measure of the size of effective, kin-based, political subunits. For 66 of the societies the Paiges' score is used. For the remaining 34 which are not in their sample, brideprice and patrilineality were coded from Murdock (1967: column 12) and Murdock and Wilson (1972), while the size of effective kin groups is estimated using a recoded version of Murdock and Wilson's (1972) community size measure. This measure is highly correlated with that of Paige and Paige for those societies where both are available.

Polygyny is a three-point measure—monogamous, less than 20% polygynous marriage, and more than 20% polygynous, derived from the Murdock and Wilson (1972) form of family variable—and measures the rates of polygyny, not the behavioral norms associated with it.

Socioeconomic complexity is a scale made up of eight different measures which are loaded on a single dimension when factor analyzed, and weighted as explained above: the importance of agriculture as a contribution to subsistence; the importance of animal husbandry; the low importance of hunting; the low importance of gathering; the degree to which food is stored; the size of the average community in the society; the degree of social stratification; and cultural complexity. The first five measures are from Murdock and Morrow (1970), the size measure is from Murdock and Wilson (1972), and the stratification and complexity measures are from Murdock and Provost (1973).

Political complexity is measured by a 13-variable scale called *political power concentration* based on factor analysis (Ross 1983). The crucial variables are: the extent to which leaders act independently in a community; the presence or absence of checks on political leaders; the degree of political role differentiation in a society; the importance of decision-making bodies; and the level of taxation.

Harsh socialization is a scale derived from a factor analysis of socialization measures from Barry and Paxson (1971) and Barry et al. (1976, 1977) which are appropriate to measure either harshness of socialization, affectionate socialization, or male gender identity conflict. The variables and their loadings on the harsh socialization dimension are: the severity of pain infliction (0.69); the extent to which corporal punishment is used (0.63); the degree to which children are not indulged (0.57); the extent to which children are scolded (0.51); the importance of caretakers other than the mother (0.44); the degree to which fortitude is stressed as a value (0.37); and the degree to which aggressiveness is stressed as a value (0.28).

Affectionate socialization is a second scale derived from the factor analysis just cited. The variables loading on this dimension are: the degree to which trust is emphasized as a value during childhood (0.74); the degree to which honesty is stressed as a value during childhood (0.67); the closeness of the father in childhood (0.65); the degree to which generosity is stressed as a value during childhood (0.53); the degree to which affection is expressed towards the child (0.49); and the extent to which children are valued by the society (0.34).

Male gender identity conflict is measured following Whiting and others by the length of abstinence from sexual intercourse by the mother after birth, described as the cultural norm. The seven point measure is from Barry and Paxson (1971). Whiting also suggests that the nature of mother–infant sleeping arrangements can be used to measure this variable, but the Barry and Paxson (1971) measure of sleeping arrangements is not sufficiently precise. Another measure which Whiting has also used is polygyny (see preceding text).

Appendix: The Seville Statement on Violence

EDITOR'S NOTE: The Seville Statement on Violence was drafted by an international committee of 20 scholars at the 6th International Colloquium on Brain and Aggression held at the University of Seville, Spain, in May 1986, with support from the Spanish Commission for UNESCO. The Statement's purpose is to dispel the widespread belief that human beings are inevitably disposed to war as a result of innate, biologically determined aggressive traits.

*UNESCO adopted the Seville Statement at its 25th General Conference Session in Paris, 17 October–16 November, 1989. The Statement has been formally endorsed by scientific organizations and published in journals around the world. UNESCO is preparing a brochure to be used in teaching young people about the Statement.**

Believing that it is our responsibility to address from our particular disciplines the most dangerous and destructive activities of our species, violence and war; recognizing that science is a human cultural product which cannot be definitive or all-encompassing; and gratefully acknowledging the support of the authorities of Seville and representatives of Spanish UNESCO; we, the undersigned scholars from around the world and from relevant sciences, have met and arrived at the following Statement on Violence. In it, we challenge a number of alleged biological findings that have been used, even by some in our disciplines, to justify violence and war. Because the alleged findings have contributed to an atmosphere of pessimism in our time, we submit that the open, considered rejection of these misstatements can contribute significantly to the International Year of Peace.

Misuse of scientific theories and data to justify violence and war is not new but has been made since the advent of modern science. For example, the theory of evolution has been made to justify not only war, but also genocide, colonialism, and suppression of the weak.

We state our position in the form of five propositions. We are aware that there are many other issues about violence and war that could be fruitfully addressed from the standpoint of our disciplines, but we restrict ourselves here to what we consider a most important first step.

It is scientifically incorrect to say that we have inherited a tendency to make war from our animal ancestors. Although fighting occurs widely throughout

---

* From Editor's Note, *American Psychologist* 45 (10):1167–1168.

animal species, only a few cases of destructive intra-species fighting between organized groups have ever been reported among naturally living species, and none of these involve the use of tools designed to be weapons. Normal predatory feeding upon other species cannot be equated with intra-species violence. Warfare is a peculiarly human phenomenon and does not occur in other animals.

The fact that warfare has changed so radically over time indicates that it is a product of culture. Its biological connection is primarily through language which makes possible the coordination of groups, the transmission of technology, and the use of tools. War is biologically possible, but it is not inevitable, as evidenced by its variation in occurrence and nature over time and space. There are cultures which have not engaged in war for centuries, and there are cultures which have engaged in war frequently at some times and not at others.

It is scientifically incorrect to say that war or any other violent behavior is genetically programmed into our human nature. While genes are involved at all levels of nervous system function, they provide a developmental potential that can be actualized only in conjunction with the ecological and social environment. While individuals vary in their predispositions to be affected by their experience, it is the interaction between their genetic endowment and conditions of nurturance that determines their personalities. Except for rare pathologies, the genes do not produce individuals necessarily predisposed to violence. Neither do they determine the opposite. While genes are co-involved in establishing our behavioral capacities, they do not by themselves specify the outcome.

It is scientifically incorrect to say that in the course of human evolution there has been a selection for aggressive behavior more than for other kinds of behavior. In all well-studied species, status within the group is achieved by the ability to cooperate and to fulfill social functions relevant to the structure of that group. "Dominance" involves social bondings and affiliations; it is not simply a matter of the possession and use of superior physical power, although it does involve aggressive behaviors. Where genetic selection for aggressive behavior has been artificially instituted in animals, it has rapidly succeeded in producing hyper-aggressive individuals; this indicates that aggression was not maximally selected under natural conditions. When such experimentally-created hyper-aggressive animals are present in a social group, they either disrupt its social structure or are driven out. Violence is neither in our evolutionary legacy nor in our genes.

It is scientifically incorrect to say that humans have a "violent brain." While we do have the neural apparatus to act violently, it is not automatically activated by internal or external stimuli. Like higher primates and unlike other animals, our higher neural processes filter such stimuli before they can be acted upon. How we act is shaped by how we have been conditioned and socialized. There is nothing in our neurophysiology that compels us to react violently.

It is scientifically incorrect to say that war is caused by "instinct" or any single motivation. The emergence of modern warfare has been a journey from the primacy of emotional and motivational factors, sometimes called "instincts," to the primacy of cognitive factors. Modern war involves institutional use of personal characteristics such as obedience, suggestibility, and idealism; social skills such as language; and rational considerations such as cost-calculation, planning, and information processing. The technology of modern war has exaggerated traits associated with violence both in the training of actual combatants and in the preparation of support for war in the general population. As a result of this exaggeration, such traits are often mistaken to be the causes rather than the consequences of the process.

We conclude that biology does not condemn humanity to war, and that humanity can be freed from the bondage of biological pessimism and empowered with confidence to undertake the transformative tasks needed in this International Year of Peace and in the years to come. Although these tasks are mainly institutional and collective, they also rest upon the consciousness of individual participants for whom pessimism and optimism are crucial factors. Just as "wars begin in the minds of men", peace also begins in our minds. The same species who invented war is capable of inventing peace. The responsibility lies with each of us.

Seville, 16 May 1986.

SIGNATORIES

David Adams, Psychlogy, Wesleyan University, Middletown, Connecticut, U.S.A.

S. A. Barnett, Ethology, The Australian National University, Canberra, Australia.

N. P. Bechtereva, Neurophysiology, Institute for Experimental Medicine of Academy of Medical Sciences of U.S.S.R., Leningrad, U.S.S.R.

Bonnie Frank Carter, Psychology, Albert Einstein Medical Center, Philadelphia, Pennsylvania U.S.A.

José M. Rodríguez Delgado, Neurophysiology, Centro de Estudios Neurobiológicos, Madrid, Spain.

José Luis Díaz, Ethology, Instituto Mexicano de Psiquiatría, Mexico D.F., Mexico.

Andrzej Eliasz, Individual Differences Psychology, Polish Academy of Sciences, Warsaw, Poland.

Santiago Genovés, Biological Anthropology, Instituto de Estudios Antropológicos, Mexico D.F., Mexico.

Benson E. Ginsburg, Behavior Genetics, University of Connecticut, Storrs, Connecticut, U.S.A.

Jo Groebel. Social Psychology, Erziehungswissenschaftliche Hochschule, Landau, Federal Republic of Germany.

Samir-Kumar Ghosh, Sociology, Indian Institute of Human Sciences, Calcutta, India.

Robert Hinde, Animal Behavior, Cambridge University, United Kingdom.

Richard E. Leakey, Physical Anthropology, National Museums of Kenya, Nairobi, Kenya.

Taha M. Malasi, Psychiatry, Kuwait University, Kuwait.

J. Martin Ramírez, Psychobiology, Universidad de Sevilla, Spain.

Federico Mayor Zaragoza, Biochemistry, Universidad Autónoma, Madrid, Spain.

Diana L. Mendoza, Ethology, Universidad de Sevilla, Spain.

Ashis Nandy, Political Psychology, Center for the Study of Developing Societies, Delhi, India.

John Paul Scott, Animal Behavior, Bowling Green State University, Bowling Green, Ohio, U.S.A.

Riitta Wahlström, Psychology, University of Jyväskylä, Finland.

Correspondence concerning the Seville Statement on Violence or the UNESCO brochure should be addressed to David Adams, Psychology Department, Wesleyan University, Middletown, CT 06457.

Index

Abuse, 2; vocalized, 10; *see also* Agonistic
    acts
Acculturation, Waorani: Violent (warlike) to
    nonviolent (peaceable), *see*
    Missionary-initiated culture change;
    violence, explanations, conscious
    motivation
Acts vs. conscious motivations about violence, 9,
    117, 150, 161, 172; *see also* Emic/etic
    distinction; Violence continuum; Violence
    definition
Adult interference, *see* Agonistic bouts
Affectionate socialization, *see* Socialization,
    affectionate
Affiliative acts (behavior), 3, 6–7, 22–24, 25,
    31, 32, 49, 108–110, 112, 118, 140, 151,
    152, 153, 154, 156, 157, 158, 162–163;
    see also Anti-violent acts; Popularity;
    Pro-social acts;
  cohesive functions of, *see* Cohesion vs.
    dispersion;
  in directional dyads, 153
Affinitive acts (behavior), 118, 140; *see also*
    Affiliative acts; Friend(ship)
Age and affiliative vs. agonistic acts, 32,
    153–154, 156, 158, 159, 161, 165,
    166–167, 169; *see also* Growth
    trajectories, sex differences
Age-gender ranking, 32, 237
Aggression and sociality as behavioral
    potentialities, *see* Aggression, violence
    and peacefulness as behavioral
    potentialities
Aggression, costs/benefits of, 2, 19, 24, 31, 37,
    39, 82, 83, 88–89, 92, 93, 102, 103,
    107, 112, 136, 172, 173, 183–184, 186,
    272; *see also* Pain; Reinforcers and
    punishers in learning
Aggression, definition, 2–12, 31, 125–127, 150,
    172, 177; cohesive vs. dispersive
    consequences, *see* Cohesion vs. dispersion
Aggression, explanations of, *see* Violence,
    explanations
Aggression, human nature and, 1, 9–10, 27; *see*
    also Violence, explanations

Aggression, level of, *see* Competition;
    Nonaggression; Violence continuum
Aggression (nonaggression), variations in:
  adult vs. young, 73, 120; *see also* Age and
    affiliative vs. agonistic acts
  artificial (selective breeding for exaggerated
    aggression), 40; laboratory vs. natural
    conditions, 88
  constructive, 22, 42–49; *see also* Pro-social
    acts
  intraspecific population differences, 74–79,
    172, 177, 178, 285–286; *see also*
    Nonviolent (peaceable) societies; Violent
    societies
  male vs. female, 73, 91, 100, 117, 119, 120,
    121, 130–134, 173, 179, 183
  maternal, 5, 45–49, 86
  mating season, 73, 75, 78, 80, 82, 134, 136
  minimal, 73; *see also* Nonaggression;
  moralistic, 22, 43–46, 50, 53; *see also*
    Pro-social acts
  passive, 231
  projective, 284
  taxonomic (e.g., interspecific) differences, 81,
    96n4, 117, 121–122, 124, 134–138, 141;
    see also Agonistic bouts, taxonomic
    differences; Cross-fostering experiments;
    Dominance acquisition, taxonomic
    differences; Human/nonhuman comparisons
Aggression reproductive success and, 40, 41, 49,
    78, 105; *see also* Rank and reproductive
    success; Reproductive strategies; Resource
    competition Violence, explanations
Aggression, violence and peacefulness
    (peaceability) as behavioral potentialities,
    10, 40, 41
Aggression, violence and testosterone levels,
    91–92, 95; *see also* Violence,
    explanations, genetic-environmental
    interplay
Aggressive, definition, 3, 4, 122–124, 150, 151,
    172; *see also* Aggressiveness
Aggressive motivation, 16–17, 26; *see also*
    Aggressiveness; Violence, explanations,
    conscious motivation

299